Python Data Analysis Cookbook

Over 140 practical recipes to help you make sense of your
data with ease and build production-ready data apps

Ivan Idris

[PACKT] open source *
PUBLISHING   community experience distilled

BIRMINGHAM - MUMBAI

Python Data Analysis Cookbook

First published: July 2016

Production reference: 1150716

Published by Packt Publishing Ltd.
Livery Place
35 Livery Street
Birmingham B3 2PB, UK.

ISBN 978-1-78528-228-7

www.packtpub.com

Credits

Author
Ivan Idris

Reviewers
Bill Chambers
Alexey Grigorev
Dr. Vahid Mirjalili
Michele Usuelli

Commissioning Editor
Akram Hussain

Acquisition Editor
Prachi Bisht

Content Development Editor
Rohit Singh

Technical Editor
Vivek Pala

Copy Editor
Pranjali Chury

Project Coordinator
Izzat Contractor

Proofreader
Safis Editing

Indexer
Rekha Nair

Graphics
Jason Monteiro

Production Coordinator
Aparna Bhagat

Cover Work
Aparna Bhagat

About the Author

Ivan Idris was born in Bulgaria to Indonesian parents. He moved to the Netherlands and graduated in experimental physics. His graduation thesis had a strong emphasis on applied computer science. After graduating, he worked for several companies as a software developer, data warehouse developer, and QA analyst.

His professional interests are business intelligence, big data, and cloud computing. He enjoys writing clean, testable code and interesting technical articles. He is the author of *NumPy Beginner's Guide*, *NumPy Cookbook*, *Learning NumPy*, and *Python Data Analysis*, all by Packt Publishing.

About the Reviewers

Bill Chambers is a data scientist from the UC Berkeley School of Information. He's focused on building technical systems and performing large-scale data analysis. At Berkeley, he has worked with everything from data science with Scala and Apache Spark to creating online Python courses for UC Berkeley's master of data science program. Prior to Berkeley, he was a business analyst at a software company where he was charged with the task of integrating multiple software systems and leading internal analytics and reporting. He contributed as a technical reviewer to the book *Learning Pandas* by Packt Publishing.

Alexey Grigorev is a skilled data scientist and software engineer with more than 5 years of professional experience. Currently, he works as a data scientist at Searchmetrics Inc. In his day-to-day job, he actively uses R and Python for data cleaning, data analysis, and modeling. He has contributed as a technical reviewer to other books on data analysis by Packt Publishing, such as *Test-Driven Machine Learning* and *Mastering Data Analysis with R*.

Dr. Vahid Mirjalili is a data scientist with a diverse background in engineering, mathematics, and computer science. Currently, he is working toward his graduate degree in computer science at Michigan State University. With his specialty in data mining, he is very interested in predictive modeling and getting insights from data. As a Python developer, he likes to contribute to the open source community. He has developed Python packages, such as PyClust, for data clustering. Furthermore, he is also focused on making tutorials for different directions of data science, which can be found at his Github repository at `http://github.com/mirjalil/DataScience`.

The other books that he has reviewed include *Python Machine Learning* by Sebastian Raschka and *Python Machine Learning Cookbook* by Parteek Joshi. Furthermore, he is currently working on a book focused on big data analysis, covering the algorithms specifically suited to analyzing massive datasets.

Michele Usuelli is a data scientist, writer, and R enthusiast specializing in the fields of big data and machine learning. He currently works for Microsoft and joined through the acquisition of Revolution Analytics, the leading R-based company that builds a big data package for R. Michele graduated in mathematical engineering, and before Revolution, he worked with a big data start-up and a big publishing company. He is the author of *R Machine Learning Essentials* and *Building a Recommendation System with R*.

www.PacktPub.com

eBooks, discount offers, and more

Did you know that Packt offers eBook versions of every book published, with PDF and ePub files available? You can upgrade to the eBook version at www.PacktPub.com and as a print book customer, you are entitled to a discount on the eBook copy. Get in touch with us at customercare@packtpub.com for more details.

At www.PacktPub.com, you can also read a collection of free technical articles, sign up for a range of free newsletters and receive exclusive discounts and offers on Packt books and eBooks.

https://www2.packtpub.com/books/subscription/packtlib

Do you need instant solutions to your IT questions? PacktLib is Packt's online digital book library. Here, you can search, access, and read Packt's entire library of books.

Why subscribe?

- ▸ Fully searchable across every book published by Packt
- ▸ Copy and paste, print, and bookmark content
- ▸ On demand and accessible via a web browser

Table of Contents

Preface   vii

Chapter 1: Laying the Foundation for Reproducible Data Analysis   1
Introduction   2
Setting up Anaconda   2
Installing the Data Science Toolbox   4
Creating a virtual environment with virtualenv and virtualenvwrapper   6
Sandboxing Python applications with Docker images   8
Keeping track of package versions and history in IPython Notebook   10
Configuring IPython   13
Learning to log for robust error checking   16
Unit testing your code   19
Configuring pandas   22
Configuring matplotlib   24
Seeding random number generators and NumPy print options   28
Standardizing reports, code style, and data access   30

Chapter 2: Creating Attractive Data Visualizations   35
Introduction   36
Graphing Anscombe's quartet   36
Choosing seaborn color palettes   39
Choosing matplotlib color maps   42
Interacting with IPython Notebook widgets   43
Viewing a matrix of scatterplots   47
Visualizing with d3.js via mpld3   49
Creating heatmaps   51
Combining box plots and kernel density plots with violin plots   54
Visualizing network graphs with hive plots   55
Displaying geographical maps   58

Using ggplot2-like plots 60
Highlighting data points with influence plots 62

Chapter 3: Statistical Data Analysis and Probability 67

Introduction 68
Fitting data to the exponential distribution 68
Fitting aggregated data to the gamma distribution 71
Fitting aggregated counts to the Poisson distribution 72
Determining bias 75
Estimating kernel density 78
Determining confidence intervals for mean, variance, and
standard deviation 81
Sampling with probability weights 83
Exploring extreme values 87
Correlating variables with Pearson's correlation 91
Correlating variables with the Spearman rank correlation 94
Correlating a binary and a continuous variable with the point
biserial correlation 97
Evaluating relations between variables with ANOVA 99

Chapter 4: Dealing with Data and Numerical Issues 103

Introduction 103
Clipping and filtering outliers 104
Winsorizing data 107
Measuring central tendency of noisy data 109
Normalizing with the Box-Cox transformation 112
Transforming data with the power ladder 114
Transforming data with logarithms 116
Rebinning data 118
Applying logit() to transform proportions 120
Fitting a robust linear model 122
Taking variance into account with weighted least squares 125
Using arbitrary precision for optimization 128
Using arbitrary precision for linear algebra 131

Chapter 5: Web Mining, Databases, and Big Data 135

Introduction 136
Simulating web browsing 136
Scraping the Web 139
Dealing with non-ASCII text and HTML entities 142
Implementing association tables 144
Setting up database migration scripts 147

Adding a table column to an existing table 148
Adding indices after table creation 150
Setting up a test web server 151
Implementing a star schema with fact and dimension tables 153
Using HDFS 159
Setting up Spark 160
Clustering data with Spark 161

Chapter 6: Signal Processing and Timeseries 167
Introduction 167
Spectral analysis with periodograms 168
Estimating power spectral density with the Welch method 170
Analyzing peaks 172
Measuring phase synchronization 174
Exponential smoothing 177
Evaluating smoothing 180
Using the Lomb-Scargle periodogram 183
Analyzing the frequency spectrum of audio 185
Analyzing signals with the discrete cosine transform 188
Block bootstrapping time series data 191
Moving block bootstrapping time series data 193
Applying the discrete wavelet transform 197

Chapter 7: Selecting Stocks with Financial Data Analysis 201
Introduction 202
Computing simple and log returns 202
Ranking stocks with the Sharpe ratio and liquidity 204
Ranking stocks with the Calmar and Sortino ratios 206
Analyzing returns statistics 208
Correlating individual stocks with the broader market 211
Exploring risk and return 214
Examining the market with the non-parametric runs test 216
Testing for random walks 219
Determining market efficiency with autoregressive models 221
Creating tables for a stock prices database 223
Populating the stock prices database 225
Optimizing an equal weights two-asset portfolio 230

Chapter 8: Text Mining and Social Network Analysis 235
Introduction 235
Creating a categorized corpus 236
Tokenizing news articles in sentences and words 239

Stemming, lemmatizing, filtering, and TF-IDF scores 240
Recognizing named entities 244
Extracting topics with non-negative matrix factorization 246
Implementing a basic terms database 248
Computing social network density 252
Calculating social network closeness centrality 254
Determining the betweenness centrality 255
Estimating the average clustering coefficient 257
Calculating the assortativity coefficient of a graph 258
Getting the clique number of a graph 259
Creating a document graph with cosine similarity 261

Chapter 9: Ensemble Learning and Dimensionality Reduction 265
Introduction 266
Recursively eliminating features 266
Applying principal component analysis for dimension reduction 269
Applying linear discriminant analysis for dimension reduction 271
Stacking and majority voting for multiple models 272
Learning with random forests 276
Fitting noisy data with the RANSAC algorithm 279
Bagging to improve results 283
Boosting for better learning 286
Nesting cross-validation 289
Reusing models with joblib 292
Hierarchically clustering data 294
Taking a Theano tour 296

Chapter 10: Evaluating Classifiers, Regressors, and Clusters 299
Introduction 300
Getting classification straight with the confusion matrix 300
Computing precision, recall, and F1-score 303
Examining a receiver operating characteristic and the area under a curve 306
Visualizing the goodness of fit 309
Computing MSE and median absolute error 310
Evaluating clusters with the mean silhouette coefficient 313
Comparing results with a dummy classifier 316
Determining MAPE and MPE 319
Comparing with a dummy regressor 321
Calculating the mean absolute error and the residual sum of squares 324
Examining the kappa of classification 326
Taking a look at the Matthews correlation coefficient 329

Chapter 11: Analyzing Images

	333
Introduction	333
Setting up OpenCV	334
Applying Scale-Invariant Feature Transform (SIFT)	337
Detecting features with SURF	339
Quantizing colors	341
Denoising images	343
Extracting patches from an image	345
Detecting faces with Haar cascades	348
Searching for bright stars	351
Extracting metadata from images	355
Extracting texture features from images	357
Applying hierarchical clustering on images	360
Segmenting images with spectral clustering	361

Chapter 12: Parallelism and Performance

	365
Introduction	365
Just-in-time compiling with Numba	367
Speeding up numerical expressions with Numexpr	369
Running multiple threads with the threading module	370
Launching multiple tasks with the concurrent.futures module	374
Accessing resources asynchronously with the asyncio module	377
Distributed processing with execnet	380
Profiling memory usage	384
Calculating the mean, variance, skewness, and kurtosis on the fly	385
Caching with a least recently used cache	390
Caching HTTP requests	393
Streaming counting with the Count-min sketch	395
Harnessing the power of the GPU with OpenCL	398

Appendix A: Glossary

	401

Appendix B: Function Reference

	407
IPython	407
Matplotlib	408
NumPy	409
pandas	410
Scikit-learn	411
SciPy	412
Seaborn	412
Statsmodels	413

Appendix C: Online Resources 415

IPython notebooks and open data 415

Mathematics and statistics 416

Appendix D: Tips and Tricks for Command-Line and Miscellaneous Tools 419

IPython notebooks 419

Command-line tools 420

The alias command 420

Command-line history 421

Reproducible sessions 421

Docker tips 422

Index 425

Preface

"Data analysis is Python's killer app"

—Unknown

This book is the follow-up to *Python Data Analysis*. The obvious question is, "what does this new book add?" as *Python Data Analysis* is pretty great (or so I like to believe) already. This book, *Python Data Analysis Cookbook*, is targeted at slightly more experienced Pythonistas. A year has passed, so we are using newer versions of software and software libraries that I didn't cover in *Python Data Analysis*. Also, I've had time to rethink and research, and as a result I decided the following:

- ▸ I need to have a toolbox in order to make my life easier and increase reproducibility. I called the toolbox **dautil** and made it available via PyPi (which can be installed with `pip/easy_install`).

- ▸ My soul-searching exercise led me to believe that I need to make it easier to obtain and install the required software. I published a Docker container (pydacbk) with some of the software we need via DockerHub. You can read more about the setup in *Chapter 1, Laying the Foundation for Reproducible Data Analysis,* and the online chapter. The Docker container is not ideal because it grew quite large, so I had to make some tough decisions. Since the container is not really part of the book, I think it will be appropriate if you contact me directly if you have any issues. However, please keep in mind that I can't change the image drastically.

- ▸ This book uses the IPython Notebook, which has become a standard tool for analysis. I have given some related tips in the online chapter and other books I have written.

- ▸ I am using Python 3 with very few exceptions because Python 2 will not be maintained after 2020.

Why do you need this book?

Some people will tell you that you don't need books, just get yourself an interesting project and figure out the rest as you go along. Although there are plenty of resources out there, this may be a very frustrating road. If you want to make a delicious soup, for example, you can of course ask friends and family, search the Internet, or watch cooking shows. However, your friends and family are not available full time for you and the quality of Internet content varies. And in my humble opinion, Packt Publishing, the reviewers, and I have spent so much time and energy on this book, that I will be surprised if you don't get any value out of it.

Data analysis, data science, big data – what is the big deal?

You probably have seen Venn diagrams depicting data science as the intersection of mathematics/statistics, computer science, and domain expertise. Data analysis is timeless and was there before data science and even before computer science. You could do data analysis with a pen and paper and, in more modern times, with a pocket calculator.

Data analysis has many aspects, with goals such as making decisions or coming up with new hypotheses and questions. The hype, status, and financial rewards surrounding data science and big data remind me of the time when datawarehousing and business intelligence were the buzz words. The ultimate goal of business intelligence and datawarehousing was to build dashboards for management. This involved a lot of politics and organizational aspects, but on the technical side, it was mostly about databases. Data science, on the other hand, is not database-centric and leans heavily on machine learning. Machine learning techniques have become necessary because of the bigger volumes of data. The data growth is caused by the growth of the world population and the rise of new technologies, such as social media and mobile devices. The data growth is, in fact, probably the only trend that we can be sure of continuing. The difference between constructing dashboards and applying machine learning is analogous to the way search engines evolved.

Search engines (if you can call them that) were initially nothing more than well-organized collections of links created manually. Eventually, the automated approach won. Since, in time, more data will be created (and not destroyed), we can expect an increase in automated data analysis.

A brief of history of data analysis with Python

The history of the various Python software libraries is quite interesting. I am not a historian, so the following notes are written from my own perspective:

- ▶ 1989: Guido van Rossum implements the very first version of Python at the CWI in the Netherlands as a Christmas "hobby" project.

- ▶ 1995: Jim Hugunin creates Numeric—the predecessor to NumPy.

- ▶ 1999: Pearu Peterson wrote f2py as a bridge between Fortran and Python.

- ▶ 2000: Python 2.0 is released.

- ▶ 2001: The SciPy library is released. Also, Numarray, a competing library of Numeric is created. Fernando Perez releases IPython, which starts out as an "afternoon hack". NLTK is released as a research project.

- ▶ 2002: John Hunter creates the Matplotlib library.

- ▶ 2005: NumPy is released by Travis Oliphant. NumPy, initially, is Numeric extended with features inspired by Numarray.

- ▶ 2006: NumPy 1.0 is released. The first version of SQLAlchemy is released.

- ▶ 2007: The scikit-learn project is initiated as a Google Summer of Code project by David Cournapeau. Cython was forked from Pyrex. Cython is later intensively used in pandas and scikit-learn to improve performance.

- ▶ 2008: Wes McKinney starts working on pandas. Python 3.0 is released.

- ▶ 2011: The IPython 0.12 release introduces the IPython notebook. Packt Publishing releases *NumPy 1.5 Beginner's Guide*.

- ▶ 2012: Packt Publishing releases *NumPy Cookbook*.

- ▶ 2013: Packt Publishing releases *NumPy Beginner's Guide, Second Edition*.

- ▶ 2014: Fernando Perez announces Project Jupyter, which aims to make a language-agnostic notebook. Packt Publishing releases *Learning NumPy Array* and *Python Data Analysis*.

- ▶ 2015: Packt Publishing releases *NumPy Beginner's Guide, Third Edition* and *NumPy Cookbook, Second Edition*.

A conjecture about the future

The future is a bright place, where an incredible amount of data lives in the Cloud and software runs on any imaginable device with an intuitive customizable interface. (I know young people who can't stop talking about how awesome their phone is and how one day we will all be programming on tablets by dragging and dropping). It seems there is a certain angst in the Python community about not being relevant in the future. Of course, the more you have invested in Python, the more it matters.

To figure out what to do, we need to know what makes Python special. A school of thought claims that Python is a glue language gluing C, Fortran, R, Java, and other languages; therefore, we just need better glue. This probably also means "borrowing" features from other languages. Personally, I like the way Python works, its flexible nature, its data structures, and the fact that it has so many libraries and features. I think the future is in more delicious syntactic sugar and just-in-time compilers. Somehow we should be able to continue writing Python code, which automatically is converted for us in concurrent (machine) code. Unseen machinery under the hood manages lower level details and sends data and instructions to CPUs, GPUs, or the Cloud. The code should be able to easily communicate with whatever storage backend we are using. Ideally, all of this magic will be just as convenient as automatic garbage collection. It may sound like an impossible "click of a button" dream, but I think it is worth pursuing.

What this book covers

Chapter 1, Laying the Foundation for Reproducible Data Analysis, is a pretty important chapter, and I recommend that you do not skip it. It explains Anaconda, Docker, unit testing, logging, and other essential elements of reproducible data analysis.

Chapter 2, Creating Attractive Data Visualizations, demonstrates how to visualize data and mentions frequently encountered pitfalls.

Chapter 3, Statistical Data Analysis and Probability, discusses statistical probability distributions and correlation between two variables.

Chapter 4, Dealing with Data and Numerical Issues, is about outliers and other common data issues. Data is almost never perfect, so a large portion of the analysis effort goes into dealing with data imperfections.

Chapter 5, Web Mining, Databases, and Big Data, is light on mathematics, but more focused on technical topics, such as databases, web scraping, and big data.

Chapter 6, Signal Processing and Timeseries, is about time series data, which is abundant and requires special techniques. Usually, we are interested in trends and seasonality or periodicity.

Chapter 7, Selecting Stocks with Financial Data Analysis, focuses on stock investing because stock price data is abundant. This is the only chapter on finance and the content should be at least partially relevant if stocks don't interest you.

Chapter 8, Text Mining and Social Network Analysis, helps you cope with the floods of textual and social media information.

Chapter 9, Ensemble Learning and Dimensionality Reduction, covers ensemble learning, classification and regression algorithms, as well as hierarchical clustering.

Chapter 10, Evaluating Classifiers, Regressors, and Clusters, evaluates the classifiers and regressors from *Chapter 9, Ensemble Learning and Dimensionality Reduction*, the preceding chapter.

Chapter 11, Analyzing Images, uses the OpenCV library quite a lot to analyze images.

Chapter 12, Parallelism and Performance, is about software performance and I discuss various options to improve performance, including caching and just-in-time compilers.

Appendix A, Glossary, is a brief glossary of technical concepts used throughout the book. The goal is to have a reference that is easy to look up.

Appendix B, Function Reference, is a short reference of functions meant as an extra aid in case you are temporarily unable to look up documentation.

Appendix C, Online Resources, lists resources including presentations, links to documentation, and freely available IPython notebooks and data. This appendix is available as an online chapter.

Appendix D, Tips and Tricks for Command-Line and Miscellaneous Tools, in this book we use various tools such as the IPython notebook, Docker, and Unix shell commands. I give a short list of tips that is not meant to be exhaustive. This appendix is also available as online chapter.

What you need for this book

First, you need a Python 3 distribution. I recommend the full Anaconda distribution as it comes with the majority of the software we need. I tested the code with Python 3.4 and the following packages:

- joblib 0.8.4
- IPython 3.2.1
- NetworkX 1.9.1
- NLTK 3.0.2

- Numexpr 2.3.1
- pandas 0.16.2
- SciPy 0.16.0
- seaborn 0.6.0
- sqlalchemy 0.9.9
- statsmodels 0.6.1
- matplotlib 1.5.0
- NumPy 1.10.1
- scikit-learn 0.17
- dautil 0.0.1a29

For some recipes, you need to install extra software, but this is explained whenever the software is required.

Who this book is for

This book is hands-on and low on theory. You should have better than beginner Python knowledge and have some knowledge of linear algebra, calculus, machine learning and statistics. Ideally, you would have read *Python Data Analysis*, but this is not a requirement. I also recommend the following books:

- *Building Machine Learning Systems with Python* by Willi Richert and Luis Pedro Coelho, 2013
- *Learning NumPy Array* by Ivan Idris, 2014
- *Learning scikit-learn: Machine Learning in Python* by Guillermo Moncecchi, 2013
- *Learning SciPy for Numerical and Scientific Computing* by Francisco J. Blanco-Silva, 2013
- *Matplotlib for Python Developers* by Sandro Tosi, 2009
- *NumPy Beginner's Guide - Third Edition* by Ivan Idris, 2015
- *NumPy Cookbook – Second Edition* by Ivan Idris, 2015
- *Parallel Programming with Python* by Jan Palach, 2014
- *Python Data Visualization Cookbook* by Igor Milovanović, 2013
- *Python for Finance* by Yuxing Yan, 2014
- *Python Text Processing with NLTK 2.0 Cookbook* by Jacob Perkins, 2010

Sections

In this book, you will find several headings that appear frequently (Getting ready, How to do it, How it works, There's more, and See also).

To give clear instructions on how to complete a recipe, we use these sections as follows:

Getting ready

This section tells you what to expect in the recipe, and describes how to set up any software or any preliminary settings required for the recipe.

How to do it...

This section contains the steps required to follow the recipe.

How it works...

This section usually consists of a detailed explanation of what happened in the previous section.

There's more...

This section consists of additional information about the recipe in order to make the reader more knowledgeable about the recipe.

See also

This section provides helpful links to other useful information for the recipe.

Conventions

In this book, you will find a number of text styles that distinguish between different kinds of information. Here are some examples of these styles and an explanation of their meaning.

Code words in text, database table names, folder names, filenames, file extensions, pathnames, dummy URLs, user input, and Twitter handles are shown as follows: "Plot the data and corresponding linear fits with the Seaborn `lmplot()` function."

A block of code is set as follows:

```
population = dawb.download(indicator=[dawb.get_name('pop_grow'), dawb.get_name('gdp_pcap'),
                                      dawb.get_name('primary_
education')],
                          country=countries['iso2c'], start=2014,
end=2014)

population = dawb.rename_columns(population)
```

When we wish to draw your attention to a particular part of a code block, the relevant lines or items are set in bold:

```
plt.figure()
plt.title('Rainy Weather vs Wind Speed')
categorical = df
categorical['RAIN'] = categorical['RAIN'] > 0
ax = sns.violinplot(x="RAIN", y="WIND_SPEED",
                    data=categorical)
```

Any command-line input or output is written as follows:

```
$ conda install -c scitools cartopy
```

New terms and **important words** are shown in bold. Words that you see on the screen, for example, in menus or dialog boxes, appear in the text like this: "In the next screenshot, the **Day of year 31** text comes from the tooltip:"

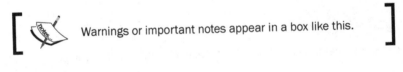

Warnings or important notes appear in a box like this.

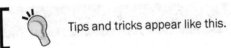

Tips and tricks appear like this.

Reader feedback

Feedback from our readers is always welcome. Let us know what you think about this book—what you liked or disliked. Reader feedback is important for us as it helps us develop titles that you will really get the most out of.

To send us general feedback, simply e-mail feedback@packtpub.com, and mention the book's title in the subject of your message.

If there is a topic that you have expertise in and you are interested in either writing or contributing to a book, see our author guide at www.packtpub.com/authors.

Customer support

Now that you are the proud owner of a Packt book, we have a number of things to help you to get the most from your purchase.

Downloading the example code

You can download the example code files for this book from your account at http://www.packtpub.com. If you purchased this book elsewhere, you can visit http://www.packtpub.com/support and register to have the files e-mailed directly to you.

You can download the code files by following these steps:

1. Log in or register to our website using your e-mail address and password.
2. Hover the mouse pointer on the **SUPPORT** tab at the top.
3. Click on **Code Downloads & Errata**.
4. Enter the name of the book in the **Search** box.
5. Select the book for which you're looking to download the code files.
6. Choose from the drop-down menu where you purchased this book from.
7. Click on **Code Download**.

Once the file is downloaded, please make sure that you unzip or extract the folder using the latest version of:

- WinRAR / 7-Zip for Windows
- Zipeg / iZip / UnRarX for Mac
- 7-Zip / PeaZip for Linux

The code bundle for the book is also hosted on GitHub at https://github.com/PacktPublishing/PythonDataAnalysisCookbook. We also have other code bundles from our rich catalog of books and videos available at https://github.com/PacktPublishing/. Check them out!

Errata

Although we have taken every care to ensure the accuracy of our content, mistakes do happen. If you find a mistake in one of our books—maybe a mistake in the text or the code— we would be grateful if you could report this to us. By doing so, you can save other readers from frustration and help us improve subsequent versions of this book. If you find any errata, please report them by visiting http://www.packtpub.com/submit-errata, selecting your book, clicking on the **Errata Submission Form** link, and entering the details of your errata. Once your errata are verified, your submission will be accepted and the errata will be uploaded to our website or added to any list of existing errata under the Errata section of that title.

To view the previously submitted errata, go to https://www.packtpub.com/books/content/support and enter the name of the book in the search field. The required information will appear under the **Errata** section.

Piracy

Piracy of copyrighted material on the Internet is an ongoing problem across all media. At Packt, we take the protection of our copyright and licenses very seriously. If you come across any illegal copies of our works in any form on the Internet, please provide us with the location address or website name immediately so that we can pursue a remedy.

Please contact us at copyright@packtpub.com with a link to the suspected pirated material.

We appreciate your help in protecting our authors and our ability to bring you valuable content.

Questions

If you have a problem with any aspect of this book, you can contact us at questions@packtpub.com, and we will do our best to address the problem.

1
Laying the Foundation for Reproducible Data Analysis

In this chapter, we will cover the following recipes:

- ▸ Setting up Anaconda
- ▸ Installing the Data Science Toolbox
- ▸ Creating a virtual environment with virtualenv and virtualenvwrapper
- ▸ Sandboxing Python applications with Docker images
- ▸ Keeping track of package versions and history in IPython Notebooks
- ▸ Configuring IPython
- ▸ Learning to log for robust error checking
- ▸ Unit testing your code
- ▸ Configuring pandas
- ▸ Configuring matplotlib
- ▸ Seeding random number generators and NumPy print options
- ▸ Standardizing reports, code style, and data access

Introduction

Reproducible data analysis is a cornerstone of good science. In today's rapidly evolving world of science and technology, reproducibility is a hot topic. Reproducibility is about lowering barriers for other people. It may seem strange or unnecessary, but reproducible analysis is essential to get your work acknowledged by others. If a lot of people confirm your results, it will have a positive effect on your career. However, reproducible analysis is hard. It has important economic consequences, as you can read in *Freedman LP, Cockburn IM, Simcoe TS (2015) The Economics of Reproducibility in Preclinical Research*. PLoS Biol 13(6): e1002165. doi:10.1371/journal.pbio.1002165.

So reproducibility is important for society and for you, but how does it apply to Python users? Well, we want to lower barriers for others by:

- Giving information about the software and hardware we used, including versions.
- Sharing virtual environments.
- Logging program behavior.
- Unit testing the code. This also serves as documentation of sorts.
- Sharing configuration files.
- Seeding random generators and making sure program behavior is as deterministic as possible.
- Standardizing reporting, data access, and code style.

I created the `dautil` package for this book, which you can install with pip or from the source archive provided in this book's code bundle. If you are in a hurry, run `$ python install_ch1.py` to install most of the software for this chapter, including `dautil`. I created a test Docker image, which you can use if you don't want to install anything except Docker (see the recipe, *Sandboxing Python applications with Docker images*).

Setting up Anaconda

Anaconda is a free Python distribution for data analysis and scientific computing. It has its own package manager, **conda**. The distribution includes more than 200 Python packages, which makes it very convenient. For casual users, the **Miniconda** distribution may be the better choice. Miniconda contains the conda package manager and Python. The technical editors use Anaconda, and so do I. But don't worry, I will describe in this book alternative installation instructions for readers who are not using Anaconda. In this recipe, we will install Anaconda and Miniconda and create a virtual environment.

Getting ready

The procedures to install Anaconda and Miniconda are similar. Obviously, Anaconda requires more disk space. Follow the instructions on the Anaconda website at `http://conda.pydata.org/docs/install/quick.html` (retrieved Mar 2016). First, you have to download the appropriate installer for your operating system and Python version. Sometimes, you can choose between a GUI and a command-line installer. I used the Python 3.4 installer, although my system Python version is v2.7. This is possible because Anaconda comes with its own Python. On my machine, the Anaconda installer created an `anaconda` directory in my home directory and required about 900 MB. The Miniconda installer installs a `miniconda` directory in your home directory.

How to do it...

1. Now that Anaconda or Miniconda is installed, list the packages with the following command:

    ```
    $ conda list
    ```

2. For reproducibility, it is good to know that we can export packages:

    ```
    $ conda list --export
    ```

3. The preceding command prints packages and versions on the screen, which you can save in a file. You can install these packages with the following command:

    ```
    $ conda create -n ch1env --file <export file>
    ```

    This command also creates an environment named `ch1env`.

4. The following command creates a simple `testenv` environment:

    ```
    $ conda create --name testenv python=3
    ```

5. On Linux and Mac OS X, switch to this environment with the following command:

    ```
    $ source activate testenv
    ```

6. On Windows, we don't need `source`. The syntax to switch back is similar:

    ```
    $ [source] deactivate
    ```

7. The following command prints export information for the environment in the YAML (explained in the following section) format:

    ```
    $ conda env export -n testenv
    ```

8. To remove the environment, type the following (note that even after removing, the name of the environment still exists in `~/.conda/environments.txt`):

    ```
    $ conda remove -n testenv --all
    ```

9. Search for a package as follows:

```
$ conda search numpy
```

In this example, we searched for the NumPy package. If NumPy is already present, Anaconda shows an asterisk in the output at the corresponding entry.

10. Update the distribution as follows:

```
$ conda update conda
```

There's more...

The `.condarc` configuration file follows the **YAML** syntax.

YAML is a human-readable configuration file format with the extension `.yaml` or `.yml`. YAML was initially released in 2011, with the latest release in 2009. The YAML homepage is at `http://yaml.org/` (retrieved July 2015).

You can find a sample configuration file at `http://conda.pydata.org/docs/install/sample-condarc.html` (retrieved July 2015). The related documentation is at `http://conda.pydata.org/docs/install/config.html` (retrieved July 2015).

See also

- Martins, L. Felipe (November 2014). *IPython Notebook Essentials* (1st Edition.). Packt Publishing. p. 190. ISBN 1783988347

- The conda user cheat sheet at `http://conda.pydata.org/docs/_downloads/conda-cheatsheet.pdf` (retrieved July 2015)

Installing the Data Science Toolbox

The **Data Science Toolbox (DST)** is a virtual environment based on Ubuntu for data analysis using Python and R. Since DST is a virtual environment, we can install it on various operating systems. We will install DST locally, which requires **VirtualBox** and **Vagrant**. VirtualBox is a virtual machine application originally created by Innotek GmbH in 2007. Vagrant is a wrapper around virtual machine applications such as VirtualBox created by Mitchell Hashimoto.

Getting ready

You need to have in the order of 2 to 3 GB free for VirtualBox, Vagrant, and DST itself. This may vary by operating system.

How to do it...

Installing DST requires the following steps:

1. Install VirtualBox by downloading an installer for your operating system and architecture from `https://www.virtualbox.org/wiki/Downloads` (retrieved July 2015) and running it. I installed VirtualBox 4.3.28-100309 myself, but you can just install whatever the most recent VirtualBox version at the time is.

2. Install Vagrant by downloading an installer for your operating system and architecture from `https://www.vagrantup.com/downloads.html` (retrieved July 2015). I installed Vagrant 1.7.2 and again you can install a more recent version if available.

3. Create a directory to hold the DST and navigate to it with a terminal. Run the following command:

   ```
   $ vagrant init data-science-toolbox/dst
   
   $ vagrant up
   ```

   The first command creates a `VagrantFile` configuration file. Most of the content is commented out, but the file does contain links to documentation that might be useful. The second command creates the DST and initiates a download that could take a couple of minutes.

4. Connect to the virtual environment as follows (on Windows use putty):

   ```
   $ vagrant ssh
   ```

5. View the preinstalled Python packages with the following command:

   ```
   vagrant@data-science-toolbox:~$ pip freeze
   ```

   The list is quite long; in my case it contained 32 packages. The DST Python version as of July 2015 was 2.7.6.

6. When you are done with the DST, log out and suspend (you can also halt it completely) the VM:

   ```
   vagrant@data-science-toolbox:~$ logout
   Connection to 127.0.0.1 closed.
   $ vagrant suspend
   ==> default: Saving VM state and suspending execution...
   ```

How it works...

Virtual machines (VMs) emulate computers in software. **VirtualBox** is an application that creates and manages VMs. VirtualBox stores its VMs in your home folder, and this particular VM takes about 2.2 GB of storage.

Ubuntu is an open source Linux operating system, and we are allowed by its license to create virtual machines. Ubuntu has several versions; we can get more info with the `lsb_release` command:

```
vagrant@data-science-toolbox:~$ lsb_release -a
No LSB modules are available.
Distributor ID:     Ubuntu
Description:     Ubuntu 14.04 LTS
Release:     14.04
Codename:     trusty
```

Vagrant used to only work with VirtualBox, but currently it also supports VMware, KVM, Docker, and Amazon EC2. Vagrant calls virtual machines boxes. Some of these boxes are available for everyone at `http://www.vagrantbox.es/` (retrieved July 2015).

See also

  ▶ *Run Ubuntu Linux Within Windows Using VirtualBox* at `http://linux.about.com/od/howtos/ss/Run-Ubuntu-Linux-Within-Windows-Using-VirtualBox.htm#step11` (retrieved July 2015)

  ▶ *VirtualBox manual chapter 10* Technical Information at `https://www.virtualbox.org/manual/ch10.html` (retrieved July 2015)

Creating a virtual environment with virtualenv and virtualenvwrapper

Virtual environments provide dependency isolation for small projects. They also keep your `site-packages` directory small. Since Python 3.3, `virtualenv` has been part of the standard Python distribution. The virtualenvwrapper Python project has some extra convenient features for virtual environment management. I will demonstrate virtualenv and virtualenvwrapper functionality in this recipe.

Getting ready

You need Python 3.3 or later. You can install `virtualenvwrapper` with `pip` command as follows:

```
$ [sudo] pip install virtualenvwrapper
```

On Linux and Mac, it's necessary to do some extra work—specifying a directory for the virtual environments and sourcing a script:

```
$ export WORKON_HOME=/tmp/envs
$ source /usr/local/bin/virtualenvwrapper.sh
```

Windows has a separate version, which you can install with the following command:

```
$ pip install virtualenvwrapper-win
```

How to do it...

1. Create a virtual environment for a given directory with the `pyvenv` script part of your Python distribution:

    ```
    $ pyvenv /tmp/testenv
    $ ls
    bin            include          lib          pyvenv.cfg
    ```

2. In this example, we created a `testenv` directory in the `/tmp` directory with several directories and a configuration file. The configuration file `pyvenv.cfg` contains the Python version and the home directory of the Python distribution.

3. Activate the environment on Linux or Mac by sourcing the `activate` script, for example, with the following command:

    ```
    $ source bin/activate
    ```

    On Windows, use the `activate.bat` file.

4. You can now install packages in this environment in isolation. When you are done with the environment, switch back on Linux or Mac with the following command:

    ```
    $ deactivate
    ```

    On Windows, use the `deactivate.bat` file.

5. Alternatively, you could use virtualenvwrapper. Create and switch to a virtual environment with the following command:

    ```
    vagrant@data-science-toolbox:~$ mkvirtualenv env2
    ```

6. Deactivate the environment with the `deactivate` command:

```
(env2)vagrant@data-science-toolbox:~$ deactivate
```

7. Delete the environment with the `rmvirtualenv` command:

```
vagrant@data-science-toolbox:~$ rmvirtualenv env2
```

See also

▶ The Python standard library documentation for virtual environments at `https://docs.python.org/3/library/venv.html#creating-virtual-environments` (retrieved July 2015)

▶ The virtualenvwrapper documentation is at `https://virtualenvwrapper.readthedocs.org/en/latest/index.html` (retrieved July 2015)

Sandboxing Python applications with Docker images

Docker uses Linux kernel features to provide an extra virtualization layer. Docker was created in 2013 by Solomon Hykes. **Boot2Docker** allows us to install Docker on Windows and Mac OS X too. Boot2Docker uses a VirtualBox VM that contains a Linux environment with Docker. In this recipe, we will set up Docker and download the `continuumio/miniconda3` Docker image.

Getting ready

The Docker installation docs are saved at `https://docs.docker.com/index.html` (retrieved July 2015). I installed Docker 1.7.0 with Boot2Docker. The installer requires about 133 MB. However, if you want to follow the whole recipe, you will need several gigabytes.

How to do it...

1. Once Boot2Docker is installed, you need to initialize the environment. This is only necessary once, and Linux users don't need this step:

```
$ boot2docker init
Latest release for github.com/boot2docker/boot2docker is v1.7.0
Downloading boot2docker ISO image...
Success: downloaded https://github.com/boot2docker/boot2docker/
releases/download/v1.7.0/boot2docker.iso
```

2. In the preceding step, you downloaded a VirtualBox VM to a directory such as `/VirtualBox\ VMs/boot2docker-vm/`.

   The next step for Mac OS X and Windows users is to start the VM:

   ```
   $ boot2docker start
   ```

3. Check the Docker environment by starting a sample container:

   ```
   $ docker run hello-world
   ```

    Some people reported a hopefully temporary issue of not being able to connect. The issue can be resolved by issuing commands with an extra argument, for instance:

   ```
   $ docker [--tlsverify=false] run hello-world
   ```

4. Docker images can be made public. We can search for such images and download them. In *Setting up Anaconda*, we installed Anaconda; however, Anaconda and Miniconda Docker images also exist. Use the following command:

   ```
   $ docker search continuumio
   ```

5. The preceding command shows a list of Docker images from **Continuum Analytics** – the company that developed Anaconda and Miniconda. Download the Miniconda 3 Docker image as follows (if you prefer using my container, skip this):

   ```
   $ docker pull continuumio/miniconda3
   ```

6. Start the image with the following command:

   ```
   $ docker run -t -i continuumio/miniconda3 /bin/bash
   ```

   We start out as root in the image.

7. The command `$ docker images` should list the `continuumio/miniconda3` image as well. If you prefer not to install too much software (possibly only Docker and Boot2Docker) for this book, you should use the image I created. It uses the `continuumio/miniconda3` image as template. This image allows you to execute Python scripts in the current working directory on your computer, while using installed software from the Docker image:

   ```
   $ docker run -it -p 8888:8888 -v $(pwd):/usr/data -w /usr/data
   "ivanidris/pydacbk:latest" python <somefile>.py
   ```

8. You can also run a IPython notebook in your current working directory with the following command:

   ```
   $ docker run -it -p 8888:8888 -v $(pwd):/usr/data -w /usr/data
   "ivanidris/pydacbk:latest" sh -c "ipython notebook --ip=0.0.0.0
   --no-browser"
   ```

9. Then, go to either `http:// 192.168.59.103:8888` or `http:// localhost:8888` to view the IPython home screen. You might have noticed that the command lines are quite long, so I will post additional tips and tricks to make life easier on `https://pythonhosted.org/dautil` (work in progress).

   The Boot2Docker VM shares the `/Users` directory on Mac OS X and the `C:\Users` directory on Windows. In general and on other operating systems, we can mount directories and copy files from the container as described in `https://docs.docker.com/userguide/dockervolumes/` (retrieved July 2015).

10. Shut down the VM (unless you are on Linux, where you use the `docker` command instead) with the following command:

```
$ boot2docker down
```

How it works...

Docker Hub acts as a central registry for public and private Docker images. In this recipe, we downloaded images via this registry. To push an image to Docker Hub, we need to create a local registry first. The way Docker Hub works is in many ways comparable to the way source code repositories such as GitHub work. You can commit changes as well as push, pull, and tag images. The `continuumio/miniconda3` image is configured with a special file, which you can find at `https://github.com/ContinuumIO/docker-images/blob/master/miniconda3/Dockerfile` (retrieved July 2015). In this file, you can read which image was used as base, the name of the maintainer, and the commands used to build the image.

See also

▶ The Docker user guide at `http://docs.docker.com/userguide/` (retrieved July 2015)

Keeping track of package versions and history in IPython Notebook

The **IPython Notebook** was added to IPython 0.12 in December 2011. Many Pythonistas feel that the IPython Notebook is essential for reproducible data analysis. The IPython Notebook is comparable to commercial products such as Mathematica, MATLAB, and Maple. It is an interactive web browser-based environment. In this recipe, we will see how to keep track of package versions and store IPython sessions in the context of reproducible data analysis. By the way, the IPython Notebook has been renamed Jupyter Notebook.

Getting ready

For this recipe, you will need a recent IPython installation. The instructions to install IPython are at `http://ipython.org/install.html` (retrieved July 2015). Install it using the pip command:

```
$ [sudo] pip install ipython/jupyter
```

If you have installed IPython via Anaconda already, check for updates with the following commands:

```
$ conda update conda
$ conda update ipython ipython-notebook ipython-qtconsole
```

I have IPython 3.2.0 as part of the Anaconda distribution.

How to do it...

We will install log a Python session and use the **watermark** extension to track package versions and other information. Start an IPython shell or notebook. When we start a session, we can use the command line switch `--logfile=<file name>.py`. In this recipe, we use the `%logstart` magic (IPython terminology) function:

```
In [1]: %logstart cookbook_log.py rotate
Activating auto-logging. Current session state plus future input saved.
Filename        : cookbook_log.py
Mode            : rotate
Output logging  : False
Raw input log   : False
Timestamping    : False
State           : active
```

This example invocation started logging to a file in rotate mode. Both the filename and mode are optional. Turn logging off and back on again as follows:

```
In [2]: %logoff
Switching logging OFF


In [3]: %logon
Switching logging ON
```

Install the `watermark` magic from Github with the following command:

```
In [4]: %install_ext https://raw.githubusercontent.com/rasbt/watermark/
master/watermark.py
```

The preceding line downloads a Python file, in my case, to `~/.ipython/extensions/watermark.py`. Load the extension by typing the following line:

```
%load_ext watermark
```

The extension can place timestamps as well as software and hardware information. Get additional usage documentation and version (I installed watermark 1.2.2) with the following command:

```
%watermark?
```

For example, call `watermark` without any arguments:

```
In [7]: %watermark
... Omitting time stamp ...

CPython 3.4.3
IPython 3.2.0

compiler   : Omitting
system     : Omitting
release    : 14.3.0
machine    : x86_64
processor  : i386
CPU cores  : 8
interpreter: 64bit
```

I omitted the timestamp and other information for personal reasons. A more complete example follows with author name (`-a`), versions of packages specified as a comma-separated string (`-p`), and custom time (`-c`) in a `strftime()` based format:

```
In [8]: %watermark -a "Ivan Idris" -v -p numpy,scipy,matplotlib -c '%b
%Y' -w
Ivan Idris 'Jul 2015'

CPython 3.4.3
IPython 3.2.0

numpy 1.9.2
```

```
scipy 0.15.1
matplotlib 1.4.3
watermark v. 1.2.2
```

How it works...

The IPython logger writes commands you type to a Python file. Most of the lines are in the following format:

```
get_ipython().magic('STRING_YOU_TYPED')
```

You can replay the session with `%load <log file>`. The logging modes are described in the following table:

Mode	Description
over	This mode overwrites existing log files.
backup	If a log file exists with the same name, the old file is renamed.
append	This mode appends lines to already existing files.
rotate	This mode rotates log files by incrementing numbers, so that log files don't get too big.

We used a custom magic function available on the Internet. The code for the function is in a single Python file and it should be easy for you to follow. If you want different behavior, you just need to modify the file.

See also

- The custom magics documentation at http://ipython.org/ipython-doc/dev/config/custommagics.html (retrieved July 2015)
- Helen Shen (2014). *Interactive notebooks: Sharing the code*. Nature 515 (7525): 151–152. doi:10.1038/515151a
- IPython reference documentation at https://ipython.org/ipython-doc/dev/interactive/reference.html (retrieved July 2015)

Configuring IPython

IPython has an elaborate configuration and customization system. The components of the system are as follows:

- IPython provides default profiles, but we can create our own profiles
- Various settable options for the shell, kernel, Qt console, and notebook

- ▶ Customization of prompts and colors
- ▶ Extensions we saw in *Keeping track of package versions and history in IPython notebooks*
- ▶ Startup files per profile

I will demonstrate some of these components in this recipe.

Getting ready

You need IPython for this recipe, so (if necessary) have a look at the *Getting ready* section of *Keeping track of package versions and history in IPython notebooks*.

How to do it...

Let's start with a startup file. I have a directory in my home directory at `.ipython/profile_default/startup`, which belongs to the default profile. This directory is meant for startup files. IPython detects Python files in this directory and executes them in lexical order of filenames. Because of the lexical order, it is convenient to name the startup files with a combination of digits and strings, for example, `0000-watermark.py`. Put the following code in the startup file:

```
get_ipython().magic('%load_ext watermark')
get_ipython().magic('watermark -a "Ivan Idris" -v -p
numpy,scipy,matplotlib -c \'%b %Y\' -w')
```

This startup file loads the extension we used in *Keeping track of package versions and history in IPython notebooks* and shows information about package versions. Other use cases include importing modules and defining functions. IPython stores commands in a SQLite database, so you could gather statistics to find common usage patterns. The following script prints source lines and associated counts from the database for the default profile sorted by counts (the code is in the `ipython_history.py` file in this book's code bundle):

```
import sqlite3
from IPython.utils.path import get_ipython_dir
import pprint
import os


def print_history(file):
    with sqlite3.connect(file) as con:
        c = con.cursor()
        c.execute("SELECT count(source_raw) as csr,\
                source_raw FROM history\
                GROUP BY source_raw\
                ORDER BY csr")
        result = c.fetchall()
```

```
    pprint.pprint(result)
    c.close()

hist_file = '%s/profile_default/history.sqlite' % get_ipython_dir()

if os.path.exists(hist_file):
    print_history(hist_file)
else:
    print("%s doesn't exist" % hist_file)
```

The highlighted SQL query does the bulk of the work. The code is self-explanatory. If it is not clear, I recommend reading *Chapter 8*, *Text Mining and Social Network*, of my book *Python Data Analysis*, *Packt Publishing*.

The other configuration option I mentioned is profiles. We can use the default profiles or create our own profiles on a per project or functionality basis. Profiles act as sandboxes and you can configure them separately. Here's the command to create a profile:

```
$ ipython profile create [newprofile]
```

The configuration files are Python files and their names end with _config.py. In these files, you can set various IPython options. Set the option to automatically log the IPython session as follows:

```
c = get_config()

c.TerminalInteractiveShell.logstart=True
```

The first line is usually included in configuration files and gets the root IPython configuration object. The last line tells IPython that we want to start logging immediately on startup so you don't have to type %logstart.

Alternatively, you can also set the log file name with the following command:

```
c.TerminalInteractiveShell.logfile='mylog_file.py'
```

You can also use the following configuration line that ensures logging in append mode:

```
c.TerminalInteractiveShell.logappend='mylog_file.py'
```

See also

- *Introduction to IPython configuration* at http://ipython.org/ipython-doc/dev/config/intro.html#profiles (retrieved July 2015)
- *Terminal IPython options documentation* at http://ipython.org/ipython-doc/dev/config/options/terminal.html (retrieved July 2015)

Learning to log for robust error checking

Notebooks are useful to keep track of what you did and what went wrong. Logging works in a similar fashion, and we can log errors and other useful information with the standard Python `logging` library.

For reproducible data analysis, it is good to know the modules our Python scripts import. In this recipe, I will introduce a minimal API from `dautil` that logs package versions of imported modules in a best effort manner.

Getting ready

In this recipe, we import NumPy and pandas, so you may need to import them. See the *Configuring pandas* recipe for pandas installation instructions. Installation instructions for NumPy can be found at `http://docs.scipy.org/doc/numpy/user/install.html` (retrieved July 2015). Alternatively, install NumPy with pip using the following command:

```
$ [sudo] pip install numpy
```

The command for Anaconda users is as follows:

```
$ conda install numpy
```

I have installed NumPy 1.9.2 via Anaconda. We also require `AppDirs` to find the appropriate directory to store logs. Install it with the following command:

```
$ [sudo] pip install appdirs
```

I have AppDirs 1.4.0 on my system.

How to do it...

To log, we need to create and set up loggers. We can either set up the loggers with code or use a configuration file. Configuring loggers with code is the more flexible option, but configuration files tend to be more readable. I use the `log.conf` configuration file from `dautil`:

```
[loggers]
keys=root

[handlers]
keys=consoleHandler,fileHandler

[formatters]
keys=simpleFormatter
```

```
[logger_root]
level=DEBUG
handlers=consoleHandler,fileHandler

[handler_consoleHandler]
class=StreamHandler
level=INFO
formatter=simpleFormatter
args=(sys.stdout,)

[handler_fileHandler]
class=dautil.log_api.VersionsLogFileHandler
formatter=simpleFormatter
args=('versions.log',)

[formatter_simpleFormatter]
format=%(asctime)s - %(name)s - %(levelname)s - %(message)s
datefmt=%d-%b-%Y
```

The file configures a logger to log to a file with the DEBUG level and to the screen with the INFO level. So, the logger logs more to the file than to the screen. The file also specifies the format of the log messages. I created a tiny API in dautil, which creates a logger with its get_logger() function and uses it to log the package versions of a client program with its log() function. The code is in the log_api.py file of dautil:

```
from pkg_resources import get_distribution
from pkg_resources import resource_filename
import logging
import logging.config
import pprint
from appdirs import AppDirs
import os


def get_logger(name):
    log_config = resource_filename(__name__, 'log.conf')
    logging.config.fileConfig(log_config)
    logger = logging.getLogger(name)

    return logger


def shorten(module_name):
```

```
        dot_i = module_name.find('.')

        return module_name[:dot_i]


    def log(modules, name):
        skiplist = ['pkg_resources', 'distutils']

        logger = get_logger(name)
        logger.debug('Inside the log function')

        for k in modules.keys():
            str_k = str(k)

            if '.version' in str_k:
                short = shorten(str_k)

                if short in skiplist:
                    continue

                try:
                    logger.info('%s=%s' % (short,
                            get_distribution(short).version))
                except ImportError:
                    logger.warn('Could not impport', short)


    class VersionsLogFileHandler(logging.FileHandler):
        def __init__(self, fName):
            dirs = AppDirs("PythonDataAnalysisCookbook",
                        "Ivan Idris")
            path = dirs.user_log_dir
            print(path)

            if not os.path.exists(path):
                os.mkdir(path)

            super(VersionsLogFileHandler, self).__init__(
                os.path.join(path, fName))
```

The program that uses the API is in the `log_demo.py` file in this book's code bundle:

```
    import sys
    import numpy as np
```

```
import matplotlib.pyplot as plt
import pandas as pd
from dautil import log_api

log_api.log(sys.modules, sys.argv[0])
```

How it works...

We configured a handler (`VersionsLogFileHandler`) that writes to file and a handler (`StreamHandler`) that displays messages on the screen. `StreamHandler` is a class in the Python standard library. To configure the format of the log messages, we used the `SimpleFormater` class from the Python standard library.

The API I made goes through modules listed in the `sys.modules` variable and tries to get the versions of the modules. Some of the modules are not relevant for data analysis, so we skip them. The `log()` function of the API logs a `DEBUG` level message with the `debug()` method. The `info()` method logs the package version at `INFO` level.

See also

- ▶ The logging tutorial at `https://docs.python.org/3.5/howto/logging.html` (retrieved July 2015)

- ▶ The logging cookbook at `https://docs.python.org/3.5/howto/logging-cookbook.html#logging-cookbook` (retrieved July 2015)

Unit testing your code

If code doesn't do what you want, it's hard to do reproducible data analysis. One way to gain control of your code is to test it. If you have tested code manually, you know it is repetitive and boring. When a task is boring and repetitive, you should automate it.

Unit testing automates testing and I hope you are familiar with it. When you learn unit testing for the first time, you start with simple tests such as comparing strings or numbers. However, you hit a wall when file I/O or other resources come into the picture. It turns out that in Python we can mock resources or external APIs easily. The packages needed are even part of the standard Python library. In the *Learning to log for robust error checking* recipe, we logged messages to a file. If we unit test this code, we don't want to trigger logging from the test code. In this recipe, I will show you how to mock the logger and other software components we need.

Getting ready

Familiarize yourself with the code under test in `log_api.py`.

How to do it...

The code for this recipe is in the `test_log_api.py` file of `dautil`. We start by importing the module under test and the Python functionality we need for unit testing:

```python
from dautil import log_api
import unittest
from unittest.mock import create_autospec
from unittest.mock import patch
```

Define a class that contains the test code:

```python
class TestLogApi(unittest.TestCase):
```

Make the unit tests executable with the following lines:

```python
if __name__ == '__main__':
    unittest.main()
```

If we call Python functions with the wrong number of arguments, we expect to get a `TypeError`. The following tests check for that:

```python
    def test_get_logger_args(self):
        mock_get_logger =           create_autospec(log_api.get_logger,
    return_value=None)
        mock_get_logger('test')
        mock_get_logger.assert_called_once_with('test')

    def test_log_args(self):
        mock_log = create_autospec(log_api.log, return_value=None)
        mock_log([], 'test')
        mock_log.assert_called_once_with([], 'test')

        with self.assertRaises(TypeError):
            mock_log()

        with self.assertRaises(TypeError):
            mock_log('test')
```

We used the `unittest.create_autospec()` function to mock the functions under test. Mock the Python `logging` package as follows:

```python
    @patch('dautil.log_api.logging')
    def test_get_logger_fileConfig(self, mock_logging):
        log_api.get_logger('test')
        self.assertTrue(mock_logging.config.fileConfig.called)
```

The @patch decorator replaces logging with a mock. We can also patch with similarly named functions. The patching trick is quite useful. Test our get_logger() function with the following method:

```
@patch('dautil.log_api.get_logger')
def test_log_debug(self, amock):
    log_api.log({}, 'test')
    self.assertTrue(amock.return_value.debug.called)
    amock.return_value.debug.assert_called_once_with(
        'Inside the log function')
```

The previous lines check whether debug() was called and with which arguments. The following two test methods demonstrate how to use multiple @patch decorators:

```
@patch('dautil.log_api.get_distribution')
@patch('dautil.log_api.get_logger')
def test_numpy(self, m_get_logger, m_get_distribution):
    log_api.log({'numpy.version': ''}, 'test')
    m_get_distribution.assert_called_once_with('numpy')
    self.assertTrue(m_get_logger.return_value.info.called)

@patch('dautil.log_api.get_distribution')
@patch('dautil.log_api.get_logger')
def test_distutils(self, amock, m_get_distribution):
    log_api.log({'distutils.version': ''}, 'test')
    self.assertFalse(m_get_distribution.called)
```

How it works...

Mocking is a technique to spy on objects and functions. We substitute them with our own spies, which we give just enough information to avoid detection. The spies report to us who contacted them and any useful information they received.

See also

▶ The unittest.mock library documentation at https://docs.python.org/3/library/unittest.mock.html#patch-object (retrieved July 2015)

▶ The unittest documentation at https://docs.python.org/3/library/unittest.html (retrieved July 2015)

Configuring pandas

The pandas library has more than a dozen configuration options, as described in `http://pandas.pydata.org/pandas-docs/dev/options.html` (retrieved July 2015).

 The pandas library is Python open source software originally created for econometric data analysis. It uses data structures inspired by the R programming language.

You can set and get properties using dotted notation or via functions. It is also possible to reset options to defaults and get information about them. The `option_context()` function allows you to limit the scope of the option to a context using the Python `with` statement. In this recipe, I will demonstrate pandas configuration and a simple API to set and reset options I find useful. The two options are `precision` and `max_rows`. The first option specifies floating point precision of output. The second option specifies the maximum rows of a pandas `DataFrame` to print on the screen.

Getting ready

You need pandas and NumPy for this recipe. Instructions to install NumPy are given in *Learning to log for robust error checking*. The pandas installation documentation can be found at `http://pandas.pydata.org/pandas-docs/dev/install.html` (retrieved July 2015). The recommended way to install pandas is via Anaconda. I have installed pandas 0.16.2 via Anaconda. You can update your Anaconda pandas with the following command:

```
$ conda update pandas
```

How to do it...

The following code from the `options.py` file in `dautil` defines a simple API to set and reset options:

```python
import pandas as pd

def set_pd_options():
    pd.set_option('precision', 4)
    pd.set_option('max_rows', 5)

def reset_pd_options():
    pd.reset_option('precision')
    pd.reset_option('max_rows')
```

The script in `configure_pd.py` in this book's code bundle uses the following API:

```
from dautil import options
import pandas as pd
import numpy as np
from dautil import log_api

printer = log_api.Printer()
print(pd.describe_option('precision'))
print(pd.describe_option('max_rows'))

printer.print('Initial precision', pd.get_option('precision'))
printer.print('Initial max_rows', pd.get_option('max_rows'))

# Random pi's, should use random state if possible
np.random.seed(42)
df = pd.DataFrame(np.pi * np.random.rand(6, 2))
printer.print('Initial df', df)

options.set_pd_options()
printer.print('df with different options', df)

options.reset_pd_options()
printer.print('df after reset', df)
```

If you run the script, you get descriptions for the options that are a bit too long to display here. The getter gives the following output:

```
'Initial precision'
7


'Initial max_rows'
60
```

Then, we create a pandas `DataFrame` table with random data. The initial printout looks like this:

```
'Initial df'
          0         1
0  1.176652  2.986757
1  2.299627  1.880741
2  0.490147  0.490071
3  0.182475  2.721173
4  1.888459  2.224476
5  0.064668  3.047062
```

The printout comes from the following class in `log_api.py`:

```
class Printer():
    def __init__(self, modules=None, name=None):
        if modules and name:
            log(modules, name)

    def print(self, *args):
        for arg in args:
            pprint.pprint(arg)
```

After setting the options with the `dautil` API, pandas hides some of the rows and the floating point numbers look different too:

```
'df with different options'
        0       1
0   1.177   2.987
1   2.300   1.881
..    ...     ...
4   1.888   2.224
5   0.065   3.047


[6 rows x 2 columns]
```

Because of the truncated rows, pandas tells us how many rows and columns the `DataFrame` table has. After we reset the options, we get the original printout back.

Configuring matplotlib

The matplotlib library allows configuration via the `matplotlibrc` files and Python code. The last option is what we are going to do in this recipe. Small configuration tweaks should not matter if your data analysis is strong. However, it doesn't hurt to have consistent and attractive plots. Another option is to apply stylesheets, which are files comparable to the `matplotlibrc` files. However, in my opinion, the best option is to use Seaborn on top of matplotlib. I will discuss Seaborn and matplotlib in more detail in *Chapter 2, Creating Attractive Data Visualizations*.

Getting ready

You need to install matplotlib for this recipe. Visit `http://matplotlib.org/users/installing.html` (retrieved July 2015) for more information. I have matplotlib 1.4.3 via Anaconda. Install Seaborn using Anaconda:

```
$ conda install seaborn
```

I have installed Seaborn 0.6.0 via Anaconda.

How to do it...

We can set options via a dictionary-like variable. The following function from the `options.py` file in `dautil` sets three options:

```
def set_mpl_options():
    mpl.rcParams['legend.fancybox'] = True
    mpl.rcParams['legend.shadow'] = True
    mpl.rcParams['legend.framealpha'] = 0.7
```

The first three options have to do with legends. The first option specifies rounded corners for the legend, the second options enables showing a shadow, and the third option makes the legend slightly transparent. The matplotlib `rcdefaults()` function resets the configuration.

To demonstrate these options, let's use sample data made available by matplotlib. The imports are as follows:

```
import matplotlib.cbook as cbook
import pandas as pd
import matplotlib.pyplot as plt
from dautil import options
import matplotlib as mpl
from dautil import plotting
import seaborn as sns
```

The data is in a CSV file and contains stock price data for AAPL. Use the following commands to read the data and stores them in a pandas `DataFrame`:

```
data = cbook.get_sample_data('aapl.csv', asfileobj=True)
df = pd.read_csv(data, parse_dates=True, index_col=0)
```

Resample the data to average monthly values as follows:

```
df = df.resample('M')
```

The full code is in the `configure_matplotlib.ipynb` file in this book's code bundle:

```python
import matplotlib.cbook as cbook
import pandas as pd
import matplotlib.pyplot as plt
from dautil import options
import matplotlib as mpl
from dautil import plotting
import seaborn as sns


data = cbook.get_sample_data('aapl.csv', asfileobj=True)
df = pd.read_csv(data, parse_dates=True, index_col=0)
df = df.resample('M')
close = df['Close'].values
dates = df.index.values
fig, axes = plt.subplots(4)


def plot(title, ax):
    ax.set_title(title)
    ax.set_xlabel('Date')

    plotter = plotting.CyclePlotter(ax)
    plotter.plot(dates, close, label='Close')
    plotter.plot(dates, 0.75 * close, label='0.75 * Close')
    plotter.plot(dates, 1.25 * close, label='1.25 * Close')

    ax.set_ylabel('Price ($)')
    ax.legend(loc='best')

plot('Initial', axes[0])
sns.reset_orig()
options.set_mpl_options()

plot('After setting options', axes[1])

sns.reset_defaults()
plot('After resetting options', axes[2])

with plt.style.context(('dark_background')):
    plot('With dark_background stylesheet', axes[3])
    fig.autofmt_xdate()
    plt.show()
```

The program plots the data and arbitrary upper and lower band with the default options, custom options, and after a reset of the options. I used the following helper class from the `plotting.py` file of `dautil`:

```
from itertools import cycle


class CyclePlotter():
    def __init__(self, ax):
        self.STYLES = cycle(["-", "--", "-.", ":"])
        self.LW = cycle([1, 2])
        self.ax = ax

    def plot(self, x, y, *args, **kwargs):
        self.ax.plot(x, y, next(self.STYLES),
                     lw=next(self.LW), *args, **kwargs)
```

The class cycles through different line styles and line widths. Refer to the following plot for the end result:

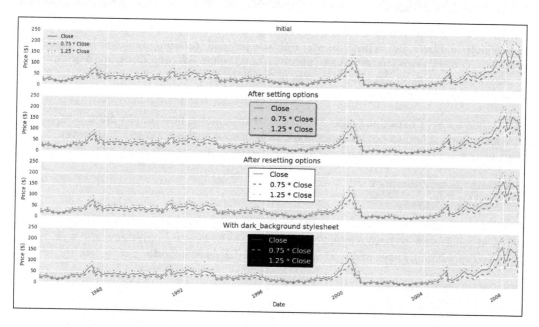

How it works...

Importing Seaborn dramatically changes the look and feel of matplotlib plots. Just temporarily comment the `seaborn` lines out to convince yourself. However, Seaborn doesn't seem to play nicely with the matplotlib options we set, unless we use the Seaborn functions `reset_orig()` and `reset_defaults()`.

See also

- The matplotlib customization documentation at `http://matplotlib.org/users/customizing.html` (retrieved July 2015)
- The matplotlib documentation about stylesheets at `http://matplotlib.org/users/style_sheets.html` (retrieved July 2015)

Seeding random number generators and NumPy print options

For reproducible data analysis, we should prefer deterministic algorithms. Some algorithms use random numbers, but in practice we rarely use perfectly random numbers. The algorithms provided in `numpy.random` allow us to specify a seed value. For reproducibility, it is important to always provide a seed value but it is easy to forget. A utility function in `sklearn.utils` provides a solution for this issue.

NumPy has a `set_printoptions()` function, which controls how NumPy prints arrays. Obviously, printing should not influence the quality of your analysis too much. However, readability is important if you want people to understand and reproduce your results.

Getting ready

Install NumPy using the instructions in the *Learning to log for robust error checking* recipe. We will need scikit-learn, so have a look at `http://scikit-learn.org/dev/install.html` (retrieved July 2015). I have installed scikit-learn 0.16.1 via Anaconda.

How to do it...

The code for this example is in the `configure_numpy.py` file in this book's code bundle:

```
from sklearn.utils import check_random_state
import numpy as np
from dautil import options
```

```
from dautil import log_api

random_state = check_random_state(42)
a = random_state.randn(5)

random_state = check_random_state(42)
b = random_state.randn(5)

np.testing.assert_array_equal(a, b)

printer = log_api.Printer()
printer.print("Default options", np.get_printoptions())

pi_array = np.pi * np.ones(30)
options.set_np_options()
print(pi_array)

# Reset
options.reset_np_options()
print(pi_array)
```

The highlighted lines show how to get a NumPy `RandomState` object with `42` as the seed. In this example, the arrays `a` and `b` are equal, because we used the same seed and the same procedure to draw the numbers. The second part of the preceding program uses the following functions I defined in `options.py`:

```
def set_np_options():
    np.set_printoptions(precision=4, threshold=5,
                        linewidth=65)


def reset_np_options():
    np.set_printoptions(precision=8, threshold=1000,
                        linewidth=75)
```

Here's the output after setting the options:

```
[ 3.1416  3.1416  3.1416 ...,  3.1416  3.1416  3.1416]
```

As you can see, NumPy replaces some of the values with an ellipsis and it shows only four digits after the decimal sign. The NumPy defaults are as follows:

```
'Default options'
{'edgeitems': 3,
 'formatter': None,
```

```
'infstr': 'inf',
'linewidth': 75,
'nanstr': 'nan',
'precision': 8,
'suppress': False,
'threshold': 1000}
```

See also

► The scikit-learn documentation at `http://scikit-learn.org/stable/developers/utilities.html` (retrieved July 2015)

► The NumPy `set_printoptions()` documentation at `http://docs.scipy.org/doc/numpy/reference/generated/numpy.set_printoptions.html` (retrieved July 2015)

► The NumPy `RandomState` documentation at `http://docs.scipy.org/doc/numpy/reference/generated/numpy.random.RandomState.html` (retrieved July 2015)

Standardizing reports, code style, and data access

Following a code style guide helps improve code quality. Having high-quality code is important if you want people to easily reproduce your analysis. One way to adhere to a coding standard is to scan your code with static code analyzers. You can use many code analyzers. In this recipe, we will use the **pep8** analyzer. In general, code analyzers complement or maybe slightly overlap each other, so you are not limited to pep8.

Convenient data access is crucial for reproducible analysis. In my opinion, the best type of data access is with a specialized API and local data. I will introduce a `dautil` module I created to load weather data provided by the Dutch KNMI.

Reporting is often the last phase of a data analysis project. We can report our findings using various formats. In this recipe, we will focus on tabulating our report with the `tabulate` module. The `landslide` tool creates slide shows from various formats such as reStructured text.

Getting ready

You will need pep8 and tabulate. A quick guide to pep8 is available at `https://pep8.readthedocs.org/en/latest/intro.html` (retrieved July 2015). I have installed pep8 1.6.2 via Anaconda. You can install joblib, tabulate, and landslide with the `pip` command.

I have tabulate 0.7.5 and landslide 1.1.3.

How to do it...

Here's an example pep8 session:

```
$ pep8 --first log_api.py
log_api.py:21:1: E302 expected 2 blank lines, found 1
log_api.py:44:33: W291 trailing whitespace
log_api.py:50:60: E225 missing whitespace around operator
```

The `--first` switch finds the first occurrence of an error. In the previous example, pep8 reports the line number where the error occurred, an error code, and a short description of the error. I prepared a module dedicated to data access of datasets we will use in several chapters. We start with access to a pandas `DataFrame` stored in a pickle, which contains selected weather data from the De Bilt weather station in the Netherlands. I created the pickle by downloading a zip file, extracting the data file, and loading the data in a pandas `DataFrame` table. I applied minimal data transformation, including multiplication of values and converting empty fields to NaNs. The code is in the `data.py` file in `dautil`. I will not discuss this code in detail, because we only need to load data from the pickle. However, if you want to download the data yourself, you can use the static method I defined in `data.py`. Downloading the data will of course give you more recent data, but you will get slightly different results if you substitute my pickle. The following code shows the basic descriptive statistics with the `pandas.DataFrame.describe()` method in the `report_weather.py` file in this book's code bundle:

```
from dautil import data
from dautil import report
import pandas as pd
import numpy as np
from tabulate import tabulate


df = data.Weather.load()
headers = [data.Weather.get_header(header)
           for header in df.columns.values.tolist()]
df = df.describe()
```

Then, the code creates a `slides.rst` file in the reStructuredText format with `dautil.RSTWriter`. This is just a matter of simple string concatenation and writing to a file. The highlighted lines in the following code show the `tabulate()` calls that create table grids from the `pandas.DataFrame` objects:

```
writer = report.RSTWriter()
writer.h1('Weather Statistics')
writer.add(tabulate(df, headers=headers,
        tablefmt='grid', floatfmt='.2f'))
writer.divider()
headers = [data.Weather.get_header(header)
            for header in df.columns.values.tolist()]
builder = report.DFBuilder(df.columns)
builder.row(df.iloc[7].values - df.iloc[3].values)
builder.row(df.iloc[6].values - df.iloc[4].values)
df = builder.build(['ptp', 'iqr'])]

writer.h1('Peak-to-peak and Interquartile Range')

writer.add(tabulate(df, headers=headers,
        tablefmt='grid', floatfmt='.2f'))
writer.write('slides.rst')
generator = report.Generator('slides.rst', 'weather_report.html')
generator.generate()
```

I use the `dautil.reportDFBuilder` class to create the `pandas.DataFrame` objects incrementally using a dictionary where the keys are columns of the final `DataFrame` table and the values are the rows:

```
import pandas as pd

class DFBuilder():
    def __init__(self, cols, *args):
        self.columns = cols
        self.df = {}

        for col in self.columns:
            self.df.update({col: []})

        for arg in args:
            self.row(arg)

    def row(self, row):
        assert len(row) == len(self.columns)

        for col, val in zip(self.columns, row):
```

```
        self.df[col].append(val)

    return self.df

def build(self, index=None):
    self.df = pd.DataFrame(self.df)

    if index:
        self.df.index = index

    return self.df
```

I eventually generate a HTML file using `landslide` and my own custom CSS. If you open `weather_report.html`, you will see the first slide with basic descriptive statistics:

Weather Statistics

	Wind Dir	W Speed, m/s	Temp, °C	Rain, mm	Pres, hPa
count	37907.00	37907.00	39032.00	37176.00	38667.00
mean	190.02	4.29	9.52	2.34	1014.93
std	93.83	1.94	6.36	4.47	9.90
min	0.00	0.00	-14.90	0.00	962.10
25%	120.00	3.10	5.00	0.00	1008.90
50%	207.00	4.10	9.70	0.20	1015.60
75%	256.00	5.10	14.50	2.80	1021.60
max	360.00	16.50	27.90	63.90	1048.30

The second slide looks like this and contains the peak-to-peak (difference between minimum and maximum values) and the interquartile range (difference between the third and first quartile):

Peak-to-peak And Interquartile Range

	Pres, hPa	Rain, mm	Temp, °C	Wind Dir	W Speed, m/s
ptp	86.20	63.90	42.80	360.00	16.50
iqr	12.70	2.80	9.50	136.00	2.00

See also

▶ The tabulate PyPi page at `https://pypi.python.org/pypi/tabulate` (retrieved July 2015)

▶ The landslide Github page at `https://github.com/adamzap/landslide` (retrieved July 2015)

2
Creating Attractive Data Visualizations

In this chapter, we will cover:

- ▶ Graphing Anscombe's quartet
- ▶ Choosing seaborn color palettes
- ▶ Choosing matplotlib color maps
- ▶ Interacting with IPython notebook widgets
- ▶ Viewing a matrix of scatterplots
- ▶ Visualizing with d3.js via mpld3
- ▶ Creating heatmaps
- ▶ Combining box plots and kernel density plots with violin plots
- ▶ Visualizing network graphs with hive plots
- ▶ Displaying geographical maps
- ▶ Using ggplot2-like plots
- ▶ Highlighting data points with influence plots

Introduction

Data analysis is more of an art than a science. Creating attractive visualizations is an integral part of this art. Obviously, what one person finds attractive, other people may find completely unacceptable. Just as in art, in the rapidly evolving world of data analysis, opinions, and taste change over time; however, in principle, nobody is absolutely right or wrong. As data artists and Pythonistas, we can choose from among several libraries of which I will cover matplotlib, seaborn, Bokeh, and ggplot. Installation instructions for some of the packages we use in this chapter were already covered in *Chapter 1, Laying the Foundation for Reproducible Data Analysis*, so I will not repeat them. I will provide an installation script (which uses pip only) for this chapter; you can even use the Docker image I described in the previous chapter. I decided to not include the Proj cartography library and the R-related libraries in the image because of their size. So for the two recipes involved in this chapter, you may have to do extra work.

Graphing Anscombe's quartet

Anscombe's quartet is a classic example that illustrates why visualizing data is important. The quartet consists of four datasets with similar statistical properties. Each dataset has a series of x values and dependent y values. We will tabulate these metrics in an IPython notebook. However, if you plot the datasets, they look surprisingly different compared to each other.

How to do it...

For this recipe, you need to perform the following steps:

1. Start with the following imports:

```
import pandas as pd
import seaborn as sns
import matplotlib.pyplot as plt
import matplotlib as mpl
from dautil import report
from dautil import plotting
import numpy as np
from tabulate import tabulate
```

2. Define the following function to compute the mean, variance, and correlation of x and y within a dataset, the slope, and the intercept of a linear fit for each of the datasets:

```
df = sns.load_dataset("anscombe")

agg = df.groupby('dataset')\
        .agg([np.mean, np.var])\
        .transpose()
```

```
    groups = df.groupby('dataset')

    corr = [g.corr()['x'][1] for _, g in groups]
    builder = report.DFBuilder(agg.columns)
    builder.row(corr)

    fits = [np.polyfit(g['x'], g['y'], 1) for _, g in groups]
    builder.row([f[0] for f in fits])
    builder.row([f[1] for f in fits])
    bottom = builder.build(['corr', 'slope', 'intercept'])

    return df, pd.concat((agg, bottom))
```

3. The following function returns a string, which is partly Markdown, partly restructured text, and partly HTML, because core Markdown does not officially support tables:

```
def generate(table):
    writer = report.RSTWriter()
    writer.h1('Anscombe Statistics')
    writer.add(tabulate(table, tablefmt='html', floatfmt='.3f'))

    return writer.rst
```

4. Plot the data and corresponding linear fits with the Seaborn lmplot() function:

```
def plot(df):
    sns.set(style="ticks")
    g = sns.lmplot(x="x", y="y", col="dataset",
        hue="dataset", data=df,
        col_wrap=2, ci=None, palette="muted", size=4,
        scatter_kws={"s": 50, "alpha": 1})

    plotting.embellish(g.fig.axes)
```

5. Display a table with statistics, as follows:

```
df, table = aggregate()
from IPython.display import display_markdown
display_markdown(generate(table), raw=True)
```

The following table shows practically identical statistics for each dataset (I modified the `custom.css` file in my IPython profile to get the colors):

Anscombe Statistics

('x', 'mean')	9.000	9.000	9.000	9.000
('x', 'var')	11.000	11.000	11.000	11.000
('y', 'mean')	7.501	7.501	7.500	7.501
('y', 'var')	4.127	4.128	4.123	4.123
corr	0.816	0.816	0.816	0.817
slope	0.500	0.500	0.500	0.500
intercept	3.000	3.001	3.002	3.002

6. The following lines plot the datasets:

```
%matplotlib inline
plot(df)
```

Refer to the following plot for the end result:

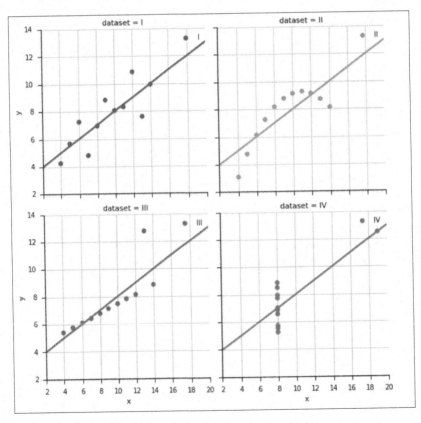

A picture says more than a thousand words. The source code is in the `anscombe.ipynb` file in this book's code bundle.

See also

- ► The Anscombe's quartet Wikipedia page at `https://en.wikipedia.org/wiki/Anscombe%27s_quartet` (retrieved July 2015)

- ► The seaborn documentation for the `lmplot()` function at `https://web.stanford.edu/~mwaskom/software/seaborn/generated/seaborn.lmplot.html` (retrieved July 2015)

Choosing seaborn color palettes

Seaborn color palettes are similar to matplotlib colormaps. Color can help you discover patterns in data and is an important visualization component. Seaborn has a wide range of color palettes, which I will try to visualize in this recipe.

How to do it...

1. The imports are as follows:

```
import seaborn as sns
import matplotlib.pyplot as plt
import matplotlib as mpl
import numpy as np
from dautil import plotting
```

2. Use the following function that helps plot the palettes:

```
def plot_palette(ax, plotter, pal, i, label, ncol=1):
    n = len(pal)
    x = np.linspace(0.0, 1.0, n)
    y = np.arange(n) + i * n
    ax.scatter(x, y, c=x,
               cmap=mpl.colors.ListedColormap(list(pal)),
               s=200)
    plotter.plot(x,y, label=label)
    handles, labels = ax.get_legend_handles_labels()
    ax.legend(loc='best', ncol=ncol, fontsize=18)
```

3. **Categorical palettes** are useful for categorical data, for instance, gender or blood type. The following function plots some of the Seaborn categorical palettes:

```
def plot_categorical_palettes(ax):
    palettes = ['deep', 'muted', 'pastel', 'bright', 'dark',
'colorblind']
```

```
plotter = plotting.CyclePlotter(ax)
ax.set_title('Categorical Palettes')

for i, p in enumerate(palettes):
    pal = sns.color_palette(p)
    plot_palette(ax, plotter, pal, i, p, 4)
```

4. **Circular color systems** usually use **HLS (Hue Lightness Saturation)** instead of **RGB (red green blue)** color spaces. They are useful if you have many categories. The following function plots palettes using HSL systems:

```
def plot_circular_palettes(ax):
    ax.set_title('Circular Palettes')
    plotter = plotting.CyclePlotter(ax)

    pal = sns.color_palette("hls", 6)
    plot_palette(ax, plotter, pal, 0, 'hls')

    sns.hls_palette(6, l=.3, s=.8)
    plot_palette(ax, plotter, pal, 1, 'hls l=.3 s=.8')

    pal = sns.color_palette("husl", 6)
    plot_palette(ax, plotter, pal, 2, 'husl')

    sns.husl_palette(6, l=.3, s=.8)
    plot_palette(ax, plotter, pal, 3, 'husl l=.3 s=.8')
```

5. Seaborn also has palettes, which are based on the online ColorBrewer tool (http://colorbrewer2.org/). Plot them as follows:

```
def plot_brewer_palettes(ax):
    ax.set_title('Brewer Palettes')
    plotter = plotting.CyclePlotter(ax)

    pal = sns.color_palette("Paired")
    plot_palette(ax, plotter, pal, 0, 'Paired')

    pal = sns.color_palette("Set2", 6)
    plot_palette(ax, plotter, pal, 1, 'Set2')
```

6. **Sequential palettes** are useful for wide ranging data, for instance, differing by orders of magnitude. Use the following function to plot them:

```
def plot_sequential_palettes(ax):
    ax.set_title('Sequential Palettes')
    plotter = plotting.CyclePlotter(ax)

    pal = sns.color_palette("Blues")
    plot_palette(ax, plotter, pal, 0, 'Blues')
```

```
pal = sns.color_palette("BuGn_r")
plot_palette(ax, plotter, pal, 1, 'BuGn_r')

pal = sns.color_palette("GnBu_d")
plot_palette(ax, plotter, pal, 2, 'GnBu_d')

pal = sns.color_palette("cubehelix", 6)
plot_palette(ax, plotter, pal, 3, 'cubehelix')
```

7. The following lines call the functions we defined:

```
%matplotlib inline

fig, axes = plt.subplots(2, 2, figsize=(16, 12))
plot_categorical_palettes(axes[0][0])
plot_circular_palettes(axes[0][1])
plot_brewer_palettes(axes[1][0])
plot_sequential_palettes(axes[1][1])
plotting.hide_axes(axes)
plt.tight_layout()
```

The complete code is available in the `choosing_palettes.ipynb` file in this book's code bundle. Refer to the following plot for the end result:

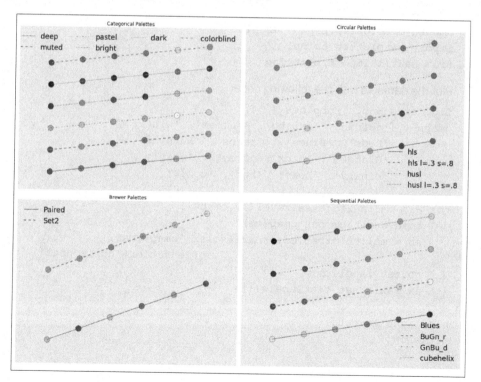

See also

▶ The seaborn color palettes documentation at `https://web.stanford.edu/~mwaskom/software/seaborn/tutorial/color_palettes.html` (retrieved July 2015)

Choosing matplotlib color maps

The matplotlib color maps are getting a lot of criticism lately because they can be misleading; however, most colormaps are just fine in my opinion. The defaults are getting a makeover in matplotlib 2.0 as announced at `http://matplotlib.org/style_changes.html` (retrieved July 2015). Of course, there are some good arguments that do not support using certain matplotlib colormaps, such as `jet`. In art, as in data analysis, almost nothing is absolutely true, so I leave it up to you to decide. In practical terms, I think it is important to consider how to deal with print publications and the various types of color blindness. In this recipe, I visualize relatively safe colormaps with colorbars. This is a tiny selection of the many colormaps in matplotlib.

How to do it...

1. The imports are as follows:

```
import matplotlib.pyplot as plt
import matplotlib as mpl
from dautil import plotting
```

2. Plot the datasets with the following code:

```
fig, axes = plt.subplots(4, 4)
cmaps = ['autumn', 'spring', 'summer', 'winter',
         'Reds', 'Blues', 'Greens', 'Purples',
         'Oranges', 'pink', 'Greys', 'gray',
         'binary', 'bone', 'hot', 'cool']

for ax, cm in zip(axes.ravel(), cmaps):
    cmap = plt.cm.get_cmap(cm)
    cb = mpl.colorbar.ColorbarBase(ax, cmap=cmap,
                                   orientation='horizontal')

    cb.set_label(cm)
    ax.xaxis.set_ticklabels([])

plt.tight_layout()
plt.show()
```

Refer to the following plot for the end result:

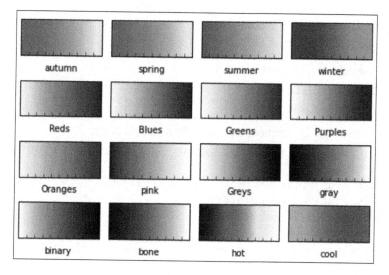

The notebook is in the `choosing_colormaps.ipynb` file in this book's code bundle. The color maps are used in various visualizations in this book.

See also

▶ The related matplotlib documentation at `http://matplotlib.org/users/colormaps.html` (retrieved July 2015)

Interacting with IPython Notebook widgets

Interactive IPython notebook widgets are, at the time of writing (July 2015), an experimental feature. I, and as far as I know, many other people, hope that this feature will remain. In a nutshell, the widgets let you select values as you would with HTML forms. This includes sliders, drop-down boxes, and check boxes. As you can read, these widgets are very convenient for visualizing the weather data I introduced in *Chapter 1, Laying the Foundation for Reproducible Data Analysis.*

How to do it...

1. Import the following:

```
import seaborn as sns
import numpy as np
import pandas as pd
```

```
import matplotlib.pyplot as plt
from IPython.html.widgets import interact
from dautil import data
from dautil import ts
```

2. Load the data and request inline plots:

```
%matplotlib inline
df = data.Weather.load()
```

3. Define the following function, which displays bubble plots:

```
def plot_data(x='TEMP', y='RAIN', z='WIND_SPEED', f='A', size=10,
cmap='Blues'):
    dfx = df[x].resample(f)
    dfy = df[y].resample(f)
    dfz = df[z].resample(f)

    bubbles = (dfz - dfz.min())/(dfz.max() - dfz.min())
    years = dfz.index.year
    sc = plt.scatter(dfx, dfy, s= size * bubbles + 9, c = years,
                cmap=cmap, label=data.Weather.get_header(z),
alpha=0.5)
    plt.colorbar(sc, label='Year')

    freqs = {'A': 'Annual', 'M': 'Monthly', 'D': 'Daily'}
    plt.title(freqs[f] + ' Averages')
    plt.xlabel(data.Weather.get_header(x))
    plt.ylabel(data.Weather.get_header(y))
    plt.legend(loc='best')
```

4. Call the function we just defined with the following code:

```
vars = df.columns.tolist()
freqs = ('A', 'M', 'D')
cmaps = [cmap for cmap in plt.cm.datad if not cmap.endswith("_r")]
cmaps.sort()
interact(plot_data, x=vars, y=vars, z=vars, f=freqs,
size=(100,700), cmap=cmaps)
```

5. This is one of the recipes where you really should play with the code to understand how it works. The following is an example bubble plot:

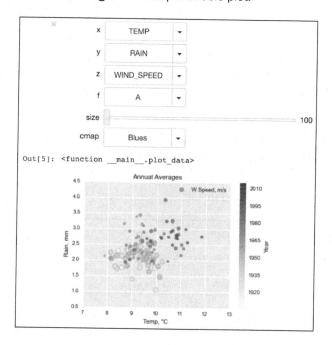

6. Define another function (actually, it has the same name), but this time the function groups the data by day of year or month:

```
def plot_data(x='TEMP', y='RAIN', z='WIND_SPEED', groupby='ts.
groupby_yday', size=10, cmap='Blues'):
    if groupby == 'ts.groupby_yday':
        groupby = ts.groupby_yday
    elif groupby == 'ts.groupby_month':
        groupby = ts.groupby_month
    else:
        raise AssertionError('Unknown groupby ' + groupby)

    dfx = groupby(df[x]).mean()
    dfy = groupby(df[y]).mean()
    dfz = groupby(df[z]).mean()

    bubbles = (dfz - dfz.min())/(dfz.max() - dfz.min())
    colors = dfx.index.values
    sc = plt.scatter(dfx, dfy, s= size * bubbles + 9, c = colors,
            cmap=cmap, label=data.Weather.get_header(z),
alpha=0.5)
```

```
        plt.colorbar(sc, label='Day of Year')

        by_dict = {ts.groupby_yday: 'Day of Year', ts.groupby_month:
    'Month'}
        plt.title('Grouped by ' + by_dict[groupby])
        plt.xlabel(data.Weather.get_header(x))
        plt.ylabel(data.Weather.get_header(y))
        plt.legend(loc='best')
```

7. Call this function with the following snippet:

```
groupbys = ('ts.groupby_yday', 'ts.groupby_month')
interact(plot_data, x=vars, y=vars, z=vars, groupby=groupbys,
size=(100,700), cmap=cmaps)
```

Refer to the following plot for the end result:

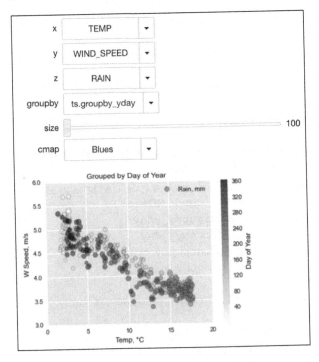

My first impression of this plot is that the temperature and wind speed seem to be correlated. The source code is in the `Interactive.ipynb` file in this book's code bundle.

See also

▸ The documentation on interactive IPython widgets at `https://ipython.org/ipython-doc/dev/api/generated/IPython.html.widgets.interaction.html` (retrieved July 2015)

Viewing a matrix of scatterplots

If you don't have many variables in your dataset, it is a good idea to view all the possible scatterplots for your data. You can do this with one function call from either seaborn or pandas. These functions display a matrix of plots with kernel density estimation plots or histograms on the diagonal.

How to do it...

1. Imports the following:

```
import pandas as pd
from dautil import data
from dautil import ts
import matplotlib.pyplot as plt
import seaborn as sns
import matplotlib as mpl
```

2. Load the weather data with the following lines:

```
df = data.Weather.load()
df = ts.groupby_yday(df).mean()
df.columns = [data.Weather.get_header(c) for c in df.columns]
```

3. Plot with the Seaborn `pairplot()` function, which plots histograms on the diagonal by default:

```
%matplotlib inline

# Seaborn plotting, issues due to NaNs
sns.pairplot(df.fillna(0))
```

The following plots are the result:

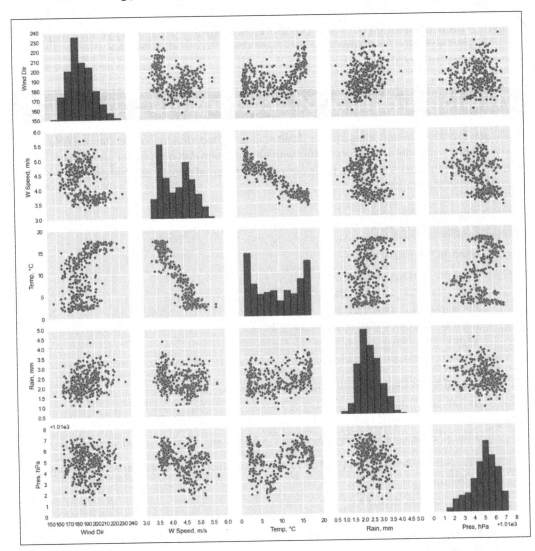

4. Plot similarly with the pandas `scatter_matrix()` function and request kernel density estimation plots on the diagonal:

```
sns.set({'figure.figsize': '16, 12'})
mpl.rcParams['axes.linewidth'] = 9
mpl.rcParams['lines.linewidth'] = 2
plots = pd.scatter_matrix(df, marker='o', diagonal='kde')
plt.show()
```

Refer to the following plots for the end result:

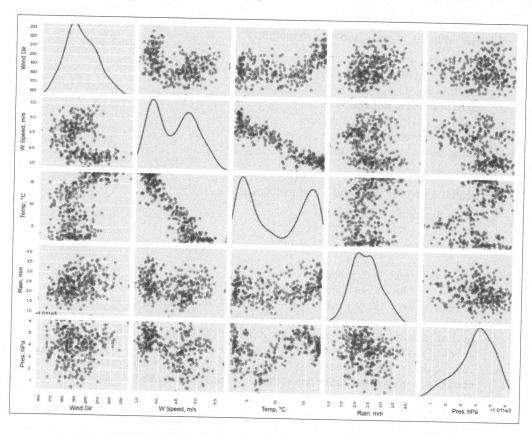

The complete code is available in the `scatter_matrix.ipynb` file in this book's code bundle.

Visualizing with d3.js via mpld3

D3.js is a JavaScript data visualization library released in 2011, which we can also use in an IPython notebook. We will add hovering tooltips to a regular matplotlib plot. As a bridge, we need the `mpld3` package. This recipe doesn't require any JavaScript coding whatsoever.

Getting ready

I installed mpld3 0.2 with the following command:

```
$ [sudo] pip install mpld3
```

How to do it...

1. Start with the imports and enable mpld3:

```
%matplotlib inline
import matplotlib.pyplot as plt
import mpld3
mpld3.enable_notebook()
from mpld3 import plugins
import seaborn as sns
from dautil import data
from dautil import ts
```

2. Load the weather data and plot it as follows:

```
df = data.Weather.load()
df = df[['TEMP', 'WIND_SPEED']]
df = ts.groupby_yday(df).mean()

fig, ax = plt.subplots()
ax.set_title('Averages Grouped by Day of Year')
points = ax.scatter(df['TEMP'], df['WIND_SPEED'],
                    s=30, alpha=0.3)
ax.set_xlabel(data.Weather.get_header('TEMP'))
ax.set_ylabel(data.Weather.get_header('WIND_SPEED'))
labels = ["Day of year {0}".format(i) for i in range(366)]
tooltip = plugins.PointLabelTooltip(points, labels)

plugins.connect(fig, tooltip)
```

The highlighted lines are responsible for the tooltips. In the following screenshot, the **Day of year 31** text comes from the tooltip:

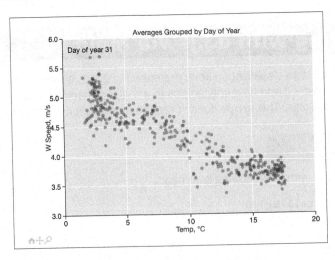

As you can see, at the bottom of the plot, you also have widgets for panning and zooming (refer to the `mpld3_demo.ipynb` file in this book's code bundle).

Creating heatmaps

Heat maps visualize data in a matrix using a set of colors. Originally, heat maps were used to represent prices of financial assets, such as stocks. Bokeh is a Python package that can display heatmaps in an IPython notebook or produce a standalone HTML file.

Getting ready

I have Bokeh 0.9.1 via Anaconda. The Bokeh installation instructions are available at `http://bokeh.pydata.org/en/latest/docs/installation.html` (retrieved July 2015).

How to do it...

1. The imports are as follows:

```
from collections import OrderedDict
from dautil import data
from dautil import ts
from dautil import plotting
import numpy as np
import bokeh.plotting as bkh_plt
from bokeh.models import HoverTool
```

2. The following function loads temperature data and groups it by year and month:

```
def load():
    df = data.Weather.load()['TEMP']
    return ts.groupby_year_month(df)
```

3. Define a function that rearranges data in a special Bokeh structure:

```
def create_source():
    colors = plotting.sample_hex_cmap()

    month = []
    year = []
    color = []
    avg = []

    for year_month, group in load():
        month.append(ts.short_month(year_month[1]))
        year.append(str(year_month[0]))
```

```
    monthly_avg = np.nanmean(group.values)
    avg.append(monthly_avg)
    color.append(colors[min(int(abs(monthly_avg)) - 2, 8)])

source = bkh_plt.ColumnDataSource(
    data=dict(month=month, year=year, color=color, avg=avg)
)

return year, source
```

4. Define a function that returns labels for the horizontal axis:

```
def all_years():
    years = set(year)
    start_year = min(years)
    end_year = max(years)

    return [str(y) for y in range(int(start_year), int(end_year),
5)]
```

5. Define a plotting function for the heat map that also sets up hover tooltips:

```
def plot(year, source):
    fig = bkh_plt.figure(title="De Bilt, NL Temperature (1901 -
2014)",
                         x_range=all_years(),
                         y_range=list(reversed(ts.short_
months())),
                         toolbar_location="left",
                         tools="resize,hover,save,pan,box_
zoom,wheel_zoom")

    fig.rect("year", "month", 1, 1, source=source,
        color="color", line_color=None)

    fig.xaxis.major_label_orientation = np.pi/3

    hover = fig.select(dict(type=HoverTool))
    hover.tooltips = OrderedDict([
        ('date', '@month @year'),
        ('avg', '@avg'),
    ])

    bkh_plt.output_notebook()
    bkh_plt.show(fig)
```

6. Call the functions you defined:

```
year, source = create_source()
plot(year, source)
```

Refer to the following plot for the end result:

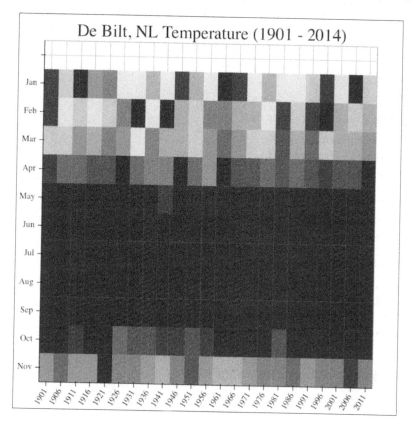

The source code is available in the `heat_map.ipynb` file in this book's code bundle.

▸ The Bokeh documentation about embedding Bokeh plots at `http://bokeh.pydata.org/en/latest/docs/user_guide/embed.html` (retrieved July 2015)

Combining box plots and kernel density plots with violin plots

Violin plots combine box plots and kernel density plots or histograms in one type of plot. Seaborn and matplotlib both offer violin plots. We will use Seaborn in this recipe on z-scores of weather data. The z-scoring is not essential, but without it, the violins will be more spread out.

How to do it...

1. Import the required libraries as follows:

```
import seaborn as sns
from dautil import data
import matplotlib.pyplot as plt
```

2. Load the weather data and calculate z-scores:

```
df = data.Weather.load()
zscores = (df - df.mean())/df.std()
```

3. Plot a violin plot of the z-scores:

```
%matplotlib inline
plt.figure()
plt.title('Weather Violin Plot')
sns.violinplot(zscores.resample('M'))
plt.ylabel('Z-scores')
```

Refer to the following plot for the first violin plot:

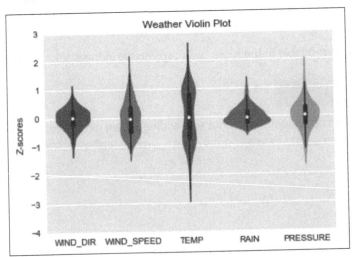

4. Plot a violin plot of rainy and dry (the opposite of rainy) days against wind speed:

```
plt.figure()
plt.title('Rainy Weather vs Wind Speed')
categorical = df
categorical['RAIN'] = categorical['RAIN'] > 0
ax = sns.violinplot(x="RAIN", y="WIND_SPEED",
                    data=categorical)
```

Refer to the following plot for the second violin plot:

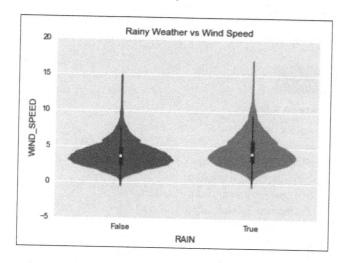

The source code is available in the `violins.ipynb` file in this book's code bundle.

See also

▶ The Seaborn documentation about violin plots at `https://web.stanford.edu/~mwaskom/software/seaborn/generated/seaborn.violinplot.html` (retrieved July 2015)

Visualizing network graphs with hive plots

A **hive plot** is a visualization technique for plotting network graphs. In hive plots, we draw edges as curved lines. We group nodes by some property and display them on radial axes. NetworkX is one of the most famous Python network graph libraries; however, it doesn't support hive plots yet (July 2015). Luckily, several libraries exist that specialize in hive plots. Also, we will use an API to partition the graph of Facebook users available at `https://snap.stanford.edu/data/egonets-Facebook.html` (retrieved July 2015). The data belongs to the **Stanford Network Analysis Project** (**SNAP**), which also has a Python API. Unfortunately, the SNAP API doesn't support Python 3 yet.

Getting ready

I have NetworkX 1.9.1 via Anaconda. The instructions to install NetworkX are at `https://networkx.github.io/documentation/latest/install.html` (retrieved July 2015). We also need the `community` package at `https://bitbucket.org/taynaud/python-louvain` (retrieved July 2015). There is another package with the same name on PyPi, which is completely unrelated. Install the `hiveplot` package hosted at `https://github.com/ericmjl/hiveplot` (retrieved July 2015):

```
$ [sudo] pip install hiveplot
```

I wrote the code with hiveplot 0.1.7.4.

How to do it...

1. The imports are as follows:

   ```
   import networkx as nx
   import community
   import matplotlib.pyplot as plt
   from hiveplot import HivePlot
   from collections import defaultdict
   from dautil import plotting
   from dautil import data
   ```

2. Load the data and create a NetworkX `Graph` object:

   ```
   fb_file = data.SPANFB().load()
   G = nx.read_edgelist(fb_file,
                        create_using = nx.Graph(),
                        nodetype = int)
   print(nx.info(G))
   ```

3. Partition the graph and create a `nodes` dictionary as follows:

   ```
   parts = community.best_partition(G)
   nodes = defaultdict(list)

   for n, d in parts.items():
       nodes[d].append(n)
   ```

4. The graph is pretty big, so we will just create three groups of edges:

```
edges = defaultdict(list)

for u, v in nx.edges(G, nodes[0]):
    edges[0].append((u, v, 0))

for u, v in nx.edges(G, nodes[1]):
    edges[1].append((u, v, 1))

for u, v in nx.edges(G, nodes[2]):
    edges[2].append((u, v, 2))
```

5. Plotting will take about six minutes:

```
%matplotlib inline
cmap = plotting.sample_hex_cmap(name='hot', ncolors=len(nodes.
keys()))
h = HivePlot(nodes, edges, cmap, cmap)
h.draw()
plt.title('Facebook Network Hive Plot')
```

After the waiting period, we get the following plot:

The code is in the `hive_plot.ipynb` file in this book's code bundle.

Displaying geographical maps

Whether dealing with local of global data, geographical maps are a suitable visualization. To plot data on a map, we need coordinates, usually in the form of latitude and longitude values. Several file formats exist with which we can save geographical data. In this recipe, we will use the special **shapefile** format and the more common **tab separated values** (**TSV**) format. The shapefile format was created by the Esri company and uses three mandatory files with the extensions `.shp`, `.shx`, and `.dbf`. The `.dbf` file contains a database with extra information for each geographical location in the shapefile. The shapefile we will use contains information about country borders, population, and **Gross Domestic Product** (**GDP**). We can download the shapefile with the `cartopy` library. The TSV file holds population data for more than 4000 cities as a timeseries. It comes from `https://nordpil.com/resources/world-database-of-large-cities/` (retrieved July 2015).

Getting ready

First, we need to install Proj.4 from source or, if you are lucky, using a binary distribution from `https://github.com/OSGeo/proj.4/wiki` (retrieved July 2015). The instructions to install Proj.4 are available at `https://github.com/OSGeo/proj.4` (retrieved July 2015). Then, install `cartopy` with pip—I wrote the code with cartopy-0.13.0. Alternatively, we can run the following command:

```
$ conda install -c scitools cartopy
```

How to do it...

1. The imports are as follows:

   ```
   import cartopy.crs as ccrs
   import matplotlib.pyplot as plt
   import cartopy.io.shapereader as shpreader
   import matplotlib as mpl
   import pandas as pd
   from dautil import options
   from dautil import data
   ```

2. We will use color to visualize country populations and populous cities. Load the data as follows:

   ```
   countries = shpreader.natural_earth(resolution='110m',
                                       category='cultural',
                                       name='admin_0_countries')
   ```

```
cities = pd.read_csv(data.Nordpil().load_urban_tsv(),
                     sep='\t', encoding='ISO-8859-1')
mill_cities = cities[cities['pop2005'] > 1000]
```

3. Draw a map, a corresponding colorbar, and mark populous cities on the map with the following code:

```
%matplotlib inline
plt.figure(figsize=(16, 12))
gs = mpl.gridspec.GridSpec(2, 1,
                           height_ratios=[20, 1])
ax = plt.subplot(gs[0], projection=ccrs.PlateCarree())

norm = mpl.colors.Normalize(vmin=0, vmax=2 * 10 ** 9)
cmap = plt.cm.Blues
ax.set_title('Population Estimates by Country')

for country in shpreader.Reader(countries).records():
    ax.add_geometries(country.geometry, ccrs.PlateCarree(),
                      facecolor=cmap(
                          norm(country.attributes['pop_est'])))

plt.plot(mill_cities['Longitude'],
         mill_cities['Latitude'], 'r.',
         label='Populous city',
         transform=ccrs.PlateCarree())

options.set_mpl_options()
plt.legend(loc='lower left')

cax = plt.subplot(gs[1])
cb = mpl.colorbar.ColorbarBase(cax,
                               cmap=cmap,
                               norm=norm,
                               orientation='horizontal')

cb.set_label('Population Estimate')
plt.tight_layout()
```

Refer to the following plot for the end result:

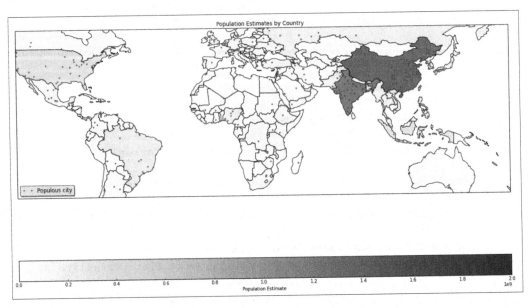

You can find the code in the `plot_map.ipynb` file in this book's code bundle.

Using ggplot2-like plots

Ggplot2 is an R library for data visualization popular among R users. The main idea of ggplot2 is that the product of data visualization consists of many layers. Like a painter, we start with an empty canvas and then gradually add layers of paint. Usually, we interface with R code from Python with `rpy2` (I will discuss several interoperability options in Chapter 11, of my book *Python Data Analysis*). However, if we only want to use `ggplot2`, it is more convenient to use the `pyggplot` library. In this recipe, we will visualize population growth for three countries using Worldbank data retrievable through `pandas`. The data consists of various indicators and related metadata. The spreadsheet at `http://api.worldbank.org/v2/en/topic/19?downloadformat=excel` (retrieved July 2015) has descriptions of the indicators. I think that we can consider the Worldbank dataset to be static; however, similar datasets have frequent changes quite often enough to keep an analyst busy almost full time. Obviously, changing the name of an indicator (probably) could break the code, so I decided to cache the data via the `joblib` library. The `joblib` library is related to **scikit-learn**, and we will discuss it in more detail in *Chapter 9, Ensemble Learning and Dimensionality Reduction*. Unfortunately, this approach has some limitations; in particular, we are not able to pickle all Python objects.

Getting ready

First, you need R with ggplot2 installed. If you are not going to seriously use ggplot2, maybe you should skip this recipe altogether. The homepage of R is `http://www.r-project.org/` (retrieved July 2015). The documentation of ggplot2 is at `http://docs.ggplot2.org/current/index.html` (retrieved July 2015). You can install pyggplot with pip—I used pyggplot-23. To install `joblib`, visit `https://pythonhosted.org/joblib/installing.html` (retrieved July 2015). I have `joblib` 0.8.4 via Anaconda.

How to do it...

1. The imports are as follows:

    ```
    import pyggplot
    from dautil import data
    ```

2. Load the data with the following code:

    ```
    dawb = data.Worldbank()
    pop_grow = dawb.get_name('pop_grow')
    df = dawb.download(indicator=pop_grow, start=1984, end=2014)
    df = dawb.rename_columns(df, use_longnames=True)
    ```

3. The following line initializes pyggplot with the pandas `DataFrame` object we created:

    ```
    p = pyggplot.Plot(df)
    ```

4. Add a bar chart with the following line:

    ```
    p.add_bar('country', dawb.get_longname(pop_grow), color='year')
    ```

5. Flip the chart so that the bars point to the right and render:

    ```
    p.coord_flip()
    p.render_notebook()
    ```

Refer to the following plot for the end result:

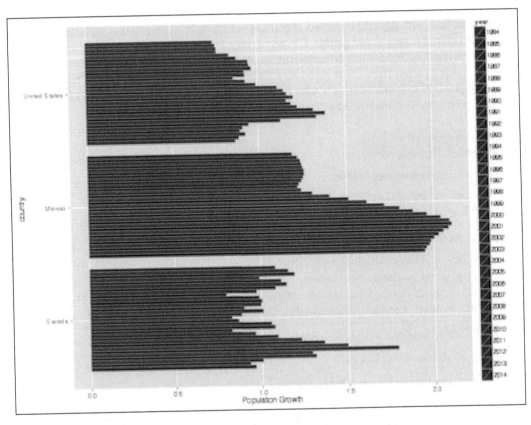

The code is in the `using_ggplot.ipynb` file in this book's code bundle.

Highlighting data points with influence plots

Influence plots take into account residuals after a fit, influence, and leverage for individual data points similar to bubble plots. The size of the residuals is plotted on the vertical axis and can indicate that a data point is an outlier. To understand influence plots, take a look at the following equations:

$$(2.1) \quad \mathrm{var}\left(\hat{\varepsilon}_i\right) = \hat{\sigma}_i^2 \left(1 - h_{ii}\right)$$

$$(2.2) \quad \hat{\sigma}_i^2 = \frac{1}{n - p - 1} \sum_j^n \quad \forall \; j \neq i$$

$$(2.3) \quad H = X\left(X'X\right)^{-1} X'$$

$$(2.4) \quad CookD = \frac{\sum_{j=1}^n \left(\hat{Y}_j - \hat{Y}_{j(i)}\right)^2}{p\,MSE}$$

$$(2.5) \quad DFFITS = \frac{\hat{Y}_i - \hat{Y}_{i(i)}}{s_{(i)}\sqrt{h_{ii}}}$$

The residuals according to the `statsmodels` documentation are scaled by standard deviation **(2.1)**. In **(2.2)**, n is the number of observations and p is the number of regressors. We have a so-called **hat-matrix**, which is given by **(2.3)**.

The diagonal elements of the hat matrix give the special metric called leverage. **Leverage** serves as the horizontal axis and indicates potential influence of influence plots. In influence plots, influence determines the size of plotted points. Influential points tend to have high residuals and leverage. To measure influence, `statsmodels` can use either **Cook's distance (2.4)** or **DFFITS (2.5)**.

How to do it...

1. The imports are as follows:

```
import matplotlib.pyplot as plt
import statsmodels.api as sm
from statsmodels.formula.api import ols
from dautil import data
```

2. Get the available country codes:

```
dawb = data.Worldbank()

countries = dawb.get_countries()[['name', 'iso2c']]
```

3. Load the data from the Worldbank:

```
population = dawb.download(indicator=[dawb.get_name('pop_grow'),
dawb.get_name('gdp_pcap'),
                                dawb.get_name('primary_
education')],
```

```
                                    country=countries['iso2c'], start=2014,
    end=2014)

    population = dawb.rename_columns(population)
```

4. Define an ordinary least squares model, as follows:

```
    population_model = ols("pop_grow ~ gdp_pcap + primary_education",
                           data=population).fit()
```

5. Display an influence plot of the model using Cook's distance:

```
    %matplotlib inline
    fig, ax = plt.subplots(figsize=(19.2, 14.4))
    fig = sm.graphics.influence_plot(population_model, ax=ax,
    criterion="cooks")
    plt.grid()
```

Refer to the following plot for the end result:

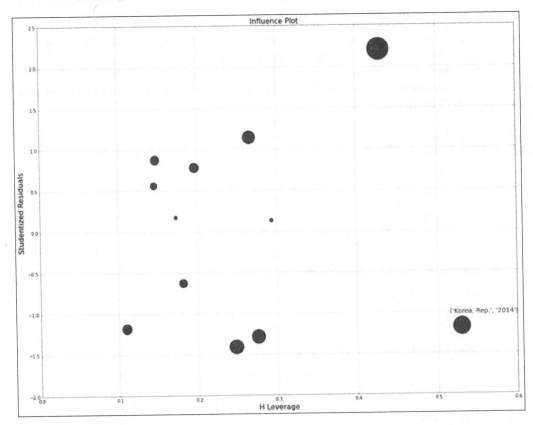

The code is in the `highlighting_influence.ipynb` file in this book's code bundle.

See also

▸ The Wikipedia page about the Cook's distance at `https://en.wikipedia.org/wiki/Cook%27s_distance` (retrieved July 2015)

▸ The Wikipedia page about DFFITS at `https://en.wikipedia.org/wiki/DFFITS` (retrieved July 2015)

3
Statistical Data Analysis and Probability

We will cover the following recipes in this chapter:

- ▶ Fitting data to the exponential distribution
- ▶ Fitting aggregated data to the gamma distribution
- ▶ Fitting aggregated counts to the Poisson distribution
- ▶ Determining bias
- ▶ Estimating kernel density
- ▶ Determining confidence intervals for mean, variance, and standard deviation
- ▶ Sampling with probability weights
- ▶ Exploring extreme values
- ▶ Correlating variables with the Pearson's correlation
- ▶ Correlating variables with the Spearman rank correlation
- ▶ Correlating a binary and a continuous variable with the point-biserial correlation
- ▶ Evaluating relationships between variables with ANOVA

Introduction

Various statistical distributions have been invented, which are the equivalent of the wheel for data analysts. Just as whatever I think of comes out differently in print, data in our world doesn't follow strict mathematical laws. Nevertheless, after visualizing our data, we can see that the data follows (to certain extent) a distribution. Even without visualization, we can find a candidate distribution using rules of thumb. The next step is to try to fit the data to a known distribution. If the data is very complex, possibly due to a high number of variables, it is useful to estimate its kernel density (also useful with one variable). In all scenarios, it is good to estimate the confidence intervals or p-values of our results. When we have at least two variables, it is sometimes appropriate to have a look at the correlation between variables. In this chapter, we will apply three types of correlation.

Fitting data to the exponential distribution

The **exponential distribution** is a special case of the **gamma distribution**, which we will also encounter in this chapter. The exponential distribution can be used to analyze extreme values for rainfall. It can also be used to model the time it takes to serve a customer in a queue. For zero and negative values, the **probability distribution function** (**PDF**) of the exponential distribution is zero. For positive values, the PDF decays exponentially:

$$(3.1) \quad f(x;\lambda) = \begin{cases} \lambda e^{-\lambda x} & x \geq 0, \\ 0 & x < 0. \end{cases}$$

We will use rain data as an example, which is a good candidate for an exponential distribution fit. Obviously, the amount of rain cannot be negative and we know that heavy rain is less likely than no rain at all. In fact, a day without rain is very likely.

How to do it...

The following steps fit the rain data to the exponential distribution:

1. The imports are as follows:

```
from scipy.stats.distributions import expon
import matplotlib.pyplot as plt
import dautil as dl
from IPython.display import HTML
```

2. I made a wrapper class that calls the `scipy.stats.expon` methods. First, call the `fit()` method:

```
rain = dl.data.Weather.load()['RAIN'].dropna()
dist = dl.stats.Distribution(rain, expon)
dl.options.set_pd_options()
html_builder = dl.report.HTMLBuilder()
html_builder.h1('Fitting Data to the Exponential Distribution')
loc, scale = dist.fit()
table = dl.report.DFBuilder(['loc', 'scale'])
table.row([loc, scale])
html_builder.h2('Distribution Parameters')
html_builder.add_df(table.build())
```

3. The following code calls the `scipy.stats.expon.pdf()` method and the `scipy.stats.describe()` function on the fit residuals:

```
pdf = dist.pdf(loc, scale)
html_builder.h2('Residuals of the Fit')
residuals = dist.describe_residuals()
html_builder.add(residuals.to_html())
```

4. To evaluate the fit, we can use metrics. Compute fit metrics with the following code snippet:

```
table2 = dl.report.DFBuilder(['Mean_AD', 'RMSE'])
table2.row([dist.mean_ad(), dist.rmse()])
html_builder.h2('Fit Metrics')
html_builder.add_df(table2.build())
```

5. Plot the fit and display the analysis report as follows:

```
plt.hist(rain, bins=dist.nbins, normed=True, label='Rain')
plt.plot(dist.x, pdf, label='PDF')
plt.title('Fitting to the exponential distribution')

# Limiting the x-asis for a better plot
plt.xlim([0, 15])
plt.xlabel(dl.data.Weather.get_header('RAIN'))
plt.ylabel('Probability')
plt.legend(loc='best')
HTML(html_builder.html)
```

Refer to the following screenshot for the end result (the code is in the `fitting_expon.ipynb` file in this book's code bundle):

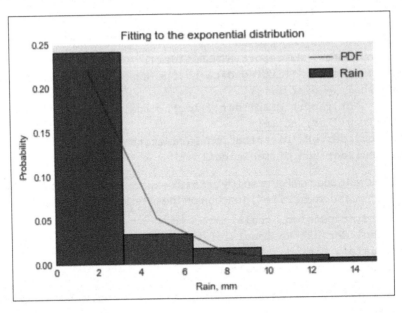

How it works...

The `scale` parameter returned by `scipy.stats.expon.fit()` is the inverse of the decay parameter from **(3.1)**. We get about 2 for the `scale` value, so the decay is about half. The probability for no rain is therefore about half. The fit residuals should have a mean and skew close to 0. If we have a nonzero skew, something strange must be going on, because we don't expect the residuals to be skewed in any direction. The **mean absolute deviation** (**MAD**) and **root mean square error** (**RMSE**) are regression metrics, which we will cover in more detail in *Chapter 10, Evaluating Classifiers, Regressors, and Clusters*.

See also

▸ The exponential distribution Wikipedia page at `https://en.wikipedia.org/wiki/Exponential_distribution` (retrieved August 2015)

▸ The relevant SciPy documentation at `http://docs.scipy.org/doc/scipy-dev/reference/generated/scipy.stats.expon.html` (retrieved August 2015)

Fitting aggregated data to the gamma distribution

The gamma distribution can be used to model the size of insurance claims, rainfall, and the distribution of inter-spike intervals in brains. The PDF for the gamma distribution is defined by shape k and scale θ as follows:

$$(3.2) \quad f\left(x;k,\theta\right)=\frac{x^{k-1}e^{-\frac{x}{\theta}}}{\theta^k\Gamma\left(k\right)} \quad for\ x>0\ and\ k,\theta>0$$

$$(3.3) \quad \mathrm{E}\left[X\right]=k\theta$$

$$(3.4) \quad Var\left[X\right]=k\theta^2$$

There is also a definition that uses an inverse scale parameter (used by SciPy). The mean and variance of the gamma distribution are described by (3.3) and (3.4). As you can see, we can estimate the shape parameter from the mean and variance using simple algebra.

How to do it...

Let's fit aggregates for the rain data for January to the gamma distribution:

1. Start with the following imports:

```
from scipy.stats.distributions import gamma
import matplotlib.pyplot as plt
import dautil as dl
import pandas as pd
from IPython.display import HTML
```

2. Load the data and select aggregates for January:

```
rain = dl.data.Weather.load()['RAIN'].resample('M').dropna()
rain = dl.ts.groupby_month(rain)
rain = rain.get_group(1)
```

3. Derive a value for k from the mean and variance of the distribution, and use it to fit the data:

```
dist = dl.stats.Distribution(rain, gamma)

a = (dist.mean() ** 2)/dist.var()
shape, loc, scale = dist.fit(a)
```

The rest of the code is similar to the code in *Fitting data to the exponential distribution*. Refer to the following screenshot for the end result (the code is in the `fitting_gamma.ipynb` file in this book's code bundle):

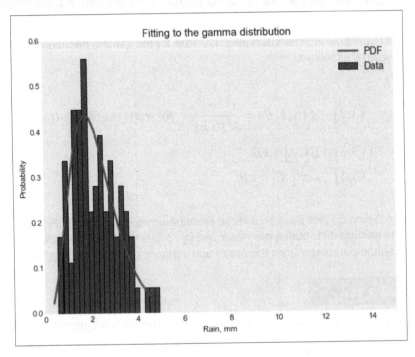

See also

▸ The relevant SciPy documentation at `http://docs.scipy.org/doc/scipy-dev/reference/generated/scipy.stats.gamma.html#scipy.stats.gamma` (retrieved August 2015)

▸ The Wikipedia page for the gamma distribution at `https://en.wikipedia.org/wiki/Gamma_distribution` (retrieved August 2015)

Fitting aggregated counts to the Poisson distribution

The **Poisson distribution** is named after the French mathematician Poisson, who published a thesis about it in 1837. The Poisson distribution is a discrete distribution usually associated with counts for a fixed interval of time or space. It is only defined for integer values k. For instance, we could apply it to monthly counts of rainy days. In this case, we implicitly assume that the event of a rainy day occurs at a fixed monthly rate. The goal of fitting the data to the Poisson distribution is to find the fixed rate.

The following equations describe the probability mass function **(3.5)** and rate parameter **(3.6)** of the Poisson distribution:

$$(3.5) \quad f(k; \lambda) = \Pr(X = k) = \frac{\lambda^k e^{-\lambda}}{k!}$$

$$(3.6) \quad \lambda = \mathrm{E}(X) = \mathrm{Var}(X)$$

How to do it...

The following steps fit using the **maximum likelihood estimation** (**MLE**) method:

1. The imports are as follows:

```
from scipy.stats.distributions import poisson
import matplotlib.pyplot as plt
import dautil as dl
from scipy.optimize import minimize
from IPython.html.widgets.interaction import interactive
from IPython.core.display import display
from IPython.core.display import HTML
```

2. Define the function to maximize:

```
def log_likelihood(k, mu):
    return poisson.logpmf(k, mu).sum()
```

3. Load the data and group it by month:

```
def count_rain_days(month):
    rain = dl.data.Weather.load()['RAIN']
    rain = (rain > 0).resample('M', how='sum')
    rain = dl.ts.groupby_month(rain)
    rain = rain.get_group(month)

    return rain
```

4. Define the following visualization function:

```
def plot(rain, dist, params, month):
    fig, ax = plt.subplots()
    plt.title('Fitting to the Poisson distribution ({})'.
format(dl.ts.short_month(month)))

    # Limiting the x-asis for a better plot
    plt.xlim([0, 15])
    plt.figtext(0.5, 0.7, 'rate {:.3f}'.format(params.x[0]),
alpha=0.7,
```

```
                    fontsize=14)
        plt.xlabel('# Rainy days in a month')
        plt.ylabel('Probability')
        ax.hist(dist.train, bins=dist.nbins, normed=True,
    label='Data')
        ax.plot(dist.x, poisson.pmf(dist.x, params.x))
```

5. Define a function to serve as the entry point:

```
    def fit_poisson(month):
        month_index = dl.ts.month_index(month)
        rain = count_rain_days(month_index)

        dist = dl.stats.Distribution(rain, poisson, range=[-0.5,
    19.5])
        params = minimize(log_likelihood, x0=rain.mean(),
    args=(rain,))
        plot(rain, dist, params, month_index)
```

6. Use interactive widgets so we can display a plot for each month:

```
    display(interactive(fit_poisson, month=dl.nb.create_month_
    widget(month='May')))
    HTML(dl.report.HTMLBuilder().watermark())
```

Refer to the following screenshot for the end result (see the `fitting_poisson.ipynb` file in this book's code bundle):

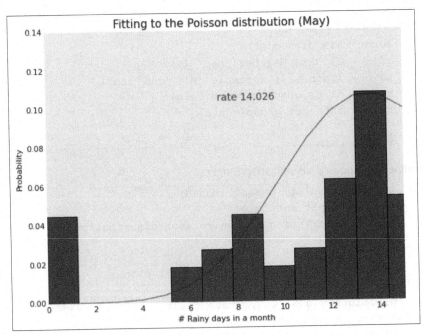

See also

▸ The Poisson distribution Wikipedia page at `https://en.wikipedia.org/wiki/Poisson_distribution` (retrieved August 2015)

▸ The related SciPy documentation at `http://docs.scipy.org/doc/scipy/reference/generated/scipy.stats.poisson.html#scipy.stats.poisson` (retrieved August 2015)

Determining bias

When teaching probability, it is customary to give examples of coin tosses. Whether it is going to rain or not is more or less like a coin toss. If we have two possible outcomes, the **binomial distribution** is appropriate. This distribution requires two parameters: the probability and the sample size.

In statistics, there are two generally accepted approaches. In the **frequentist** approach, we measure the number of coin tosses and use that frequency for further analysis. **Bayesian** analysis is named after its founder the Reverend Thomas Bayes. The Bayesian approach is more incremental and requires a **prior distribution**, which is the distribution we assume before performing experiments. The **posterior distribution** is the distribution we are interested in and which we obtain after getting new data from experiments. Let's first have a look at the following equations:

$$(3.7) \quad f(k;n,p) = \Pr(X=k) = \binom{n}{k} p^k (1-p)^{n-k}$$

$$(3.8) \quad \binom{n}{k} = \frac{n!}{k!(n-k)!}$$

$$(3.9) \quad P(a < p < b \,|\, m;n) = \frac{\int_a^b \binom{n+m}{m} p^m (1-p)^n \, dp}{\int_0^1 \binom{n+m}{m} p^m (1-p)^n \, dp}$$

(3.7) and **(3.8)** describe the probability mass function for the binomial distribution. **(3.9)** comes from an essay published by Bayes. The equation is about an experiment with m successes and n failures and assumes a uniform prior distribution for the probability parameter of the binomial distribution.

How to do it...

In this recipe, we will apply the frequentist and Bayesian approach to rain data:

1. The imports are as follows:

```
import dautil as dl
from scipy import stats
import matplotlib.pyplot as plt
import numpy as np
from IPython.html.widgets.interaction import interact
from IPython.display import HTML
```

2. Define the following function to load the data:

```
def load():
    rainy = dl.data.Weather.rain_values() > 0
    n = len(rainy)
    nrains = np.cumsum(rainy)

    return n, nrains
```

3. Define the following function to compute the posterior:

```
def posterior(i, u, data):
    return stats.binom(i, u).pmf(data[i])
```

4. Define the following function to plot the posterior for the subset of the data:

```
def plot_posterior(ax, day, u, nrains):
    ax.set_title('Posterior distribution for day {}'.format(day))
    ax.plot(posterior(day, u, nrains),
            label='rainy days in period={}'.format(nrains[day]))
    ax.set_xlabel('Uniform prior parameter')
    ax.set_ylabel('Probability rain')
    ax.legend(loc='best')
```

5. Define the following function to do the plotting:

```
def plot(day1=1, day2=30):
    fig, [[upleft, upright], [downleft, downright]] = plt.
subplots(2, 2)
    plt.suptitle('Determining bias of rain data')
    x = np.arange(n) + 1
    upleft.set_title('Frequentist Approach')
    upleft.plot(x, nrains/x, label='Probability rain')
    upleft.set_xlabel('Days')
    set_ylabel(upleft)

    max_p = np.zeros(n)
    u = np.linspace(0, 1, 100)
```

```
for i in x - 1:
    max_p[i] = posterior(i, u, nrains).argmax()/100

downleft.set_title('Bayesian Approach')
downleft.plot(x, max_p)
downleft.set_xlabel('Days')
set_ylabel(downleft)

plot_posterior(upright, day1, u, nrains)
plot_posterior(downright, day2, u, nrains)
plt.tight_layout()
```

6. The following lines call the other functions and place a watermark:

```
interact(plot, day1=(1, n), day2=(1, n))
HTML(dl.report.HTMLBuilder().watermark())
```

Refer to the following screenshot for the end result (see the `determining_bias.ipynb` file in this book's code bundle):

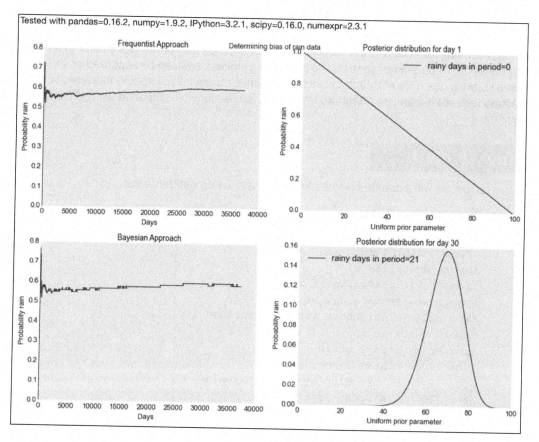

See also

 ▶ The Wikipedia page about the essay mentioned in this recipe is at `https://en.wikipedia.org/wiki/An_Essay_towards_solving_a_Problem_in_the_Doctrine_of_Chances` (retrieved August 2015)

Estimating kernel density

Often, we have an idea about the kind of distribution that is appropriate for our data. If that is not the case, we can apply a procedure called **kernel density estimation**. This method doesn't make any assumptions and is nonparametric. We basically smooth the data in an attempt to get a handle on the probability density. To smooth data, we can use various functions. These functions are called kernel functions in this context. The following equation defines the estimator:

$$(3.10) \quad \hat{f}_h(x) = \frac{1}{n}\sum_{i=1}^{n} K_h(x - x_i) = \frac{1}{nh}\sum_{i=1}^{n} K\left(\frac{x - x_i}{h}\right)$$

In the preceding formula, K is the kernel function, a function with properties similar to a PDF. The bandwidth h parameter controls the smoothing process and can be kept fixed or varied. Some libraries use rules of thumb to calculate h, while others let you specify its value. SciPy, statsmodels, scikit-learn, and Seaborn implement kernel density estimation using different algorithms.

How to do it...

In this recipe, we will estimate bivariate kernel density using weather data:

1. The imports are as follows:

```
import seaborn as sns
import matplotlib.pyplot as plt
import dautil as dl
from dautil.stats import zscores
import statsmodels.api as sm
from sklearn.neighbors import KernelDensity
import numpy as np
from scipy import stats
from IPython.html import widgets
from IPython.core.display import display
from IPython.display import HTML
```

2. Define the following function to plot the estimated kernel density:

```
def plot(ax, a, b, c, xlabel, ylabel):
    dl.plotting.scatter_with_bar(ax, 'Kernel Density', a.values,
b.values, c=c, cmap='Blues')
    ax.set_xlabel(xlabel)
    ax.set_ylabel(ylabel)
```

3. In the following notebook cell, load the data and define widgets for the selection of weather variables:

```
df = dl.data.Weather.load().resample('M').dropna()
columns = [str(c) for c in df.columns.values]
var1 = widgets.Dropdown(options=columns, selected_label='RAIN')
display(var1)
var2 = widgets.Dropdown(options=columns, selected_label='TEMP')
display(var2)
```

4. In the next notebook cell, define variables using the values of the widgets we created:

```
x = df[var1.value]
xlabel = dl.data.Weather.get_header(var1.value)
y = df[var2.value]
ylabel = dl.data.Weather.get_header(var2.value)
X = [x, y]
```

5. The next notebook cell does the heavy lifting with the most important lines highlighted:

```
# need to use zscores to avoid errors
Z = [zscores(x), zscores(y)]
kde = stats.gaussian_kde(Z)


_, [[sp_ax, sm_ax], [sk_ax, sns_ax]] = plt.subplots(2, 2)
plot(sp_ax, x, y, kde.pdf(Z), xlabel, ylabel)
sp_ax.set_title('SciPy')


sm_kde = sm.nonparametric.KDEMultivariate(data=X, var_type='cc',
                                          bw='normal_reference')
sm_ax.set_title('statsmodels')
plot(sm_ax, x, y, sm_kde.pdf(X), xlabel, ylabel)


XT = np.array(X).T
sk_kde = KernelDensity(kernel='gaussian', bandwidth=0.2).fit(XT)
sk_ax.set_title('Scikit Learn')
plot(sk_ax, x, y, sk_kde.score_samples(XT), xlabel, ylabel)
```

```
sns_ax.set_title('Seaborn')
sns.kdeplot(x, y, ax=sns_ax)
sns.rugplot(x, color="b", ax=sns_ax)
sns.rugplot(y, vertical=True, ax=sns_ax)
sns_ax.set_xlabel(xlabel)
sns_ax.set_ylabel(ylabel)


plt.tight_layout()
HTML(dl.report.HTMLBuilder().watermark())
```

Refer to the following screenshot for the end result (see the `kernel_density_estimation.ipynb` file in this book's code bundle):

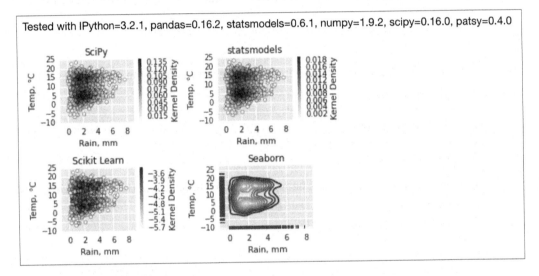

See also

▸ The kernel density estimation Wikipedia page at `https://en.wikipedia.org/wiki/Kernel_density_estimation` (retrieved August 2015)

▸ The related statsmodels documentation at `http://statsmodels.sourceforge.net/devel/generated/statsmodels.nonparametric.kernel_density.KDEMultivariate.html` (retrieved August 2015)

▸ The related scikit-learn documentation at `http://scikit-learn.org/stable/modules/density.html` (retrieved August 2015)

Determining confidence intervals for mean, variance, and standard deviation

It is sometimes useful to imagine that the data we observe is just the tip of an iceberg. If you get into this mindset, then you probably will want to know how big this iceberg actually is. Obviously, if you can't see the whole thing, you can still try to extrapolate from the data you have. In statistics we try to estimate confidence intervals, which are an estimated range usually associated with a certain confidence level quoted in percentages.

The `scipy.stats.bayes_mvs()` function estimates confidence intervals for mean, variance, and standard deviation. The function uses Bayesian statistics to estimate confidence assuming that the data is independent and normally distributed. **Jackknifing** is an alternative deterministic algorithm to estimate confidence intervals. It falls under the family of resampling algorithms. Usually, we generate new datasets under the jackknifing algorithm by deleting one value (we can also delete two or more values). We generate data *N* times, where *N* is the number of values in the dataset. Typically, if we want a 5 percent confidence level, we estimate the means or variances for the new datasets and determine the 2.5 and 97.5 percentile values.

How to do it...

In this recipe, we estimate confidence intervals with the `scipy.stats.bayes_mvs()` function and jackknifing:

1. The imports are as follows:

    ```
    from scipy import stats
    import dautil as dl
    from dautil.stats import jackknife
    import pandas as pd
    import matplotlib.pyplot as plt
    import numpy as np
    from IPython.html.widgets.interaction import interact
    from IPython.display import HTML
    ```

2. Define the following function to visualize the Scipy result using error bars:

    ```
    def plot_bayes(ax, metric, var, df):
        vals = np.array([[v.statistic, v.minmax[0], v.minmax[1]] for v
    in
                        df[metric].values])

        ax.set_title('Bayes {}'.format(metric))
        ax.errorbar(np.arange(len(vals)), vals.T[0], yerr=(vals.T[1],
    vals.T[2]))
        set_labels(ax, var)
    ```

3. Define the following function to visualize the jackknifing result using error bars:

```
def plot_jackknife(ax, metric, func, var, df):
    vals = df.apply(lambda x: jackknife(x, func, alpha=0.95))
    vals = np.array([[v[0], v[1], v[2]] for v in vals.values])

    ax.set_title('Jackknife {}'.format(metric))
    ax.errorbar(np.arange(len(vals)), vals.T[0], yerr=(vals.T[1],
vals.T[2]))
    set_labels(ax, var)
```

4. Define the following function, which will be called with the help of an IPython interactive widget:

```
def confidence_interval(var='TEMP'):
    df = dl.data.Weather.load().dropna()
    df = dl.ts.groupby_yday(df)

    def f(x):
        return stats.bayes_mvs(x, alpha=0.95)

    bayes_df = pd.DataFrame([[v[0], v[1], v[2]] for v in
                            df[var].apply(f).values],
columns=['Mean', 'Var',

'Std'])

    fig, axes = plt.subplots(2, 2)
    fig.suptitle('Confidence Intervals')

    plot_bayes(axes[0][0], 'Mean', var, bayes_df)
    plot_bayes(axes[0][1], 'Var', var, bayes_df)
    plot_jackknife(axes[1][0], 'Mean', np.mean, var, df[var])
    plot_jackknife(axes[1][1], 'Mean', np.var, var, df[var])

    plt.tight_layout()
```

5. Set up an interactive IPython widget:

```
interact(confidence_interval, var=dl.data.Weather.get_headers())
HTML(dl.report.HTMLBuilder().watermark())
```

Refer to the following screenshot for the end result (see the `bayes_confidence.ipynb` file in this book's code bundle):

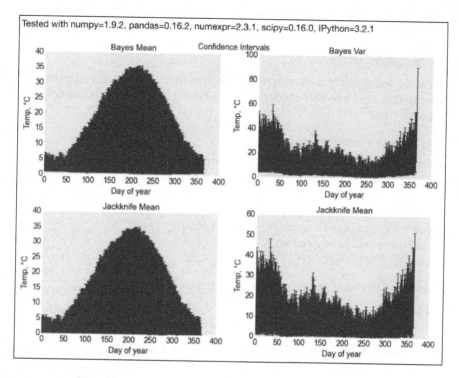

> ▸ The Wikipedia page on jackknife resampling at `https://en.wikipedia.org/wiki/Jackknife_resampling` (retrieved August 2015)
> ▸ T.E. Oliphant, "*A Bayesian perspective on estimating mean, variance, and standard-deviation from data*" (`http://hdl.handle.net/1877/438`, 2006)

Sampling with probability weights

To create the nuclear bomb during the Second World War, physicists needed to perform pretty complicated calculations. Stanislaw Ulam got the idea to treat this challenge as a game of chance. Later, the method he came up with was given the code name **Monte Carlo**. Games of chance usually have very simple rules, but playing in an optimal way can be difficult. According to quantum mechanics, subatomic particles are also unpredictable. If we simulate many experiments with subatomic particles, we still can get an idea of how they are likely to behave. The Monte Carlo method is not deterministic, but it approaches the correct result for a complex computation for a sufficiently large number of simulations.

The `statsmodels.distributions.empirical_distribution.ECDF` class defines the cumulative distribution function of a data array. We can use its output to simulate a complex process. This simulation is not perfect, because we lose information in the process.

How to do it...

In this recipe, we will simulate weather processes. In particular, I am interested in annual temperature values. I am interested in finding out whether the simulated data sets also show an upward trend:

1. The imports are as follows:

    ```
    from statsmodels.distributions.empirical_distribution import ECDF
    import dautil as dl
    import numpy as np
    import matplotlib.pyplot as plt
    from sklearn.utils import check_random_state
    from IPython.html.widgets.interaction import interact
    from IPython.core.display import HTML
    ```

2. Define the following function to calculate the slope:

    ```
    def slope(x, y):
        return np.polyfit(x, y, 1)[0]
    ```

3. Define the following function to generate data for a single year:

    ```
    def simulate(x, years, rs, p):
        N = len(years)
        means = np.zeros(N)

        for i in range(N):
            sample = rs.choice(x, size=365, p=p)
            means[i] = sample.mean()

        return means, np.diff(means).mean(), slope(years, means)
    ```

4. Define the following function to run multiple simulations:

```
def run_multiple(times, x, years, p):
    sims = []
    rs = check_random_state(20)

    for i in range(times):
        sims.append(simulate(x, years, rs, p))

    return np.array(sims)
```

5. Define the following function, which by default loads temperature values:

```
def main(var='TEMP'):
    df = dl.data.Weather.load().dropna()[var]
    cdf = ECDF(df)
    x = cdf.x[1:]
    p = np.diff(cdf.y)

    df = df.resample('A')
    years = df.index.year
    sims = run_multiple(500, x, years, p)

    sp = dl.plotting.Subplotter(2, 1, context)
    plotter = dl.plotting.CyclePlotter(sp.ax)
    plotter.plot(years, df.values, label='Data')
    plotter.plot(years, sims[0][0], label='Sim 1')
    plotter.plot(years, sims[1][0], label='Sim 2')
    header = dl.data.Weather.get_header(var)
    sp.label(title_params=header, ylabel_params=header)
    sp.ax.legend(loc='best')

    sp.next_ax()
    sp.label()
    sp.ax.hist(sims.T[2], normed=True)
    plt.figtext(0.2, 0.3, 'Slope of the Data {:.3f}'.
format(slope(years, df.values)))
    plt.tight_layout()
```

The notebook stored in the `sampling_weights.ipynb` file in this book's code bundle gives you the option to select other weather variables too. Refer to the following screenshot for the end result:

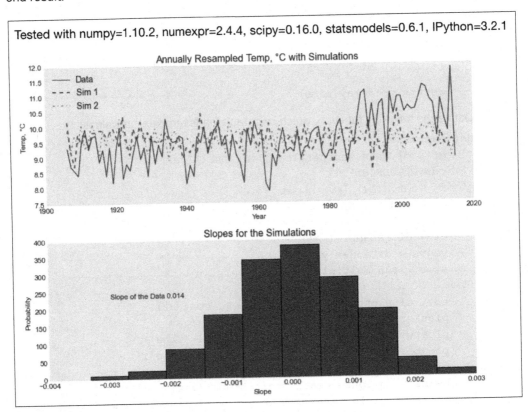

See also

▶ The Wikipedia page for the Monte Carlo method at `https://en.wikipedia.org/wiki/Monte_Carlo_method` (retrieved August 2015)

▶ The documentation for the `ECDF` class at `http://statsmodels.sourceforge.net/0.6.0/generated/statsmodels.distributions.empirical_distribution.ECDF.html` (retrieved August 2015)

Exploring extreme values

Worldwide, there are almost a million dams, roughly 5 percent of which are higher than 15 m. A civil engineer designing a dam will have to consider many factors, including rainfall. Let's assume, for the sake of simplicity, that the engineer wants to know the cumulative annual rainfall. We can also take monthly maximums and fit those to a **generalized extreme value** (**GEV**) distribution. Using this distribution, we can then bootstrap to get our estimate. Instead, I select values that are above the 95th percentile in this recipe.

The GEV distribution is implemented in `scipy.stats` and is a mixture of the Gumbel, Frechet, and Weibull distributions. The following equations describe the cumulative distribution function **(3.11)** and a related constraint **(3.12)**:

$$(3.11) \quad F\left(x;\mu,\sigma,\xi\right)=\exp\left\{-\left[1+\xi\left(\frac{x-\mu}{\sigma}\right)\right]^{-1/\xi}\right\}$$

$$(3.12) \quad 1+\xi\left(x-\mu\right)/\sigma>0$$

In these equations, μ is the location parameter, σ is the scale parameter, and ξ is the shape parameter.

How to do it...

Let's analyze the data using the GEV distribution:

1. The imports are as follows:

```
from scipy.stats.distributions import genextreme
import matplotlib.pyplot as plt
import dautil as dl
import numpy as np
from IPython.display import HTML
```

2. Define the following function to sample the GEV distribution:

```
def run_sims(nsims):
    sums = []

    np.random.seed(19)

    for i in range(nsims):
        for j in range(len(years)):
            sample_sum = dist.rvs(shape, loc, scale, size=365).
    sum()
```

```
                    sums.append(sample_sum)

        a = np.array(sums)
        low, high = dl.stats.ci(a)

        return a, low, high
```

3. Load the data and select the extreme values:

```
rain = dl.data.Weather.load()['RAIN'].dropna()
annual_sums = rain.resample('A', how=np.sum)
years = np.unique(rain.index.year)
limit = np.percentile(rain, 95)
rain = rain[rain > limit]
dist = dl.stats.Distribution(rain, genextreme)
```

4. Fit the extreme values to the GEV distribution:

```
shape, loc, scale = dist.fit()
table = dl.report.DFBuilder(['shape', 'loc', 'scale'])
table.row([shape, loc, scale])
dl.options.set_pd_options()
html_builder = dl.report.HTMLBuilder()
html_builder.h1('Exploring Extreme Values')
html_builder.h2('Distribution Parameters')
html_builder.add_df(table.build())
```

5. Get statistics on the fit residuals:

```
pdf = dist.pdf(shape, loc, scale)
html_builder.h2('Residuals of the Fit')
residuals = dist.describe_residuals()
html_builder.add(residuals.to_html())
```

6. Get the fit metrics:

```
table2 = dl.report.DFBuilder(['Mean_AD', 'RMSE'])
table2.row([dist.mean_ad(), dist.rmse()])
html_builder.h2('Fit Metrics')
html_builder.add_df(table2.build())
```

7. Plot the data and the result of the bootstrap:

```
sp = dl.plotting.Subplotter(2, 2, context)

sp.ax.hist(annual_sums, normed=True, bins=dl.stats.sqrt_
bins(annual_sums))
sp.label()
set_labels(sp.ax)

sp.next_ax()
sp.label()
sp.ax.set_xlim([5000, 10000])
sims = []
nsims = [25, 50, 100, 200]

for n in nsims:
    sims.append(run_sims(n))

sims = np.array(sims)
sp.ax.hist(sims[2][0], normed=True, bins=dl.stats.sqrt_
bins(sims[2][0]))
set_labels(sp.ax)

sp.next_ax()
sp.label()
sp.ax.set_xlim([10, 40])
sp.ax.hist(rain, bins=dist.nbins, normed=True, label='Rain')
sp.ax.plot(dist.x, pdf, label='PDF')
set_labels(sp.ax)
sp.ax.legend(loc='best')

sp.next_ax()
sp.ax.plot(nsims, sims.T[1], 'o', label='2.5 percentile')
sp.ax.plot(nsims, sims.T[2], 'x', label='97.5 percentile')
sp.ax.legend(loc='center')
sp.label(ylabel_params=dl.data.Weather.get_header('RAIN'))

plt.tight_layout()
HTML(html_builder.html)
```

Refer to the following screenshot for the end result (see the `extreme_values.ipynb` file in this book's code bundle):

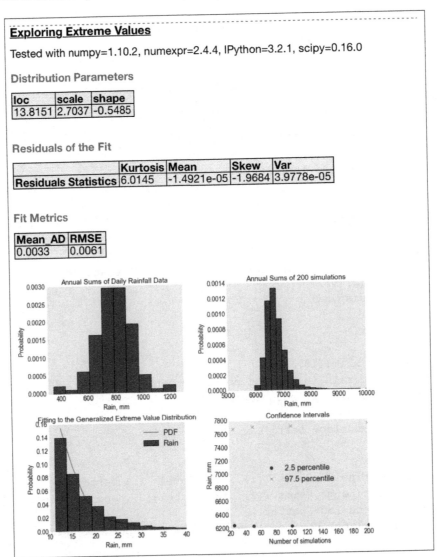

Exploring Extreme Values

Tested with numpy=1.10.2, numexpr=2.4.4, IPython=3.2.1, scipy=0.16.0

Distribution Parameters

loc	scale	shape
13.8151	2.7037	-0.5485

Residuals of the Fit

	Kurtosis	Mean	Skew	Var
Residuals Statistics	6.0145	-1.4921e-05	-1.9684	3.9778e-05

Fit Metrics

Mean_AD	RMSE
0.0033	0.0061

See also

▶ The Wikipedia page on the GEV distribution at https://en.wikipedia.org/wiki/Generalized_extreme_value_distribution (retrieved August 2015).

Correlating variables with Pearson's correlation

Pearson's r, named after its developer Karl Pearson (1896), measures linear correlation between two variables. Let's look at the following equations:

$$(3.13) \quad r = r_{xy} = \frac{\sum_{i=1}^{n}(x_i - \bar{x})(y_i - \bar{y})}{\sqrt{\sum_{i=1}^{n}(x_i - \bar{x})^2}\sqrt{\sum_{i=1}^{n}(y_i - \bar{y})^2}}$$

$$(3.14) \quad F(r) = \frac{1}{2}\ln\frac{1+r}{1-r} = \operatorname{arctanh}(r)$$

$$(3.15) \quad SE = \frac{1}{\sqrt{n-3}}$$

$$(3.16) \quad z = \frac{x - mean}{SE} = \left[F(r) - F(\rho_0)\right]\sqrt{n-3}$$

(3.13) defines the coefficient and **(3.14)** describes the **Fisher transformation** used to compute confidence intervals. **(3.15)** gives the standard error of the correlation. **(3.16)** is about the z-score of the Fisher transformed correlation. If we assume a normal distribution, we can use the z-score to compute confidence intervals. Alternatively, we can bootstrap by resampling pairs of values with replacement. Also, the `scipy.stats.pearsonr()` function returns a p-value, which (according to the documentation) is not accurate for samples of less than 500 values. Unfortunately, we are going to use such a small sample in this recipe. We are going to correlate carbon dioxide emission data from the Worldbank with related temperature data for the Netherlands.

How to do it...

In this recipe, we will compute the correlation coefficient and estimate confidence intervals using z-scores and bootstrapping with the following steps:

1. The imports are as follows:

```
import dautil as dl
import pandas as pd
from scipy import stats
import numpy as np
import math
from sklearn.utils import check_random_state
import matplotlib.pyplot as plt
from IPython.display import HTML
from IPython.display import display
```

2. Download the data and set up appropriate data structures:

```
wb = dl.data.Worldbank()
indicator = wb.get_name('co2')
co2 = wb.download(country='NL', indicator=indicator, start=1900,
                  end=2014)
co2.index = [int(year) for year in co2.index.get_level_values(1)]
temp = pd.DataFrame(dl.data.Weather.load()['TEMP'].resample('A'))
temp.index = temp.index.year
temp.index.name = 'year'
df = pd.merge(co2, temp, left_index=True, right_index=True).
dropna()
```

3. Compute the correlation as follows:

```
stats_corr = stats.pearsonr(df[indicator].values, df['TEMP'].
values)
print('Correlation={0:.4g}, p-value={1:.4g}'.format(stats_corr[0],
stats_corr[1]))
```

4. Calculate the confidence interval with the Fisher transform:

```
z = np.arctanh(stats_corr[0])
n = len(df.index)
se = 1/(math.sqrt(n - 3))
ci = z + np.array([-1, 1]) * se * stats.norm.ppf((1 + 0.95)/2)

ci = np.tanh(ci)
dl.options.set_pd_options()
ci_table = dl.report.DFBuilder(['Low', 'High'])
ci_table.row([ci[0], ci[1]])
```

5. Bootstrap by resampling pairs with replacement:

```
rs = check_random_state(34)

ranges = []

for j in range(200):
    corrs = []

    for i in range(100):
        indices = rs.choice(n, size=n)
        pairs = df.values
        gen_pairs = pairs[indices]
        corrs.append(stats.pearsonr(gen_pairs.T[0], gen_
pairs.T[1])[0])

    ranges.append(dl.stats.ci(corrs))
```

```
ranges = np.array(ranges)
bootstrap_ci = dl.stats.ci(corrs)
ci_table.row([bootstrap_ci[0], bootstrap_ci[1]])
ci_table = ci_table.build(index=['Formula', 'Bootstrap'])
```

6. Plot the results and produce a report:

```
x = np.arange(len(ranges)) * 100
plt.plot(x, ranges.T[0], label='Low')
plt.plot(x, ranges.T[1], label='High')
plt.plot(x, stats_corr[0] * np.ones_like(x), label='SciPy
estimate')
plt.ylabel('Pearson Correlation')
plt.xlabel('Number of bootstraps')
plt.title('Bootstrapped Pearson Correlation')
plt.legend(loc='best')
result = dl.report.HTMLBuilder()
result.h1('Pearson Correlation Confidence intervals')
result.h2('Confidence Intervals')
result.add(ci_table.to_html())
HTML(result.html)
```

Refer to the following screenshot for the end result (see the `correlating_pearson.ipynb` file in this book's code bundle):

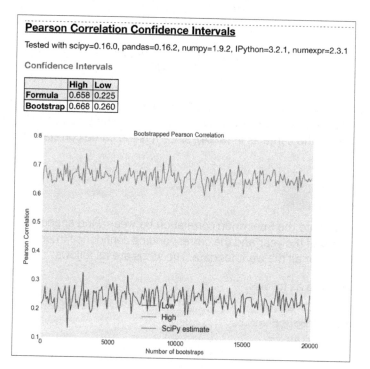

See also

▸ The related SciPy documentation at `http://docs.scipy.org/doc/scipy/reference/generated/scipy.stats.pearsonr.html#scipy.stats.pearsonr` (retrieved August 2015).

Correlating variables with the Spearman rank correlation

The **Spearman rank correlation** uses ranks to correlate two variables with the Pearson Correlation. Ranks are the positions of values in sorted order. Items with equal values get a rank, which is the average of their positions. For instance, if we have two items of equal value assigned position 2 and 3, the rank is 2.5 for both items. Have a look at the following equations:

$$(3.17) \quad \rho = 1 - \frac{6\sum d_i^2}{n(n^2 - 1)}$$

$$(3.18) \quad d_i = x_i - y_i$$

$$(3.19) \quad \sigma = \frac{0.6325}{\sqrt{n-1}}$$

$$(3.20) \quad z = \sqrt{\frac{n-3}{1.06}} F(r)$$

In these equations, n is the sample size. **(3.17)** shows how the correlation is calculated. **(3.19)** gives the standard error. **(3.20)** is about the z-score, which we assume to be normally distributed. $F(r)$ is here the same as in **(3.14)**, since it is the same correlation but applied to ranks.

How to do it...

In this recipe we calculate the Spearman correlation between wind speed and temperature aggregated by the day of the year and the corresponding confidence interval. Then, we display the correlation matrix for all the weather data. The steps are as follows:

1. The imports are as follows:

    ```
    import dautil as dl
    from scipy import stats
    import numpy as np
    import math
    ```

```
import seaborn as sns
import matplotlib.pyplot as plt
from IPython.html import widgets
from IPython.display import display
from IPython.display import HTML
```

2. Define the following function to compute the confidence interval:

```
def get_ci(n, corr):
    z = math.sqrt((n - 3)/1.06) * np.arctanh(corr)
    se = 0.6325/(math.sqrt(n - 1))
    ci = z + np.array([-1, 1]) * se * stats.norm.ppf((1 + 0.95)/2)

    return np.tanh(ci)
```

3. Load the data and display widgets so that you can correlate a different pair if you want:

```
df = dl.data.Weather.load().dropna()
df = dl.ts.groupby_yday(df).mean()

drop1 = widgets.Dropdown(options=dl.data.Weather.get_headers(),
                         selected_label='TEMP',
description='Variable 1')
drop2 = widgets.Dropdown(options=dl.data.Weather.get_headers(),
                         selected_label='WIND_SPEED',
description='Variable 2')
display(drop1)
display(drop2)
```

4. Compute the Spearman rank correlation with SciPy:

```
var1 = df[drop1.value].values
var2 = df[drop2.value].values
stats_corr = stats.spearmanr(var1, var2)
dl.options.set_pd_options()
html_builder = dl.report.HTMLBuilder()
html_builder.h1('Spearman Correlation between {0} and {1}'.format(
    dl.data.Weather.get_header(drop1.value), dl.data.Weather.get_
header(drop2.value)))
html_builder.h2('scipy.stats.spearmanr()')
dfb = dl.report.DFBuilder(['Correlation', 'p-value'])
dfb.row([stats_corr[0], stats_corr[1]])
html_builder.add_df(dfb.build())
```

5. Compute the confidence interval as follows:

```
n = len(df.index)
ci = get_ci(n, stats_corr)
html_builder.h2('Confidence intervale')
dfb = dl.report.DFBuilder(['2.5 percentile', '97.5 percentile'])
dfb.row(ci)
html_builder.add_df(dfb.build())
```

6. Display the correlation matrix as a Seaborn heatmap:

```
corr = df.corr(method='spearman')

%matplotlib inline
plt.title('Spearman Correlation Matrix')
sns.heatmap(corr)
HTML(html_builder.html)
```

Refer to the following screenshot for the end result (see the `correlating_spearman.ipynb` file in this book's code bundle):

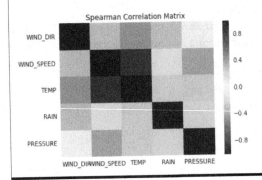

Spearman Correlation Between Temp, °C And W Speed, M/S

Tested with statsmodels=0.6.1, scipy=0.16.0, pandas=0.16.2, IPython=3.2.1, numpy=1.9.2

scipy.stats.spearmanr()

Correlation	p-value
-0.891	3.220e-127

Confidence intervale

2.5 percentile	97.5 percentile
-1	0.065

▶ The Spearman rank correlation Wikipedia page at `https://en.wikipedia.org/wiki/Spearman%27s_rank_correlation_coefficient` (retrieved August 2015)

Correlating a binary and a continuous variable with the point biserial correlation

The **point-biserial correlation** correlates a binary variable Y and a continuous variable X. The coefficient is calculated as follows:

$$(3.21) \quad r_{pb} = \frac{M_1 - M_0}{s_n} \sqrt{\frac{n_1 n_0}{n^2}}$$

$$(3.22) \quad s_n = \sqrt{\frac{1}{n} \sum_{i=1}^{n} (X_i - \bar{X})^2}$$

The subscripts in **(3.21)** correspond to the two groups of the binary variable. *M1* is the mean of X for values corresponding to group 1 of Y. *M2* is the mean of X for values corresponding to group 0 of Y.

In this recipe, the binary variable we will use is rain or no rain. We will correlate this variable with temperature.

How to do it...

We will calculate the correlation with the `scipy.stats.pointbiserialr()` function. We will also compute the rolling correlation using a 2 year window with the `np.roll()` function. The steps are as follows:

1. The imports are as follows:

```
import dautil as dl
from scipy import stats
import numpy as np
import matplotlib.pyplot as plt
import pandas as pd
from IPython.display import HTML
```

2. Load the data and correlate the two relevant arrays:

```
df = dl.data.Weather.load().dropna()
df['RAIN'] = df['RAIN'] > 0

stats_corr = stats.pointbiserialr(df['RAIN'].values, df['TEMP'].
values)
```

3. Compute the 2 year rolling correlation as follows:

```
N = 2 * 365
corrs = []

for i in range(len(df.index) - N):
    x = np.roll(df['RAIN'].values, i)[:N]
    y = np.roll(df['TEMP'].values, i)[:N]
    corrs.append(stats.pointbiserialr(x, y)[0])

corrs = pd.DataFrame(corrs,
                index=df.index[N:],
                columns=['Correlation']).resample('A')
```

4. Plot the results with the following code:

```
plt.plot(corrs.index.values, corrs.values)
plt.hlines(stats_corr[0], corrs.index.values[0], corrs.index.
values[-1],
          label='Correlation using the whole data set')
plt.title('Rolling Point-biserial Correlation of Rain and
Temperature with a 2 Year Window')
plt.xlabel('Year')
plt.ylabel('Correlation')
plt.legend(loc='best')
HTML(dl.report.HTMLBuilder().watermark())
```

Refer to the following screenshot for the end result (see `correlating_pointbiserial.ipynb` file in this book's code bundle):

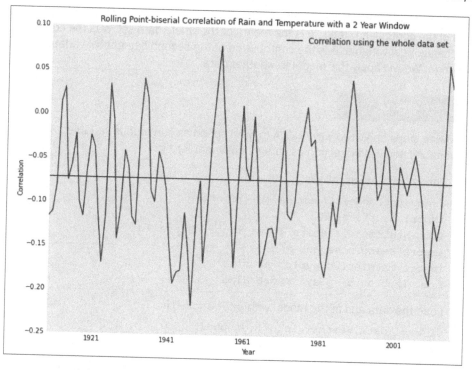

See also

▸ The relevant SciPy documentation at `http://docs.scipy.org/doc/scipy/reference/generated/scipy.stats.pointbiserialr.html#scipy.stats.pointbiserialr` (retrieved August 2015).

Evaluating relations between variables with ANOVA

Analysis of variance (ANOVA) is a statistical data analysis method invented by statistician Ronald Fisher. This method partitions data of a continuous variable using the values of one or more corresponding categorical variables to analyze variance. ANOVA is a form of linear modeling. If we are modeling with one categorical variable, we speak of **one-way ANOVA**. In this recipe, we will use two categorical variables so we have **two-way ANOVA**. In two-way ANOVA, we create a **contingency table**—a table containing counts for all combinations of the two categorical variables (we will see a contingency table example soon). The linear model is then given by the equation:

$$(3.23) \quad \mu_{ij} = \mu + \alpha_i + \beta_j + \gamma_{ij}$$

This is an additive model where μ_{ij} is the mean of the continuous variable corresponding to one cell of the contingency table, μ is the mean for the whole data set, α_i is the contribution of the first categorical variable, β_j is the contribution of the second categorical variable, and y_{ij} is a cross-term. We will apply this model to weather data.

How to do it...

The following steps apply two-way ANOVA to wind speed as continuous variable, rain as a binary variable, and wind direction as categorical variable:

1. The imports are as follows:

   ```
   from statsmodels.formula.api import ols
   import dautil as dl
   from statsmodels.stats.anova import anova_lm
   import seaborn as sns
   import matplotlib.pyplot as plt
   from IPython.display import HTML
   ```

2. Load the data and fit the model with `statsmodels`:

   ```
   df = dl.data.Weather.load().dropna()
   df['RAIN'] = df['RAIN'] > 0
   formula = 'WIND_SPEED ~ C(RAIN) + C(WIND_DIR)'
   lm = ols(formula, df).fit()
   hb = dl.HTMLBuilder()
   hb.h1('ANOVA Applied to Weather Data')
   hb.h2('ANOVA results')
   hb.add_df(anova_lm(lm), index=True)
   ```

3. Display a truncated contingency table and visualize the data with Seaborn:

   ```
   df['WIND_DIR'] = dl.data.Weather.categorize_wind_dir(df)
   hb.h2('Truncated Contingency table')
   hb.add_df(df.groupby([df['RAIN'], df['WIND_DIR']]).count().
   head(3),index=True)

   sns.pointplot(y='WIND_SPEED', x='WIND_DIR',
                 hue='RAIN', data=df[['WIND_SPEED', 'RAIN', 'WIND_
   DIR']])
   HTML(hb.html)
   ```

Refer to the following screenshot for the end result (see `anova.ipynb` file in this book's code bundle):

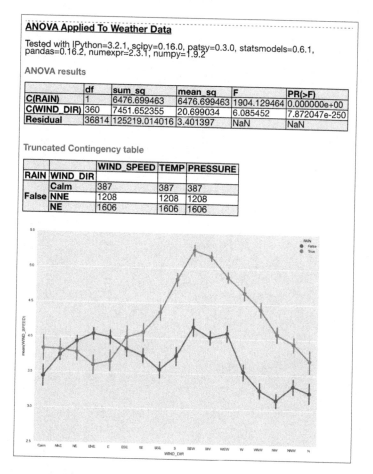

ANOVA Applied To Weather Data

Tested with IPython=3.2.1, scipy=0.16.0, patsy=0.3.0, statsmodels=0.6.1, pandas=0.16.2, numexpr=2.3.1, numpy=1.9.2

ANOVA results

	df	sum_sq	mean_sq	F	PR(>F)
C(RAIN)	1	6476.699463	6476.699463	1904.129464	0.000000e+00
C(WIND_DIR)	360	7451.652355	20.699034	6.085452	7.872047e-250
Residual	36814	125219.014016	3.401397	NaN	NaN

Truncated Contingency table

RAIN	WIND_DIR	WIND_SPEED	TEMP	PRESSURE
	Calm	387	387	387
False	NNE	1208	1208	1208
	NE	1606	1606	1606

See also

- The Wikipedia page for two-way ANOVA at https://en.wikipedia.org/wiki/Two-way_analysis_of_variance (retrieved August 2015)
- The Wikipedia page about the contingency table is https://en.wikipedia.org/wiki/Contingency_table (retrieved August 2015)

4

Dealing with Data and Numerical Issues

The recipes in this chapter are as follows:

- Clipping and filtering outliers
- Winsorizing data
- Measuring central tendency of noisy data
- Normalizing with the Box-Cox transformation
- Transforming data with the power ladder
- Transforming data with logarithms
- Rebinning data
- Applying `logit()` to transform proportions
- Fitting a robust linear model
- Taking variance into account with weighted least squares
- Using arbitrary precision for optimization
- Using arbitrary precision for linear algebra

Introduction

In the real world, data rarely matches textbook definitions and examples. We have to deal with issues such as faulty hardware, uncooperative customers, and disgruntled colleagues. It is difficult to predict what kind of issues you will run into, but it is safe to assume that they will be plentiful and challenging. In this chapter, I will sketch some common approaches to deal with noisy data, which are based more on rules of thumb than strict science. Luckily, the trial and error part of data analysis is limited.

Most of this chapter is about outlier management. Outliers are values that we consider to be abnormal. Of course, this is not the only issue that you will encounter, but it is a sneaky one. A common issue is that of missing or invalid values, so I will briefly mention masked arrays and pandas features such as the `dropna()` function, which I have used throughout this book.

I have also written two recipes about using **mpmath** for arbitrary precision calculations. I don't recommend using mpmath unless you really have to because of the performance penalty you have to pay. Usually we can work around numerical issues, so arbitrary precision libraries are rarely needed.

Clipping and filtering outliers

Outliers are a common issue in data analysis. Although an exact definition of outliers doesn't exist, we know that outliers can influence means and regression results. Outliers are values that are anomalous. Usually, outliers are caused by a measurement error, but the outliers are sometimes real. In the second case, we may be dealing with two or more types of data related to different phenomena.

The data for this recipe is described at `https://vincentarelbundock.github.io/Rdatasets/doc/robustbase/starsCYG.html` (retrieved August 2015). It consists of logarithmic effective temperature and logarithmic light intensity for 47 stars in a certain star cluster. Any astronomers reading this paragraph will know the **Hertzsprung-Russell diagram**. In data analysis terms, the diagram is a scatter plot, but for astronomers, it is of course more than that. The Hertzsprung Russell diagram was defined around 1910 and features a diagonal line (not entirely straight) called the **main sequence**. Most stars in our data set should be on the main sequence with four outliers in the upper-left corner. These outliers are classified as giants.

We have many strategies to deal with outliers. In this recipe, we will use the two simplest strategies: clipping with the NumPy `clip()` function and completely removing the outliers. For this example, I define outliers as values 1.5 interquartile ranges removed from the box defined by the 1st and 3rd quartile.

How to do it...

The following steps show how to clip and filter outliers:

1. The imports are as follows:

```
import statsmodels.api as sm
import matplotlib.pyplot as plt
import numpy as np
import seaborn as sns
import dautil as dl
from IPython.display import HTML
```

2. Define the following function to filter outliers:

```
def filter_outliers(a):
    b = a.copy()
    bmin, bmax = dl.stats.outliers(b)
    b[bmin > b] = np.nan
    b[b > bmax] = np.nan

    return b
```

3. Load and clip outliers as follows:

```
starsCYG = sm.datasets.get_rdataset("starsCYG", "robustbase",
cache=True).data

clipped = starsCYG.apply(dl.stats.clip_outliers)
```

4. Filter outliers as follows:

```
filtered = starsCYG.copy()
filtered['log.Te'] = filter_outliers(filtered['log.Te'].values)
filtered['log.light'] = filter_outliers(filtered['log.light'].
values)
filtered.dropna()
```

5. Plot the result with the following code:

```
sp = dl.plotting.Subplotter(3, 1, context)
sp.label()
sns.regplot(x='log.Te', y='log.light', data=starsCYG, ax=sp.ax)
sp.label(advance=True)
sns.regplot(x='log.Te', y='log.light', data=clipped, ax=sp.ax)
sp.label(advance=True)
sns.regplot(x='log.Te', y='log.light', data=filtered, ax=sp.ax)
plt.tight_layout()
HTML(dl.report.HTMLBuilder().watermark())
```

Refer to the following screenshot for the end result (refer to the `outliers.ipynb` file in this book's code bundle):

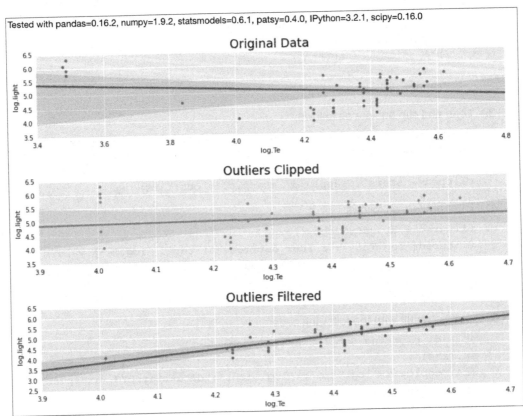

See also

► The NumPy `clip()` function documented at `https://docs.scipy.org/doc/numpy/reference/generated/numpy.clip.html#numpy.clip` (retrieved August 2015)

► You can read more about the Hertzsprung-Russell diagram at `https://en.wikipedia.org/wiki/Hertzsprung%E2%80%93Russell_diagram` (retrieved August 2015)

Winsorizing data

Winsorizing is another technique to deal with outliers and is named after Charles Winsor. In effect, Winsorization clips outliers to given percentiles in a symmetric fashion. For instance, we can clip to the 5th and 95th percentile. SciPy has a `winsorize()` function, which performs this procedure. The data for this recipe is the same as that for the *Clipping and filtering outliers* recipe.

How to do it...

Winsorize the data with the following procedure:

1. The imports are as follows:

```
rom scipy.stats.mstats import winsorize
import statsmodels.api as sm
import seaborn as sns
import matplotlib.pyplot as plt
import dautil as dl
from IPython.display import HTML
```

2. Load and winsorize the data for the effective temperature (limit is set to 15%):

```
starsCYG = sm.datasets.get_rdataset("starsCYG", "robustbase",
cache=True).data
limit = 0.15
winsorized_x = starsCYG.copy()
winsorized_x['log.Te'] = winsorize(starsCYG['log.Te'],
limits=limit)
```

3. Winsorize the light intensity as follows:

```
winsorized_y = starsCYG.copy()
winsorized_y['log.light'] = winsorize(starsCYG['log.light'],
limits=limit)
winsorized_xy = starsCYG.apply(winsorize, limits=[limit, limit])
```

4. Plot the Hertzsprung-Russell diagram with regression lines (not part of the usual astronomical diagram):

```
sp = dl.plotting.Subplotter(2, 2, context)
sp.label()
sns.regplot(x='log.Te', y='log.light', data=starsCYG, ax=sp.ax)

sp.label(advance=True)
sns.regplot(x='log.Te', y='log.light', data=winsorized_x, ax=sp.
ax)
```

```
sp.label(advance=True)
sns.regplot(x='log.Te', y='log.light', data=winsorized_y, ax=sp.
ax)

sp.label(advance=True)
sns.regplot(x='log.Te', y='log.light', data=winsorized_xy, ax=sp.
ax)
plt.tight_layout()
HTML(dl.report.HTMLBuilder().watermark())
```

Refer to the following screenshot for the end result (refer to the `winsorising_data.ipynb` file in this book's code bundle):

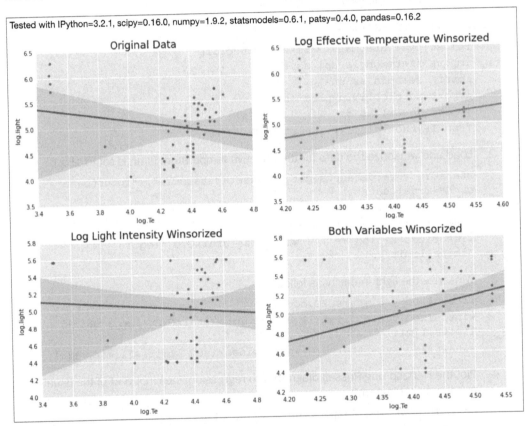

See also

▶ The relevant Wikipedia page at `https://en.wikipedia.org/wiki/Winsorising` (retrieved August 2015)

Measuring central tendency of noisy data

We can measure central tendency with the mean and median. These measures use all the data available. It is a generally accepted idea to get rid of outliers by discarding data on the higher and lower end of a data set. The **truncated mean** or **trimmed mean**, and derivatives of it such as the **interquartile mean (IQM)** and **trimean**, use this idea too. Take a look at the following equations:

$$(4.1) \quad TM = \frac{Q_1 + 2Q_2 + Q_3}{4}$$

$$(4.2) \quad x_{IQM} = \frac{2}{n} \sum_{i=\frac{n}{4}+1}^{\frac{3n}{4}} x_i$$

The truncated mean discards the data at given percentiles—for instance, from the lowest value to the 5th percentile and from the 95th percentile to the highest value. The **trimean** (4.1) is a weighted average of the median, first quartile, and third quartile. For the IQM (4.2), we discard the lowest and highest quartile of the data, so it is a special case of the truncated mean. We will calculate these measures with the SciPy `tmean()` and `trima()` functions.

How to do it...

We will take a look at the central tendency for varying levels of truncation with the following steps:

1. The imports are as follows:

```
import matplotlib.pyplot as plt
from scipy.stats import tmean
from scipy.stats.mstats import trima
import numpy as np
import dautil as dl
import seaborn as sns
from IPython.display import HTML

context = dl.nb.Context('central_tendency')
```

2. Define the following function to calculate the interquartile mean:

```
def iqm(a):
    return truncated_mean(a, 25)
```

3. Define the following function to plot distributions:

```
def plotdists(var, ax):
    displot_label = 'From {0} to {1} percentiles'
    cyc = dl.plotting.Cycler()

    for i in range(1, 9, 3):
        limits = dl.stats.outliers(var, method='percentiles',
                                   percentiles=(i, 100 - i))
        truncated = trima(var, limits=limits).compressed()
        sns.distplot(truncated, ax=ax, color=cyc.color(),
                     hist_kws={'histtype': 'stepfilled', 'alpha':
1/i,
                               'linewidth': cyc.lw()},
                     label=displot_label.format(i, 100 - i))
```

4. Define the following function to compute the truncated mean:

```
def truncated_mean(a, percentile):
    limits = dl.stats.outliers(a, method='percentiles',
                               percentiles=(percentile, 100 -
percentile))

    return tmean(a, limits=limits)
```

5. Load the data and calculate means as follows:

```
df = dl.data.Weather.load().resample('M').dropna()
x = range(9)
temp_means = [truncated_mean(df['TEMP'], i) for i in x]
ws_means = [truncated_mean(df['WIND_SPEED'], i) for i in x]
```

6. Plot the means and distributions with the following code:

```
sp = dl.plotting.Subplotter(2, 2, context)
cp = dl.plotting.CyclePlotter(sp.ax)
cp.plot(x, temp_means, label='Truncated mean')
cp.plot(x, dl.stats.trimean(df['TEMP']) * np.ones_like(x),
label='Trimean')
cp.plot(x, iqm(df['TEMP']) * np.ones_like(x), label='IQM')
sp.label(ylabel_params=dl.data.Weather.get_header('TEMP'))

cp = dl.plotting.CyclePlotter(sp.next_ax())
cp.plot(x, ws_means, label='Truncated mean')
cp.plot(x, dl.stats.trimean(df['WIND_SPEED']) * np.ones_like(x),
        label='Trimean')
cp.plot(x, iqm(df['WIND_SPEED']) * np.ones_like(x), label='IQM')
sp.label(ylabel_params=dl.data.Weather.get_header('WIND_SPEED'))

plotdists(df['TEMP'], sp.next_ax())
```

```
sp.label(xlabel_params=dl.data.Weather.get_header('TEMP'))

plotdists(df['WIND_SPEED'], sp.next_ax())
sp.label(xlabel_params=dl.data.Weather.get_header('WIND_SPEED'))
plt.tight_layout()
HTML(dl.report.HTMLBuilder().watermark())
```

Refer to the following screenshot for the end result (refer to the `central_tendency.ipynb` file in this book's code bundle):

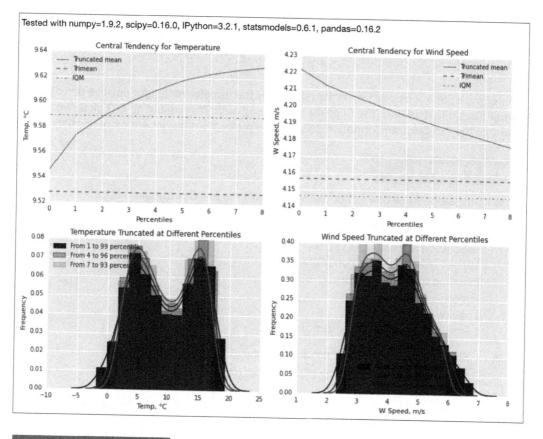

See also

▸ The SciPy documentation for `trima()` at https://docs.scipy.org/doc/
scipy/reference/generated/scipy.stats.mstats.trima.html (retrieved
August 2015)

▸ The SciPy documentation for `tmean()` at https://docs.scipy.org/doc/
scipy/reference/generated/scipy.stats.tmean.html#scipy.stats.
tmean (retrieved August 2015)

Normalizing with the Box-Cox transformation

Data that doesn't follow a known distribution, such as the normal distribution, is often difficult to manage. A popular strategy to get control of the data is to apply the Box-Cox transformation. It is given by the following equation:

$$(4.3) \quad y_i^{(\lambda)} = \begin{cases} \dfrac{y_i^{\lambda} - 1}{\lambda} & \text{if } \lambda \neq 0, \\ \ln(y_i) & \text{if } \lambda = 0, \end{cases}$$

The `scipy.stats.boxcox()` function can apply the transformation for positive data. We will use the same data as in the *Clipping and filtering outliers* recipe. With Q-Q plots, we will show that the Box-Cox transformation does indeed make the data appear more normal.

How to do it...

The following steps show how to normalize data with the Box-Cox transformation:

1. The imports are as follows:

```
import statsmodels.api as sm
import matplotlib.pyplot as plt
from scipy.stats import boxcox
import seaborn as sns
import dautil as dl
from IPython.display import HTML
```

2. Load the data and transform it as follows:

```
context = dl.nb.Context('normalizing_boxcox')

starsCYG = sm.datasets.get_rdataset("starsCYG", "robustbase",
cache=True).data

var = 'log.Te'

# Data must be positive
transformed, _ = boxcox(starsCYG[var])
```

3. Display the Q-Q plots and the distribution plots as follows:

```
sp = dl.plotting.Subplotter(2, 2, context)
sp.label()
sm.qqplot(starsCYG[var], fit=True, line='s', ax=sp.ax)


sp.label(advance=True)
sm.qqplot(transformed, fit=True, line='s', ax=sp.ax)


sp.label(advance=True)
sns.distplot(starsCYG[var], ax=sp.ax)


sp.label(advance=True)
sns.distplot(transformed, ax=sp.ax)
plt.tight_layout()
HTML(dl.report.HTMLBuilder().watermark())
```

Refer to the following screenshot for the end result (refer to the `normalizing_boxcox.ipynb` file in this book's code bundle):

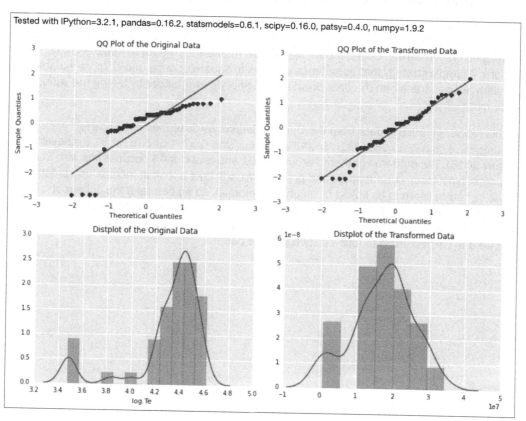

How it works

The Q-Q plots, in the previous screenshot, graph theoretical quantiles for the normal distribution against the quantiles of the actual data. To help evaluate conformance to the normal distribution, I displayed a line that should correspond with perfectly normal data. The more the data fits the line, the more normal it is. As you can see, the transformed data fits the line better and is, therefore, more normal. The distribution plots should help you to confirm this.

See also

▶ The relevant Wikipedia page at `https://en.wikipedia.org/wiki/Power_transform` (retrieved August 2015)

▶ G.E.P. Box and D.R. Cox, *An Analysis of Transformations*, Journal of the Royal Statistical Society B, 26, 211-252 (1964).

Transforming data with the power ladder

Linear relations are commonplace in science and data analysis. Obviously, linear models are easier to understand than non-linear models. So historically, tools for linear models were developed first. In certain cases, it pays to linearize (make linear) data to make analysis simpler. A simple strategy that sometimes works is to square or cube one or more variables. Similarly, we can transform the data down an imaginary power ladder by taking the square or cube root.

In this recipe, we will use data from the Duncan dataset as described in `https://vincentarelbundock.github.io/Rdatasets/doc/car/Duncan.html` (retrieved August 2015). The data was gathered around 1961 and is about 45 occupations with four columns—type, income, education, and prestige. We will take a look at income and prestige. These variables seem to be linked by a cubic polynomial, so we can take the cube root of income or the cube of prestige. To check the result, we will visualize the residuals of regression. The expectation is that the residuals are randomly distributed, which means that we don't expect them to follow a recognizable pattern.

How to do it...

In the following steps, I will demonstrate the basic data transformation:

1. The imports are as follows:

```
import matplotlib.pyplot as plt
import numpy as np
import dautil as dl
import seaborn as sns
import statsmodels.api as sm
from IPython.display import HTML
```

2. Load and transform the data as follows:

```
df = sm.datasets.get_rdataset("Duncan", "car", cache=True).data
transformed = df.copy()
transformed['income'] = np.power(transformed['income'], 1.0/3)
```

3. Plot the original data with a Seaborn regression plot (cubic polynomial) as follows:

```
sp = dl.plotting.Subplotter(2, 2, context)
sp.label()
sns.regplot(x='income', y='prestige', data=df, order=3, ax=sp.ax)
```

4. Plot the transformed data with the following lines:

```
sp.label(advance=True)
sns.regplot(x='income', y='prestige', data=transformed, ax=sp.ax)
```

5. Plot the residuals plot for the cubic polynomial:

```
sp.label(advance=True)
sns.residplot(x='income', y='prestige', data=df, order=3, ax=sp.
ax)
```

6. Plot the residuals plot for the transformed data as follows:

```
sp.label(advance=True)
sp.ax.set_xlim([1, 5])
sns.residplot(x='income', y='prestige', data=transformed, ax=sp.
ax)
plt.tight_layout()
HTML(dl.report.HTMLBuilder().watermark())
```

Refer to the following screenshot for the end result (refer to the `transforming_up.ipynb` file in this book's code bundle):

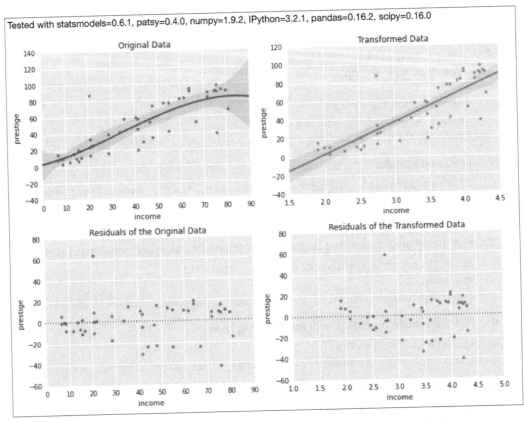

Transforming data with logarithms

When data varies by orders of magnitude, transforming the data with logarithms is an obvious strategy. In my experience, it is less common to do the opposite transformation using an exponential function. Usually when exploring, we visualize a log-log or semi-log scatter plot of paired variables.

To demonstrate this transformation, we will use the Worldbank data for infant mortality rate per 1000 livebirths and **Gross Domestic Product (GDP)** per capita for the available countries. If we apply the logarithm of base 10 to both variables, the slope of the line we get by fitting the data has a useful property. A one percent increase in one variable corresponds to a percentage change given by the slope of the other variable.

How to do it...

Transform the data using logarithms with the following procedure:

1. The imports are as follows:

```
import dautil as dl
import matplotlib.pyplot as plt
import numpy as np
from IPython.display import HTML
```

2. Download the data for 2010 with the following code:

```
wb = dl.data.Worldbank()
countries = wb.get_countries()[['name', 'iso2c']]
inf_mort = wb.get_name('inf_mort')
gdp_pcap = wb.get_name('gdp_pcap')
df = wb.download(country=countries['iso2c'],
                 indicator=[inf_mort, gdp_pcap],
                 start=2010, end=2010).dropna()
```

3. Apply the log transform with the following snippet:

```
loglog = df.applymap(np.log10)
x = loglog[gdp_pcap]
y = loglog[inf_mort]
```

4. Plot the data before and after the transformation:

```
sp = dl.plotting.Subplotter(2, 1, context)
xvar = 'GDP per capita'
sp.label(xlabel_params=xvar)
sp.ax.set_ylim([0, 200])
sp.ax.scatter(df[gdp_pcap], df[inf_mort])

sp.next_ax()
sp.ax.scatter(x, y, label='Transformed')
dl.plotting.plot_polyfit(sp.ax, x, y)
sp.label(xlabel_params=xvar)
plt.tight_layout()
HTML(dl.report.HTMLBuilder().watermark())
```

Refer to the following screenshot for the end result (refer to the `transforming_down. ipynb` file in this book's code bundle):

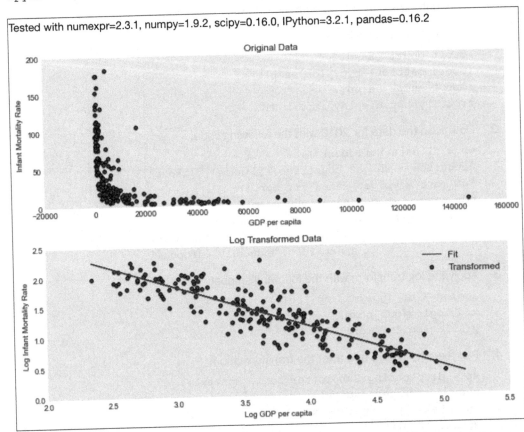

Rebinning data

Often, the data we have is not structured the way we want to use it. A structuring technique we can use is called (statistical) **data binning** or **bucketing**. This strategy replaces values within an interval (a bin) with one representative value. In the process, we may lose information; however, we gain better control over the data and efficiency.

In the weather dataset, we have wind direction in degrees and wind speed in m/s, which can be represented in a different way. In this recipe, I chose to present wind direction with cardinal directions (north, south, and so on). For the wind speed, I used the Beaufort scale (visit `https://en.wikipedia.org/wiki/Beaufort_scale`).

How to do it...

Follow these instructions to rebin the data:

1. The imports are as follows:

```
import dautil as dl
import seaborn as sns
import matplotlib.pyplot as plt
import pandas as pd
import numpy as np
from IPython.display import HTML
```

2. Load and rebin the data as follows (wind direction is in degree 0-360; we rebin to cardinal directions such as north, southwest, and so on):

```
df = dl.data.Weather.load()[['WIND_SPEED', 'WIND_DIR']].dropna()
categorized = df.copy()
categorized['WIND_DIR'] = dl.data.Weather.categorize_wind_dir(df)
categorized['WIND_SPEED'] = dl.data.Weather.beaufort_scale(df)
```

3. Show distributions and countplots with the following code:

```
sp = dl.plotting.Subplotter(2, 2, context)
sns.distplot(df['WIND_SPEED'], ax=sp.ax)
sp.label(xlabel_params=dl.data.Weather.get_header('WIND_SPEED'))

sns.distplot(df['WIND_DIR'], ax=sp.next_ax())
sp.label(xlabel_params=dl.data.Weather.get_header('WIND_DIR'))

sns.countplot(x='WIND_SPEED', data=categorized, ax=sp.next_ax())
sp.label()

sns.countplot(x='WIND_DIR', data=categorized, ax=sp.next_ax())
sp.label()
plt.tight_layout()
HTML(dl.report.HTMLBuilder().watermark())
```

Refer to the following screenshot for the end result (refer to the `rebinning_data.ipynb` file in this book's code bundle):

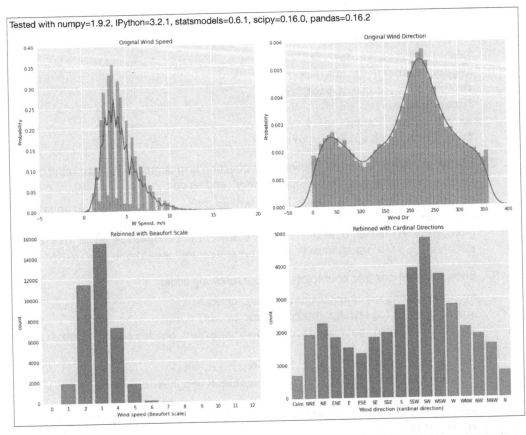

Applying logit() to transform proportions

We can transform proportions or ratios with the SciPy `logit()` function. The result should be a more Gaussian distribution. This function is defined by the following equation:

$$(4.4) \quad \text{logit}(p) = \log\left(\frac{p}{1-p}\right) = \log(p) - \log(1-p) = -\log\left(\frac{1}{p}-1\right)$$

As you can see in equation (4.4), the logit is the logarithm of the odds. What we want to achieve with this transformation is getting a more symmetric distribution—a skew close to zero. As the proportions approach zero and one, the logit asymptotically approaches minus infinity and infinity, so we have to be careful in those cases.

As an example of a proportion, we will take the monthly proportions of rainy days. We get these proportions by turning rain amounts into a binary variable and then averaging over each month.

How to do it...

Transform the ratios by following this guide:

1. The imports are as follows:

```
import dautil as dl
import seaborn as sns
import matplotlib.pyplot as plt
import pandas as pd
import math
import statsmodels.api as sm
from scipy.special import logit
from IPython.display import HTML
```

2. Load the data and transform it with the following code:

```
rain = dl.data.Weather.load()['RAIN'].dropna()
rain = rain > 0
rain = rain.resample('M').dropna()
transformed = rain.apply(logit)
transformed = dl.data.dropinf(transformed.values)
```

3. Plot the result of the transformation with distribution plots and Q-Q plots:

```
sp = dl.plotting.Subplotter(2, 2, context)
sns.distplot(rain, ax=sp.ax)
sp.label()

sp.label(advance=True)
sns.distplot(transformed, ax=sp.ax)

sp.label(advance=True)
sm.qqplot(rain, line='s', ax=sp.ax)

sp.label(advance=True)
sm.qqplot(transformed, line='s', ax=sp.ax)
plt.tight_layout()
HTML(dl.report.HTMLBuilder().watermark())
```

Refer to the following screenshot for the end result (refer to the `transforming_ratios.ipynb` file in this book's code bundle):

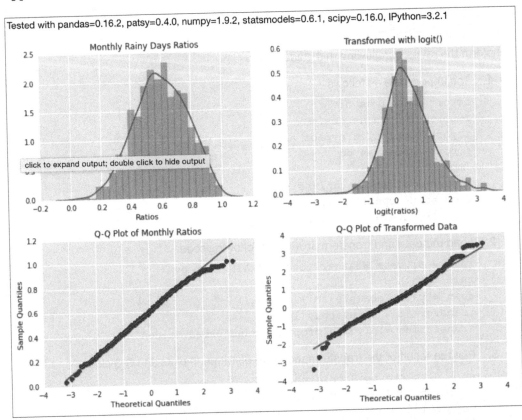

Tested with pandas=0.16.2, patsy=0.4.0, numpy=1.9.2, statsmodels=0.6.1, scipy=0.16.0, IPython=3.2.1

Fitting a robust linear model

Robust regression is designed to deal better with outliers in data than ordinary regression. This type of regression uses special robust estimators, which are also supported by statsmodels. Obviously, there is no best estimator, so the choice of estimator depends on the data and the model.

In this recipe, we will fit data about annual sunspot counts available in statsmodels. We will define a simple model where the current count depends linearly on the previous value. To demonstrate the effect of outliers, I added a pretty big value and we will compare the robust regression model and an ordinary least squares model.

How to do it...

The following steps describe how to apply the robust linear model:

1. The imports are as follows:

```
import statsmodels.api as sm
import matplotlib.pyplot as plt
import dautil as dl
from IPython.display import HTML
```

2. Define the following function to set the labels of the plots:

```
def set_labels(ax):
    ax.set_xlabel('Year')
    ax.set_ylabel('Sunactivity')
```

3. Define the following function to plot the model fits:

```
def plot_fit(df, ax, results):
    x = df['YEAR']
    cp = dl.plotting.CyclePlotter(ax)
    cp.plot(x[1:], df['SUNACTIVITY'][1:], label='Data')
    cp.plot(x[2:], results.predict()[1:], label='Fit')
    ax.legend(loc='best')
```

4. Load the data and add an outlier for demonstration purposes:

```
df = sm.datasets.sunspots.load_pandas().data
vals = df['SUNACTIVITY'].values

# Outlier added by malicious person, because noone
# laughs at his jokes.
vals[0] = 100
```

5. Fit the robust model as follows:

```
rlm_model = sm.RLM(vals[1:], sm.add_constant(vals[:-1]),
                   M=sm.robust.norms.TrimmedMean())

rlm_results = rlm_model.fit()
hb = dl.report.HTMLBuilder()
hb.h1('Fitting a robust linear model')
hb.h2('Robust Linear Model')
hb.add(rlm_results.summary().tables[1].as_html())
```

6. Fit an ordinary least squares model:

```
hb.h2('Ordinary Linear Model')
ols_model = sm.OLS(vals[1:], sm.add_constant(vals[:-1]))
ols_results = ols_model.fit()
hb.add(ols_results.summary().tables[1].as_html())
```

7. Plot the data and the model results with the following code:

```
fig, [ax, ax2] = plt.subplots(2, 1)

plot_fit(df, ax, rlm_results)
ax.set_title('Robust Linear Model')
set_labels(ax)

ax2.set_title('Ordinary Least Squares')
plot_fit(df, ax2, ols_results)
set_labels(ax2)
plt.tight_layout()
HTML(hb.html)
```

Refer to the following screenshot for the end result (refer to the `rlm_demo.ipynb` file in this book's code bundle):

Fitting A Robust Linear Model

Tested with scipy=0.16.0, patsy=0.4.0, pandas=0.16.2, statsmodels=0.6.1, IPython=3.2.1, numpy=1.9.2

Robust Linear Model

	coef	std err	z	P>|z|	[95.0% Conf. Int.]
const	4.9464	1.399	3.536	0.000	2.205 7.688
x1	0.7815	0.022	36.000	0.000	0.739 0.824

Ordinary Linear Model

	coef	std err	t	P>|t|	[95.0% Conf. Int.]
const	8.9405	2.129	4.199	0.000	4.751 13.130
x1	0.8157	0.033	24.684	0.000	0.751 0.881

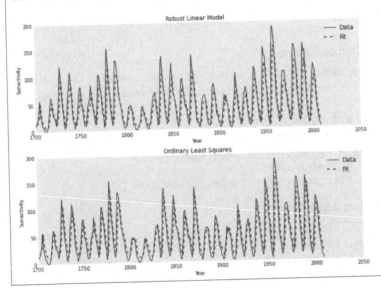

▶ The relevant statsmodels documentation at `http://statsmodels.` `sourceforge.net/0.6.0/generated/statsmodels.robust.robust_` `linear_model.RLM.html` (retrieved August 2015)

Taking variance into account with weighted least squares

The statsmodels library allows us to define arbitrary weights per data point for regression. Outliers are sometimes easy to spot with simple rules of thumbs. One of these rules of thumb is based on the interquartile range, which is the difference between the first and third quartile of data. With the interquartile ranges, we can define weights for the **weighted least squares** regression.

We will use the data and model from *Fitting a robust linear mode*, but with arbitrary weights. The points we suspect are outliers will get a lower weight, which is the inverse of the interquartile range values just mentioned.

How to do it...

Fit the data with weighted least squares using the following method:

1. The imports are as follows:

```
import dautil as dl
import matplotlib.pyplot as plt
import statsmodels.api as sm
import numpy as np
from IPython.display import HTML
```

2. Load the data and add an outlier:

```
temp = dl.data.Weather.load()['TEMP'].dropna()
temp = dl.ts.groupby_yday(temp).mean()

# Outlier added by malicious person, because noone
# laughs at his jokes.
temp.values[0] = 100
```

3. Fit using an ordinary least squares model:

```
ntemp = len(temp)
x = np.arange(1, ntemp + 1)
factor = 2 * np.pi/365.25
```

```
cos_x = sm.add_constant(np.cos(-factor * x - factor * 337))
ols_model = sm.OLS(temp, cos_x)
ols_results = ols_model.fit()
hb = dl.report.HTMLBuilder()
hb.h1('Taking variance into account with weighted least squares')
hb.h2('Ordinary least squares')
hb.add(ols_results.summary().tables[1].as_html())
ols_preds = ols_results.predict()
```

4. Compute weights using interquartile ranges and fit the weighted least squares model:

```
box = dl.stats.Box(temp)
iqrs = box.iqr_from_box()
# Adding 1 to avoid div by 0
weights = 1./(iqrs + 1)
wls_model = sm.WLS(temp, cos_x, weights=weights)
wls_results = wls_model.fit()

hb.h2('Weighted least squares')
hb.add(wls_results.summary().tables[1].as_html())
```

5. Plot the model results and weights:

```
sp = dl.plotting.Subplotter(2, 2, context)

sp.ax.plot(x[1:], temp[1:], 'o', label='Data')
sp.ax.plot(x[1:], ols_preds[1:], label='Fit')
sp.label(ylabel_params=dl.data.Weather.get_header('TEMP'))

sp.label(advance=True)
sp.ax.plot(x, iqrs, 'o')

sp.next_ax().plot(x[1:], temp[1:], 'o', label='Data')
sp.ax.plot(x[1:], wls_results.predict()[1:], label='Fit')
sp.label(ylabel_params=dl.data.Weather.get_header('TEMP'))

sp.label(advance=True)
sp.ax.plot(x, weights, 'o')
plt.tight_layout()
HTML(hb.html)
```

Refer to the following screenshot for the end result (refer to the `weighted_ls.ipynb` file in this book's code bundle):

Taking Variance Into Account With Weighted Least Squares

Tested with statsmodels=0.6.1, patsy=0.4.0, numpy=1.9.2, IPython=3.2.1, scipy=0.16.0, pandas=0.16.2

Ordinary least squares

	coef	std err	t	P>|t|	[95.0% Conf. Int.]
const	9.7902	0.269	36.433	0.000	9.262 10.319
x1	-7.0908	0.380	-18.670	0.000	-7.838 -6.344

Weighted least squares

	coef	std err	t	P>|t|	[95.0% Conf. Int.]
const	9.5604	0.105	90.637	0.000	9.353 9.768
x1	-7.5123	0.147	-51.103	0.000	-7.801 -7.223

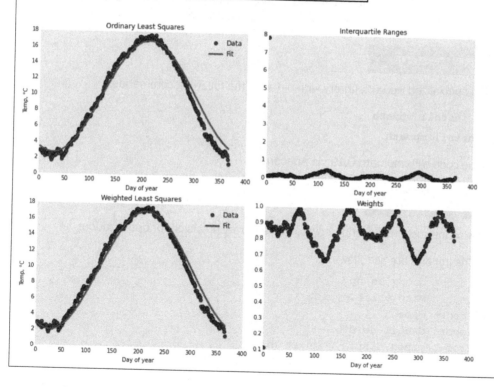

See also

▶ The relevant statsmodels documentation at `http://statsmodels.`
`sourceforge.net/0.5.0/examples/generated/example_wls.html`
(retrieved August 2015).

Using arbitrary precision for optimization

The intended readers of this book should be aware of floating point number issues. I will remind you that we are not able to represent floating point numbers exactly. Even integer representation is limited. For certain applications, for instance financial calculations or work involving known analytic expressions, we need a higher precision than available with numerical software such as NumPy. The Python standard library provides the `Decimal` class, which we can use to achieve arbitrary precision. However, the specialized `mpmath` library is a better fit for more advanced use.

Temperature follows a seasonal pattern, so a model involving the cosine seems natural. We will apply such a model. The nice thing about using arbitrary precision is that you can easily do analysis, differentiate, find roots, and approximate polynomials.

Getting ready

Install the specialized `mpmath` library with either of the following commands:

```
$ conda install mpmath
$ pip install mpmath
```

I tested the code with mpmath 0.19 via Anaconda.

How to do it...

The following instructions describe how to use arbitrary precision for optimization:

1. The imports are as follows:

```
import numpy as np
import matplotlib.pyplot as plt
import mpmath
import dautil as dl
from IPython.display import HTML
```

2. Define the following functions for the model and the first derivative:

```
def model(t):
    mu, C, w, phi = (9.6848106, -7.59870042, -0.01766333,
    -5.83349705)

    return mu + C * mpmath.cos(w * t + phi)

def diff_model(t):
    return mpmath.diff(model, t)
```

3. Load the data and find the root of the first derivative:

```
vals = dl.data.Weather.load()['TEMP'].dropna()
vals = dl.ts.groupby_yday(vals).mean()
diff_root = mpmath.findroot(diff_model, (1, 366),
solver='anderson')
```

4. Get a polynomial approximation for the model as follows:

```
days = range(1, 367)
poly = mpmath.chebyfit(model, (1, 366), 3)
poly = np.array([float(c) for c in poly])
```

5. Plot the data, model results, and approximation with the following code:

```
sp = dl.plotting.Subplotter(2, 1, context)
cp = dl.plotting.CyclePlotter(sp.ax)
cp.plot(days, [model(i) for i in days], label='Model')
cp.plot(days, vals, label='Data')
sp.ax.annotate(s='Root of derivative', xy=(diff_root, vals.max() -
1),
                xytext=(diff_root, vals.max() - 8),
                arrowprops=dict(arrowstyle='->'))
yvar = dl.data.Weather.get_header('TEMP')
sp.label(ylabel_params=yvar)

cp = dl.plotting.CyclePlotter(sp.next_ax())
cp.plot(days, vals, label='Data')
cp.plot(days, np.polyval(poly, days), label='Approximation')
sp.label(ylabel_params=yvar)
plt.tight_layout()
HTML(dl.report.HTMLBuilder().watermark())
```

Refer to the following screenshot for the end result (refer to the `mpmath_fit.ipynb` file in this book's code bundle):

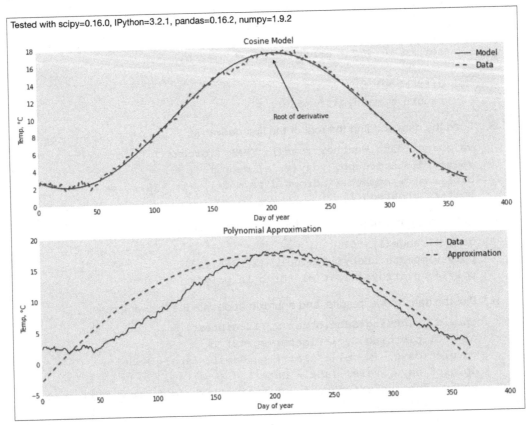

▸ The documentation for the `chebyfit()` function at `https://mpmath.readthedocs.org/en/latest/calculus/approximation.html#mpmath.chebyfit` (retrieved August 2015)

▸ The documentation for the `findroot()` function at `https://mpmath.readthedocs.org/en/latest/calculus/optimization.html` (retrieved August 2015)

Using arbitrary precision for linear algebra

A lot of models can be reduced to systems of linear equations, which are the domain of linear algebra. The mpmath library mentioned in the *Using arbitrary precision for optimization* recipe can do arbitrary precision linear algebra too.

Theoretically, we can approximate any differentiable function as a polynomial series. To find the coefficients of the polynomial, we can define a system of linear equations, basically taking powers of a data vector (vector as mathematical term) and using a vector of ones to represent the constant in the polynomial. We will solve such a system with the mpmath `lu_solve()` function. As example data, we will use wind speed data grouped by the day of year.

Getting ready

For the relevant instructions, refer to the *Using arbitrary precision for optimization* recipe.

How to do it...

Follow these steps to use arbitrary precision for linear algebra:

1. The imports are as follows:

```
import mpmath
import dautil as dl
import numpy as np
import matplotlib.pyplot as plt
from IPython.display import HTML
```

2. Define the following function to compute the arithmetic mean with mpmath:

```
def mpmean(arr):
    mpfs = [mpmath.mpf(a) for a in arr]

    return sum(mpfs)/len(arr)
```

3. Load the data and solve the system with `lu_solve()`:

```
vals = dl.data.Weather.load()['WIND_SPEED'].dropna()
vals = dl.ts.groupby_yday(vals).apply(mpmean)

days = np.arange(1, 367, dtype=int)
A = [[], [], []]
A[0] = np.ones_like(days, dtype=int).tolist()
A[1] = days.tolist()
```

```
A[2] = (days ** 2).tolist()
A = mpmath.matrix(A).transpose()

params = mpmath.lu_solve(A, vals)

result = dl.report.HTMLBuilder()
result.h1('Arbitrary Precision Linear Algebra')
result.h2('Polynomial fit')
dfb = dl.report.DFBuilder(['Coefficient 0', 'Coefficient 1',
'Coefficient 2'])
dfb.row(params)
result.add_df(dfb.build())
```

4. Define the following function to evaluate the polynomial we got:

```
def poly(x):
    return mpmath.polyval(params[::-1], x)
```

5. Use the `fourier()` function to get a trigonometric approximation:

```
cs = mpmath.fourier(poly, days.tolist(), 1)
result.h2('Cosine and sine terms')
dfb = dl.report.DFBuilder(['Coefficient 1', 'Coefficient 2'])
dfb.row(cs[0])
dfb.row(cs[1])
result.add_df(dfb.build(index=['Cosine', 'Sine']), index=True)
```

6. Plot the data, model results, and approximation as follows:

```
sp = dl.plotting.Subplotter(2, 1, context)

cp = dl.plotting.CyclePlotter(sp.ax)
cp.plot(days, vals, label='Data')
cp.plot(days, poly(days), label='Fit')
yvar = dl.data.Weather.get_header('WIND_SPEED')
sp.label(ylabel_params=yvar)

cp = dl.plotting.CyclePlotter(sp.next_ax())
cp.plot(days, vals, label='Data')
cp.plot(days, [mpmath.fourierval(cs, days, d) for d in days],
label='Approximation')
sp.label(ylabel_params=yvar)
plt.tight_layout()
HTML(result.html)
```

Refer to the following screenshot for the end result (refer to the `mpmath_linalg.ipynb` file in this book's code bundle):

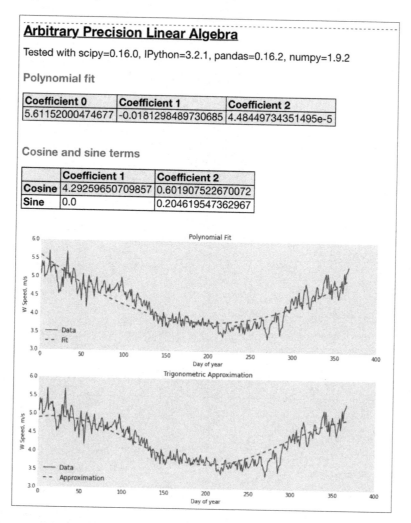

See also

- The `fourier()` function documented at https://mpmath.readthedocs.org/en/latest/calculus/approximation.html?highlight=fourier#mpmath.fourier (retrieved August 2015)

- The `lu_solve()` function documented at https://mpmath.readthedocs.org/en/latest/matrices.html?highlight=lu_solve (retrieved August 2015)

5
Web Mining, Databases, and Big Data

On the menu for this chapter are the following recipes:

- Simulating web browsing
- Scraping the Web
- Dealing with non-ASCII text and HTML entities
- Implementing association tables
- Setting up database migration scripts
- Adding a table column to an existing table
- Adding indices after table creation
- Setting up a test web server
- Implementing a star schema with fact and dimension tables
- Using HDFS
- Setting up Spark
- Clustering data with Spark

Introduction

This chapter is light on math, but it is more focused on technical topics. Technology has a lot to offer for data analysts. Databases have been around for a while, but the relational databases that most people are familiar with can be traced back to the 1970s. Edgar Codd came up with a number of ideas that later led to the creation of the relational model and SQL. Relational databases have been a dominant technology since then. In the 1980s, object-oriented programming languages caused a paradigm shift and an unfortunate mismatch with relational databases.

Object-oriented programming languages support concepts such as inheritance, which relational databases and SQL do not support (of course with some exceptions). The Python ecosystem has several **object-relational mapping** (**ORM**) frameworks that try to solve this mismatch issue. It is not possible and is unnecessary to cover them all, so I chose SQLAlchemy for the recipes here. We will also have a look at database schema migration as a common hot topic, especially for production systems.

Big data is one of the buzzwords that you may have heard of. Hadoop and Spark may probably also sound familiar. We will look at these frameworks in this chapter. If you use my Docker image, you will unfortunately not find Selenium, Hadoop, and Spark in there because I decided not to include them to save space.

Another important technological development is the World Wide Web, also known as the Internet. The Internet is the ultimate data source; however, getting this data in an easy-to-analyze form is sometimes quite a challenge. As a last resource, we may have to crawl and scrape web pages. Success is not guaranteed because the website owner can change the content without warning us. It is up to you to keep the code of the web scraping recipes up to date.

Simulating web browsing

Corporate websites are usually made by teams or departments using specialized tools and templates. A lot of the content is generated on the fly and consists of a large part of JavaScript and CSS. This means that even if we download the content, we still have to, at least, evaluate the JavaScript code. One way that we can do this from a Python program is using the **Selenium** API. Selenium's main purpose is actually testing websites, but nothing stops us from using it to scrape websites.

Instead of scraping a website, we will scrape an IPython Notebook—the `test_widget.ipynb` file in this book's code bundle. To simulate browsing this web page, we provided a unit test class in `test_simulating_browsing.py`. In case you wondered, this is not the recommended way to test IPython Notebooks.

For historic reasons, I prefer using XPath to find HTML elements. XPath is a query language, which also works with HTML. This is not the only method, you can also use CSS selectors, tag names, or IDs. To find the right XPath expression, you can either install a relevant plugin for your favorite browser, or for instance in Google Chrome, you can inspect an element's XPath.

Getting ready

Install Selenium with the following command:

```
$ pip install selenium
```

I tested the code with Selenium 2.47.1.

How to do it...

The following steps show you how to simulate web browsing using an IPython widget that I made. The code for this recipe is in the `test_simulating_browsing.py` file in this book's code bundle:

1. The first step is to run the following:

   ```
   $ ipython notebook
   ```

2. The imports are as follows:

   ```
   from selenium import webdriver
   import time
   import unittest
   import dautil as dl

   NAP_SECS = 10
   ```

3. Define the following function, which creates a Firefox browser instance:

   ```
   class SeleniumTest(unittest.TestCase):
       def setUp(self):
           self.logger = dl.log_api.conf_logger(__name__)
           self.browser = webdriver.Firefox()
   ```

4. Define the following function to clean up when the test is done:

   ```
   def tearDown(self):
       self.browser.quit()
   ```

5. The following function clicks on the widget tabs (we have to wait for the user interface to respond):

```
def wait_and_click(self, toggle, text):
        xpath = "//a[@data-toggle='{0}' and contains(text(),
'{1}')]"
        xpath = xpath.format(toggle, text)
        elem = dl.web.wait_browser(self.browser, xpath)
        elem.click()
```

6. Define the following function, which performs the test that consists of evaluating the notebook cells and clicking on a couple of tabs in the IPython widget (we use port 8888):

```
def test_widget(self):
        self.browser.implicitly_wait(NAP_SECS)
        self.browser.get('http://localhost:8888/notebooks/test_
widget.ipynb')

        try:
            # Cell menu
            xpath = '//*[@id="menus"]/div/div/ul/li[5]/a'
            link = dl.web.wait_browser(self.browser, xpath)
            link.click()
            time.sleep(1)

            # Run all
            xpath = '//*[@id="run_all_cells"]/a'
            link = dl.web.wait_browser(self.browser, xpath)
            link.click()
            time.sleep(1)

            self.wait_and_click('tab', 'Figure')
            self.wait_and_click('collapse', 'figure.figsize')
        except Exception:
            self.logger.warning('Error while waiting to click',
exc_info=True)
            self.browser.quit()

        time.sleep(NAP_SECS)
        self.browser.save_screenshot('widgets_screenshot.png')

if __name__ == "__main__":
    unittest.main()
```

The following screenshot is created by the code:

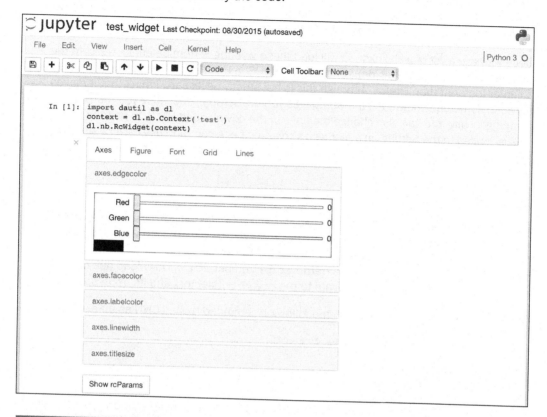

▸ The Selenium documentation is at `https://selenium-python.readthedocs.org/en/latest/installation.html` (retrieved September 2015)

▸ The Wikipedia page about XPath is at `https://en.wikipedia.org/wiki/XPath` (retrieved September 2015)

Scraping the Web

We know that search engines send out autonomous programs called bots to find information on the Internet. Usually, this leads to the creation of giant indices similar to a phonebook or a dictionary. The current situation (September 2015) for Python 3 users is not ideal when it comes to scraping the Web. Most frameworks only support Python 2. However, Guido van Rossum, **Benevolent Dictator for Life** (**BDFL**) has just contributed a crawler on GitHub that uses the AsyncIO API. All hail the BDFL!

I forked the repository and made small changes in order to save crawled URLs. I also made the crawler exit early. These changes are not very elegant, but this was all I could do in a limited time frame. Anyway, I can't hope to do better than the BDFL himself.

Once we have a list of web links, we will load these webpages from Selenium (refer to the *Simulating web browsing* recipe). I chose PhantomJS, a headless browser, which should have a lighter footprint than Firefox. Although this is not strictly necessary, I think that it makes sense to sometimes download the web pages you are scraping, because you then can test scraping locally. You can also change the links in the downloaded HTML to point to local files. This is related to the *Setting up a test web server* recipe. A common use case of scraping is to create a text corpus for linguistic analysis. This is our goal in this recipe.

Getting ready

Install Selenium as described in the *Simulating web browsing* recipe. I use PhantomJS in this recipe, but this is not a hard requirement. You can use any other browser supported by Selenium. My modifications are under the 0.0.1 tag at `https://github.com/ivanidris/500lines/releases` (retrieved September 2015). Download one of the source archives and unpack it. Navigate to the `crawler` directory and its `code` subdirectory.

Start (optional step) the crawler with the following command (I used CNN as an example):

```
$ python crawl.py edition.cnn.com
```

How to do it...

You can use the CSV file with links in this book's code bundle or make your own as I explained in the previous section. The following procedure describes how to create a text corpus of news articles (refer to the `download_html.py` file in this book's code bundle):

1. The imports are as follows:

```
import dautil as dl
import csv
import os
from selenium import webdriver
from selenium.webdriver.support.ui import WebDriverWait
from selenium.webdriver.support import expected_conditions as EC
from selenium.webdriver.common.by import By
import urllib.parse as urlparse
import urllib.request as urlrequest
```

2. Define the following global constants:

```
LOGGER = dl.log_api.conf_logger('download_html')
DRIVER = webdriver.PhantomJS()
NAP_SECONDS = 10
```

3. Define the following function to extract text from a HTML page and save it:

```
def write_text(fname):
    elems = []

    try:
        DRIVER.get(dl.web.path2url(fname))

        elems = WebDriverWait(DRIVER, NAP_SECONDS).until(
            EC.presence_of_all_elements_located((By.XPATH, '//p'))
        )

        LOGGER.info('Elems', elems)

        with open(fname.replace('.html', '_phantomjs.html'), 'w')
as pjs_file:
            LOGGER.warning('Writing to %s', pjs_file.name)
            pjs_file.write(DRIVER.page_source)

    except Exception:
        LOGGER.error("Error processing HTML", exc_info=True)


    new_name = fname.replace('html', 'txt')

    if not os.path.exists(new_name):
        with open(new_name, 'w') as txt_file:
            LOGGER.warning('Writing to %s', txt_file.name)

            lines = [e.text for e in elems]
            LOGGER.info('lines', lines)
            txt_file.write(' \n'.join(lines))
```

4. Define the following `main()` function, which reads the CSV file with links and calls the functions in the previous steps:

```
def main():
    filedir = os.path.join(dl.data.get_data_dir(), 'edition.cnn.
com')

    with open('saved_urls.csv') as csvfile:
        reader = csv.reader(csvfile)

        for line in reader:
            timestamp, count, basename, url = line
```

```
                    fname = '_'.join([count, basename])
                    fname = os.path.join(filedir, fname)

                    if not os.path.exists(fname):
                        dl.data.download(url, fname)

                    write_text(fname)

        if __name__ == '__main__':
            DRIVER.implicitly_wait(NAP_SECONDS)
            main()
            DRIVER.quit()
```

Dealing with non-ASCII text and HTML entities

HTML is not as structured as data from a database query or a pandas `DataFrame`. You may be tempted to manipulate HTML with regular expressions or string functions. However, this approach works only in a limited number of cases. You are better off using specialized Python libraries to process HTML. In this recipe, we will use the `clean_html()` function of the lxml library. This function strips all JavaScript and CSS from a HTML page.

American Standard Code for Information Interchange (ASCII) was the dominant encoding standard on the Internet until the end of 2007 with UTF-8 (8-bit Unicode) taking over first place. ASCII is limited to the English alphabet and has no support for alphabets of different languages. Unicode has a much broader support for alphabets. However, we sometimes need to limit ourselves to ASCII, so this recipe gives you an example of how to ignore non-ASCII characters.

Getting ready

Install lxml with pip or conda, as follows:

```
$ pip install lxml
$ conda install lxml
```

I tested the code with lxml 3.4.2 from Anaconda.

How to do it...

The code is in the `processing_html.py` file in this book's code bundle and is broken up in the following steps:

1. The imports are as follows:

```
from lxml.html.clean import clean_html
from difflib import Differ
import unicodedata
import dautil as dl


PRINT = dl.log_api.Printer()
```

2. Define the following function to diff two files:

```
def diff_files(text, cleaned):
    d = Differ()
    diff = list(d.compare(text.splitlines(keepends=True),
                          cleaned.splitlines(keepends=True)))
    PRINT.print(diff)
```

3. The following code block opens a HTML file, cleans it, and compares the cleaned file with the original:

```
with open('460_cc_phantomjs.html') as html_file:
    text = html_file.read()
    cleaned = clean_html(text)
    diff_files(text, cleaned)
    PRINT.print(dl.web.find_hrefs(cleaned))
```

4. The following snippet demonstrates handling of non-ASCII text:

```
bulgarian = 'Питон is Bulgarian for Python'
PRINT.print('Bulgarian', bulgarian)
PRINT.print('Bulgarian ignored', unicodedata.normalize('NFKD',
bulgarian).encode('ascii', 'ignore'))
```

Refer to the following screenshot for the end result (I omitted some of the output for brevity):

```
'- </body></html>',
'+ \n',
'+ \n',
'+ </body></div>']

['',
 'http://hraunfoss.fcc.gov/edocs_public/attachmatch/FCC-12-9A1.doc',
 'mailto:IPClosedCaptioning@turner.com']

'Bulgarian'
'Питон is Bulgarian for Python'

'Bulgarian ignored'
b' is Bulgarian for Python'
```

See also

▸ The lxml documentation is at `http://lxml.de/index.html` (retrieved September 2015)

Implementing association tables

The association table acts as a bridge between database tables, which have a many-to-many relationship. The table contains foreign keys that are linked to the primary keys of the tables it connects.

In this recipe, we will associate web pages with links within the page. A page has many links, and links can be in many pages. We will concern ourselves only with links to other websites, but this is not a requirement. If you are trying to reproduce a website on your local machine for testing or analysis, you will want to store image and JavaScript links as well. Have a look at the following relational schema diagram:

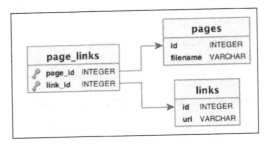

Getting ready

I installed SQLAlchemy 0.9.9 with Anaconda, as follows:

```
$ conda install sqlalchemy
```

If you prefer, you can also install SQLAlchemy with the following command:

```
$ pip install sqlalchemy
```

How to do it...

The following code from the `impl_association.py` file in this book's code bundle implements the association table pattern:

1. The imports are as follows:

```
from sqlalchemy import create_engine
from sqlalchemy import Column
```

```
from sqlalchemy import ForeignKey
from sqlalchemy import Integer
from sqlalchemy import String
from sqlalchemy import Table
from sqlalchemy.orm import backref
from sqlalchemy.orm import relationship
from sqlalchemy.ext.declarative import declarative_base
from sqlalchemy.orm import sessionmaker
from sqlalchemy.exc import IntegrityError
import dautil as dl
import os

Base = declarative_base()
```

2. Define the following class to represent a web page:

```
class Page(Base):
    __tablename__ = 'pages'
    id = Column(Integer, primary_key=True)
    filename = Column(String, nullable=False, unique=True)
    links = relationship('Link', secondary='page_links')

    def __repr__(self):
        return "Id=%d filename=%s" % (self.id, self.filename)
```

3. Define the following class to represent a web link:

```
class Link(Base):
    __tablename__ = 'links'
    id = Column(Integer, primary_key=True)
    url = Column(String, nullable=False, unique=True)

    def __repr__(self):
        return "Id=%d url=%s" % (self.id, self.url)
```

4. Define the following class to represent the association between pages and links:

```
class PageLink(Base):
    __tablename__ = 'page_links'
    page_id = Column(Integer, ForeignKey('pages.id'), primary_
key=True)
    link_id = Column(Integer, ForeignKey('links.id'), primary_
key=True)
    page = relationship('Page', backref=backref('link_assoc'))
    link = relationship('Link', backref=backref('page_assoc'))

    def __repr__(self):
        return "page_id=%s link_id=%s" % (self.page_id, self.link_
id)
```

5. Define the following function to go through HTML files and update the related tables:

```
def process_file(fname, session):
    with open(fname) as html_file:
        text = html_file.read()

        if dl.db.count_where(session, Page.filename, fname):
            # Cowardly refusing to continue
            return

        page = Page(filename=fname)
        hrefs = dl.web.find_hrefs(text)

        for href in set(hrefs):
            # Only saving http links
            if href.startswith('http'):
                if dl.db.count_where(session, Link.url, href):
                    continue

                link = Link(url=href)
                session.add(PageLink(page=page, link=link))

        session.commit()
```

6. Define the following function to populate the database:

```
def populate():
    dir = dl.data.get_data_dir()
    path = os.path.join(dir, 'crawled_pages.db')
    engine = create_engine('sqlite:///' + path)
    DBSession = sessionmaker(bind=engine)
    Base.metadata.create_all(engine)
    session = DBSession()

    files = ['460_cc_phantomjs.html', '468_live_phantomjs.html']

    for file in files:
        process_file(file, session)

    return session
```

7. The following code snippet uses the functions and classes that we defined:

```
if __name__ == "__main__":
    session = populate()
    printer = dl.log_api.Printer(nelems=3)
```

```
pages = session.query(Page).all()
printer.print('Pages', pages)

links = session.query(Link).all()
printer.print('Links', links)

page_links = session.query(PageLink).all()
printer.print('PageLinks', page_links)
```

Refer to the following screenshot for the end result:

```
'Pages'
[Id=1 filename=460_cc_phantomjs.html, Id=2 filename=468_live_pha
ntomjs.html]

'Links'
[Id=1 url=http://hraunfoss.fcc.gov/edocs_public/attachmatch/FCC-
12-9A1.doc,
 '...',
 Id=4 url=http://www.cnn.com/feedback/forms/form1.html?43,
 '...',
 Id=7 url=http://www.macromedia.com/support/documentation/en/fla
shplayer/help/settings_manager03.html]

'PageLinks'
[page_id=1 link_id=1, '...', page_id=2 link_id=4, '...', page_id
=2 link_id=7]
```

Setting up database migration scripts

One of the first things that you learn in programming classes is that nobody can get a complex program right the very first time. Software evolves over time, and we hope for the best. Automation in automated testing helps ensure that our programs improve over time. However, when it comes to evolving database schemas, automation doesn't seem to be so obvious. Especially in large enterprises, database schemas are the domain of database administrators and specialists. Of course, there are security and operational issues related to changing schemas, even more so in production databases. In any case, you can always implement database migration in your local test environment and document proposed changes for the production team.

We will use Alembic to demonstrate how you can go about setting up migration scripts. In my opinion, Alembic is the right tool for the job, although it is in beta as of September 2015.

Getting ready

Install Alembic with the following command:

```
$ pip install alembic
```

Alembic depends on SQLAlchemy, and it will automatically install SQLAlchemy if needed. You should now have the `alembic` command in your path. I used Alembic 0.8.2 for this chapter.

How to do it...

The following steps describe how to set up Alembic migration steps. When we run the Alembic initialization script in a directory, it creates an `alembic` directory and a configuration file named `alembic.ini`:

1. Navigate to the appropriate directory and initialize the migration project, as follows:

    ```
    $ alembic init alembic
    ```

2. Edit the `alembic.ini` file as required. For instance, change the `sqlalchemy.url` property to point to the correct database.

See also

▸   The relevant Alembic documentation is at `https://alembic.readthedocs.org/en/latest/tutorial.html` (retrieved September 2015)

Adding a table column to an existing table

If we use an object-relational mapper (ORM), such as SQLAlchemy, we map classes to tables and class attributes to table columns. Often, due to new business requirements, we need to add a table column and corresponding class attribute. We will probably need to populate the column immediately after adding it.

If we deal with a production database, then probably you do not have direct access. Luckily, we can generate SQL with Alembic, which a database administrator can review.

Getting ready

Refer to the *Setting up database migration scripts* recipe.

How to do it...

Alembic has its own versioning system, which requires extra tables. It also creates a versions directory under the `alembic` directory with generated Python code files. We need to specify the types of change necessary for migration in these files:

1. Create a new revision, as follows:

   ```
   $ alembic revision -m "Add a column"
   ```

2. Open the generated Python file (for instance, `27218d73000_add_a_column.py`). Replace the two functions in there with the following code, which adds the `link_type` string column:

   ```python
   def upgrade():
       # MODIFIED Ivan Idris
       op.add_column('links', sa.Column('link_type', sa.String(20)))


   def downgrade():
       # MODIFIED Ivan Idris
       op.drop_column('links', 'link_type')
   ```

3. Generate SQL, as follows:

   ```
   $ alembic upgrade head --sql
   ```

Refer to the following screenshot for the end result:

```
INFO  [alembic.runtime.migration] Context impl SQLiteImpl.
INFO  [alembic.runtime.migration] Generating static SQL
INFO  [alembic.runtime.migration] Will assume non-transactional
DDL.
CREATE TABLE alembic_version (
    version_num VARCHAR(32) NOT NULL
);

INFO  [alembic.runtime.migration] Running upgrade  -> 27218d7300
0, Add a column
-- Running upgrade  -> 27218d73000

ALTER TABLE links ADD COLUMN link_type VARCHAR(20);

INSERT INTO alembic_version (version_num) VALUES ('27218d73000')
;
```

Adding indices after table creation

Indices are a general concept in computing. This book also has an index for faster lookup, which matches concepts to page numbers. An index takes up space; in the case of this book, a couple of pages. Database indices have the added disadvantage that they make inserts and updates slower because of the extra overhead of updating the index. Usually, primary and foreign keys automatically get an index, but this depends on the database implementation.

Adding indices should not be taken lightly, and this is best done after consulting database administrators. Alembic has features for index addition similar to the features that we saw in the *Adding a table column to an existing table* recipe.

Getting ready

Refer to the *Setting up database migration scripts* recipe.

How to do it...

This recipe has some overlap with the *Adding a table column to an existing table* recipe, so I will not repeat all the details:

1. Create a new revision, as follows:

   ```
   $ alembic revision -m "Add indices"
   ```

2. Open the generated Python file (for instance, `21579ecccd8_add_indices.py`) and modify the code to have the following functions, which take care of adding indices:

   ```python
   def upgrade():
       # MODIFIED Ivan Idris
       op.create_index('idx_links_url', 'links', ['url'])
       op.create_index('idx_pages_filename', 'pages', ['filename'])


   def downgrade():
       # MODIFIED Ivan Idris
       op.drop_index('idx_links_url')
       op.drop_index('idx_pages_filename')
   ```

3. Generate SQL, as follows:

   ```
   $ alembic upgrade head --sql
   ```

Refer to the following screenshot for the end result:

```
INFO  [alembic.runtime.migration] Context impl SQLiteImpl.
INFO  [alembic.runtime.migration] Generating static SQL
INFO  [alembic.runtime.migration] Will assume non-transactional
DDL.
CREATE TABLE alembic_version (
    version_num VARCHAR(32) NOT NULL
);

INFO  [alembic.runtime.migration] Running upgrade  -> 21579ecccd
8, Add indices
-- Running upgrade  -> 21579ecccd8

CREATE INDEX idx_links_url ON links (url);

CREATE INDEX idx_pages_filename ON pages (filename);

INSERT INTO alembic_version (version_num) VALUES ('21579ecccd8')
;
```

How it works...

The `create_index()` function adds indices given an index name, a table, and a list of table columns. The `drop_index()` function does the opposite, removing indices given an index name.

See also

▸ The Wikipedia page about database indices is at `https://en.wikipedia.org/wiki/Database_index` (retrieved September 2015)

Setting up a test web server

In *Chapter 1, Laying the Foundation for Reproducible Data Analysis*, we discussed why unit testing is a good idea. Purists will tell you that you only need unit tests. However, the general consensus is that higher-level testing can also be useful.

Obviously, this book is about data analysis and not about web development. Still, sharing your results or data via a website or web service is a common requirement. When you mine the Web or do something else related to the Web, it often becomes necessary to reproduce certain use cases, such as login forms. As you expect of a mature language, Python has many great web frameworks. I chose Flask, a simple Pythonic web framework for this recipe because it seemed easy to set up, but you should use your own judgment because I have no idea what your requirements are.

Getting ready

I tested the code with Flask 0.10.1 from Anaconda. Install Flask with `conda` or `pip`, as follows:

```
$ conda install flask
$ pip install flask
```

How to do it...

In this recipe, we will set up a secure page with a login form, which you can use for testing. The code consists of a `app.py` Python file and a HTML file in the `templates` directory (I will not discuss the HTML in detail):

1. The imports are as follows:

```
from flask import Flask
from flask import render_template
from flask import request
from flask import redirect
from flask import url_for

app = Flask(__name__)
```

2. Define the following function to handle requests for the home page:

```
@app.route('/')
def home():
    return "Test Site"
```

3. Define the following function to process login attempts:

```
@app.route('/secure', methods=['GET', 'POST'])
def login():
    error = None
    if request.method == 'POST':
        if request.form['username'] != 'admin' or\
                request.form['password'] != 'admin':
            error = 'Invalid password or user name.'
        else:
            return redirect(url_for('home'))
    return render_template('admin.html', error=error)
```

4. The following block runs the server (don't use `debug=True` for public-facing websites):

```
if __name__ == '__main__':
    app.run(debug=True)
```

5. Run `$ python app.py` and open a web browser at `http://127.0.0.1:5000/` and `http://127.0.0.1:5000/secure`.

Refer to the following screenshot for the end result:

Implementing a star schema with fact and dimension tables

The **star schema** is a database pattern that facilitates reporting. Star schemas are appropriate for the processing of events, such as website visits, ad clicks, or financial transactions. Event information (metrics, such as temperature or purchase amount) is stored in fact tables linked to much smaller dimension tables. Star schemas are denormalized, which places the responsibility of integrity checks to the application code. For this reason, we should only write to the database in a controlled manner. If you use SQLAlchemy for bulk inserts, you should choose the Core API over the ORM API or use straight SQL. You can read more about the reasons at `http://docs.sqlalchemy.org/en/rel_1_0/faq/performance.html` (retrieved September 2015).

Time is a common dimension in reporting. For instance, we can store dates of daily weather measurements in a dimension table. For each date in our data, we can save the date, year, month, and day of year. We can prepopulate this table before processing events and then add new dates as needed. We don't even have to add new records to the time dimension table if we assume that we only need to maintain the database for a century. In such a case, we will just prepopulate the time dimension table with all the possible dates in the range that we want to support. If we are dealing with binary or categorical variables, pre-populating the dimension tables should be possible too.

In this recipe, we will implement a star schema for direct marketing data described in `http://blog.minethatdata.com/2008/03/minethatdata-e-mail-analytics-and-data.html` (retrieved September 2015). The data is in a CSV file from a direct marketing campaign. For the sake of simplicity, we will ignore some of the columns. As a metric, we will take the `spend` column with purchase amounts. For the dimensions, I chose the channel (Phone, Web, or Multichannel), the zip code (Rural, Suburban, or Urban) and segment (Mens, Womens, or no e-mail). Refer to the following entity-relationship diagram:

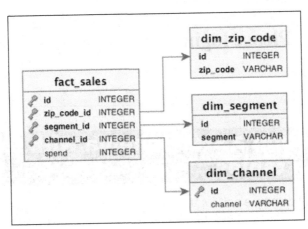

How to do it...

The following code downloads the data, loads it in a database, and then queries the database (refer to the `star_schema.py` file in this book's code bundle):

1. The imports are as follows:

```python
from sqlalchemy import Column
from sqlalchemy import create_engine
from sqlalchemy.ext.declarative import declarative_base
from sqlalchemy import ForeignKey
from sqlalchemy import Integer
from sqlalchemy import String
from sqlalchemy.orm import sessionmaker
from sqlalchemy import func
import dautil as dl
from tabulate import tabulate
import sqlite3
import os
from joblib import Memory

Base = declarative_base()
memory = Memory(cachedir='.')
```

2. Define the following class to represent the ZIP code dimension:

```python
class DimZipCode(Base):
    __tablename__ = 'dim_zip_code'
    id = Column(Integer, primary_key=True)
    # Urban, Suburban, or Rural.
    zip_code = Column(String(8), nullable=False, unique=True)
```

3. Define the following class to represent the segment dimension:

```python
class DimSegment(Base):
    __tablename__ = 'dim_segment'
    id = Column(Integer, primary_key=True)
    # Mens E-Mail, Womens E-Mail or No E-Mail
    segment = Column(String(14), nullable=False, unique=True)
```

4. Define the following class to represent the channel dimension:

```python
class DimChannel(Base):
    __tablename__ = 'dim_channel'
    id = Column(Integer, primary_key=True)
    channel = Column(String)
```

5. Define the following class to represent the fact table:

```python
class FactSales(Base):
    __tablename__ = 'fact_sales'
    id = Column(Integer, primary_key=True)
    zip_code_id = Column(Integer, ForeignKey('dim_zip_code.id'),
                         primary_key=True)
    segment_id = Column(Integer, ForeignKey('dim_segment.id'),
                        primary_key=True)
    channel_id = Column(Integer, ForeignKey('dim_channel.id'),
                        primary_key=True)

    # Storing amount as cents
    spend = Column(Integer)

    def __repr__(self):
        return "zip_code_id={0} channel_id={1} segment_id={2}".format(
            self.zip_code_id, self.channel_id, self.segment_id)
```

6. Define the following function to create a SQLAlchemy session:

```python
def create_session(dbname):
    engine = create_engine('sqlite:///{}'.format(dbname))
    DBSession = sessionmaker(bind=engine)
    Base.metadata.create_all(engine)

    return DBSession()
```

7. Define the following function to populate the segment dimension table:

```
def populate_dim_segment(session):
    options = ['Mens E-Mail', 'Womens E-Mail', 'No E-Mail']

    for option in options:
        if not dl.db.count_where(session, DimSegment.segment,
option):
            session.add(DimSegment(segment=option))

    session.commit()
```

8. Define the following function to populate the ZIP code dimension table:

```
def populate_dim_zip_code(session):
    # Note the interesting spelling
    options = ['Urban', 'Surburban', 'Rural']

    for option in options:
        if not dl.db.count_where(session, DimZipCode.zip_code,
option):
            session.add(DimZipCode(zip_code=option))

    session.commit()
```

9. Define the following function to populate the channel dimension table:

```
def populate_dim_channels(session):
    options = ['Phone', 'Web', 'Multichannel']

    for option in options:
        if not dl.db.count_where(session, DimChannel.channel,
option):
            session.add(DimChannel(channel=option))

    session.commit()
```

10. Define the following function to populate the fact table (it uses straight SQL for performance reasons):

```
def load(csv_rows, session, dbname):
    channels = dl.db.map_to_id(session, DimChannel.channel)
    segments = dl.db.map_to_id(session, DimSegment.segment)
    zip_codes = dl.db.map_to_id(session, DimZipCode.zip_code)
    conn = sqlite3.connect(dbname)
    c = conn.cursor()
```

```
logger = dl.log_api.conf_logger(__name__)

for i, row in enumerate(csv_rows):
    channel_id = channels[row['channel']]
    segment_id = segments[row['segment']]
    zip_code_id = zip_codes[row['zip_code']]
    spend = dl.data.centify(row['spend'])

    insert = "INSERT INTO fact_sales (id, segment_id,\
        zip_code_id, channel_id, spend) VALUES({id}, \
        {sid}, {zid}, {cid}, {spend})"
    c.execute(insert.format(id=i, sid=segment_id,
                            zid=zip_code_id, cid=channel_id,
    spend=spend))


    if i % 1000 == 0:
        logger.info("Progress %s/64000", i)
        conn.commit()

conn.commit()
c.close()
conn.close()
```

11. Define the following function to download and parse the data:

```
@memory.cache
def get_and_parse():
    out = dl.data.get_direct_marketing_csv()
    return dl.data.read_csv(out)
```

12. The following block uses the functions and classes we defined:

```
if __name__ == "__main__":
    dbname = os.path.join(dl.data.get_data_dir(), 'marketing.db')
    session = create_session(dbname)
    populate_dim_segment(session)
    populate_dim_zip_code(session)
    populate_dim_channels(session)

    if session.query(FactSales).count() < 64000:
        load(get_and_parse(), session, dbname)

    fsum = func.sum(FactSales.spend)
    query = session.query(DimSegment.segment, DimChannel.channel,
                          DimZipCode.zip_code, fsum)
```

```
    dim_cols = (DimSegment.segment, DimChannel.channel,
DimZipCode.zip_code)
    dim_entities = [dl.db.entity_from_column(col) for col in dim_
cols]
    spend_totals = query.join(FactSales,
                            *dim_entities)\
                    .group_by(*dim_cols).order_by(fsum.
desc()).all()
    print(tabulate(spend_totals, tablefmt='psql',
                 headers=['Segment', 'Channel', 'Zip Code',
'Spend']))
```

Refer to the following screenshot for the end result (spending amounts in cents):

```
+----------------+--------------+-------------+---------+
| Segment        | Channel      | Zip Code    |  Spend  |
|----------------+--------------+-------------+---------|
| Mens E-Mail    | Web          | Surburban   | 753965  |
| Mens E-Mail    | Phone        | Urban       | 475161  |
| Womens E-Mail  | Web          | Urban       | 465327  |
| Mens E-Mail    | Phone        | Surburban   | 447702  |
| Mens E-Mail    | Web          | Urban       | 437970  |
| Womens E-Mail  | Phone        | Urban       | 397354  |
| Womens E-Mail  | Web          | Surburban   | 333875  |
| No E-Mail      | Phone        | Surburban   | 292136  |
| No E-Mail      | Web          | Surburban   | 289213  |
| Womens E-Mail  | Phone        | Surburban   | 273985  |
| Mens E-Mail    | Web          | Rural       | 252286  |
| No E-Mail      | Web          | Urban       | 244141  |
| Mens E-Mail    | Multichannel | Urban       | 224474  |
| Womens E-Mail  | Web          | Rural       | 218235  |
| Womens E-Mail  | Multichannel | Urban       | 216351  |
| No E-Mail      | Phone        | Urban       | 211589  |
| Womens E-Mail  | Multichannel | Surburban   | 209122  |
| Mens E-Mail    | Multichannel | Surburban   | 198106  |
| Mens E-Mail    | Phone        | Rural       | 193816  |
| Womens E-Mail  | Phone        | Rural       | 157707  |
| No E-Mail      | Phone        | Rural       |  97356  |
| No E-Mail      | Web          | Rural       |  95936  |
| No E-Mail      | Multichannel | Surburban   |  62989  |
| No E-Mail      | Multichannel | Urban       |  49961  |
| Mens E-Mail    | Multichannel | Rural       |  47689  |
| No E-Mail      | Multichannel | Rural       |  47512  |
| Womens E-Mail  | Multichannel | Rural       |  31855  |
+----------------+--------------+-------------+---------+
```

See also

▶ The Star schema Wikipedia page at `https://en.wikipedia.org/wiki/Star_schema` (retrieved September 2015)

Using HDFS

Hadoop Distributed File System (**HDFS**) is the storage component of the Hadoop framework for Big Data. HDFS is a distributed filesystem, which spreads data on multiple systems, and is inspired by the Google File System used by Google for its search engine. HDFS requires a **Java Runtime Environment** (**JRE**), and it uses a `NameNode` server to keep track of the files. The system also replicates the data so that losing a few nodes doesn't lead to data loss. The typical use case for HDFS is processing large read-only files. Apache Spark, also covered in this chapter, can use HDFS too.

Getting ready

Install Hadoop and a JRE. As these are not Python frameworks, you will have to check what the appropriate procedure is for your operating system. I used Hadoop 2.7.1 with Java 1.7.0_60 for this recipe. This can be a complicated process, but there are many resources online that can help you troubleshoot for your specific system.

How to do it...

We can configure HDFS with several XML files found in your Hadoop install. Some of the steps in this section serve only as example and you should implement them as appropriate for your operating system, environment, and personal preferences:

1. Edit the `core-site.xml` file so that it has the following content (comments omitted):

   ```
   <?xml version="1.0" encoding="UTF-8"?>
   <?xml-stylesheet type="text/xsl" href="configuration.xsl"?>
   <configuration>
       <property>
           <name>fs.default.name</name>
           <value>hdfs://localhost:8020</value>
       </property>
   </configuration>
   ```

2. Edit the `hdfs-site.xml` file so that it has the following content (comments omitted), setting the replication of each file to just 1, to run HDFS locally:

   ```
   <?xml version="1.0" encoding="UTF-8"?>
   <?xml-stylesheet type="text/xsl" href="configuration.xsl"?>
   <configuration>
       <property>
           <name>dfs.replication</name>
           <value>1</value>
       </property>
   </configuration>
   ```

3. If necessary, enable Remote login on your system to SSH into localhost and generate keys (Windows users can use putty):

    ```
    $ ssh-keygen -t dsa -f ~/.ssh/id_dsa
    $ cat ~/.ssh/id_dsa.pub >> ~/.ssh/authorized_keys
    ```

4. Format the filesystem from the root of the Hadoop directory:

    ```
    $ bin/hdfs namenode -format
    ```

5. Start the NameNode server, as follows (the opposite command is `$ sbin/stop-dfs.sh`):

    ```
    $ sbin/start-dfs.sh
    ```

6. Create a directory in HDFS with the following command:

    ```
    $ hadoop fs -mkdir direct_marketing
    ```

7. Optionally, if you want to use the `direct_marketing.csv` file in the Spark recipe, you need to copy it into HDFS, as follows:

    ```
    $ hadoop fs -copyFromLocal <path to file>/direct_marketing.csv
    direct_marketing
    ```

See also

▶   The HDFS user guide at `https://hadoop.apache.org/docs/r2.6.0/hadoop-project-dist/hadoop-hdfs/HdfsUserGuide.html` (retrieved September 2015)

Setting up Spark

Apache Spark is a project in the Hadoop ecosystem (refer to the *Using HDFS* recipe), which purportedly performs better than Hadoop's MapReduce. Spark loads data into memory as much as possible, and it has good support for machine learning. In the *Clustering data with Spark* recipe, we will apply a machine learning algorithm via Spark.

Spark can work standalone, but it is designed to work with Hadoop using HDFS. **Resilient Distributed Datasets** (**RDDs**) are the central structure in Spark, and they represent distributed data. Spark has good support for Scala, which is a JVM language, and a somewhat lagging support for Python. For instance, the support to stream in the pyspark API lags a bit. Spark also has the concept of DataFrames, but it is not implemented through pandas, but through a Spark implementation.

Getting ready

Download Spark from the downloads page at `https://spark.apache.org/downloads.html` (retrieved September 2015). I downloaded the `spark-1.5.0-bin-hadoop2.6.tgz` archive for Spark 1.5.0.

Unpack the archive in an appropriate directory.

How to do it...

The following steps illustrate a basic setup for Spark with a few optional steps:

1. If you want to use a different Python version than the system Python, set the `PYSPARK_PYTHON` environment variable via the GUI of your operating system or the CLI, as follows:

   ```
   $ export PYSPARK_PYTHON=/path/to/anaconda/bin/python
   ```

2. Set the `SPARK_HOME` environment variable, as follows:

   ```
   $ export SPARK_HOME=<path/to/spark/>spark-1.5.0-bin-hadoop2.6
   ```

3. Add the `python` directory to your `PYTHONPATH` environment variable, as follows:

   ```
   $ export PYTHONPATH=$SPARK_HOME/python:$PYTHONPATH
   ```

4. Add the ZIP of `py4j` to your `PYTHONPATH` environment variable, as follows:

   ```
   $ export PYTHONPATH=$SPARK_HOME/python/lib/py4j-0.8.2.1-src.zip:$PYTHONPATH
   ```

5. If the logging of Spark is too verbose, copy the `log4j.properties.template` file in the `$SPARK_HOME/conf` directory to `log4j.properties` and change the INFO levels to WARN.

See also

The official Spark website is at `http://spark.apache.org/` (retrieved September 2015)

Clustering data with Spark

In the previous recipe, *Setting up Spark*, we covered a basic setup of Spark. If you followed the *Using HDFS* recipe, you can optionally serve the data from Hadoop. In this case, you need to specify the URL of the file in this manner, `hdfs://hdfs-host:port/path/direct_marketing.csv`.

We will use the same data as we did in the *Implementing a star schema with fact and dimension tables* recipe. However, this time we will use the spend, history, and recency columns. The first column corresponds to recent purchase amounts after a direct marketing campaign, the second to historical purchase amounts, and the third column to the recency of purchase in months. The data is described in http://blog.minethatdata.com/2008/03/minethatdata-e-mail-analytics-and-data.html (retrieved September 2015). We will apply the popular K-means machine-learning algorithm to cluster the data. *Chapter 9, Ensemble Learning and Dimensionality Reduction*, pays more attention to machine learning algorithms. The K-means algorithm attempts to find the best clusters for a dataset given a number of clusters. We are supposed to either know this number or find it through trial and error. In this recipe, I evaluate the clusters through the **Within Set Sum Squared Error** (**WSSSE**), also known as **Within Cluster Sum of Squares** (**WCSS**). This metric calculates the sum of the squared error of the distance between each point and its assigned cluster. You can read more about evaluation metrics in *Chapter 10, Evaluating Classifiers, Regressors, and Clusters*.

Getting ready

Follow the instructions in the *Setting up Spark* recipe.

How to do it...

The code for this recipe is in the clustering_spark.py file in this book's code bundle:

1. The imports are as follows:

```
from pyspark.mllib.clustering import KMeans
from pyspark import SparkContext
import dautil as dl
import csv
import matplotlib.pyplot as plt
import matplotlib as mpl
from matplotlib.colors import Normalize
```

2. Define the following function to compute the error:

```
def error(point, clusters):
    center = clusters.centers[clusters.predict(point)]

    return dl.stats.wssse(point, center)
```

3. Read and parse the data, as follows:

```
sc = SparkContext()
csv_file = dl.data.get_direct_marketing_csv()
lines = sc.textFile(csv_file)
header = lines.first().split(',')
```

```
cols_set = set(['recency', 'history', 'spend'])
select_cols = [i for i, col in enumerate(header) if col in cols_
set]
```

4. Set up the following RDDs:

```
header_rdd = lines.filter(lambda l: 'recency' in l)
noheader_rdd = lines.subtract(header_rdd)
temp = noheader_rdd.map(lambda v: list(csv.reader([v]))[0])\
                .map(lambda p: (int(p[select_cols[0]]),
                        dl.data.centify(p[select_cols[1]]),
                        dl.data.centify(p[select_cols[2]])))

# spend > 0
temp = temp.filter(lambda x: x[2] > 0)
```

5. Cluster the data with the k-means algorithm:

```
points = []
clusters = None

for i in range(2, 28):
    clusters = KMeans.train(temp, i, maxIterations=10,
                        runs=10, initializationMode="random")

    val = temp.map(lambda point: error(point, clusters))\
            .reduce(lambda x, y: x + y)
    points.append((i, val))
```

6. Plot the clusters, as follows:

```
dl.options.mimic_seaborn()
fig, [ax, ax2] = plt.subplots(2, 1)
ax.set_title('k-means Clusters')
ax.set_xlabel('Number of clusters')
ax.set_ylabel('WSSSE')
dl.plotting.plot_points(ax, points)

collected = temp.collect()
recency, history, spend = zip(*collected)
indices = [clusters.predict(c) for c in collected]
ax2.set_title('Clusters for spend, history and recency')
ax2.set_xlabel('history (cents)')
ax2.set_ylabel('spend (cents)')
markers = dl.plotting.map_markers(indices)
```

```
colors = dl.plotting.sample_hex_cmap(name='hot',
ncolors=len(set(recency)))

for h, s, r, m in zip(history, spend, recency, markers):
    ax2.scatter(h, s, s=20 + r, marker=m, c=colors[r-1])

cma = mpl.colors.ListedColormap(colors, name='from_list', N=None)
norm = Normalize(min(recency), max(recency))
msm = mpl.cm.ScalarMappable(cmap=cma, norm=norm)
msm.set_array([])
fig.colorbar(msm, label='Recency')

for i, center in enumerate(clusters.clusterCenters):
    recency, history, spend = center
    ax2.text(history, spend, str(i))

plt.tight_layout()
plt.show()
```

Refer to the following screenshot for the end result (the numbers in the plot correspond to cluster centers):

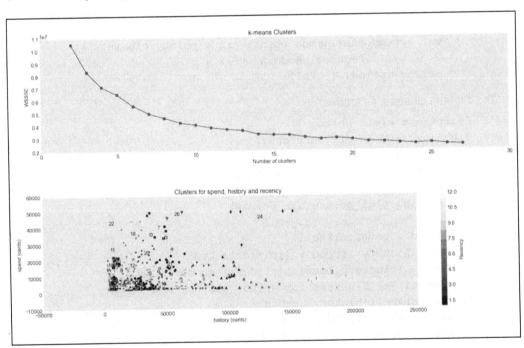

How it works...

K-means clustering assigns data points to k clusters. The problem of clustering is not solvable directly, but we can apply heuristics, which achieve an acceptable result. The algorithm for k-means iterates between two steps not including the (usually random) initialization of k-means:

- ▸ Assign each data point a cluster with the lowest WCSS mean
- ▸ Recalculate the center of the cluster as the mean of the cluster points coordinates

The algorithm stops when the cluster assignments become stable.

There's more...

Spark 1.5.0 added experimental support to stream K-means. Due to the experimental nature of these new features, I decided to not discuss them in detail. I have added the following example code in the `streaming_clustering.py` file in this book's code bundle:

```
import dautil as dl
from pyspark.mllib.clustering import StreamingKMeansModel
from pyspark import SparkContext

csv_file = dl.data.get_direct_marketing_csv()
csv_rows = dl.data.read_csv(csv_file)

stkm = StreamingKMeansModel(28 * [[0., 0., 0.]], 28 * [1.])
sc = SparkContext()

for row in csv_rows:
    spend = dl.data.centify(row['spend'])

    if spend > 0:
        history = dl.data.centify(row['history'])
        data = sc.parallelize([[int(row['recency']),
                                history, spend]])
        stkm = stkm.update(data, 0., 'points')

print(stkm.centers)
```

See also

- ▸ *Building Machine Learning Systems with Python*, Willi Richert, and Luis Pedro Coelho (2013)
- ▸ The Wikipedia page about K-means clustering is at https://en.wikipedia.org/wiki/K-means_clustering (retrieved September 2015)

6

Signal Processing and Timeseries

In this chapter, we will cover the following recipes:

- ▶ Spectral analysis with periodograms
- ▶ Estimating power spectral density with the Welch method
- ▶ Analyzing peaks
- ▶ Measuring phase synchronization
- ▶ Exponential smoothing
- ▶ Evaluating smoothing
- ▶ Using the Lomb-Scargle periodogram
- ▶ Analyzing the frequency spectrum of audio
- ▶ Analyzing signals with the discrete cosine transform
- ▶ Block bootstrapping time series data
- ▶ Moving block bootstrapping time series data
- ▶ Applying the discrete wavelet transform

Introduction

Time is an important dimension in science and daily life. Time series data is abundant and requires special techniques. Usually, we are interested in trends and seasonality or periodicity. In mathematical terms, this means that we try to represent the data by (usually linear) polynomial or trigonometric functions, or a combination of both.

When we investigate seasonality, we generally distinguish between time domain and frequency domain analysis. In the time domain, we can use a dozen pandas functions for rolling windows. We can also smooth data to remove noise while hopefully keeping enough of the signal. Smoothing is in many respects similar to fitting, which is convenient because we can reuse some of the regression tools we know.

To get in the frequency domain, we apply transforms such as the **fast Fourier Transform** and **discrete cosine transform**. We can then further analyze signals with periodograms.

Spectral analysis with periodograms

We can think of periodic signals as being composed of multiple frequencies. For instance, sound is composed of multiple tones and light is composed of multiple colors. The range of frequencies is called the **frequency spectrum**. When we analyze the frequency spectrum of a signal, it's natural to take a look at the result of the Fourier Transform of the signal. The periodogram extends this and is equal to the squared magnitude of the Fourier Transform, as follows:

$$(6.1) \quad S(f) = \frac{\Delta t}{N} \left| \sum_{n=0}^{N-1} x_n e^{-i2\pi n f} \right|^2, \quad -\frac{1}{2\Delta t} < f \leq \frac{1}{2\Delta t}$$

We will look at the periodograms of the following variables:

▸ Rain values from the KNMI De Bilt weather data

▸ The second difference (comparable to second derivative in calculus) of the rain values

▸ The rolling sum of the rain values using a window of 365 days

▸ The rolling mean of the rain values using a window of 365 days

How to do it...

1. The imports are as follows:

```
from scipy import signal
import matplotlib.pyplot as plt
import dautil as dl
import numpy as np
import pandas as pd
from IPython.display import HTML
```

2. Load the data as follows:

```
fs = 365
rain = dl.data.Weather.load()['RAIN'].dropna()
```

3. Define the following function to plot periodograms:

```
def plot_periodogram(arr, ax):
    f, Pxx_den = signal.periodogram(arr, fs)
    ax.set_xlabel('Frequency (Hz)')
    ax.set_ylabel('PSD')
    ax.semilogy(f, Pxx_den)
```

4. Plot the periodograms with the following code:

```
sp = dl.plotting.Subplotter(2, 2, context)
sp.label()
plot_periodogram(rain, sp.ax)
sp.label(advance=True)
plot_periodogram(np.diff(rain, 2), sp.ax)
sp.label(advance=True)
plot_periodogram(pd.rolling_sum(rain, fs).dropna(), sp.ax)
sp.label(advance=True)
plot_periodogram(pd.rolling_mean(rain, fs).dropna(), sp.ax)
HTML(sp.exit())
```

Refer to the following screenshot for the end result:

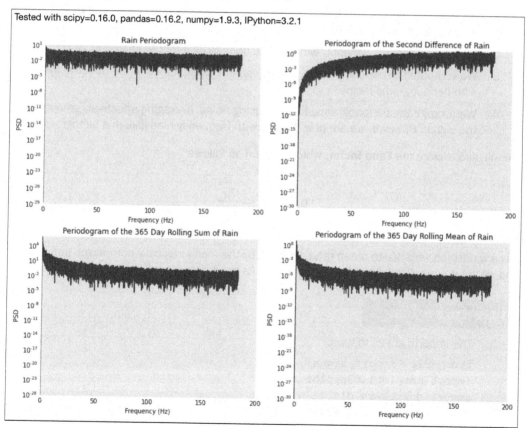

The code is from the `periodograms.ipynb` file in this book's code bundle demonstrates periodograms.

See also

▸ The documentation for the `periodogram()` function at `https://docs.scipy.org/doc/scipy-0.16.0/reference/generated/scipy.signal.periodogram.html#scipy.signal.periodogram` (retrieved September 2015)

▸ The relevant Wikipedia page at `https://en.wikipedia.org/wiki/Spectral_density_estimation` (retrieved September 2015)

Estimating power spectral density with the Welch method

The **Welch method** is an improvement (it reduces noise) of the periodogram technique and is named after P.D. Welch. The noise of the power spectrum is reduced with the following steps:

1. We split the signal with a fixed number of overlapping points. If the overlap is 0, then we have **Bartlett's method**.

2. In the time domain, we apply window functions to each of the segments of step 1.

3. We compute the periodogram for each segment as explained in the *Spectral analysis with periodograms* recipe.

4. We average the periodograms, thus reducing noise. Averaging effectively smoothens the signal. However, we are now dealing with frequency bins (like in a histogram).

We will also explore the **Fano factor**, which is given as follows:

$$(6.2) \quad F = \frac{\sigma_W^2}{\mu_W}$$

It is a windowed variance-to-mean ratio. Dividing by the mean basically normalizes the values, and we get a normalized measure of dispersion. As input data we will use temperature data.

How to do it...

1. The imports are as follows:

```
from scipy import signal
import matplotlib.pyplot as plt
import dautil as dl
from IPython.display import HTML
```

2. Load the data and compute the Fano factor:

```
fs = 365
temp = dl.data.Weather.load()['TEMP'].dropna()
fano_factor = dl.ts.fano_factor(temp, fs)
```

3. Define the following function to plot the periodograms:

```
def plot_welch(arr, ax):
    f, Pxx_den = signal.welch(arr, fs)
    ax.semilogy(f, Pxx_den)
```

4. Plot the input data and corresponding periodograms:

```
sp = dl.plotting.Subplotter(2, 2, context)
temp.plot(ax=sp.ax)
sp.label(ylabel_params=dl.data.Weather.get_header('TEMP'))
sp.label(advance=True)
sp.ax.plot(temp.index, fano_factor)
sp.label(advance=True)
plot_welch(temp, sp.ax)
sp.label(advance=True)
plot_welch(fano_factor.dropna(), sp.ax)
HTML(sp.exit())
```

Refer to the following screenshot for the end result:

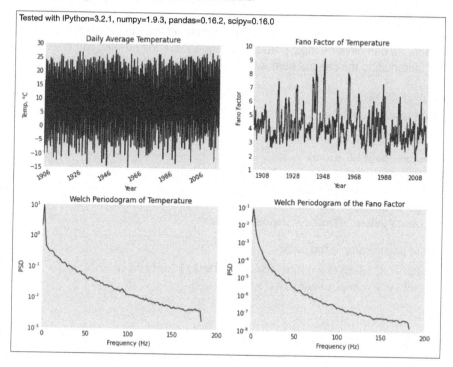

The code is in the `estimating_welch.ipynb` file in this book's code bundle.

See also

▶ The Wikipedia page about the Fano factor at `https://en.wikipedia.org/wiki/Fano_factor` (retrieved September 2015)

▶ The Wikipedia page about the Welch method at `https://en.wikipedia.org/wiki/Welch's_method` (retrieved September 2015)

▶ The `welch()` function documented at `https://docs.scipy.org/doc/scipy/reference/generated/scipy.signal.welch.html#scipy.signal.welch` (retrieved September 2015)

Analyzing peaks

The analysis of peaks is similar to that of valleys, since both are extreme values. SciPy has the `argrelmax()` function that finds the relative maxima. When we apply this function to daily temperature values, it not only finds hot days in summer but also hot days in winter unless we make the function consider a larger time frame. Of course, we can also check whether values are above a threshold or only select summer data using prior knowledge.

When we analyze peaks in time series data, we can apply two approaches. The first approach is to consider the highest peaks in a year, a month, or another fixed time interval and build a series with those values. The second approach is to define any value above a threshold as a peak. In this recipe, we will use the 95th percentile as the threshold. In the context of this approach, we can have multiple peaks in a sequence. Long streaks can have a negative impact, for instance, in the case of heat waves.

How to do it...

1. The imports are as follows:

```
import dautil as dl
from scipy import signal
import matplotlib.pyplot as plt
import seaborn as sns
from IPython.display import HTML
```

2. Load and resample the data:

```
temp = dl.data.Weather.load()['TEMP'].dropna()
monthly = temp.resample('M')
```

3. Plot peaks and note that hot days in winter are also considered:

```
sp = dl.plotting.Subplotter(2, 2, context)
max_locs = signal.argrelmax(monthly.values)
sp.ax.plot(monthly.index, monthly, label='Monthly means')
sp.ax.plot(monthly.index[max_locs], monthly.values[max_locs],
           'o', label='Tops')
sp.label(ylabel_params=dl.data.Weather.get_header('TEMP'))
```

4. Plot the annual maximum series:

```
annual_max = dl.ts.groupby_year(temp).max()
sp.next_ax().plot(annual_max.index, annual_max, label='Annual
Maximum Series')
dl.plotting.plot_polyfit(sp.ax, annual_max.index, annual_max.
values)
sp.label(ylabel_params=dl.data.Weather.get_header('TEMP'))
```

5. Plot the longest annual streaks of hot days over the 95th percentile threshold:

```
_, threshhold = dl.stats.outliers(temp, method='percentiles')
over_threshhold = temp > threshhold
streaks = dl.ts.groupby_year(over_threshhold).apply(
    lambda x: dl.collect.longest_streak(x, 1))
sp.next_ax().plot(streaks.index, streaks)
dl.plotting.plot_polyfit(sp.ax, streaks.index, streaks.values)
over_threshhold = dl.ts.groupby_year(over_threshhold).mean()
sp.label()
```

6. Plot the annual maximum series distribution:

```
sp.label(advance=True)
sns.distplot(annual_max, ax=sp.ax)
sp.label(xlabel_params=dl.data.Weather.get_header('TEMP'))
HTML(sp.exit())
```

Refer to the following screenshot for the end result:

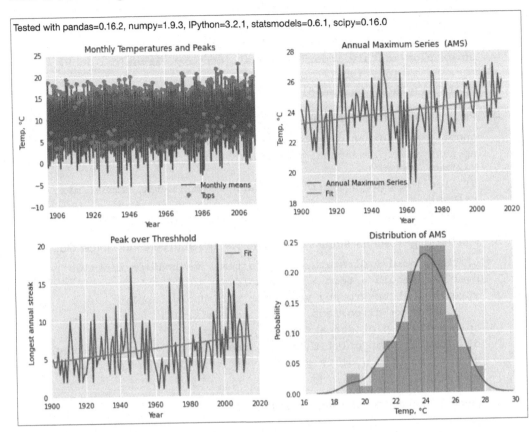

The code is in the `analyzing_peaks.ipynb` file in this book's code bundle.

See also

▶ The `argrelmax()` function documented at https://docs.scipy.org/doc/scipy/reference/generated/scipy.signal.argrelmax.html (retrieved September 2015)

Measuring phase synchronization

Two signals can be fully synchronized, not synchronized, or somewhere in between. We usually measure **phase synchronization** in radians. The related quantity of **instantaneous phase** can be measured with the NumPy `angle()` function. For real-valued data, we need to obtain the analytic representation of the signal, which is given by the Hilbert transform. The Hilbert transform is also available in SciPy and NumPy.

Cross-correlation measures the correlation between two signals using a sliding inner product. We can use cross-correlation to measure the time delay between two signals. NumPy offers the `correlate()` function, which calculates the cross-correlation between two arrays.

How to do it...

1. The imports are as follows:

```
import dautil as dl
import matplotlib.pyplot as plt
import numpy as np
from IPython.display import HTML
```

2. Load the data and calculate the instantaneous phase:

```
df = dl.data.Weather.load().dropna()
df = dl.ts.groupby_yday(df).mean().dropna()
ws_phase = dl.ts.instant_phase(df['WIND_SPEED'])
wd_phase = dl.ts.instant_phase(df['WIND_DIR'])
```

3. Plot the wind direction and speed z-scores:

```
sp = dl.plotting.Subplotter(2, 2, context)
cp = dl.plotting.CyclePlotter(sp.ax)
cp.plot(df.index, dl.stats.zscores(df['WIND_DIR'].values),
        label='Wind direction')
cp.plot(df.index, dl.stats.zscores(df['WIND_SPEED'].values),
        label='Wind speed')
sp.label()
```

4. Plot the instantaneous phase as follows:

```
cp = dl.plotting.CyclePlotter(sp.next_ax())
cp.plot(df.index, ws_phase, label='Wind speed')
cp.plot(df.index, wd_phase, label='Wind direction')
sp.label()
```

5. Plot the correlation of wind speed and direction:

```
sp.label(advance=True)
sp.ax.plot(np.correlate(df['WIND_SPEED'], df['WIND_DIR'], 'same'))
```

6. Plot the phase shift with the fast Fourier Transform:

```
sp.label(advance=True)
sp.ax.plot(np.angle(np.fft.fft(df['WIND_SPEED'])/np.fft.
fft(df['WIND_DIR'])))
HTML(sp.exit())
```

Refer to the following screenshot for the end result:

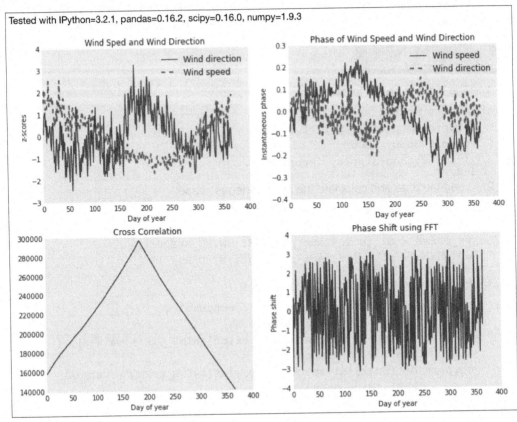

The code for this recipe is in the `phase_synchrony.ipynb` file in this book's code bundle.

See also

▶ The instantaneous phase Wikipedia page at `https://en.wikipedia.org/wiki/Instantaneous_phase` (retrieved September 2015)

▶ The analytic signal Wikipedia page at `https://en.wikipedia.org/wiki/Analytic_signal` (retrieved September 2015)

▶ The Wikipedia page about cross-correlation at `https://en.wikipedia.org/wiki/Cross-correlation` (retrieved September 2015)

▶ The documentation for the `angle()` function at `https://docs.scipy.org/doc/numpy/reference/generated/numpy.angle.html` (retrieved September 2015)

▶ The documentation for the `correlate()` function at `https://docs.scipy.org/doc/numpy/reference/generated/numpy.correlate.html` (retrieved September 2015)

Exponential smoothing

Exponential smoothing is a low-pass filter that aims to remove noise. In this recipe, we will apply single and double exponential smoothing, as shown by the following equations:

$$(6.3) \quad s_t = \alpha x_t + (1 - \alpha) s_{t-1}, t > 0$$

$$(6.4) \quad s_t = \alpha x_t + (1 - \alpha)(s_{t-1} + b_{t-1})$$

$$(6.5) \quad b_t = \beta(s_t - s_{t-1}) + (1 - \beta) b_{t-1}$$

Single exponential smoothing (6.3) requires the **smoothing factor** α, where $0 < \alpha < 1$. Double exponential smoothing (6.4 and 6.5) attempts to handle trends in data via the **trend smoothing factor** β, where $0 < \beta < 1$.

We will also take a look at rolling deviations of wind speed, which are similar to z-scores, but they are applied to a rolling window. Smoothing is associated with regression, although the goal of smoothing is to get rid of noise. Nevertheless, metrics related to regression, such as the **Mean Squared Error** (**MSE**), are also appropriate for smoothing.

How to do it...

1. The imports are as follows:

```
import dautil as dl
import pandas as pd
import matplotlib.pyplot as plt
import numpy as np
import seaborn as sns
from IPython.display import HTML
```

2. Define the following function to help visualize the result of double exponential smoothing:

```
def grid_mse(i, j, devs):
    alpha = 0.1 * i
    beta = 0.1 * j
    cell = dl.ts.double_exp_smoothing(devs.values, alpha, beta)

    return dl.stats.mse(devs, cell)
```

3. Load the wind speed data and calculate annual means and rolling deviations:

```
wind = dl.data.Weather.load()['WIND_SPEED'].dropna()
wind = dl.ts.groupby_year(wind).mean()
devs = dl.ts.rolling_deviations(wind, 12).dropna()
```

4. Plot the annual means of the wind speed data:

```
sp = dl.plotting.Subplotter(2, 2, context)
sp.label(ylabel_params=dl.data.Weather.get_header('WIND_SPEED'))
sp.ax.plot(wind.index, wind)
```

5. Plot the rolling deviations with an α of 0.7:

```
cp = dl.plotting.CyclePlotter(sp.next_ax())
cp.plot(devs.index, devs, label='Rolling Deviations')
cp.plot(devs.index, dl.ts.exp_smoothing(devs.values, 0.7),
label='Smoothing')
sp.label()
```

6. Plot the MSE for varying smoothing factors:

```
alphas = 0.01 * np.arange(1, 100)
errors = [dl.stats.mse(devs, dl.ts.exp_smoothing(devs.values,
alpha)
            for alpha in alphas]
sp.label(advance=True)
sp.ax.plot(alphas, errors)
```

7. Plot the MSE for a grid of α and β values:

```
sp.label(advance=True)
rng = range(1, 10)
df = dl.report.map_grid(rng, rng, ["alpha", "beta", "mse"], grid_
mse, devs)
sns.heatmap(df, cmap='Blues', square=True, annot=True, fmt='.1f',
            ax=sp.ax)


HTML(sp.exit())
```

Refer to the following screenshot for the end result:

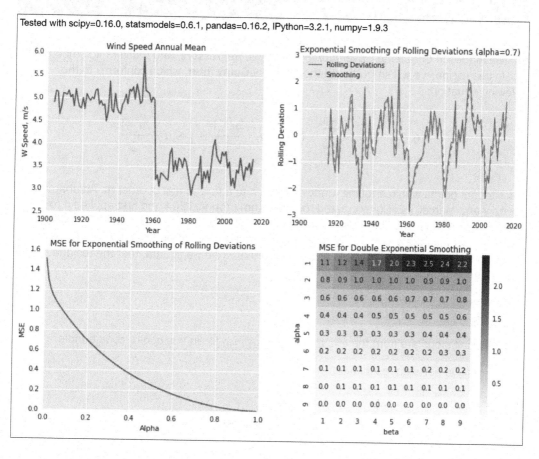

The code is in the `exp_smoothing.ipynb` file in this book's code bundle.

▶ The Wikipedia page about exponential smoothing at `https://en.wikipedia.org/wiki/Exponential_smoothing` (retrieved September 2015)

Evaluating smoothing

Many aspects of smoothing are comparable to regression; therefore, you can apply some of the techniques in *Chapter 10, Evaluating Classifiers, Regressors, and Clusters*, to smoothing too. In this recipe, we will smooth with the **Savitzky-Golay filter**, which conforms to the following equation:

$$(6.6) \quad Y_j = \sum_{i=-(m-1)/2}^{i=(m-1)/2} C_i y_j + i \quad \frac{m+1}{2} \leq j \leq n - \frac{m-1}{2}$$

The filter fits points within a rolling window of size *n* to a polynomial of order *m*. Abraham Savitzky and Marcel J. E. Golay created the algorithm around 1964 and first applied it to chemistry problems. The filter has two parameters that naturally form a grid. As in regression problems, we will take a look at a difference, in this case, the difference between the original signal and the smoothed signal. We assume, just like when we fit data, that the residuals are random and follow a Gaussian distribution.

How to do it...

The following steps are from the `eval_smooth.ipynb` file in this book's code bundle:

1. The imports are as follows:

```
import dautil as dl
import matplotlib.pyplot as plt
from scipy.signal import savgol_filter
import pandas as pd
import numpy as np
import seaborn as sns
from IPython.display import HTML
```

2. Define the following helper functions:

```
def error(data, fit):
    return data - fit


def win_rng():
    return range(3, 25, 2)


def calc_mape(i, j, pres):
    return dl.stats.mape(pres, savgol_filter(pres, i, j))
```

3. Load the atmospheric pressure data as follows:

```
pres = dl.data.Weather.load()['PRESSURE'].dropna()
pres = pres.resample('A')
```

4. Plot the original data and the filter with window size 11 and various polynomial orders:

```
sp = dl.plotting.Subplotter(2, 2, context)
cp = dl.plotting.CyclePlotter(sp.ax)
cp.plot(pres.index, pres, label='Pressure')
cp.plot(pres.index, savgol_filter(pres, 11, 2), label='Poly order
2')
cp.plot(pres.index, savgol_filter(pres, 11, 3), label='Poly order
3')
cp.plot(pres.index, savgol_filter(pres, 11, 4), label='Poly order
4')
sp.label(ylabel_params=dl.data.Weather.get_header('PRESSURE'))
```

5. Plot the standard deviations of the filter residuals for varying window sizes:

```
cp = dl.plotting.CyclePlotter(sp.next_ax())
stds = [error(pres, savgol_filter(pres, i, 2)).std()
        for i in win_rng()]
cp.plot(win_rng(), stds, label='Filtered')
stds = [error(pres, pd.rolling_mean(pres, i)).std()
        for i in win_rng()]
cp.plot(win_rng(), stds, label='Rolling mean')
sp.label()
```

6. Plot the box plots of the filter residuals:

```
sp.label(advance=True)
sp.ax.boxplot([error(pres, savgol_filter(pres, i, 2))
              for i in win_rng()])
sp.ax.set_xticklabels(win_rng())
```

7. Plot the MAPE for a grid of window sizes and polynomial orders:

```
sp.label(advance=True)
df = dl.report.map_grid(win_rng()[1:], range(1, 5),
                  ['win_size', 'poly', 'mape'], calc_mape, pres)
sns.heatmap(df, cmap='Blues', ax=sp.ax)
HTML(sp.exit())
```

Refer to the following screenshot for the end result:

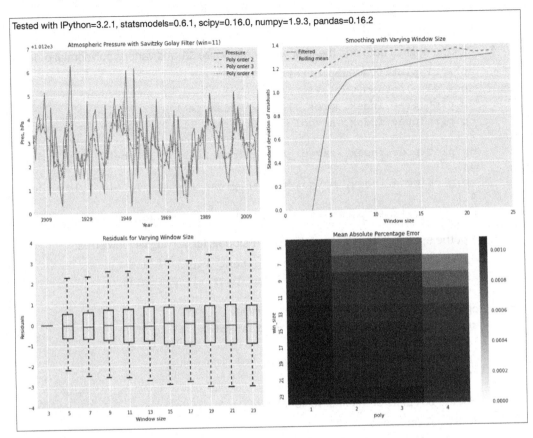

- ▶ The Wikipedia page about the Savitzky-Golay filter at `https://en.wikipedia.org/wiki/Savitzky%E2%80%93Golay_filter` (retrieved September 2015)

- ▶ The `savgol_filter()` function documented at `https://docs.scipy.org/doc/scipy/reference/generated/scipy.signal.savgol_filter.html` (retrieved September 2015)

Using the Lomb-Scargle periodogram

The Lomb-Scargle periodogram is a frequency spectrum estimation method that fits sines to data, and it is frequently used with unevenly sampled data. The method is named after Nicholas R. Lomb and Jeffrey D. Scargle. The algorithm was published around 1976 and has been improved since then. Scargle introduced a time delay parameter, which separates the sine and cosine waveforms. The following equations define the time delay (6.7) and periodogram (6.8).

$$(6.7) \quad \tan 2\omega\tau = \frac{\sum_j \sin 2\omega t_j}{\sum_j \cos 2\omega t_j}$$

$$(6.8) \quad P_x(\omega) = \frac{1}{2}\left(\frac{\left[\sum_j X_j \cos\omega(t_j - \tau)\right]^2}{\sum_j \cos^2\omega(t_j - \tau)} + \frac{\left[\sum_j X_j \sin\omega(t_j - \tau)\right]^2}{\sum_j \sin^2\omega(t_j - \tau)} \right)$$

How to do it...

1. The imports are as follows:

```
from scipy import signal
import numpy as np
import matplotlib.pyplot as plt
import dautil as dl
import statsmodels.api as sm
from IPython.display import HTML
```

2. Load the sunspots data as follows:

```
df = sm.datasets.sunspots.load_pandas().data
sunspots = df['SUNACTIVITY'].values
size = len(sunspots)
t = np.linspace(-2 * np.pi, 2 * np.pi, size)
sine = dl.ts.sine_like(sunspots)
f = np.linspace(0.01, 2, 10 * size)
```

3. Plot a sine waveform as follows:

```
sp = dl.plotting.Subplotter(2, 2, context)
sp.ax.plot(t, sine)
sp.label()

sp.next_ax().plot(df['YEAR'], df['SUNACTIVITY'])
sp.label()
```

4. Apply the periodogram to the sine:

```
pgram = signal.lombscargle(t, sine, f)
sp.next_ax().plot(f, 2 * np.sqrt(pgram/size))
sp.label()
```

5. Apply the periodogram to the sunspots data:

```
pgram = signal.lombscargle(np.arange(size, dtype=float), sunspots,
f)
sp.next_ax().plot(f, 2 * np.sqrt(pgram/size))
sp.label()
HTML(sp.exit())
```

Refer to the following screenshot for the end result:

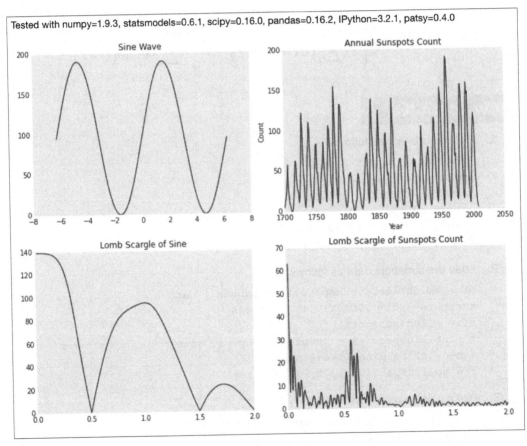

The preceding code is a breakdown of the `lomb_scargle.ipynb` file in this book's code bundle.

See also

▸ The relevant Wikipedia page at `https://en.wikipedia.org/wiki/Least-squares_spectral_analysis` (retrieved September 2015)

▸ The `lombscargle()` function documented at `https://docs.scipy.org/doc/scipy/reference/generated/scipy.signal.lombscargle.html` (retrieved September 2015)

Analyzing the frequency spectrum of audio

We can apply many techniques to analyze audio, and, therefore, we can debate at length about which techniques are most appropriate. The most obvious method is purportedly the FFT. As a variation, we can use the **short-time Fourier transform (STFT)**. The STFT splits the signal in the time domain into equal parts, and it then applies the FFT to each segment. Another algorithm we will use is the **cepstrum**, which was originally used to analyze earthquakes but was later successfully applied to speech analysis. The power cepstrum is given by the following equation:

$$(6.9) \quad \left| F^{-1} \left\{ \log \left(\left| F\{f(t)\} \right|^2 \right) \right\} \right|^2$$

The algorithm is as follows:

1. Calculate the Fourier transform.
2. Compute the squared magnitude of the transform.
3. Take the logarithm of the previous result.
4. Apply the inverse Fourier transform.
5. Calculate the squared magnitude again.

The cepstrum is, in general, useful when we have large changes in the frequency domain. An important use case of the cepstrum is to form feature vectors for audio classification. This requires a mapping from frequency to the **mel scale** (refer to the Wikipedia page mentioned in the See *also* section).

How to do it...

1. The imports are as follows:

```
import dautil as dl
import matplotlib.pyplot as plt
import numpy as np
from ch6util import read_wav
from IPython.display import HTML
```

2. Define the following function to calculate the magnitude of the signal with FFT:

```
def amplitude(arr):
    return np.abs(np.fft.fft(arr))
```

3. Load the data as follows:

```
rate, audio = read_wav()
```

4. Plot the audio waveform:

```
sp = dl.plotting.Subplotter(2, 2, context)
t = np.arange(0, len(audio)/float(rate), 1./rate)
sp.ax.plot(t, audio)
freqs = np.fft.fftfreq(audio.size, 1./rate)
indices = np.where(freqs > 0)[0]
sp.label()
```

5. Plot the amplitude spectrum:

```
magnitude = amplitude(audio)
sp.next_ax().semilogy(freqs[indices], magnitude[indices])
sp.label()
```

6. Plot the cepstrum as follows:

```
cepstrum = dl.ts.power(np.fft.ifft(np.log(magnitude ** 2)))
sp.next_ax().semilogy(cepstrum)
sp.label()
```

7. Plot the STFT as a contour diagram:

```
npieces = 200
stft_amps = []

for i, c in enumerate(dl.collect.chunk(audio[: npieces ** 2],
len(audio)/npieces)):
    amps = amplitude(c)
    stft_amps.extend(amps)
```

```
stft_freqs = np.linspace(0, rate, npieces)
stft_times = np.linspace(0, len(stft_amps)/float(rate), npieces)
sp.next_ax().contour(stft_freqs/rate, stft_freqs,
            np.log(stft_amps).reshape(npieces, npieces))
sp.label()

HTML(sp.exit())
```

Refer to the following screenshot for the end result:

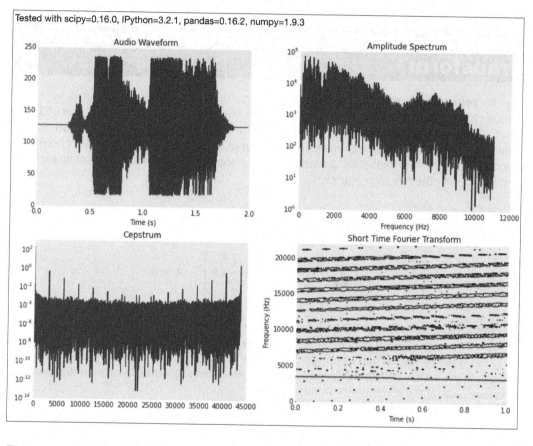

The example code is in the `analyzing_audio.ipynb` file in this book's code bundle.

- ▸ The Wikipedia page about the STFT at `https://en.wikipedia.org/wiki/Short-time_Fourier_transform` (retrieved September 2015)

- ▸ The Wikipedia page about the cepstrum at `https://en.wikipedia.org/wiki/Cepstrum` (retrieved September 2015)

- ▸ The Wikipedia page about the mel scale at `https://en.wikipedia.org/wiki/Mel_scale` (retrieved September 2015)

Analyzing signals with the discrete cosine transform

The **discrete cosine transform** (**DCT**) is a transform similar to the Fourier transform, but it tries to represent a signal by a sum of cosine terms only (refer to equation 6.11). The DCT is used for signal compression and in the calculation of the **mel frequency** spectrum, which I mentioned in the *Analyzing the frequency spectrum of audio* recipe. We can convert normal frequencies to the mel frequency (a frequency more appropriate for the analysis of speech and music) with the following equation:

$$(6.10) \quad m = 1127 \log\left(1 + \frac{f}{700}\right)$$

$$(6.11) \quad X_k = \sum_{n=0}^{N-1} x_n \cos\left[\frac{\pi}{N}\left(n + \frac{1}{2}\right)k\right] \quad k = 0, \ldots, N-1$$

The steps to create the mel frequency spectrum are not complicated, but there are quite a few of them. The relevant Wikipedia page is available at `https://en.wikipedia.org/wiki/Mel-frequency_cepstrum` (retrieved September 2015). If you do a quick web search, you can find a couple of Python libraries that implement the algorithm. I implemented a very simple version of the computation in this recipe.

How to do it...

1. The imports are as follows:

```
import dautil as dl
from scipy.fftpack import dct
import matplotlib.pyplot as plt
import ch6util
import seaborn as sns
import numpy as np
from IPython.display import HTML
```

2. Load the data and transform it as follows:

```
rate, audio = ch6util.read_wav()
transformed = dct(audio)
```

3. Plot the amplitude spectrum using DCT:

```
sp = dl.plotting.Subplotter(2, 2, context)
freqs = np.fft.fftfreq(audio.size, 1./rate)
indices = np.where(freqs > 0)[0]
sp.ax.semilogy(np.abs(transformed)[indices])
sp.label()
```

4. Plot the distribution of the amplitude:

```
sns.distplot(np.log(np.abs(transformed)), ax=sp.next_ax())
sp.label()
```

5. Plot the distribution of the phase:

```
sns.distplot(np.angle(transformed), ax=sp.next_ax())
sp.label()
```

6. Plot the mel amplitude spectrum as follows:

```
magnitude = ch6util.amplitude(audio)
cepstrum = dl.ts.power(np.fft.ifft(np.log(magnitude ** 2)))
mel = 1127 * np.log(1 + freqs[indices]/700)
sp.next_ax().plot(mel, ch6util.amplitude(dct(np.
log(magnitude[indices] ** 2))))
sp.label()
HTML(sp.exit())
```

Refer to the following screenshot for the end result:

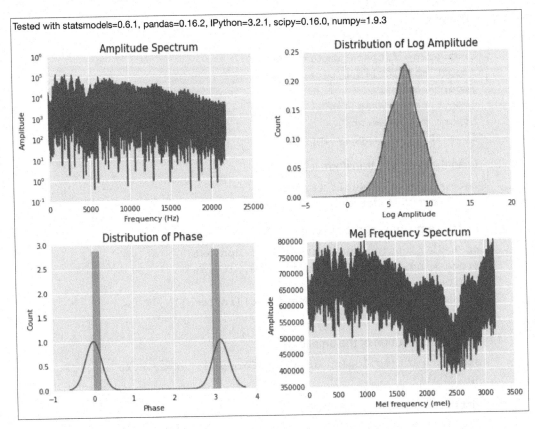

The code for this recipe is in the `analyzing_dct.ipynb` file in this book's code bundle.

See also

▸ The Wikipedia page about the mel scale at `https://en.wikipedia.org/wiki/Mel_scale` (retrieved September 2015)

▸ The Wikipedia page about the DCT at `https://en.wikipedia.org/wiki/Discrete_cosine_transform` (retrieved September 2015)

Block bootstrapping time series data

The usual bootstrapping method doesn't preserve the ordering of time series data, and it is, therefore, unsuitable for trend estimation. In the **block bootstrapping** approach, we split data into non-overlapping blocks of equal size and use those blocks to generate new samples. In this recipe, we will apply a very naive and easy-to-implement linear model with annual temperature data. The procedure for this recipe is as follows:

1. Split the data into blocks and generate new data samples.

2. Fit the data to a line or calculate the first differences of the new data.

3. Repeat the previous step to build a list of slopes or medians of the first differences.

How to do it...

1. The imports are as follows:

```
import dautil as dl
import random
import matplotlib.pyplot as plt
import pandas as pd
import numpy as np
import seaborn as sns
import ch6util
from IPython.display import HTML
```

2. Define the following function to bootstrap the data:

```
def shuffle(temp, blocks):
    random.shuffle(blocks)
    df = pd.DataFrame({'TEMP': dl.collect.flatten(blocks)},
                      index=temp.index)
    df = df.resample('A')

    return df
```

3. Load the data and create blocks from it:

```
temp = dl.data.Weather.load()['TEMP'].resample('M').dropna()
blocks = list(dl.collect.chunk(temp.values, 100))
random.seed(12033)
```

4. Plot a couple of random realizations as a sanity check:

```
sp = dl.plotting.Subplotter(2, 2, context)
cp = dl.plotting.CyclePlotter(sp.ax)
medians = []
slopes = []

for i in range(240):
    df = shuffle(temp, blocks)
    slopes.append(ch6util.fit(df))
    medians.append(ch6util.diff_median(df))

    if i < 5:
        cp.plot(df.index, df.values)

sp.label(ylabel_params=dl.data.Weather.get_header('TEMP'))
```

5. Plot the distribution of the first difference medians using the bootstrapped data:

```
sns.distplot(medians, ax=sp.next_ax(), norm_hist=True)
sp.label()
```

6. Plot the distribution of the linear regression slopes using the bootstrapped data:

```
sns.distplot(slopes, ax=sp.next_ax(), norm_hist=True)
sp.label()
```

7. Plot the confidence intervals for a varying number of bootstraps:

```
mins = []
tops = []
xrng = range(30, len(medians))

for i in xrng:
    min, max = dl.stats.outliers(medians[:i])
    mins.append(min)
    tops.append(max)

cp = dl.plotting.CyclePlotter(sp.next_ax())
cp.plot(xrng, mins, label='5 %')
cp.plot(xrng, tops, label='95 %')
sp.label()
HTML(sp.exit())
```

Refer to the following screenshot for the end result:

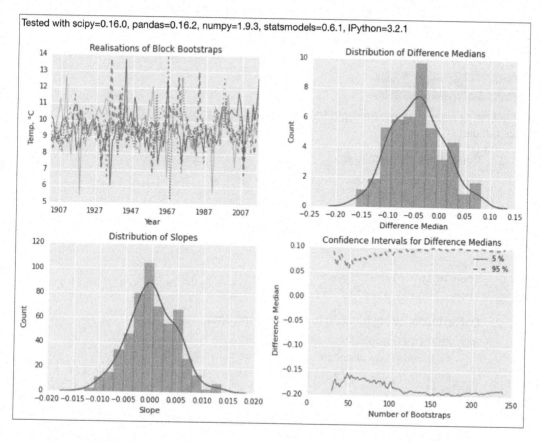

Tested with scipy=0.16.0, pandas=0.16.2, numpy=1.9.3, statsmodels=0.6.1, IPython=3.2.1

The following code comes from the `block_boot.ipynb` file in this book's code bundle.

See also

▶ The relevant Wikipedia page at https://en.wikipedia.org/wiki/Bootstrapping_%28statistics%29#Block_bootstrap (retrieved September 2015)

Moving block bootstrapping time series data

If you followed along with the *Block bootstrapping time series data* recipe, you are now aware of a simple bootstrapping scheme for time series data. The **moving block bootstrapping** algorithm is a bit more complicated. In this scheme, we generate overlapping blocks by moving a fixed size window, similar to the moving average. We then assemble the blocks to create new data samples.

In this recipe, we will apply the moving block bootstrap to annual temperature data to generate lists of second difference medians and the slope of an AR(1) model. This is an autoregressive model with lag 1. Also, we will try to neutralize outliers and noise with a median filter.

How to do it...

The following code snippets are from the `moving_boot.ipynb` file in this book's code bundle:

1. The imports are as follows:

```
import dautil as dl
import numpy as np
import pandas as pd
import matplotlib.pyplot as plt
import seaborn as sns
import ch6util
from scipy.signal import medfilt
from IPython.display import HTML
```

2. Define the following function to bootstrap the data:

```
def shuffle(temp):
    indices = np.random.choice(start, n/12)
    sample = dl.collect.flatten([temp.values[i: i + 12] for i in
indices])
    sample = medfilt(sample)
    df = pd.DataFrame({'TEMP': sample}, index=temp.
index[:len(sample)])
    df = df.resample('A', how=np.median)

    return df
```

3. Load the data as follows:

```
temp = dl.data.Weather.load()['TEMP'].resample('M', how=np.
median).dropna()
n = len(temp)
start = np.arange(n - 11)
np.random.seed(2609787)
```

4. Plot a few random realizations as a sanity check:

```
sp = dl.plotting.Subplotter(2, 2, context)
cp = dl.plotting.CyclePlotter(sp.ax)
medians = []
slopes = []

for i in range(240):
    df = shuffle(temp)
    slopes.append(dl.ts.ar1(df.values.flatten())['slope'])
    medians.append(ch6util.diff_median(df, 2))

    if i < 5:
        cp.plot(df.index, df.values)

sp.label(ylabel_params=dl.data.Weather.get_header('TEMP'))
```

5. Plot the distribution of the second difference medians using the bootstrapped data:

```
sns.distplot(medians, ax=sp.next_ax())
sp.label()
```

6. Plot the distribution of the AR(1) model slopes using the bootstrapped data:

```
sns.distplot(slopes, ax=sp.next_ax())
sp.label()
```

7. Plot the confidence intervals for a varying number of bootstraps:

```
mins = []
tops = []
xrng = range(30, len(medians))

for i in xrng:
    min, max = dl.stats.outliers(medians[:i])
    mins.append(min)
    tops.append(max)


cp = dl.plotting.CyclePlotter(sp.next_ax())
cp.plot(xrng, mins, label='5 %')
cp.plot(xrng, tops, label='95 %')
sp.label()
HTML(sp.exit())
```

Refer to the following screenshot for the end result:

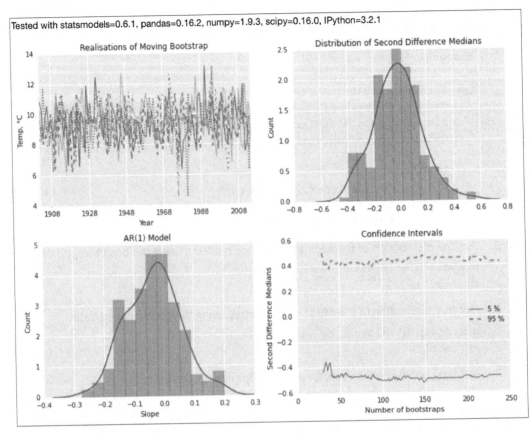

See also

▸ The relevant Wikipedia page at `https://en.wikipedia.org/wiki/Bootstrapping_%28statistics%29#Block_bootstrap` (retrieved September 2015)

▸ The `medfilt()` documentation at `https://docs.scipy.org/doc/scipy/reference/generated/scipy.signal.medfilt.html` (retrieved September 2015)

Applying the discrete wavelet transform

The **discrete wavelet transform** (**DWT**) captures information in both the time and frequency domains. The mathematician Alfred Haar created the first wavelet. We will use this **Haar wavelet** in this recipe too. The transform returns **approximation** and **detail coefficients**, which we need to use together to get the original signal back. The approximation coefficients are the result of a low-pass filter. A high-pass filter produces the detail coefficients. The Haar wavelet algorithm is of order O(n) and, similar to the STFT algorithm (refer to the *Analyzing the frequency spectrum of audio* recipe), combines frequency and time information.

The difference with the Fourier transform is that we express the signal as a sum of sine and cosine terms, while the wavelet is represented by a single wave (wavelet function). Just as in the STFT, we split the signal in the time domain and then apply the wavelet function to each segment. The DWT can have multiple levels in this recipe, we don't go further than the first level. To obtain the next level, we apply the wavelet to the approximation coefficients of the previous level. This means that we can have multiple level detail coefficients.

As the dataset, we will have a look at the famous Nile river flow, which even the Greek historian Herodotus wrote about. More recently, in the previous century, the hydrologist Hurst discovered a power law for the **rescaled range** of the Nile river flow in the year. Refer to the *See also* section for more information. The rescaled range is not difficult to compute, but there are lots of steps as described in the following equations:

$$(6.12) \quad Y_t = X_t - m \; for \; t = 1, 2, \ldots, n$$

$$(6.13) \quad Z_t = \sum_{i=1}^{t} Y_i \; for \; t = 1, 2, \ldots, n$$

$$(6.14) \quad R_t = \max\left(Z_1, Z_2, \ldots, Z_t\right) - \min\left(Z_1, Z_2, \ldots, Z_t\right) \; for \; t = 1, 2, \ldots, n$$

$$(6.15) \quad S_t = \sqrt{\frac{1}{t} \sum_{i=1}^{t} \left(X_i - m(t)\right)^2} \; for \; t = 1, 2, \ldots, n$$

$$(6.16) \quad \left(R/S\right)_t = \frac{R_t}{S_t} \; for \; t = 1, 2, \ldots, n$$

The **Hurst exponent** from the power law is an indicator of trends. We can also get the Hurst exponent with a more efficient procedure from the wavelet coefficients.

Getting started

Install `pywavelets`, as follows:

```
$ pip install pywavelets
```

I used `pywavelets` 0.3.0 for this recipe.

How to do it...

1. The imports are as follows:

```
from statsmodels import datasets
import matplotlib.pyplot as plt
import pywt
import pandas as pd
import dautil as dl
import numpy as np
import seaborn as sns
import warnings
from IPython.display import HTML
```

2. Filter warnings as follows (optional step):

```
warnings.filterwarnings(action='ignore',
                        message='.*Mean of empty slice.*')
warnings.filterwarnings(action='ignore',
                        message='.*Degrees of freedom <= 0 for
slice.*')
```

3. Define the following function to calculate the rescaled range:

```
def calc_rescaled_range(X):
    N = len(X)

    # 1. Mean
    mean = X.mean()

    # 2. Y mean adjusted
    Y = X - mean

    # 3. Z cumulative deviates
    Z = np.array([Y[:i].sum() for i in range(N)])

    # 4. Range R
    R = np.array([0] + [np.ptp(Z[:i]) for i in range(1, N)])
```

```
# 5. Standard deviation S
S = np.array([X[:i].std() for i in range(N)])

# 6. Average partial R/S
return [np.nanmean(R[:i]/S[:i]) for i in range(N)]
```

4. Load the data and transform it with a Haar wavelet:

```
data = datasets.get_rdataset('Nile', cache=True).data
cA, cD = pywt.dwt(data['Nile'].values, 'haar')
coeff = pd.DataFrame({'cA': cA, 'cD': cD})
```

5. Plot the Nile river flow as follows:

```
sp = dl.plotting.Subplotter(2, 2, context)
sp.ax.plot(data['time'], data['Nile'])
sp.label()
```

6. Plot the approximation and detail coefficients of the transformed data:

```
cp = dl.plotting.CyclePlotter(sp.next_ax())
cp.plot(range(len(cA)), cA, label='Approximation coefficients')
cp.plot(range(len(cD)), cD, label='Detail coefficients')
sp.label()
```

7. Plot the rescaled ranges of the coefficients as follows:

```
sp.next_ax().loglog(range(len(cA)), calc_rescaled_range(cA),
                    label='Approximation coefficients')
sp.ax.loglog(range(len(cD)), calc_rescaled_range(cD),
             label='Detail coefficients')
sp.label()
```

8. Plot the rescaled ranges of the Nile river flow data with a fit:

```
range_df = pd.DataFrame(data={'Year': data.index,
                              'Rescaled range':
                              calc_rescaled_range(data['Nile'])})
sp.next_ax().set(xscale="log", yscale="log")
sns.regplot('Year', 'Rescaled range', range_df, ax=sp.ax, order=1,
            scatter_kws={"s": 100})
sp.label()
HTML(sp.exit())
```

Refer to the following screenshot for the end result:

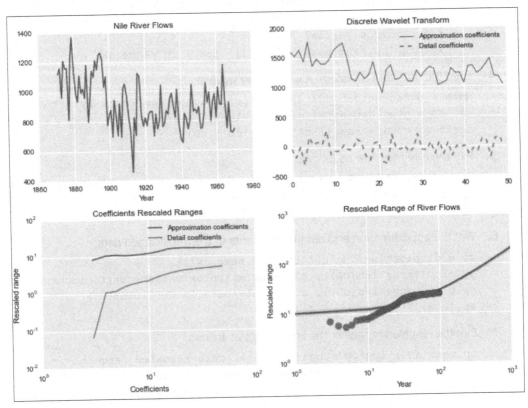

The relevant code is in the `discrete_wavelet.ipynb` file in this book's code bundle.

See also

- The Wikipedia page about the discrete wavelet transform at `https://en.wikipedia.org/wiki/Discrete_wavelet_transform` (retrieved September 2015)
- The Wikipedia page about the rescaled range at `https://en.wikipedia.org/wiki/Rescaled_range` (retrieved September 2015)
- The Wikipedia page about the Hurst exponent at `https://en.wikipedia.org/wiki/Hurst_exponent` (retrieved September 2015)

7
Selecting Stocks with Financial Data Analysis

In this chapter, we will cover the following recipes:

- ▸ Computing simple and log returns
- ▸ Ranking stocks with the Sharpe ratio and liquidity
- ▸ Ranking stocks with the Calmar and Sortino ratios
- ▸ Analyzing returns statistics
- ▸ Correlating individual stocks with the broader market
- ▸ Exploring risk and return
- ▸ Examining the market with the non-parametric runs test
- ▸ Testing for random walks
- ▸ Determining market efficiency with autoregressive models
- ▸ Creating tables for a stock prices database
- ▸ Populating the stock prices database
- ▸ Optimizing an equal weights two-asset portfolio

Introduction

Finance deals with many subjects, such as money, saving, investing, and insurance. In this chapter, we will focus on stock investing because stock price data is abundant. According to academic theory, an average investor should not invest in individual stocks, but in whole markets, for instance, a basket of stocks representing large companies within a country. Economists make several such arguments for this theory. First, financial markets are random; therefore, beating an average basket by picking stocks is very difficult. Second, individual stocks are volatile with wild price swings. These price moves get averaged in a basket, which makes investing in a group of stocks less risky.

We will analyze stock prices, but nothing prevents you from reusing the recipes to analyze mutual funds and exchange traded funds or other financial assets. To keep the analysis simple, I limited the selection to half a dozen stocks for well-known U.S. companies, which are also represented in the S&P 500 stock index.

Computing simple and log returns

Returns measure the rate of change of (stock) prices. The advantage of using returns is that returns are dimensionless, so we can easily compare the returns of different financial securities. In contrast, the price of financial assets alone doesn't tell us much. In this chapter, we calculate daily returns because our data is sampled daily. With small adjustments, you should be able to apply the same analysis on different time frames.

In fact, there are various types of returns. For the purpose of basic analysis, we only need to know about simple (7.1) and log(arithmic) returns (7.2), as given by the following equations:

$$(7.1) \quad r = \frac{V_f - V_i}{V_i}$$

$$(7.2) \quad R = \ln\left(\frac{V_f}{V_i}\right)$$

Actually these types of returns can easily be converted – from simple to log returns and back. Log returns are the ones you should prefer if you are given the choice, because they are easier to compute.

How to do it...

1. The imports are as follows:

```
import dautil as dl
import ch7util
import matplotlib.pyplot as plt
```

2. Download data for the S&P 500 index:

```
ohlc = dl.data.OHLC()
sp500 = ohlc.get('^GSPC')['Adj Close']
rets = sp500[1:]/sp500[:-1] - 1
```

3. Plot the simple and log returns:

```
_, ax = plt.subplots()
cp = dl.plotting.CyclePlotter(ax)
cp.plot(sp500.index, rets, label='Simple')
cp.plot(sp500.index[1:], ch7util.log_rets(sp500), label='Log')
ax.set_title('Simple and Log Returns')
ax.set_xlabel('Date')
ax.set_ylabel('Return')
ax.legend(loc='best')
```

Refer to the following screenshot for the end result (the values of simple and log returns are very close):

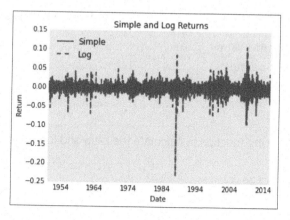

The code for this recipe is in the `simple_log_rets.ipynb` file in this book's code bundle.

See also

▸ The relevant Wikipedia page at `https://en.wikipedia.org/wiki/Rate_of_return` (retrieved October 2015)

Ranking stocks with the Sharpe ratio and liquidity

The **Sharpe ratio**, defined by William Sharpe, is a fundamental investing metric. The ratio is given as follows:

$$(7.3) \quad S_a = \frac{E[R_a - R_b]}{\sigma_a} = \frac{E[R_a - R_b]}{\sqrt{\text{var}[R_a - R_b]}}$$

The ratio depends on the returns of the asset and the returns of a benchmark. We will use the S&P 500 index as the benchmark. The ratio is supposed to represent a reward to risk ratio. We want to maximize reward while minimizing risk, which corresponds to maximizing the Sharpe ratio.

Another important investing variable is liquidity. Cash is the ultimate liquid asset, but most other assets are less liquid, which means that they change value when we try to sell or buy them. We will use trading volume in this recipe as a measure of liquidity. (Trading volume corresponds to the number of transactions for a financial asset. Liquidity measures how liquid an asset is—how easy it is to buy or sell it.)

How to do it...

You can find the code in the `sharpe_liquidity.ipynb` file in this book's code bundle:

1. The imports are as follows:

```
import numpy as np
import dautil as dl
import matplotlib.pyplot as plt
import ch7util
```

2. Define the following function to calculate the ratio and logarithm of the average trading volume:

```
def calc_metrics(ticker, ohlc):
    stock = ohlc.get(ticker)
    sp500 = ohlc.get('^GSPC')
    merged = ch7util.merge_sp500(stock, sp500)
    rets_stock = ch7util.log_rets(merged['Adj Close_stock'])
    rets_sp500 = ch7util.log_rets(merged['Adj Close_sp500'])
    stock_sp500 = rets_stock - rets_sp500
    sharpe_stock = stock_sp500.mean()/stock_sp500.std()
```

```
        avg_vol = np.log(merged['Volume_stock'].mean())

        return (sharpe_stock, avg_vol)
```

3. Calculate the metrics for our basket of stocks from the `ch7util` module:

    ```
    dfb = dl.report.DFBuilder(cols=['Ticker', 'Sharpe', 'Log(Average
    Volume)'])

    ohlc = dl.data.OHLC()

    for symbol in ch7util.STOCKS:
        sharpe, vol = calc_metrics(symbol, ohlc)
        dfb.row([symbol, sharpe, vol])

    df = dfb.build(index=ch7util.STOCKS)
    ```

4. Plot the ratio and logarithm average volume for the stocks:

    ```
    _, ax = plt.subplots()
    ax.scatter(df['Log(Average Volume)'], df['Sharpe'])
    dl.plotting.plot_polyfit(ax, df['Log(Average Volume)'],
    df['Sharpe'])

    dl.plotting.plot_text(ax, df['Log(Average Volume)'],
                        df['Sharpe'], ch7util.STOCKS)
    ax.set_xlabel('Log(Average Volume)')
    ax.set_ylabel('Sharpe')
    ax.set_title('Sharpe Ratio & Liquidity')
    ```

Refer to the following screenshot for the end result:

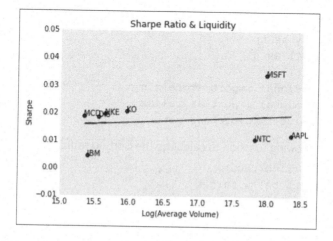

▶ The relevant Wikipedia page at `https://en.wikipedia.org/wiki/Sharpe_ratio` (retrieved October 2015)

Ranking stocks with the Calmar and Sortino ratios

The **Sortino** and **Calmar ratios** are performance ratios comparable to the Sharpe ratio (refer to the *Ranking stocks with the Sharpe ratio and liquidity* recipe). There are even more ratios; however, the Sharpe ratio has been around the longest, and is therefore very widely used.

The Sortino ratio is named after Frank Sortino, but it was defined by Brian Rom. The ratio defines risk as a downside variance below a benchmark. The benchmark can be an index or a fixed return such as zero. The ratio is defined as follows:

$$(7.4) \quad S = \frac{R - T}{DR}$$

R is the return of the asset, *T* the target benchmark, and *DR* the downside risk. The Calmar ratio was invented by Terry Young and was named after his company and newsletter. This ratio defines risk as the **maximum drawdown** (price fall from a peak to a bottom) of an asset.

How to do it...

The following is a breakdown of the `calmar_sortino.ipynb` file in this book's code bundle:

1. The imports are as follows:

```
import numpy as np
import dautil as dl
import ch7util
from scipy.signal import argrelmin
from scipy.signal import argrelmax
import matplotlib.pyplot as plt
```

2. Define the following function to calculate the Sortino ratio:

```
def calc_sortino(rets):
    # Returns below target
    semi_var = rets[rets < 0] ** 2
```

```
    semi_var = semi_var.sum()/len(rets)
    sortino = np.sqrt(semi_var)

    return rets.mean()/sortino
```

3. Define the following function to calculate the Calmar ratio:

```
def calc_calmar(rets):
    # Peaks and bottoms indexes in sequence
    mins = np.ravel(argrelmin(rets))
    maxs = np.ravel(argrelmax(rets))
    extrema = np.concatenate((mins, maxs))
    extrema.sort()

    return -rets.mean()/np.diff(rets[extrema]).min()
```

4. Compute the Calmar and Sortino ratios for our list of stocks:

```
ohlc = dl.data.OHLC()
dfb = dl.report.DFBuilder(cols=['Ticker', 'Sortino', 'Calmar'])

for symbol in ch7util.STOCKS:
    stock = ohlc.get(symbol)
    rets = ch7util.log_rets(stock['Adj Close'])
    sortino = calc_sortino(rets)
    calmar = calc_calmar(rets)
    dfb.row([symbol, sortino, calmar])

df = dfb.build(index=ch7util.STOCKS).dropna()
```

5. Plot the Sortino and Calmar ratios for the stocks:

```
_, ax = plt.subplots()
ax.scatter(df['Sortino'], df['Calmar'])
dl.plotting.plot_polyfit(ax, df['Sortino'], df['Calmar'])
dl.plotting.plot_text(ax, df['Sortino'], df['Calmar'], ch7util.
STOCKS)
ax.set_xlabel('Sortino')
ax.set_ylabel('Calmar')
ax.set_title('Sortino & Calmar Ratios')
```

Refer to the following screenshot for the end result:

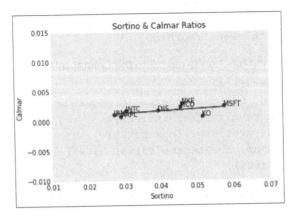

See also

▶ The Wikipedia page about the Sortino ratio at `https://en.wikipedia.org/wiki/Sortino_ratio` (retrieved October 2015)

▶ The Wikipedia page about the Calmar ratio at `https://en.wikipedia.org/wiki/Calmar_ratio` (retrieved October 2015)

Analyzing returns statistics

Returns, especially of stock indices, have been extensively studied. In the past, it was assumed that the returns are normally distributed. However, it is now clear that the returns distribution has fat tails (fatter than normal distributions). More information is available at `https://en.wikipedia.org/wiki/Fat-tailed_distribution` (retrieved October 2015). It is easy enough to check whether data fits the normal distribution. All we need is the mean and standard deviation of the sample.

There are a number of topics that we will explore in this recipe:

▶ The skewness and kurtosis of stock returns are interesting to study. Skewness is especially important in the context of stock option models. Analysts usually limit themselves to the mean and standard deviation, which are assumed to correspond to reward and risk, respectively.

▶ If we are interested in the existence of a trend, then we should take a look at an autocorrelation plot. This is a plot of autocorrelation—that is, correlation between a signal and the signal at a certain lag (also explained in *Python Data Analysis, Packt Publishing*).

▶ We will also plot negative returns (absolute value thereof) and corresponding counts on a log-log scale, as those approximately seem to follow a power law (especially the tail values).

How to do it...

The analysis can be found in the `rets_stats.ipynb` file in this book's code bundle:

1. The imports are as follows:

```
import dautil as dl
import ch7util
import matplotlib.pyplot as plt
from scipy.stats import skew
from scipy.stats import kurtosis
from pandas.tools.plotting import autocorrelation_plot
import numpy as np
from scipy.stats import norm
from IPython.display import HTML
```

2. Calculate returns for our stocks:

```
ohlc = dl.data.OHLC()
rets_dict = {}

for i, symbol in enumerate(ch7util.STOCKS):
    rets = ch7util.log_rets(ohlc.get(symbol)['Adj Close'])
    rets_dict[symbol] = rets

sp500 = ch7util.log_rets(ohlc.get('^GSPC')['Adj Close'])
```

3. Plot the histogram of the S&P 500 returns and corresponding theoretical normal distribution:

```
sp = dl.plotting.Subplotter(2, 2, context)
sp.ax.set_xlim(-0.05, 0.05)
_, bins, _ = sp.ax.hist(sp500, bins=dl.stats.sqrt_bins(sp500),
                        alpha=0.6, normed=True)
sp.ax.plot(bins, norm.pdf(bins, sp500.mean(), sp500.std()), lw=2)
```

4. Plot the skew and kurtosis of returns:

```
skews = [skew(rets_dict[s]) for s in ch7util.STOCKS]
kurts = [kurtosis(rets_dict[s]) for s in ch7util.STOCKS]
sp.label()

sp.next_ax().scatter(skews, kurts)
dl.plotting.plot_text(sp.ax, skews, kurts, ch7util.STOCKS)
sp.label()
```

5. Plot the autocorrelation plot of the S&P 500 returns:

```
autocorrelation_plot(sp500, ax=sp.next_ax())
sp.label()
```

6. Plot the log-log plot of negative returns (absolute value) and counts:

```
# Negative returns
counts, neg_rets = np.histogram(sp500[sp500 < 0])
neg_rets = neg_rets[:-1] + (neg_rets[1] - neg_rets[0])/2
# Adding 1 to avoid log(0)
dl.plotting.plot_polyfit(sp.next_ax(), np.log(np.abs(neg_rets)),
                         np.log(counts + 1), plot_points=True)

sp.label()

HTML(sp.exit())
```

Refer to the following screenshot for the end result:

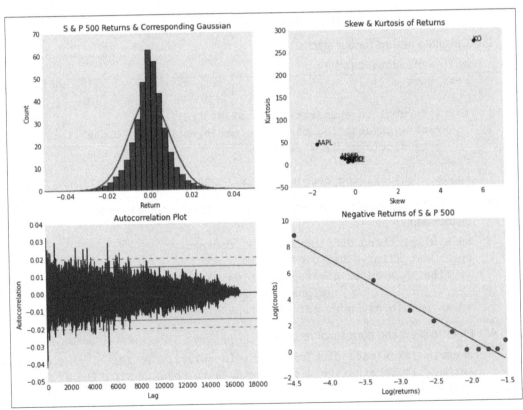

Correlating individual stocks with the broader market

When we define a stock market or index, we usually choose stocks that are similar in some way. For instance, the stocks might be in the same country or continent. The position of birds can be roughly estimated from the position of the flock they belong to. Similarly, we expect stock returns to be correlated to their market, although not necessarily perfectly.

We will explore the following metrics:

▶ The most obvious metric is purportedly the correlation coefficient of the individual stock returns and the S&P 500 index.

▶ Another metric is the slope obtained from linear regression instead of correlation.

▶ We can also analyze squared differences of returns somewhat similar to squared errors in regression diagnostics.

▶ Instead of correlating returns, we can also correlate trading volumes and volatility. To measure volatility, we will use the somewhat uncommon squared value of high and low prices difference. Actually, we are supposed to divide this value by a constant; however, this is not necessary for the correlation coefficient calculation.

How to do it...

The analysis is in the `correlating_market.ipynb` file in this book's code bundle:

1. The imports are as follows:

```
import ch7util
import dautil as dl
import numpy as np
import matplotlib.pyplot as plt
from IPython.display import HTML
```

2. Define the following function to compute the volatility:

```
def hl2(df, suffix):
    high = df['High_' + suffix]
    low = df['Low_' + suffix]

    return (high - low) ** 2
```

3. Define the following function to correlate the S&P 500 and our stocks:

```
def correlate(stock, sp500):
    merged = ch7util.merge_sp500(stock, sp500)
    rets = ch7util.log_rets(merged['Adj Close_stock'])
    sp500_rets = ch7util.log_rets(merged['Adj Close_sp500'])
    result = {}

    result['corrcoef'] = np.corrcoef(rets, sp500_rets)[0][1]
    slope, _ = np.polyfit(sp500_rets, rets, 1)
    result['slope'] = slope

    srd = (sp500_rets - rets) ** 2
    result['msrd'] = srd.mean()
    result['std_srd'] = srd.std()

    result['vols'] = np.corrcoef(merged['Volume_stock'],
                                 merged['Volume_sp500'])[0][1]

    result['hl2'] = np.corrcoef(hl2(merged, 'stock'),
                                hl2(merged, 'sp500'))[0][1]


    return result
```

4. Correlate our set of stocks with the S&P 500 index:

```
ohlc = dl.data.OHLC()
dfs = [ohlc.get(stock) for stock in ch7util.STOCKS]
sp500 = ohlc.get('^GSPC')
corrs = [correlate(df, sp500) for df in dfs]
```

5. Plot correlation coefficients for the stocks:

```
sp = dl.plotting.Subplotter(2, 2, context)
dl.plotting.bar(sp.ax, ch7util.STOCKS,
                [corr['corrcoef'] for corr in corrs])
sp.label()

dl.plotting.bar(sp.next_ax(), ch7util.STOCKS,
                [corr['slope'] for corr in corrs])
sp.label()
```

6. Plot the squared difference statistics:

```
sp.next_ax().set_xlim([0, 0.001])
dl.plotting.plot_text(sp.ax, [corr['msrd'] for corr in corrs],
                      [corr['std_srd'] for corr in corrs],
```

```
                              ch7util.STOCKS, add_scatter=True,
                              fontsize=9, alpha=0.6)
        sp.label()
```

7. Plot volume and volatility correlation coefficients:

```
dl.plotting.plot_text(sp.next_ax(), [corr['vols'] for corr in
corrs],

                      [corr['hl2'] for corr in corrs],
                      ch7util.STOCKS, add_scatter=True,
                      fontsize=9, alpha=0.6)
        sp.label()


        HTML(sp.exit())
```

Refer to the following screenshot for the end result:

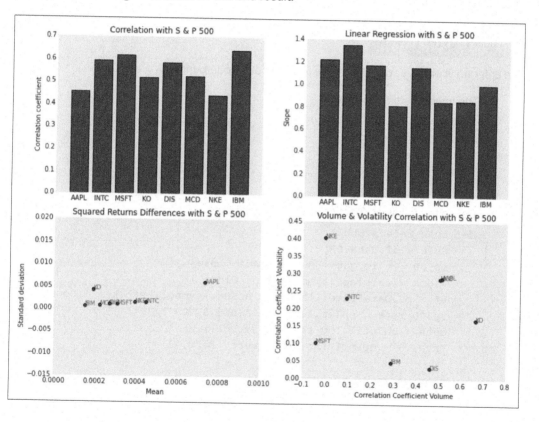

Exploring risk and return

Beta in finance is the slope of a linear regression model involving the returns of the asset and the returns of a benchmark, for instance the S&P 500 index. The model is defined as follows:

$$(7.5) \quad r_{a,t} = \alpha + \beta r_{b,t} + \varepsilon_t$$

According to the **Capital Asset Pricing Model** (**CAPM**), beta is a measure for risk. The expected return is given by the average of the returns. If we plot betas and expected returns for various securities, we obtain the **security market line** (**SML**) for the corresponding market. The intercept of the SML gives the **risk-free rate**, a return we should theoretically receive without taking any risk. In general, if an asset doesn't lie on the SML, then it is mispriced according to the CAPM.

How to do it...

The program is in the `capm.ipynb` file in this book's code bundle:

1. The imports are as follows:

```
import dautil as dl
import numpy as np
import pandas as pd
import ch7util
import matplotlib.pyplot as plt
```

2. Define the following function to calculate the beta:

```
def calc_beta(symbol):
    ohlc = dl.data.OHLC()
    sp500 = ohlc.get('^GSPC')['Adj Close']
    stock = ohlc.get(symbol)['Adj Close']
    df = pd.DataFrame({'SP500': sp500, symbol: stock}).dropna()
    sp500_rets = ch7util.log_rets(df['SP500'])
    rets = ch7util.log_rets(df[symbol])
    beta, _ = np.polyfit(sp500_rets, rets, 1)

    # annualize & percentify
    return beta, 252 * rets.mean() * 100
```

3. Compute betas and average returns for our stocks:

```
betas = []
means = []

for symbol in ch7util.STOCKS:
    beta, ret_mean = calc_beta(symbol)
    betas.append(beta)
    means.append(ret_mean)
```

4. Plot the results and the market security line:

```
_, ax = plt.subplots()
dl.plotting.plot_text(ax, betas, means, ch7util.STOCKS, add_
scatter=True)
dl.plotting.plot_polyfit(ax, betas, means)
ax.set_title('Capital Asset Pricing Model')
ax.set_xlabel('Beta')
ax.set_ylabel('Mean annual return (%)')
```

Refer to the following screenshot for the end result:

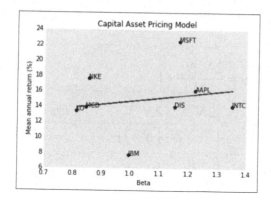

See also

- The Wikipedia page about beta at `https://en.wikipedia.org/wiki/Beta_%28finance%29` (retrieved October 2015)
- The Wikipedia page about the CAPM at `https://en.wikipedia.org/wiki/Capital_asset_pricing_model` (retrieved October 2015)

Examining the market with the non-parametric runs test

The **efficient-market hypothesis** (**EMH**) stipulates that you can't, on average, "beat the market" by picking better stocks or timing the market. According to the EMH, all information about the market is immediately available to every market participant in one form or another, and it is immediately reflected in asset prices, so investing is like playing a game of cards with all the cards revealed. The only way you can win is by betting on very risky stocks and getting lucky.

The French mathematician Bachelor developed a test for the EMH around 1900. The test examines consecutive occurrences of negative and positive price changes. We don't count events during which the price didn't change and only use them to end a run. These types of events are relatively rare anyway for liquid markets.

The statistical test itself is known outside finance and goes by the name of the **Wald-Wolfowitz runs test**. If we denote positive changes with '+' and negative changes with '-', we can have the sequence '++++---++--+++++' with 5 runs. The following equations for the mean μ (7.6), standard deviation σ (7.7), and z-score Z (7.8) of the number of runs R also require the number of negative changes $N-$, positive changes $N+$, and total number of changes N:

$$(7.6) \quad \mu = \frac{2N_+ N_-}{N} + 1$$

$$(7.7) \quad \sigma^2 = \frac{2N_+ N_- (2N_+ N_- - N)}{N^2 (N-1)} = \frac{(\mu-1)(\mu-2)}{N-1}$$

$$(7.8) \quad Z = \frac{R - \mu}{\sigma}$$

We assume that the number of runs follow a normal distribution, which gives us a way to potentially reject the randomness of runs at a confidence level of our choosing.

How to do it...

Have a look at the non_parametric.ipynb file in this book's code bundle.

1. The imports are as follows:

```
import dautil as dl
import numpy as np
import pandas as pd
import ch7util
```

```
import matplotlib.pyplot as plt
from scipy.stats import norm
from IPython.display import HTML
```

2. Define the following function to count the number of runs:

```
def count_runs(signs):
    nruns = 0
    prev = None

    for s in signs:
        if s != 0 and s != prev:
            nruns += 1

        prev = s

    return nruns
```

3. Define the following function to calculate the mean, standard deviation, and z-score:

```
def proc_runs(symbol):
    ohlc = dl.data.OHLC()
    close = ohlc.get(symbol)['Adj Close'].values
    diffs = np.diff(close)
    nplus = (diffs > 0).sum()
    nmin = (diffs < 0).sum()
    n = nplus + nmin
    mean = (2 * (nplus * nmin) / n) + 1
    var = (mean - 1) * (mean - 2) / (n - 1)
    std = np.sqrt(var)
    signs = np.sign(diffs)
    nruns = count_runs(np.diff(signs))

    return mean, std, (nruns - mean) / std
```

4. Calculate the metrics for our stocks:

```
means = []
stds = []
zscores = []

for symbol in ch7util.STOCKS:
    mean, std, zscore = proc_runs(symbol)
    means.append(mean)
    stds.append(std)
    zscores.append(zscore)
```

5. Plot the z-scores with a line indicating the 95% confidence level:

```
sp = dl.plotting.Subplotter(2, 1, context)
dl.plotting.plot_text(sp.ax, means, stds, ch7util.STOCKS, add_
scatter=True)
sp.label()

dl.plotting.bar(sp.next_ax(), ch7util.STOCKS, zscores)
sp.ax.axhline(norm.ppf(0.95), label='95 % confidence level')
sp.label()
HTML(sp.exit())
```

Refer to the following screenshot for the end result:

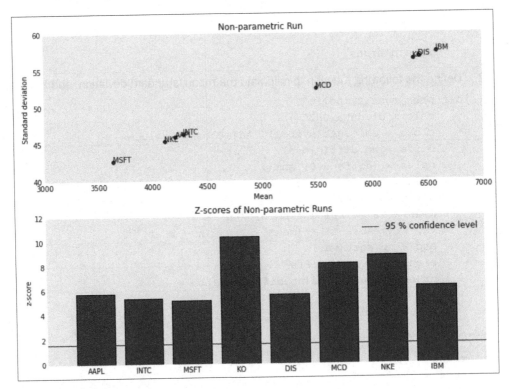

See also

► The Wikipedia page about the Wald-Wolfowitz runs test at `https://en.wikipedia.org/wiki/Wald%E2%80%93Wolfowitz_runs_test` (retrieved October 2015)

► The Wikipedia page about the EMH at `https://en.wikipedia.org/wiki/Efficient-market_hypothesis` (retrieved October 2015)

Testing for random walks

The **random walk hypothesis** (**RWH**) just like the efficient-market hypothesis (refer to the *Examining the market with the non-parametric runs test* recipe) claims that the market cannot be beaten. The RWH stipulates that asset prices perform a random walk. You can in fact generate pretty convincing stock price charts just by flipping a coin repeatedly.

In 1988, finance professors Lo and MacKinlay constructed a test for the RWH using the natural log(arithm) of asset prices as data. The test specifies the log prices to drift around a mean (7.9). We expect price changes for different frequencies (for instance, one-day and two-day periods) to be random. Furthermore, the variances (7.10 and 7.11) at two different frequencies are related, and according to the following equations, the corresponding ratio (7.12) is normally distributed around zero:

$$(7.9) \quad \hat{\mu} \equiv \frac{1}{2n}\sum_{k=1}^{2n}\left(X_k - X_{k-1}\right) = \frac{1}{2n}\left(X_{2n} - X_0\right)$$

$$(7.10) \quad \hat{\sigma}_a^2 \equiv \frac{1}{2n}\sum_{k=1}^{2n}\left(X_k - X_{k-1} - \hat{\mu}\right)^2$$

$$(7.11) \quad \hat{\sigma}_b^2 \equiv \frac{1}{2n}\sum_{k=1}^{n}\left(X_{2k} - X_{2k-2} - 2\hat{\mu}\right)^2$$

$$(7.12) \quad J_r \equiv \frac{\hat{\sigma}_b^2}{\hat{\sigma}_a^2} - 1 \quad \sqrt{2n}J_r \underset{\sim}{a} N\left(0,2\right)$$

How to do it...

The code is in the `random_walk.ipynb` file in this book's code bundle:

1. The imports are as follows:

```
import dautil as dl
import numpy as np
import matplotlib.pyplot as plt
import ch7util
```

2. Calculate the ratios for our stocks:

```
ratios = []

for symbol in ch7util.STOCKS:
    ohlc = dl.data.OHLC()
    P = ohlc.get(symbol)['Adj Close'].values
    N = len(P)
```

```
mu = (np.log(P[-1]) - np.log(P[0]))/N
var_a = 0
var_b = 0

for k in range(1, N):
    var_a = (np.log(P[k]) - np.log(P[k - 1]) - mu) ** 2
    var_a = var_a / N

for k in range(1, N//2):
    var_b = (np.log(P[2 * k]) - np.log(P[2 * k - 2]) - 2 * mu)
** 2
    var_b = var_b / N

ratios.append(np.sqrt(N) * (var_b/var_a - 1))
```

3. Plot the ratios, which we expect to be close to zero (7.12):

```
_, ax = plt.subplots()
dl.plotting.bar(ax, ch7util.STOCKS, ratios)
ax.set_title('Random Walk Test')
ax.set_ylabel('Ratio')
```

Refer to the following screenshot for the end result:

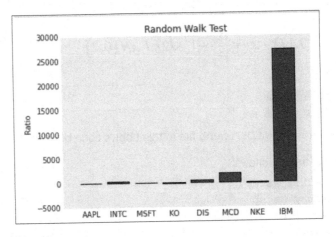

See also

▶ The Wikipedia page about the random walk hypothesis at `https://en.wikipedia.org/wiki/Random_walk_hypothesis` (retrieved October 2015)

▶ Rev. Financ. Stud. (1988) 1 (1): 41-66. doi: 10.1093/rfs/1.1.41 at `http://rfs.oxfordjournals.org/content/1/1/41.full` (retrieved October 2015)

Determining market efficiency with autoregressive models

According to the efficient-market hypothesis (refer to the *Examining the market with the non-parametric runs test* recipe), all information about an asset is immediately reflected in the price of the asset. This means that previous prices don't influence the current price. The following equations specify an autoregressive model (7. 13) and a restricted model (7. 14) with all the coefficients set to zero:

$$(7.13) \quad X_t = c + \sum_{i=1}^{p} \varphi_i X_{t-i} + \varepsilon_t$$

$$(7.14) \quad X_t = c + \varepsilon_t$$

$$(7.15) \quad MarketEfficiency = 1 - \frac{R_{Restricted}^2}{R_{Unrestricted}^2}$$

If we believe the market to be efficient, we would expect the unrestricted model to have nothing to add over the restricted model, and, therefore, the ratio (7. 15) of the respective R-squared coefficients should be close to one.

How to do it...

The script is in the `autoregressive_test.ipynb` file in this book's code bundle:

1. The imports are as follows:

   ```
   import dautil as dl
   import ch7util
   import numpy as np
   import matplotlib.pyplot as plt
   import statsmodels.api as sm
   from IPython.display import HTML
   ```

2. Fit the models using (7.13) and (7.14) and then calculate the market efficiency using (7.15) for our list of stocks:

   ```
   ohlc = dl.data.OHLC()
   efficiencies = []
   restricted_r2 = []
   unrestricted_r2 = []

   for stock in ch7util.STOCKS:
       rets = ch7util.log_rets(ohlc.get(stock)['Adj Close'])
       restricted = sm.OLS(rets, rets.mean() * np.ones_like(rets)).fit()
   ```

```
rets_1 = rets[3:-1]
rets_2 = rets[2:-2]
rets_3 = rets[1:-3]
rets_4 = rets[:-4]
x = np.vstack((rets_1, rets_2, rets_3, rets_4)).T
x = sm.add_constant(x)
y = rets[4:]
unrestricted = sm.OLS(y, x).fit()
restricted_r2.append(restricted.rsquared)
unrestricted_r2.append(unrestricted.rsquared)
efficiencies.append(1 - restricted.rsquared/unrestricted.
rsquared)
```

3. Plot the market efficiency and R-squared values as follows:

```
sp = dl.plotting.Subplotter(2, 1, context)
dl.plotting.bar(sp.ax, ch7util.STOCKS, efficiencies)
sp.label()
dl.plotting.plot_text(sp.next_ax(), unrestricted_r2,
np.array(restricted_r2)/10 ** -16,
                      ch7util.STOCKS, add_scatter=True)
sp.label()
HTML(sp.exit())
```

Refer to the following screenshot for the end result:

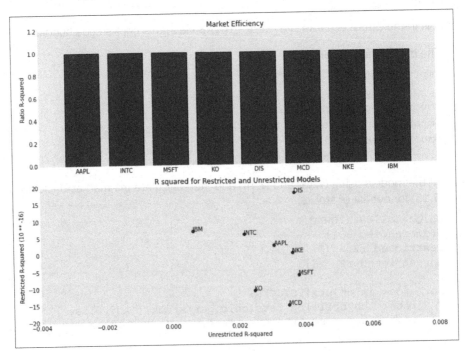

 ▸ The Wikipedia page about the autoregressive model \ at `https://en.wikipedia.org/wiki/Autoregressive_model` (retrieved October 2015)

Creating tables for a stock prices database

Storing stock prices only is in general not very useful. We usually want to store additional static information about companies and related derivatives such as stock options and futures. Economic theory tells us that looking for cycles and trends in historical price data is more or less a waste of time; therefore, creating a database seems be even more pointless. Of course you don't have to believe the theory, and anyway creating a stock prices database is a fun technical challenge. Also a database is useful for portfolio optimization (see the recipe, *Optimizing an equal weights 2 asset portfolio*).

We will base the design on the star schema pattern covered in *Implementing a star schema with fact and dimension tables*. The fact table will hold the prices, with a date dimension table, asset dimension table, and a source dimension table as in the following diagram:

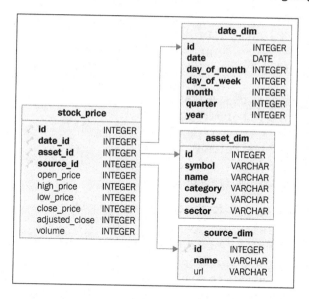

Obviously, the schema will evolve over time with tables, indexes, and columns added or removed as needed. We will use the schema in the *Populating the stock prices database* recipe.

How to do it...

The schema is defined in the `database_tables.py` file in this book's code bundle:

1. The imports are as follows:

```
from sqlalchemy import Column
from sqlalchemy.ext.declarative import declarative_base
from sqlalchemy import Date
from sqlalchemy import ForeignKey
from sqlalchemy import Integer
from sqlalchemy import String

Base = declarative_base()
```

2. Define the following class for the stock prices fact table:

```
class StockPrice(Base):
    __tablename__ = 'stock_price'
    id = Column(Integer, primary_key=True)
    date_id = Column(Integer, ForeignKey('date_dim.id'),
                        primary_key=True)
    asset_id = Column(Integer, ForeignKey('asset_dim.id'),
                        primary_key=True)
    source_id = Column(Integer, ForeignKey('source_dim.id'),
                        primary_key=True)
    open_price = Column(Integer)
    high_price = Column(Integer)
    low_price = Column(Integer)
    close_price = Column(Integer)
    adjusted_close = Column(Integer)
    volume = Column(Integer)
```

3. Define the following class for the date dimension table:

```
class DateDim(Base):
    __tablename__ = 'date_dim'
    id = Column(Integer, primary_key=True)
    date = Column(Date, nullable=False, unique=True)
    day_of_month = Column(Integer, nullable=False)
    day_of_week = Column(Integer, nullable=False)
    month = Column(Integer, nullable=False)
    quarter = Column(Integer, nullable=False)
    year = Column(Integer, nullable=False)
```

4. Define the following class to hold information about the stocks:

```
class AssetDim(Base):
    __tablename__ = 'asset_dim'
    id = Column(Integer, primary_key=True)
    symbol = Column(String, nullable=False, unique=True)
    name = Column(String, nullable=False)
    # Could make this a reference to separate table
    category = Column(String, nullable=False)
    country = Column(String, nullable=False)
    # Could make this a reference to separate table
    sector = Column(String, nullable=False)
```

5. Define the following class for the source dimension table (we only need one entry for Yahoo Finance):

```
class SourceDim(Base):
    __tablename__ = 'source_dim'
    id = Column(Integer, primary_key=True)
    name = Column(String, nullable=False)
    url = Column(String)
```

Populating the stock prices database

In the *Creating tables for a stock prices database* recipe, we defined a schema for a historical stock prices database. In this recipe, we will populate the tables with data from Yahoo Finance and plot average volumes for different time frames and business sectors.

Stock market researchers have found several strange phenomena that have to do with seasonal effects. Also, there are certain recurring events such as earnings announcements, dividend payments, and options expirations. Again, economic theory tells us that any patterns we observe are either illusions or already known to all market participants. Whether this is true or not is hard to confirm; however, this recipe is great as exercise in data analysis. Also, you can use the database to optimize your portfolio as explained in the *Optimizing an equal weights 2 asset portfolio* recipe.

How to do it...

The code is in the `populate_database.ipynb` file in this book's code bundle:

1. The imports are as follows:

```
import database_tables as tables
import pandas as pd
import os
import dautil as dl
```

```
import ch7util
import sqlite3
import matplotlib.pyplot as plt
import seaborn as sns
from IPython.display import HTML
```

2. Define the following function to populate the date dimension table:

```
def populate_date_dim(session):
    for d in pd.date_range(start='19000101', end='20250101'):
        adate = tables.DateDim(date=d.date(), day_of_month=d.day,
                               day_of_week=d.dayofweek, month=d.month,
                               quarter=d.quarter, year=d.year)
        session.add(adate)

    session.commit()
```

3. Define the following function to populate the asset dimension table:

```
def populate_asset_dim(session):
    asset = tables.AssetDim(symbol='AAPL', name='Apple Inc.',
                            category='Common Stock',
                            country='USA',
                            sector='Consumer Goods')
    session.add(asset)

    asset = tables.AssetDim(symbol='INTC', name='Intel Corporation',
                            category='Common Stock',
                            country='USA',
                            sector='Technology')
    session.add(asset)

    asset = tables.AssetDim(symbol='MSFT', name='Microsoft Corporation',
                            category='Common Stock',
                            country='USA',
                            sector='Technology')
    session.add(asset)

    asset = tables.AssetDim(symbol='KO', name='The Coca-Cola Company',
                            category='Common Stock',
                            country='USA',
```

```
                                            sector='Consumer Goods')
        session.add(asset)


        asset = tables.AssetDim(symbol='DIS', name='The Walt Disney
Company',
                                    category='Common Stock',
country='USA',
                                    sector='Services')
        session.add(asset)


        asset = tables.AssetDim(symbol='MCD', name='McDonald\'s
Corp.',
                                    category='Common Stock',
country='USA',
                                    sector='Services')
        session.add(asset)


        asset = tables.AssetDim(symbol='NKE', name='NIKE, Inc.',
                                    category='Common Stock',
country='USA',
                                    sector='Consumer Goods')
        session.add(asset)


        asset = tables.AssetDim(symbol='IBM',
                                    name='International Business Machines
Corporation',
                                    category='Common Stock',
country='USA',
                                    sector='Technology')
        session.add(asset)


        session.commit()
```

4. Define the following function to populate the source dimension table:

```
def populate_source_dim(session):
    session.add(tables.SourceDim(name='Yahoo Finance',
                                 url='https://finance.yahoo.com'))
    session.commit()
```

5. Define the following function to populate the fact table holding stock prices:

```
def populate_prices(session):
    symbols = dl.db.map_to_id(session, tables.AssetDim.symbol)
    dates = dl.db.map_to_id(session, tables.DateDim.date)
    source_id = session.query(tables.SourceDim).first().id
    ohlc = dl.data.OHLC()
```

```
conn = sqlite3.connect(dbname)
c = conn.cursor()
insert = '''INSERT INTO stock_price (id, date_id,
    asset_id, source_id, open_price, high_price, low_price,
    close_price, adjusted_close, volume) VALUES({id}, {date_
id},
    {asset_id}, {source_id}, {open_price}, {high_price},
    {low_price}, {close_price}, {adj_close}, {volume})'''
logger = dl.log_api.conf_logger(__name__)

for symbol in ch7util.STOCKS:
    df = ohlc.get(symbol)
    i = 0

    for index, row in df.iterrows():
        date_id = dates[index.date()]
        asset_id = symbols[symbol]
        i += 1
        stmt = insert.format(id=i, date_id=date_id,
                            asset_id=asset_id,
                            source_id=source_id,
                            open_price=dl.data.
centify(row['Open']),
                            high_price=dl.data.
centify(row['High']),
                            low_price=dl.data.
centify(row['Low']),
                            close_price=dl.data.
centify(row['Close']),
                            adj_close=dl.data.
centify(row['Adj Close']),
                            volume=int(row['Volume']))
        c.execute(stmt)

        if i % 1000 == 0:
            logger.info("Progress %s %s", symbol, i)

        conn.commit()

    conn.commit()

c.close()
conn.close()
```

6. Define the following function to populate all the tables:

```
def populate(session):
    if session.query(tables.SourceDim).count() == 0:
        populate_source_dim(session)
        populate_asset_dim(session)
        populate_date_dim(session)
        populate_prices(session)
```

7. Define the following function to plot the average volumes:

```
def plot_volume(col, ax):
    df = pd.read_sql(sql.format(col=col), conn)
    sns.barplot(x=col, y='AVG(P.Volume/1000)', data=df,
                hue='sector', ax=ax)

    ax.legend(loc='best')

dbname = os.path.join(dl.data.get_data_dir(), 'stock_prices.db')
session = dl.db.create_session(dbname, tables.Base)
populate(session)
sql = '''
    SELECT
        A.sector,
        D.{col},
        AVG(P.Volume/1000)
    FROM stock_price P
    INNER JOIN date_dim D  ON (P.Date_Id = D.Id)
    INNER JOIN asset_dim A ON (P.asset_id = a.Id)
    GROUP BY
        A.sector,
        D.{col}
    '''
```

8. Plot the average volumes with the following code:

```
conn = sqlite3.connect(dbname)

sp = dl.plotting.Subplotter(2, 2, context)
plot_volume('day_of_week', sp.ax)
sp.ax.set_xticklabels(['Mon', 'Tue', 'Wed', 'Thu', 'Fri'])

plot_volume('month', sp.next_ax())
sp.ax.set_xticklabels(dl.ts.short_months())

plot_volume('day_of_month', sp.next_ax())
plot_volume('quarter', sp.next_ax())
HTML(sp.exit())
```

Refer to the following screenshot for the end result:

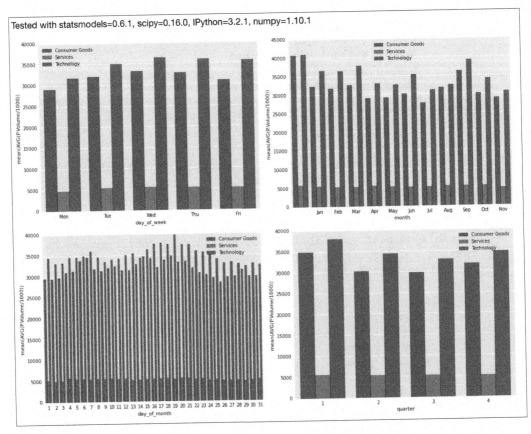

Optimizing an equal weights two-asset portfolio

Buying and selling stocks is a bit like shopping. Shopping is something that supermarkets and online bookstores know well. These types of business often apply techniques such as basket analysis and recommendation engines. If, for example, you are a fan of a writer who writes historically inaccurate novels, a recommendation engine will probably recommend another novel by the same writer or other historically inaccurate novels.

A recommendation engine for stocks can't work this way. For instance, if you only have stocks of oil producers in your portfolio and the oil price moves against you, then the whole portfolio will lose value. So, we should try to have stocks from different sectors, industries, or geographical regions. We can measure similarity with the correlation of returns.

Analogous to the Sharpe ratio (refer to the *Ranking stocks with the Sharpe ratio and liquidity* recipe), we want to maximize the average returns of our portfolio and minimize the variance of the portfolio returns. These ideas are also present in the **Modern Portfolio Theory** (**MPT**), the inventor of which was awarded the Nobel Prize. For a two-asset portfolio, we have the following equations:

$$(7.16) \quad E\left(R_p\right) = w_A E\left(R_A\right) + w_B E\left(R_B\right) = w_A E\left(R_A\right) + \left(1 - w_A\right) E\left(R_B\right)$$

$$(7.17) \quad \sigma_p^2 = w_A^2 \sigma_A^2 + w_B^2 \sigma_B^2 + 2 w_A w_B \sigma_A \sigma_B \rho_{AB}$$

The weights *wA* and *wB* are the portfolio weights and sum up to 1. The weights can be negative—as investors can sell short (selling without owning, which incurs borrowing costs) a security. We can solve the portfolio optimization problem with linear algebra methods or general optimization algorithms. However, for a two-asset portfolio with equal weights and a handful of stocks, the brute force approach is good enough.

How to do it...

The following is a breakdown of the `portfolio_optimization.ipynb` file in this book's code bundle:

1. The imports are as follows:

   ```
   import dautil as dl
   import ch7util
   import pandas as pd
   import numpy as np
   import seaborn as sns
   import matplotlib.pyplot as plt
   ```

2. Define the following function to calculated the expected return (7.16):

   ```
   def expected_return(stocka, stockb, means):
       return 0.5 * (means[stocka] + means[stockb])
   ```

3. Define the following function to calculate the variance of the portfolio return (7.17):

   ```
   def variance_return(stocka, stockb, stds):
       ohlc = dl.data.OHLC()
       dfa = ohlc.get(stocka)
       dfb = ohlc.get(stockb)
       merged = pd.merge(left=dfa, right=dfb,
                         right_index=True, left_index=True,
                         suffixes=('_A', '_B')).dropna()
       retsa = ch7util.log_rets(merged['Adj Close_A'])
       retsb = ch7util.log_rets(merged['Adj Close_B'])
   ```

```
corr = np.corrcoef(retsa, retsb)[0][1]

return 0.25 * (stds[stocka] ** 2 + stds[stockb] ** 2 +
                2 * stds[stocka] * stds[stockb] * corr)
```

4. Define the following function to calculate the ratio of the expected return and variance:

```
def calc_ratio(stocka, stockb, means, stds, ratios):
    if stocka == stockb:
        return np.nan

    key = stocka + '_' + stockb
    ratio = ratios.get(key, None)

    if ratio:
        return ratio

    expected = expected_return(stocka, stockb, means)
    var = variance_return(stocka, stockb, stds)
    ratio = expected/var
    ratios[key] = ratio

    return ratio
```

5. Compute the average return and standard deviations for each stock:

```
means = {}
stds = {}

ohlc = dl.data.OHLC()

for stock in ch7util.STOCKS:
    close = ohlc.get(stock)['Adj Close']
    rets = ch7util.log_rets(close)
    means[stock] = rets.mean()
    stds[stock] = rets.std()
```

6. Calculate the ratios in a grid for all the combinations of our stocks:

```
pairs = dl.collect.grid_list(ch7util.STOCKS)
sorted_pairs = [[sorted(row[i]) for row in pairs]
                for i in range(len(ch7util.STOCKS))]
ratios = {}

grid = [[calc_ratio(row[i][0], row[i][1], means, stds, ratios)
        for row in sorted_pairs] for i in range(len(ch7util.
STOCKS))]
```

7. Plot the grid in a heatmap as follows:

```
%matplotlib inline
plt.title('Expected Return/Return Variance for 2 Asset Portfolio')
sns.heatmap(grid, xticklabels=ch7util.STOCKS, yticklabels=ch7util.
STOCKS)
```

Refer to the following screenshot for the end result:

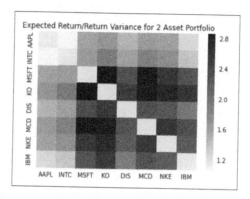

See also

▸ The Wikipedia page about the MPT at https://en.wikipedia.org/wiki/
Modern_portfolio_theory (retrieved October 2015)

8
Text Mining and Social Network Analysis

In this chapter, we will cover the following recipes:

- ▸ Creating a categorized corpus
- ▸ Tokenizing news articles in sentences and words
- ▸ Stemming, lemmatizing, filtering, and TF-IDF scores
- ▸ Recognizing named entities
- ▸ Extracting topics with non-negative matrix factorization
- ▸ Implementing a basic terms database
- ▸ Computing social network density
- ▸ Calculating social network closeness centrality
- ▸ Determining the betweenness centrality
- ▸ Estimating the average clustering coefficient
- ▸ Calculating the assortativity coefficient of a graph
- ▸ Getting the clique number of a graph
- ▸ Creating a document graph with cosine similarity

Introduction

Humans have communicated through language for thousands of years. Handwritten texts have been around for ages, the Gutenberg press was of course a huge development, but now that we have computers, the Internet, and social media, things have definitely spiraled out of control.

This chapter will help you cope with the flood of textual and social media information. The main Python libraries we will use are NLTK and NetworkX. You have to really appreciate how many features can be found in these libraries. Install NLTK with either `pip` or `conda` as follows:

```
$ conda/pip install nltk
```

The code was tested with NLTK 3.0.2. If you need to download corpora, follow the instructions given at `http://www.nltk.org/data.html` (retrieved November 2015).

Install NetworkX with either `pip` or `conda`, as follows:

```
$ conda/pip install networkx
```

The code was tested with Network 1.9.1.

Creating a categorized corpus

As Pythonistas, we are interested in news about Python programming or related technologies; however, if you search for Python articles, you may also get articles about snakes. One solution for this issue is to train a classifier, which recognizes relevant articles. This requires a training set—a categorized corpus with, for instance, the categories "Python programming" and "other".

NLTK has the `CategorizedPlaintextCorpusReader` class for the construction of a categorized corpus. To make things extra exciting, we will get the links for the news articles from RSS feeds. I chose feeds from the BBC, but of course you can use any other feeds. The BBC feeds are already categorized. I selected the world news and technology news feeds, so this gives us two categories. The feeds don't contain the full text of the articles, hence we need to do a bit of scraping using Selenium as more thoroughly described in *Chapter 5, Web Mining, Databases, and Big Data*. You may need to post-process the text files because the BBC web pages don't contain only the text of the news stories, but also side sections.

Getting ready

Install NLTK following the instructions in the *Introduction* section of this chapter. Install feedparser for the processing of RSS feeds:

```
$ pip/conda install feedparser
```

I tested this recipe with feedparser 5.2.1.

How to do it...

1. The imports are as follows:

```
import feedparser as fp
import urllib
from selenium import webdriver
from selenium.webdriver.support.ui import WebDriverWait
from selenium.webdriver.support import expected_conditions as EC
from selenium.webdriver.common.by import By
import dautil as dl
from nltk.corpus.reader import CategorizedPlaintextCorpusReader
import os
```

2. Create the following variables to help with scraping:

```
DRIVER = webdriver.PhantomJS()
NAP_SECONDS = 10
LOGGER = dl.log_api.conf_logger('corpus')
```

3. Define the following function to store text content:

```
def store_txt(url, fname, title):
    try:
        DRIVER.get(url)

        elems = WebDriverWait(DRIVER, NAP_SECONDS).until(
            EC.presence_of_all_elements_located((By.XPATH, '//p'))
        )

        with open(fname, 'w') as txt_file:
            txt_file.write(title + '\n\n')
            lines = [e.text for e in elems]
            txt_file.write(' \n'.join(lines))
    except Exception:
        LOGGER.error("Error processing HTML", exc_info=True)
```

4. Define the following function to retrieve the stories:

```
def fetch_news(dir):
    base = 'http://newsrss.bbc.co.uk/rss/newsonline_uk_edition/{}/rss.xml'

    for category in ['world', 'technology']:
        rss = fp.parse(base.format(category))
```

```
        for i, entry in enumerate(rss.entries):
            fname = '{0}_bbc_{1}.txt'.format(i, category)
            fname = os.path.join(dir, fname)

            if not dl.conf.file_exists(fname):
                store_txt(entry.link, fname, entry.title)
```

5. Call the functions with the following code:

```
if __name__ == "__main__":
    dir = os.path.join(dl.data.get_data_dir(), 'bbc_news_corpus')

    if not os.path.exists(dir):
        os.mkdir(dir)

    fetch_news(dir)
    reader = CategorizedPlaintextCorpusReader(dir, r'.*bbc.*\.
txt',
                                    cat_pattern=r'.*bbc_
(\w+)\.txt')
    printer = dl.log_api.Printer(nelems=3)
    printer.print('Categories', reader.categories())
    printer.print('World fileids', reader.
fileids(categories=['world']))
    printer.print('Technology fileids',
                    reader.fileids(categories=['technology']))
```

Refer to the following screenshot for the end result:

```
'Categories'
['technology', 'world']

'World fileids'
['0_bbc_world.txt', '...', '33_bbc_world.txt', '...', '9_bbc_world.txt']

'Technology fileids'
['0_bbc_technology.txt',
 '...',
 '23_bbc_technology.txt',
 '...',
 '9_bbc_technology.txt']
```

The code is in the `corpus.py` file in this book's code bundle.

▸ The documentation for `CategorizedPlaintextCorpusReader` at `http://www.nltk.org/api/nltk.corpus.reader.html#nltk.corpus.reader.CategorizedPlaintextCorpusReader` (retrieved October 2015)

Tokenizing news articles in sentences and words

The corpora that are part of the NLTK distribution are already tokenized, so we can easily get lists of words and sentences. For our own corpora, we should apply tokenization too. This recipe demonstrates how to implement tokenization with NLTK. The text file we will use is in this book's code bundle. This particular text is in English, but NLTK supports other languages too.

Getting ready

Install NLTK, following the instructions in the *Introduction* section of this chapter.

How to do it...

The program is in the `tokenizing.py` file in this book's code bundle:

1. The imports are as follows:

```
from nltk.tokenize import sent_tokenize
from nltk.tokenize import word_tokenize
import dautil as dl
```

2. The following code demonstrates tokenization:

```
fname = '46_bbc_world.txt'
printer = dl.log_api.Printer(nelems=3)

with open(fname, "r", encoding="utf-8") as txt_file:
    txt = txt_file.read()
    printer.print('Sentences', sent_tokenize(txt))
    printer.print('Words', word_tokenize(txt))
```

Refer to the following screenshot for the end result:

```
'Sentences'
["The day Iceland's women went on strike\n"
 '\n'
 'Forty years ago, the women of Iceland went on strike - they refused to '
 'work, cook and look after children for a day.',
 '...',
 '"I think at first they thought it was something funny, but I can\'t '
 'remember any of them being angry," says Vigdis.',
 '...',
 'The male model who slept on the streets \n'
 'Aerial images show how migrant camp at Calais has grown \n'
 'Emergency delivery raises questions in Taiwan']

'Words'
['The', '...', 'Adalheidur', '...', 'Taiwan']
```

See also

▶ The relevant documentation is at `http://www.nltk.org/api/nltk.tokenize.html?highlight=sent_tokenize#nltk.tokenize.sent_tokenize` (retrieved October 2015).

Stemming, lemmatizing, filtering, and TF-IDF scores

The bag-of-words model represents a corpus literally as a bag of words, not taking into account the position of the words—only their count. Stop words are common words such as "a", "is," and "the", which don't add information value.

TF-IDF scores can be computed for single words (**unigrams**) or combinations of multiple consecutive words (**n-grams**). TF-IDF is roughly the ratio of **term frequency** and **inverse document frequency**. I say "roughly" because we usually take the logarithm of the ratio or apply a weighting scheme. Term frequency is the frequency of a word or n-gram in a document. The inverse document frequency is the inverse of the number of documents in which the word or n-gram occurs. We can use TF-IDF scores for clustering or as a feature of classification. In the *Extracting topics with non-negative matrix factorization* recipe, we will use the scores to discover topics.

NLTK represents the scores by a sparse matrix with one row for each document in the corpus and one column for each word or n-gram. Even though the matrix is sparse, we should try to filter words as much as possible depending on the type of problems we are trying to solve. The filtering code is in `ch8util.py` and implements the following operations:

▸ Converts all words to lower case. In English, sentences start with upper case and in the bag-of-words model, we don't care about the word position. Obviously, if we want to detect named entities (as in the *Recognizing named entities* recipe), case matters.

▸ Ignores stop words, as those have no semantic value.

▸ Ignores words consisting of only one character, as those are either stop words or punctuation pretending to be words.

▸ Ignores words that only occur once, as those are unlikely to be important.

▸ Only allows words containing letters, so ignores a word like "7th" as it contains a digit.

We will also filter with **lemmatization**. Lemmatization is similar to stemming, which I will also demonstrate. The idea behind both procedures is that words have common roots, for instance, the words "analysis," "analyst," and "analysts" have a common root. In general, **stemming** cuts characters, so the result doesn't have to be a valid word. Lemmatization, in contrast, always produces valid words and performs dictionary look-ups.

The code for the `ch8util.py` file in this book's code bundle is as follows:

```
from collections import Counter
from nltk.corpus import brown
from joblib import Memory


memory = Memory(cachedir='.')


def only_letters(word):
    for c in word:
        if not c.isalpha():
            return False

    return True


@memory.cache
def filter(fid, lemmatizer, sw):
    words = [lemmatizer.lemmatize(w.lower()) for w in brown.words(fid)
            if len(w) > 1 and w.lower() not in sw]
```

```
# Ignore words which only occur once
counts = Counter(words)
rare = set([w for w, c in counts.items() if c == 1])

filtered_words = [w for w in words if w not in rare]

return [w for w in filtered_words if only_letters(w)]
```

I decided to limit the analysis to unigrams, but it's quite easy to extend the analysis to bigrams or trigrams. The scikit-learn `TfidfVectorizer` class that we will use lets us specify a `ngram_range` field, so we can consider unigrams and n-grams at the same time. We will pickle the results of this recipe to be reused by other recipes.

Getting ready

Install NLTK by following the instructions in the *Introduction* section.

How to do it...

The script is in the `stemming_lemma.py` file in this book's code bundle:

1. The imports are as follows:

    ```
    from nltk.corpus import brown
    from nltk.corpus import stopwords
    from nltk.stem import PorterStemmer
    from nltk.stem import WordNetLemmatizer
    import ch8util
    from sklearn.feature_extraction.text import TfidfVectorizer
    import numpy as np
    import pandas as pd
    import pickle
    import dautil as dl
    ```

2. Demonstrate stemming and lemmatizing as follows:

    ```
    stemmer = PorterStemmer()
    lemmatizer = WordNetLemmatizer()

    print('stem(analyses)', stemmer.stem('analyses'))
    print('lemmatize(analyses)', lemmatizer.lemmatize('analyses'))
    ```

3. Filter the words in the NLTK Brown corpus:

    ```
    sw = set(stopwords.words())
    texts = []
    ```

```
fids = brown.fileids(categories='news')

for fid in fids:
    texts.append(" ".join(ch8util.filter(fid, lemmatizer, sw)))
```

4. Calculate TF-IDF scores as follows:

```
vectorizer = TfidfVectorizer()
matrix = vectorizer.fit_transform(texts)

with open('tfidf.pkl', 'wb') as pkl:
    pickle.dump(matrix, pkl)

sums = np.array(matrix.sum(axis=0)).ravel()

ranks = [(word, val) for word, val in
         zip(vectorizer.get_feature_names(), sums)]

df = pd.DataFrame(ranks, columns=["term", "tfidf"])
df.to_pickle('tfidf_df.pkl')
df = df.sort(['tfidf'])
dl.options.set_pd_options()
print(df)
```

Refer to the following screenshot for the end result:

```
stem(analyses) analys
lemmatize(analyses) analysis

          term   tfidf
292      beyond  0.035
1460   informed  0.035
...        ...     ...
2736      state  1.831
2478       said  3.236

[3173 rows x 2 columns]
```

How it works

As you can see, stemming doesn't return a valid word. It is faster than lemmatization; however, if you want to reuse the results, it makes sense to prefer lemmatization. The TF-IDF scores are sorted in ascending order in the final pandas `DataFrame` object. A higher TF-IDF score indicates a more important word.

See also

- ▸ The Wikipedia page about the bag-of-words model at `https://en.wikipedia.org/wiki/Bag-of-words_model` (retrieved October 2015)

- ▸ The Wikipedia page about lemmatization at `https://en.wikipedia.org/wiki/Lemmatisation` (retrieved October 2015)

- ▸ The Wikipedia page about the TF-IDF at `https://en.wikipedia.org/wiki/Tf%E2%80%93idf` (retrieved October 2015)

- ▸ The Wikipedia page about stop words at `https://en.wikipedia.org/wiki/Stop_words` (retrieved October 2015)

- ▸ The documentation for the `TfidfVectorizer` class at `http://scikit-learn.org/stable/modules/generated/sklearn.feature_extraction.text.TfidfVectorizer.html` (retrieved October 2015)

- ▸ The documentation for the `WordNetLemmatizer` class at `http://www.nltk.org/api/nltk.stem.html#nltk.stem.wordnet.WordNetLemmatizer` (retrieved November 2015)

Recognizing named entities

Named-entity recognition (**NER**) tries to detect names of persons, organizations, locations, and other names in texts. Some NER systems are almost as good as humans, but it is not an easy task. Named entities usually start with upper case, such as Ivan. We should, therefore, not change the case of words when applying NER.

NLTK has support for the Stanford NER API. This is a Java API, so you need to have Java on your system. I tested the code with Java 1.8.0_65. The code in this recipe downloads the most recent Stanford NER archive (`stanford-ner-2015-04-20.zip/3.5.2`) as of October 2015. If you want another version, take a look at `http://nlp.stanford.edu/software/CRF-NER.shtml` (retrieved October 2015).

Getting ready

Install NLTK by following the instructions in the *Introduction* section. You may also need to install Java.

How to do it...

The script is in the `named_entity.py` file in this book's code bundle:

1. The imports are as follows:

```
from nltk.tag.stanford import NERTagger
import dautil as dl
import os
from zipfile import ZipFile
from nltk.corpus import brown
```

2. Define the following function to download the NER archive:

```
def download_ner():
    url = 'http://nlp.stanford.edu/software/stanford-ner-2015-04-20.zip'
    dir = os.path.join(dl.data.get_data_dir(), 'ner')

    if not os.path.exists(dir):
        os.mkdir(dir)

    fname = 'stanford-ner-2015-04-20.zip'
    out = os.path.join(dir, fname)

    if not dl.conf.file_exists(out):
        dl.data.download(url, out)

        with ZipFile(out) as nerzip:
            nerzip.extractall(path=dir)

    return os.path.join(dir, fname.replace('.zip', ''))
```

3. Apply NER to one of the files in the Brown corpus:

```
dir = download_ner()
st = NERTagger(os.path.join(dir, 'classifiers',
                            'english.all.3class.distsim.crf.ser.gz'),
               os.path.join(dir, 'stanford-ner.jar'))
fid = brown.fileids(categories='news')[0]
printer = dl.log_api.Printer(nelems=9)

tagged = [pair for pair in dl.collect.flatten(st.tag(brown.words(fid)))
          if pair[1] != 'O']
printer.print(tagged)
```

Refer to the following screenshot for the end result:

```
[('Fulton', 'ORGANIZATION'),
 ('County', 'ORGANIZATION'),
 ('Grand', 'ORGANIZATION'),
 ('Jury', 'ORGANIZATION'),
 '...',
 ('Party', 'ORGANIZATION'),
 '...',
 ('Williams', 'PERSON'),
 ('Williams', 'PERSON'),
 ('Felix', 'PERSON'),
 ('Tabb', 'PERSON')]
```

How it works

We created a `NerTagger` object by specifying a pre-trained classifier and the NER JAR (Java archive). The classifier tagged words in our corpus as organization, location, person, or other. The classification is case sensitive, which means that if you lowercase all the words, you will get different results.

See also

> ▶ The Wikipedia page about NER at `https://en.wikipedia.org/wiki/Named-entity_recognition` (retrieved October 2015)

Extracting topics with non-negative matrix factorization

Topics in natural language processing don't exactly match the dictionary definition and correspond to more of a nebulous statistical concept. We speak of **topic models** and probability distributions of words linked to topics, as we know them. When we read a text, we expect certain words that appear in the title or the body of the text to capture the semantic context of the document. An article about Python programming will have words like "class" and "function", while a story about snakes will have words like "eggs" and "afraid." Texts usually have multiple topics; for instance, this recipe is about topic models and non-negative matrix factorization, which we will discuss shortly. We can, therefore, define an additive model for topics by assigning different weights to topics.

One of the topic modeling algorithms is **non-negative matrix factorization** (**NMF**). This algorithm factorizes a matrix into a product of two matrices in such a way that the two matrices have no negative values. Usually, we are only able to numerically approximate the solution of the factorization and the time complexity is polynomial. The scikit-learn NMF class implements this algorithm. NMF can also be applied to document clustering and signal processing.

How to do it...

We will reuse the results from the *Stemming, lemmatizing, filtering, and TF-IDF scores* recipe:

1. The imports are as follows:

```
from sklearn.decomposition import NMF
import ch8util
```

2. Load the TF-IDF matrix and words from a pickle:

```
terms = ch8util.load_terms()
tfidf = ch8util.load_tfidf()
```

3. Visualize topics as lists of high-ranking words:

```
nmf = NMF(n_components=44, random_state=51).fit(tfidf)

for topic_idx, topic in enumerate(nmf.components_):
    label = '{}: '.format(topic_idx)
    print(label, " ".join([terms[i] for i in topic.argsort()[:-9:-
1]]))
```

Refer to the following screenshot for the end result:

```
0:   council hawksley charter said law cd martinelli town
1:   mari mantle run yankee home baseball mickey hit
2:   bundle miss chairman daughter robert thrift drexel queen
3:   liberal committee congress lao rule battle colmer smith
4:   gin stock dallas share cotton morton equipment sale
5:   library system headquarters book librarian nassau service collection
6:   republican mitchell state hughes campaign candidate jones said
7:   palmer player hole tournament round golf stroke green
8:   fee city project hughes hemphill said license association
9:   emory theater student atlanta said acre friday letter
10:  sale farm tax income dealer billion farmer august
11:  law labor union act price collective bargaining wage
12:  portland hillsboro agency junior achievement blue company harvey
13:  recovery bank share economy debenture railroad growth camera
14:  belgian congo congolese independence lumumba province government kasavubu
15:  ballet toy san concert season francisco car television
16:  secret submarine narcotic british evanston dreadnought youth sub
17:  catholic faculty institution community college religious sense university
18:  puppet car driven formerly beverly ride lamp hill
19:  turnpike textile coal bond interest cent traffic revenue
20:  kowalski hengesbach verdict neighbor pohl said havana family
21:  garson design ramsey table dallas designer contemporary chicken
22:  wendell tomorrow chicago monroe club wedding italian burke
23:  holmes thompson georgia frankie pittsburgh chicago went university
24:  plane president kennedy paso senate beardens rickards bearden
25:  cent police said simpkins snow apartment annapolis street
26:  oriole robinson hansen double run league kansa single
27:  fulton jury county election said highway resolution department
28:  game yard moritz meek halfback play texas rice
29:  family house music concert gallery white young brevard
30:  medical care grant precinct health case million karns
31:  stein huff fiedler missile union witness buchheister leavitt
32:  khrushchev meeting premier moscow soviet summit negotiation president
33:  democratic mayor leader buckley wagner bill coalition bronx
34:  administration tax barnett legislature session davis avenue democratic
35:  motel miss bride marr honor pool meredith baker
36:  church family christian sunday kern library ballet restaurant
37:  providence hospital cranston jury board appeal said car
38:  skorich shea arnold award league palmer football eagle
39:  texas bill dallas adc would school committee austin
40:  church god board said school belief secretary district
41:  mantle team pirate benington bob season game may
42:  administration lao policy communist united state nato oslo
43:  game run bear inning liston baseball sox third
```

The code is in the `topic_extraction.py` file in this book's code bundle.

How it works

The NMF class has a `components_` attribute, which holds the non-negative components of the data. We selected the words corresponding to the highest values in the `components_` attribute. As you can see, the topics are varied, although a bit outdated.

See also

▶ The documentation for the NMF class at `http://scikit-learn.org/stable/modules/generated/sklearn.decomposition.NMF.html` (retrieved October 2015)

▶ The Wikipedia page about topic models at `https://en.wikipedia.org/wiki/Topic_model` (retrieved October 2015)

▶ The Wikipedia page about NMF at `https://en.wikipedia.org/wiki/Non-negative_matrix_factorization` (retrieved October 2015)

Implementing a basic terms database

As you know, natural language processing has many applications:

▶ Full text search as implemented by commercial and open source search engines

▶ Clustering of documents

▶ Classification, for example to determine the type of text or the sentiment in the context of a product review

To perform these tasks, we need to calculate features such as TF-IDF scores (refer to *Stemming, lemmatizing, filtering, and TF-IDF scores*). Especially, with large datasets, it makes sense to store the features for easy processing. Search engines use inverted indices, which map words to web pages. This is similar to the association table pattern (refer to *Implementing association tables*).

We will implement the association table pattern with three tables. One table contains the words, another will implement the association table pattern with three tables. One table contains the words, another table holds the information about the documents, and the third table links the other two tables as shown in the following schema:

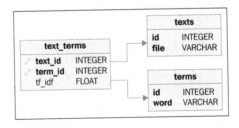

How to do it...

The program is in the `terms_database.py` file in this book's code bundle:

1. The imports are as follows:

```
from sqlalchemy.ext.declarative import declarative_base
from sqlalchemy import Column
from sqlalchemy import ForeignKey
from sqlalchemy import Float
from sqlalchemy import Integer
from sqlalchemy import String
from sqlalchemy.orm import backref
from sqlalchemy.orm import relationship
import os
import dautil as dl
from nltk.corpus import brown
from sqlalchemy import func
import ch8util

Base = declarative_base()
```

2. Define the following class for the text documents:

```
class Text(Base):
    __tablename__ = 'texts'
    id = Column(Integer, primary_key=True)
    file = Column(String, nullable=False, unique=True)
    terms = relationship('Term', secondary='text_terms')

    def __repr__(self):
        return "Id=%d file=%s" % (self.id, self.file)
```

3. Define the following class for the words in the articles:

```
class Term(Base):
    __tablename__ = 'terms'
    id = Column(Integer, primary_key=True)
    word = Column(String, nullable=False, unique=True)

    def __repr__(self):
        return "Id=%d word=%s" % (self.id, self.word)
```

4. Define the following class for the association of documents and words:

```
class TextTerm(Base):
    __tablename__ = 'text_terms'
    text_id = Column(Integer, ForeignKey('texts.id'), primary_
key=True)
    term_id = Column(Integer, ForeignKey('terms.id'), primary_
key=True)
    tf_idf = Column(Float)
    text = relationship('Text', backref=backref('term_assoc'))
    term = relationship('Term', backref=backref('text_assoc'))

    def __repr__(self):
        return "text_id=%s term_id=%s" % (self.text_id, self.term_
id)
```

5. Define the following function to insert entries in the texts table:

```
def populate_texts(session):
    if dl.db.not_empty(session, Text):
        # Cowardly refusing to continue
        return

    fids = brown.fileids(categories='news')

    for fid in fids:
        session.add(Text(file=fid))

    session.commit()
```

6. Define the following function to insert entries in the terms table:

```
def populate_terms(session):
    if dl.db.not_empty(session, Term):
        # Cowardly refusing to continue
        return

    terms = ch8util.load_terms()

    for term in terms:
        session.add(Term(word=term))

    session.commit()
```

7. Define the following function to insert entries in the association table:

```
def populate_text_terms(session):
    if dl.db.not_empty(session, TextTerm):
```

```
        # Cowardly refusing to continue
        return

    text_ids = dl.collect.flatten(session.query(Text.id).all())
    term_ids = dl.collect.flatten(session.query(Term.id).all())

    tfidf = ch8util.load_tfidf()
    logger = dl.log_api.conf_logger(__name__)

    for text_id, row, in zip(text_ids, tfidf):
        logger.info('Processing {}'.format(text_id))
        arr = row.toarray()[0]
        session.get_bind().execute(
            TextTerm.__table__.insert(),
            [{'text_id': text_id, 'term_id': term_id,
              'tf_idf': arr[i]}
             for i, term_id in enumerate(term_ids)
             if arr[i] > 0]
        )

    session.commit()
```

8. Define the following function to perform a search with keywords:

```
def search(session, keywords):
    terms = keywords.split()
    fsum = func.sum(TextTerm.tf_idf)

    return session.query(TextTerm.text_id, fsum).\
        join(Term, TextTerm).\
        filter(Term.word.in_(terms)).\
        group_by(TextTerm.text_id).\
        order_by(fsum.desc()).all()
```

9. Call the functions we defined with the following code:

```
if __name__ == "__main__":
    dbname = os.path.join(dl.data.get_data_dir(), 'news_terms.db')
    session = dl.db.create_session(dbname, Base)
    populate_texts(session)
    populate_terms(session)
    populate_text_terms(session)
    printer = dl.log_api.Printer()
    printer.print('id, tf_idf', search(session, 'baseball game'))
```

We performed a search for "baseball game." Refer to the following screenshot for the end result (file IDs and TF-IDF sums):

```
'id, tf_idf'
[(12, 2.5665254543738096),
 (13, 2.4081218366314148),
 (15, 1.5604954671497586),
 (39, 1.3231045413703009),
 (14, 0.921068156484757),
 (11, 0.8502146144930182),
 (38, 0.2519025401924042)]
```

How it works

We stored TF-IDF scores using the association table database pattern. As an example of using the database, we queried for "baseball game." The query looked up the IDs of both words in the terms table and then summed the related TF-IDF scores in the association table. The sums serve as a relevancy score. Then, we presented the corresponding file IDs with relevancy scores in descending order. If you are showing the result to end users, you will have to do at least one more query to replace the file IDs with filenames. As it happens, the files we are analyzing are named `ca01` to `ca44`, so the query is not strictly necessary.

Because I had the TF-IDF scores already, I found it convenient to store them directly. However, you can also decide to store the term frequency and inverse document frequency and derive the TF-IDF scores from those. You only need to determine the term frequency for each new document and the words in the document. All the inverse document frequencies need to be updated when documents are added or removed. However, establishing a link via the association table is already enough to calculate the term frequency, inverse document frequency, and TF-IDF scores.

See also

▶ The Wikipedia page about search engine indexing at `https://en.wikipedia.org/wiki/Search_engine_indexing` (retrieved October 2015)

Computing social network density

Humans are social animals and, therefore, social connections are very important. We can view these connections and the persons involved as a network. We represent networks or a subset as a graph. A graph consists of nodes or points connected by edges or lines. Graphs can be directed or undirected—the lines can be arrows.

We will use the Facebook SPAN data, which we also used in the *Visualizing network graphs with hive plots* recipe. Facebook started out small in 2004, but it has more than a billion users as of 2015. The data doesn't include all the users, but it is still enough for a decent analysis. The following equations describe the density of undirected (8.1) and directed (8.2) graphs:

$$(8.1) \quad d = \frac{2m}{n(n-1)}$$

$$(8.2) \quad d = \frac{m}{n(n-1)}$$

In these equations, n is the number of nodes and m is the number of edges.

Getting ready

Install NetworkX with the instructions from the *Introduction* section.

How to do it...

The code is in the net_density.ipynb file in this book's code bundle:

1. The imports are as follows:

```
import networkx as nx
import dautil as dl
```

2. Create a NetworkX graph as follows:

```
fb_file = dl.data.SPANFB().load()
G = nx.read_edgelist(fb_file,
                     create_using=nx.Graph(),
                     nodetype=int)
```

3. Call the density() function as follows:

```
print('Density', nx.density(G))
```

We get the following density:

```
Density 0.010819963503439287
```

See also

- The `density()` function documented at https://networkx.github.io/ documentation/latest/reference/generated/networkx.classes. function.density.html (retrieved October 2015)

- The Wikipedia page about graphs at https://en.wikipedia.org/wiki/ Graph_%28abstract_data_type%29 (retrieved October 2015)

Calculating social network closeness centrality

In a social network such as the Facebook SPAN data, we will have influential people. In graph terminology, these are the influential nodes. **Centrality** finds features of important nodes. **Closeness centrality** uses shortest paths between nodes as a feature, as shown in the following equation:

$$(8.3) \quad C(u) = \frac{n-1}{\sum_{v=1}^{n-1} d(v,u)}$$

In (8.3), *d(u, v)* is the shortest path between *u, v*, and *n* is the number of nodes. An influential node is close to other nodes and, therefore, the sum of the shortest paths is low. We can compute closeness centrality for each node separately, and for a large graph, this can be a lengthy calculation. NetworkX allows us to specify which node we are interested in, so we will calculate closeness centrality just for a few nodes.

Getting ready

Install NetworkX with the instructions from the *Introduction* section.

How to do it...

Have a look at the `close_centrality.ipynb` file in this book's code bundle:

1. The imports are as follows:

```
import networkx as nx
import dautil as dl
```

2. Create a NetworkX graph from the Facebook SPAN data as follows:

```
fb_file = dl.data.SPANFB().load()
G = nx.read_edgelist(fb_file,
                create_using=nx.Graph(),
                nodetype=int)
```

3. Calculate the closeness centrality for node 1 and node 4037:

```
print('Closeness Centrality Node 1',
      nx.closeness_centrality(G, 1))
print('Closeness Centrality Node 4037',
      nx.closeness_centrality(G, 4037))
```

We get the following result for the Facebook SPAN data:

```
Closeness Centrality Node 1 0.2613761408505405

Closeness Centrality Node 4037 0.18400546821599453
```

See also

▶ The Wikipedia page about closeness centrality at `https://en.wikipedia.org/wiki/Centrality#Closeness_centrality` (retrieved October 2015)

Determining the betweenness centrality

Betweenness centrality is a type of centrality similar to closeness centrality (refer to the *Calculating social network closeness centrality* recipe). This metric is given by the following equation:

$$(8.4) \quad c_B(v) = \sum_{s,t \in V} \frac{\sigma(s,t|v)}{\sigma(s,t)}$$

It is the total of the fraction of all possible pairs of shortest paths that go through a node.

Getting ready

Install NetworkX with instructions from the *Introduction* section.

How to do it...

The script is in the `between_centrality.ipynb` file in this book's code bundle:

1. The imports are as follows:

```
import networkx as nx
import dautil as dl
import pandas as pd
```

2. Load the Facebook SPAN data into a NetworkX graph:

```
fb_file = dl.data.SPANFB().load()
G = nx.read_edgelist(fb_file,
                     create_using=nx.Graph(),
                     nodetype=int)
```

3. Calculate the betweenness centrality with `k = 256` (number of nodes to use) and store the result in a pandas `DataFrame` object:

```
key_values = nx.betweenness_centrality(G, k=256)
df = pd.DataFrame.from_dict(key_values, orient='index')

dl.options.set_pd_options()
print('Betweenness Centrality', df)
```

Refer to the following screenshot for the end result:

```
Betweenness Centrality
0       1.406e-01
1       4.996e-06
...        ...
4037    0.000e+00
4038    0.000e+00

[4039 rows x 1 columns]
```

See also

- The Wikipedia page about betweenness centrality at `https://en.wikipedia.org/wiki/Betweenness_centrality` (retrieved October 2015

- The documentation for the `betweenness_centrality()` function at `https://networkx.github.io/documentation/latest/reference/generated/networkx.algorithms.centrality.betweenness_centrality.html` (retrieved October 2015)

Estimating the average clustering coefficient

From kindergarten onward, we have friends, close friends, best friends forever, social media friends, and other friends. A social network graph should, therefore, have clumps, unlike what you would observe at a high school party. The question that naturally arises is what would happen if we just invite a group of random strangers to a party or recreate this setup online? We would expect the probability of strangers connecting to be lower than for friends. In graph theory, this probability is measured by the **clustering coefficient**.

The **average clustering coefficient** is a local (single node) version of the clustering coefficient. The definition of this metric considers triangles formed by nodes. With three nodes, we can form one triangle, for instance, the three musketeers. If we add D'Artagnan to the mix, more triangles are possible, but not all the triangles have to be realized. It could happen that D'Artagnan gets in a fight with all three of the musketeers. In (8.5), we define a clustering coefficient as the ratio of realized and possible triangles and average clustering coefficient (8.6):

$$(8.5) \quad C_i = \frac{\lambda_G(v)}{\tau_G(v)}$$

$$(8.6) \quad \bar{C} = \frac{1}{n}\sum_{i=1}^{n} C_i$$

Getting ready

Install NetworkX with the instructions from the *Introduction* section.

How to do it...

The script is in the `avg_clustering.ipynb` file in this book's code bundle:

1. The imports are as follows:

```
import networkx as nx
import dautil as dl
```

2. Load the Facebook SPAN data into a NetworkX graph:

```
fb_file = dl.data.SPANFB().load()
G = nx.read_edgelist(fb_file,
                     create_using=nx.Graph(),
                     nodetype=int)
```

3. Calculate the average clustering coefficient as follows:

```
print('Average Clustering',
      nx.average_clustering(G))
```

We get the following result for the Facebook SPAN data:

```
Average Clustering 0.6055467186200871
```

See also

▶ The Wikipedia page about the clustering coefficient at `https://en.wikipedia.org/wiki/Clustering_coefficient` (retrieved October 2015)

▶ The documentation for the `average_clustering()` function at `https://networkx.github.io/documentation/latest/reference/generated/networkx.algorithms.approximation.clustering_coefficient.average_clustering.html` (retrieved October 2015).

Calculating the assortativity coefficient of a graph

In graph theory, similarity is measured by the **degree distribution**. **Degree** is the number of connections a node has to other nodes. In a directed graph, we have incoming and outgoing connections and corresponding indegree and outdegree. Friends tend to have something in common. In graph theory, this tendency is measured by the **assortativity coefficient**. This coefficient is the Pearson correlation coefficient between a pair of nodes, as given in the following equation:

$$(8.7) \quad r = \frac{\sum_{jk} jk \left(e_{jk} - q_j q_k \right)}{\sigma_q^2}$$

qk (distribution of the remaining degree) is the number of connections leaving node *k*. *ejk* is the joint probability distribution of the remaining degrees of the node pair.

Getting ready

Install NetworkX with the instructions from the *Introduction* section.

How to do it...

The code is in the `assortativity.ipynb` file in this book's code bundle:

1. The imports are as follows:

```
import networkx as nx
import dautil as dl
```

2. Load the Facebook SPAN data into a NetworkX graph:

```
fb_file = dl.data.SPANFB().load()
G = nx.read_edgelist(fb_file,
                     create_using=nx.Graph(),
                     nodetype=int)
```

3. Calculate the assortativity coefficient as follows:

```
print('Degree Assortativity Coefficient',
      nx.degree_assortativity_coefficient(G))
```

We get the following result for the Facebook SPAN data:

```
Degree Assortativity Coefficient 0.0635772291856
```

See also

▶ The Wikipedia page about degree distribution at `https://en.wikipedia.org/wiki/Degree_distribution` (retrieved October 2015)

▶ The Wikipedia page about assortativity at `https://en.wikipedia.org/wiki/Assortativity` (retrieved October 2015)

▶ The documentation for the `degree_assortativity_coefficient()` function at `https://networkx.github.io/documentation/latest/reference/generated/networkx.algorithms.assortativity.degree_assortativity_coefficient.html` (retrieved October 2015)

Getting the clique number of a graph

A **complete graph** is a graph in which every pair of nodes is connected by a unique connection. A **clique** is a subgraph that is complete. This is equivalent to the general concept of cliques in which every person knows all the other people. The **maximum clique** is the clique with the most nodes. The **clique number** is the number of nodes in the maximum clique. Unfortunately finding the clique number takes a long time, so we will not use the complete Facebook SPAN data.

Getting ready

Install NetworkX with the instructions from the *Introduction* section.

How to do it...

The code is in the `clique_number.py` file in this book's code bundle:

1. The imports are as follows:

```
import networkx as nx
import dautil as dl
```

2. Load the Facebook SPAN data into a NetworkX graph:

```
fb_file = dl.data.SPANFB().load()
G = nx.read_edgelist(fb_file,
                     create_using=nx.Graph(),
                     nodetype=int)
```

3. Determine the clique number for a subgraph:

```
print('Graph Clique Number',
      nx.graph_clique_number(G.subgraph(list(range(2048)))))
```

We get the following result for the partial Facebook SPAN data:

```
Graph Clique Number 38
```

See also

- ▶ The Wikipedia page about complete graphs at `https://en.wikipedia.org/wiki/Complete_graph` (retrieved October 2015)

- ▶ The Wikipedia page about cliques at `https://en.wikipedia.org/wiki/Clique_%28graph_theory%29` (retrieved October 2015)

- ▶ The documentation for the `graph_clique_number()` function at `https://networkx.github.io/documentation/latest/reference/generated/networkx.algorithms.clique.graph_clique_number.html` (retrieved October 2015)

Creating a document graph with cosine similarity

The Internet is a large web of documents linked to each other. We can view it as a document graph in which each node corresponds to a document. You will expect documents to link to similar documents; however, web pages sometimes link to other unrelated web pages. This can be by mistake or on purpose, for instance in the context of advertising or attempts to improve search engine rankings. A more trustworthy source such as Wikipedia will probably yield a better graph. However, some Wikipedia pages are very basic stubs, so we may be missing out on quality links.

The **cosine similarity** is a common distance metric to measure the similarity of two documents. For this metric, we need to compute the inner product of two feature vectors. The cosine similarity of vectors corresponds to the cosine of the angle between vectors, hence the name. The cosine similarity is given by the following equation:

$$(8.8) \quad k(x, y) = \frac{xy^T}{\|x\|\|y\|}$$

The feature vectors in this recipe are the TF-IDF scores, corresponding to a document. The cosine similarity of a document with itself is equal to 1 (zero angle); therefore for documents to be similar, the cosine similarity should be as close to 1 as possible.

We will perform the following steps to create a document graph of the news articles in the Brown corpus:

1. Calculate cosine similarities using the TF-IDF scores that we stored in a pickle from the code of the *Stemming, lemmatizing, filtering, and TF-IDF scores* recipe. The result is similar to a correlation matrix.

2. For each document, add a connection in the graph to each document, which is similar enough. I used the 90th percentile of similarities as threshold; however, you can use another value if you prefer.

3. For each document, select the top three words using the TF-IDF scores. I used the words to annotate the document nodes.

4. Calculate graph metrics with NetworkX, as discussed in this chapter.

How to do it...

The code to create the document graph with cosine similarity is in the `cos_similarity.ipynb` file in this book's code bundle:

1. The imports are as follows:

```
from sklearn.metrics.pairwise import cosine_similarity
import networkx as nx
import matplotlib.pyplot as plt
import numpy as np
import dautil as dl
import ch8util
```

2. Define the following function to add nodes to the NetworkX graph annotated with the top three most important words per document:

```
def add_nodes(G, nodes, start, terms):
    for n in nodes:
        words = top_3_words(tfidf, n, terms)
        G.add_node(n, words='{0}: {1}'.
                   format(n, " ".join(words.tolist())))
        G.add_edge(start, n)
```

3. Define the following function to find the top three words for a document:

```
def top_3_words(tfidf, row, terms):
    indices = np.argsort(tfidf[row].toarray().ravel())[-3:]

    return terms[indices]
```

4. Load the necessary data, calculate cosine similarities, and create a NetworkX graph:

```
tfidf = ch8util.load_tfidf()
terms = ch8util.load_terms()

sims = cosine_similarity(tfidf, tfidf)
G = nx.Graph()
```

5. Iterate through the cosine similarities and add nodes to the graph:

```
for i, row in enumerate(sims):
    over_limit = np.where(row > np.percentile(row, 90))[0]
    nodes = set(over_limit.tolist())
    nodes.remove(i)
    add_nodes(G, nodes, i, terms)
```

6. Plot the graph and print some metrics using NetworkX:

```
labels = nx.get_node_attributes(G, 'words')
nx.draw_networkx(G, pos=nx.spring_layout(G), labels=labels)
plt.axis('off')
plt.title('Graph of News Articles in the Brown Corpus')
print('Density', nx.density(G))
print('Average Clustering',
      nx.average_clustering(G))
print('Degree Assortativity Coefficient',
      nx.degree_assortativity_coefficient(G))
print('Graph Clique Number', nx.graph_clique_number(G))
```

Refer to the following screenshot for the end result:

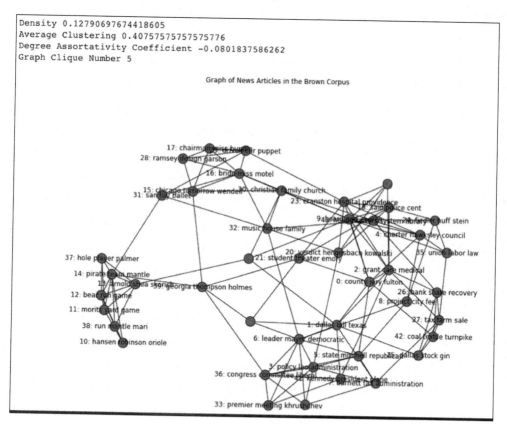

```
Density 0.12790697674418605
Average Clustering 0.40757575757575776
Degree Assortativity Coefficient -0.0801837586262
Graph Clique Number 5
```

See also

- The *Computing social network density* recipe
- The *Estimating average clustering coefficient* recipe
- The *Calculating the assortativity coefficient of a graph* recipe
- The *Getting the clique number of a graph* recipe
- The Wikipedia page about the cosine similarity at `https://en.wikipedia.org/wiki/Cosine_similarity` (retrieved October 2015)
- The documentation about the `cosine_similarity()` function at `http://scikit-learn.org/stable/modules/metrics.html#cosine-similarity` (retrieved October 2015)

9
Ensemble Learning and Dimensionality Reduction

In this chapter, we will cover the following recipes:

- ▸ Recursively eliminating features
- ▸ Applying principal component analysis for dimensionality reduction
- ▸ Applying linear discriminant analysis for dimensionality reduction
- ▸ Stacking and majority voting for multiple models
- ▸ Learning with random forests
- ▸ Fitting noisy data with the RANSAC algorithm
- ▸ Bagging to improve results
- ▸ Boosting for better learning
- ▸ Nesting cross-validation
- ▸ Reusing models with joblib
- ▸ Hierarchically clustering data
- ▸ Taking a Theano tour

Introduction

In the 1983 *War Games* movie, a computer made life and death decisions that could have resulted in World War III. As far as I know, technology wasn't able to pull off such feats at the time. However, in 1997, the Deep Blue supercomputer did manage to beat a world chess champion. In 2005, a Stanford self-driving car drove by itself for more than 130 kilometers in a desert. In 2007, the car of another team drove through regular traffic for more than 50 kilometers. In 2011, the Watson computer won a quiz against human opponents. If we assume that computer hardware is the limiting factor, then we can try to extrapolate into the future. Ray Kurzweil did just that, and according to him, we can expect human-level intelligence around 2029.

In this chapter, we will focus on the simpler problem of forecasting weather for the next day. We will assume that the weather today depends on yesterday's weather. Theoretically, if a butterfly flaps its wings at one location, this could trigger a chain of events causing a snow storm in a place thousands kilometers further away (the butterfly effect). This is not impossible, but very improbable. However, if we have many such incidents, a similar scenario will occur more often than you would suspect.

It is impossible to take into account all possible factors. In fact, we will try to make our life easier by ignoring some of the data we have available. We will apply classification and regression algorithms, as well as hierarchical clustering. Let's defer results evaluation to *Chapter 10, Evaluating Classifiers, Regressors, and Clusters*. If you are curious about the confusion matrix mentioned in the classification recipes, please jump to the *Getting classification straight with the confusion matrix* recipe.

Most artificial intelligence systems are nowadays, in fact, not so smart. A judge in a court of law could make wrong decisions because he or she is biased or having a bad day. A group of multiple judges should perform better. This is comparable to a machine learning project, in which we worry about overfitting and underfitting. **Ensemble learning** is a solution to this conundrum, and it basically means combining multiple learners in a clever way.

A major part of this chapter is about **hyperparameter** optimization—these are parameters of classifiers and regressors. To check for overfitting or underfitting, we can use **learning curves**, which show training and test scores for varying training set sizes. We can also vary the value of a single hyperparameter with **validation curves**.

Recursively eliminating features

If we have many features (explanatory variables), it is tempting to include them all in our model. However, we then run the risk of overfitting—getting a model that works very well for the training data and very badly for unseen data. Not only that, but the model is bound to be relatively slow and require a lot of memory. We have to weigh accuracy (or an other metric) against speed and memory requirements.

We can try to ignore features or create new better compound features. For instance, in online advertising, it is common to work with ratios, such as the ratio of views and clicks related to an ad. Common sense or domain knowledge can help us select features. In the worst-case scenario, we may have to rely on correlations or other statistical methods. The scikit-learn library offers the `RFE` class (recursive feature elimination), which can automatically select features. We will use this class in this recipe. We also need an external estimator. The `RFE` class is relatively new, and unfortunately there is no guarantee that all estimators will work together with the `RFE` class.

How to do it...

1. The imports are as follows:

```
from sklearn.feature_selection import RFE
from sklearn.svm import SVC
from sklearn.svm import SVR
from sklearn.preprocessing import MinMaxScaler
import dautil as dl
import warnings
import numpy as np
```

2. Create a SVC classifier and an RFE object as follows:

```
warnings.filterwarnings("ignore", category=DeprecationWarning)
clf = SVC(random_state=42, kernel='linear')
selector = RFE(clf)
```

3. Load the data, scale it using a `MinMaxScaler` function, and add the day of the year as a feature:

```
df = dl.data.Weather.load().dropna()
df['RAIN'] = df['RAIN'] == 0
df['DOY'] = [float(d.dayofyear) for d in df.index]
scaler = MinMaxScaler()

for c in df.columns:
    if c != 'RAIN':
        df[c] = scaler.fit_transform(df[c])
```

4. Print the first row of the data as a sanity check:

```
dl.options.set_pd_options()
print(df.head(1))
X = df[:-1].values
np.set_printoptions(formatter={'all': '{:.3f}'.format})
print(X[0])
np.set_printoptions()
```

5. Determine support and rankings for the features using rain or no rain as classes (in the context of classification):

```
y = df['RAIN'][1:].values
selector = selector.fit(X, y)
print('Rain support', df.columns[selector.support_])
print('Rain rankings', selector.ranking_)
```

6. Determine support and rankings for the features using temperature as a feature:

```
reg = SVR(kernel='linear')
selector = RFE(reg)
y = df['TEMP'][1:].values
selector = selector.fit(X, y)
print('Temperature support', df.columns[selector.support_])
print('Temperature ranking', selector.ranking_)
```

Refer to the following screenshot for the end result:

```
            WIND_DIR  WIND_SPEED   TEMP  RAIN  PRESSURE  DOY
YYYYMMDD
1906-01-01    0.311      0.594    0.269  True   0.712     0
[0.311 0.594 0.269 1.000 0.712 0.000]
Rain support Index(['WIND_DIR', 'RAIN', 'PRESSURE'], dtype='object')
Rain rankings [1 2 4 1 1 3]
Temperature support Index(['WIND_SPEED', 'TEMP', 'PRESSURE'], dtype='object')
Temperature ranking [4 1 1 3 1 2]
```

The code for this recipe is in the `feature_elimination.py` file in this book's code bundle.

How it works

The `RFE` class selects half of the features by default. The algorithm is as follows:

1. Train the external estimator on the data and assign weights to the features.

2. The features with smallest weights are removed.

3. Repeat the procedure until we have the necessary number of features.

See also

▸ The documentation for the `RFE` class at `http://scikit-learn.org/stable/modules/generated/sklearn.feature_selection.RFE.html` (retrieved November 2015)

Applying principal component analysis for dimension reduction

Principal component analysis (**PCA**), invented by Karl Pearson in 1901, is an algorithm that transforms data into uncorrelated orthogonal features called **principal components**. The principal components are the eigenvectors of the covariance matrix.

Sometimes, we get better results by scaling the data prior to applying PCA, although this is not strictly necessary. We can interpret PCA as projecting data to a lower dimensional space. Some of the principal components contribute relatively little information (low variance); therefore, we can omit them. We have the following transformation:

$$(9.1) \quad T_L = XW_L$$

The result is the matrix T_L, with the same number of rows as the original matrix but a lower number of columns.

Dimensionality reduction is, of course, useful for visualization and modeling and to reduce the chance of overfitting. In fact, there is a technique called **Principal component regression** (**PCR**), which uses this principle. In a nutshell, PCR performs the following steps:

1. Transforms the data to a lower dimensional space with PCA.
2. Performs linear regression in the new space.
3. Transforms the result back to the original coordinate system.

How to do it...

1. The imports are as follows:

```
import dautil as dl
from sklearn.decomposition import PCA
import matplotlib.pyplot as plt
from sklearn.preprocessing import scale
```

2. Load the data as follows and group by the day of the year:

```
df = dl.data.Weather.load().dropna()
df = dl.ts.groupby_yday(df).mean()
X = df.values
```

3. Apply PCA to project the data into a two-dimensional space:

```
pca = PCA(n_components=2)
X_r = pca.fit_transform(scale(X)).T
```

4. Plot the result of the transformation:

```
plt.scatter(X_r[0], X_r[1])
plt.xlabel('x')
plt.ylabel('y')
plt.title('Dimension Reducion with PCA')
```

Refer to the following screenshot for the end result:

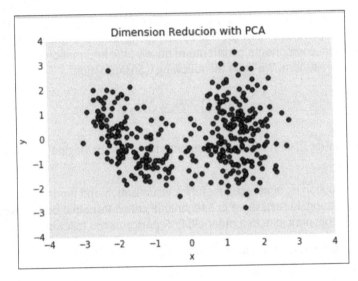

The code is in the `applying_pca.ipynb` file in this book's code bundle.

See also

▸ The Wikipedia page about PCA at `https://en.wikipedia.org/wiki/Principal_component_analysis` (retrieved November 2015)

▸ The Wikipedia page about PCR at `https://en.wikipedia.org/wiki/Principal_component_regression` (retrieved November 2015)

▸ The documentation for the PCA class at `http://scikit-learn.org/stable/modules/generated/sklearn.decomposition.PCA.html` (retrieved November 2015

Applying linear discriminant analysis for dimension reduction

Linear discriminant analysis (**LDA**) is an algorithm that looks for a linear combination of features in order to distinguish between classes. It can be used for classification or dimensionality reduction by projecting to a lower dimensional subspace. LDA requires a target attribute both for classification and dimensionality reduction.

If we represent class densities as multivariate Gaussians, then LDA assumes that the classes have the same covariance matrix. We can use training data to estimate the parameters of the class distributions.

In scikit-learn, `lda.LDA` has been deprecated in 0.17 and renamed `discriminant_analysis.LinearDiscriminantAnalysis`. The default solver of this class uses singular value decomposition, does not need to calculate the covariance matrix, and is therefore fast.

How to do it...

The code is in the `applying_lda.ipynb` file in this book's code bundle:

1. The imports are as follows:

   ```
   import dautil as dl
   from sklearn.discriminant_analysis import
   LinearDiscriminantAnalysis
   import matplotlib.pyplot as plt
   ```

2. Load the data as follows:

   ```
   df = dl.data.Weather.load().dropna()
   X = df.values
   y = df['WIND_DIR'].values
   ```

3. Apply LDA to project the data into a two-dimensional space:

   ```
   lda = LinearDiscriminantAnalysis(n_components=2)
   X_r = lda.fit(X, y).transform(X).T
   ```

4. Plot the result of the transformation:

   ```
   plt.scatter(X_r[0], X_r[1])
   plt.xlabel('x')
   plt.ylabel('y')
   plt.title('Dimension Reduction with LDA')
   ```

Refer to the following screenshot for the end result:

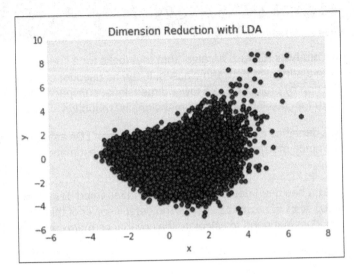

See also

▸ The Wikipedia page about LDA at `https://en.wikipedia.org/wiki/Linear_discriminant_analysis` (retrieved November 2015)

▸ The relevant scikit-learn documentation is `http://scikit-learn.org/stable/modules/generated/sklearn.discriminant_analysis.LinearDiscriminantAnalysis.html` (retrieved November 2015)

Stacking and majority voting for multiple models

It is generally believed that two people know more than one person alone. A democracy should work better than a dictatorship. In machine learning, we don't have humans making decisions, but algorithms. When we have multiple classifiers or regressors working together, we speak of **ensemble learning**.

There are many ensemble learning schemes. The simplest setup does majority voting for classification and averaging for regression. In scikit-learn 0.17, you can use the `VotingClassifier` class to do majority voting. This classifier lets you emphasize or suppress classifiers with weights.

Stacking takes the outputs of machine learning estimators and then uses those as inputs for another algorithm. You can, of course, feed the output of the higher-level algorithm to another predictor. It is possible to use any arbitrary topology, but for practical reasons, you should try a simple setup first.

How to do it...

1. The imports are as follows:

```
import dautil as dl
from sklearn.tree import DecisionTreeClassifier
import numpy as np
import ch9util
from sklearn.ensemble import VotingClassifier
from sklearn.grid_search import GridSearchCV
from IPython.display import HTML
```

2. Load the data and create three decision tree classifiers:

```
X_train, X_test, y_train, y_test = ch9util.rain_split()
default = DecisionTreeClassifier(random_state=53, min_samples_
leaf=3,
                                 max_depth=4)
entropy = DecisionTreeClassifier(criterion='entropy',
                                 min_samples_leaf=3, max_depth=4,
                                 random_state=57)
random = DecisionTreeClassifier(splitter='random', min_samples_
leaf=3,
                                max_depth=4, random_state=5)
```

3. Use the classifiers to take a vote:

```
clf = VotingClassifier([('default', default),
                        ('entropy', entropy), ('random', random)])
params = {'voting': ['soft', 'hard'],
          'weights': [None, (2, 1, 1), (1, 2, 1), (1, 1, 2)]}
gscv = GridSearchCV(clf, param_grid=params, n_jobs=-1, cv=5)
gscv.fit(X_train, y_train)
votes = gscv.predict(X_test)

preds = []
```

```
for clf in [default, entropy, random]:
    clf.fit(X_train, y_train)
    preds.append(clf.predict(X_test))

preds = np.array(preds)
```

4. Plot the confusion matrix for the votes-based forecast:

```
%matplotlib inline
context = dl.nb.Context('stacking_multiple')
dl.nb.RcWidget(context)

sp = dl.plotting.Subplotter(2, 2, context)
html = ch9util.report_rain(votes, y_test, gscv.best_params_,
sp.ax)
sp.ax.set_title(sp.ax.get_title() + ' | Voting')
```

5. Plot the confusion matrix for the stacking-based forecast:

```
default.fit(preds_train.T, y_train)
stacked_preds = default.predict(preds.T)
html += ch9util.report_rain(stacked_preds,
                            y_test, default.get_params(), sp.next_
ax())
sp.ax.set_title(sp.ax.get_title() + ' | Stacking')
ch9util.report_rain(default.predict(preds.T), y_test)
```

6. Plot the learning curves of the voting and stacking classifiers:

```
ch9util.plot_learn_curve(sp.next_ax(), gscv.best_estimator_, X_
train,
                         y_train, title='Voting')

ch9util.plot_learn_curve(sp.next_ax(), default, X_train,
                         y_train, title='Stacking')
```

Refer to the following screenshot for the end result:

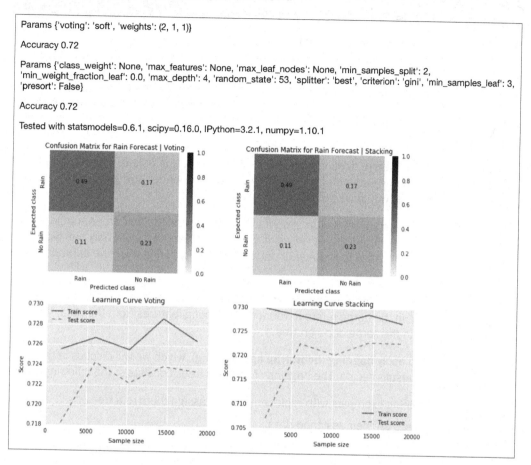

Params {'voting': 'soft', 'weights': (2, 1, 1)}

Accuracy 0.72

Params {'class_weight': None, 'max_features': None, 'max_leaf_nodes': None, 'min_samples_split': 2, 'min_weight_fraction_leaf': 0.0, 'max_depth': 4, 'random_state': 53, 'splitter': 'best', 'criterion': 'gini', 'min_samples_leaf': 3, 'presort': False}

Accuracy 0.72

Tested with statsmodels=0.6.1, scipy=0.16.0, IPython=3.2.1, numpy=1.10.1

The code is in the `stacking_multiple.ipynb` file in this book's code bundle.

See also

- The documentation for the `VotingClassifier` class at `http://scikit-learn.org/stable/modules/generated/sklearn.ensemble.VotingClassifier.html` (retrieved November 2015)

- The Wikipedia section about stacking at `https://en.wikipedia.org/wiki/Ensemble_learning#Stacking` (retrieved November 2015)

Learning with random forests

The `if a: else b` statement is one of the most common statements in Python programming. By nesting and combining such statements, we can build a so-called decision tree. This is similar to an old fashioned flowchart, although flowcharts also allow loops. The application of decision trees in machine learning is called **decision tree learning**. The end nodes of the trees in decision tree learning, also known as **leaves**, contain the class labels of a classification problem. Each non-leaf node is associated with a Boolean condition involving feature values.

Decision trees can be used to deduce relatively simple rules. Being able to produce such results is, of course, a huge advantage. However, you have to wonder how good these rules are. If we add new data, would we get the same rules?

If one decision tree is good, a whole forest should be even better. Multiple trees should reduce the chance of overfitting. However, as in a real forest, we don't want only one type of tree. Obviously, we would have to average or decide by majority voting what the appropriate result should be.

In this recipe, we will apply the **random forest** algorithm invented by Leo Breiman and Adele Cutler. The "random" in the name refers to randomly selecting features from the data. We use all the data but not in the same decision tree.

Random forests also apply **bagging** (**bootstrap aggregating**), which we will discuss in the *Bagging to improve results* recipe. The bagging of decision trees consists of the following steps:

1. Sample training examples with replacement and assign them to a tree.
2. Train the trees on their assigned data.

We can determine the correct number of trees by cross-validation or by plotting the test and train error against the number of trees.

How to do it...

The code is in the `random_forest.ipynb` file in this book's code bundle:

1. The imports are as follows:

```
import dautil as dl
from sklearn.grid_search import GridSearchCV
from sklearn.ensemble import RandomForestClassifier
import ch9util
import numpy as np
from IPython.display import HTML
```

2. Load the data and do a prediction as follows:

```
X_train, X_test, y_train, y_test = ch9util.rain_split()
clf = RandomForestClassifier(random_state=44)
params = {
    'max_depth': [2, 4],
    'min_samples_leaf': [1, 3],
    'criterion': ['gini', 'entropy'],
    'n_estimators': [100, 200]
}

rfc = GridSearchCV(estimator=RandomForestClassifier(),
                   param_grid=params, cv=5, n_jobs=-1)
rfc.fit(X_train, y_train)
preds = rfc.predict(X_test)
```

3. Plot the rain forecast confusion matrix as follows:

```
sp = dl.plotting.Subplotter(2, 2, context)
html = ch9util.report_rain(preds, y_test, rfc.best_params_, sp.ax)
```

4. Plot a validation curve for a range of forest sizes:

```
ntrees = 2 ** np.arange(9)
ch9util.plot_validation(sp.next_ax(), rfc.best_estimator_,
                        X_train, y_train, 'n_estimators', ntrees)
```

5. Plot a validation curve for a range of depths:

```
depths = np.arange(2, 9)
ch9util.plot_validation(sp.next_ax(), rfc.best_estimator_,
                        X_train, y_train, 'max_depth', depths)
```

6. Plot the learning curve of the best estimator:

```
ch9util.plot_learn_curve(sp.next_ax(),
                         rfc.best_estimator_, X_train, y_train)
HTML(html + sp.exit())
```

Refer to the following screenshot for the end result:

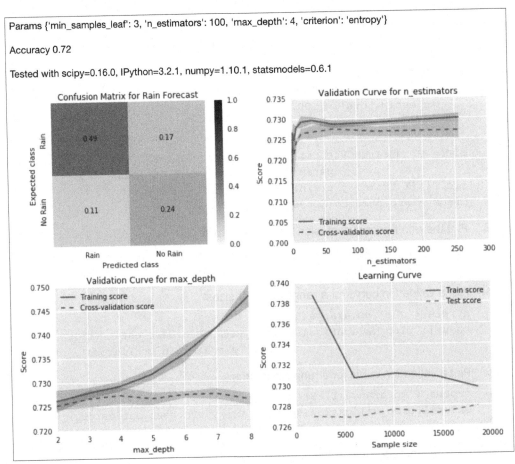

Params {'min_samples_leaf': 3, 'n_estimators': 100, 'max_depth': 4, 'criterion': 'entropy'}

Accuracy 0.72

Tested with scipy=0.16.0, IPython=3.2.1, numpy=1.10.1, statsmodels=0.6.1

There's more...

Random forests classification is considered such a versatile algorithm that we can use it for almost any classification task. **Genetic algorithms** and **genetic programming** can do a grid search or optimization in general.

We can consider a program to be a sequence of operators and operands that generates a result. This is a very simplified model of programming, of course. However, in such a model, it is possible to evolve programs using natural selection modeled after biological theories. A genetic program is self-modifying with huge adaptability, but we get a lower level of determinism.

The TPOT project is an attempt to evolve machine learning pipelines (currently uses a small number of classifiers including random forests). I forked TPOT 0.1.3 on GitHub and made some changes. TPOT uses `deap` for the genetic programming parts, which you can install as follows:

```
$ pip install deap
```

I tested the code with deap 1.0.2. Install my changes under tag `r1` as follows:

```
$ git clone git@github.com:ivanidris/tpot.git
$ cd tpot
$ git checkout r1
$ python setup.py install
```

You can also get the code from `https://github.com/ivanidris/tpot/releases/tag/r1`. The following code from the `rain_pot.py` file in this book's code bundle demonstrates how to fit and score rain predictions with TPOT:

```
import ch9util
from tpot import TPOT


X_train, X_test, y_train, y_test = ch9util.rain_split()
tpot = TPOT(generations=7, population_size=110, verbosity=2)
tpot.fit(X_train, y_train)
print(tpot.score(X_train, y_train, X_test, y_test))
```

See also

▸ The Wikipedia page about random forests at `https://en.wikipedia.org/wiki/Random_forest` (retrieved November 2015)

▸ The documentation for the `RandomForestClassifier` class at `http://scikit-learn.org/stable/modules/generated/sklearn.ensemble.RandomForestClassifier.html` (retrieved November 2015)

Fitting noisy data with the RANSAC algorithm

We discussed the issue of outliers in the context of regression elsewhere in this book (refer to the *See also* section at the end of this recipe). The issue is clear—the outliers make it difficult to properly fit our models. The **RANdom SAmple Consensus algorithm** (**RANSAC**) does a best effort attempt to fit our data in an iterative manner. RANSAC was introduced by Fishler and Bolles in 1981.

We often have some knowledge about our data, for instance the data may follow a normal distribution. Or, the data may be a mix produced by multiple processes with different characteristics. We could also have abnormal data due to glitches or errors in data transformation. In such cases, it should be easy to identify outliers and deal with them appropriately. The RANSAC algorithm doesn't know your data, but it also assumes that there are inliers and outliers.

The algorithm goes through a fixed number of iterations. The object is to find a set of inliers of specified size (**consensus set**).

RANSAC performs the following steps:

1. Randomly select as small a subset of the data as possible and fit the model.
2. Check whether each data point is consistent with the fitted model in the previous step. Mark inconsistent points as outliers using a residuals threshold.
3. Accept the model if enough inliers have been found.
4. Re-estimate parameters with the full consensus set.

The scikit-learn `RANSACRegressor` class can use a suitable estimator for fitting. We will use the default `LinearRegression` estimator. We can also specify the minimum number of samples for fitting, the residuals threshold, a decision function for outliers, a function that decides whether a model is valid, the maximum number of iterations, and the required number of inliers in the consensus set.

How to do it...

The code is in the `fit_ransac.ipynb` file in this book's code bundle:

1. The imports are as follows:

```
import ch9util
from sklearn import linear_model
from sklearn.grid_search import GridSearchCV
import numpy as np
import dautil as dl
from IPython.display import HTML
```

2. Load the data and do a temperature prediction as follows:

```
X_train, X_test, y_train, y_test = ch9util.temp_split()
ransac = linear_model.RANSACRegressor(random_state=27)
params = {
    'max_trials': [50, 100, 200],
    'stop_probability': [0.98, 0.99]
}

gscv = GridSearchCV(estimator=ransac, param_grid=params, cv=5)
gscv.fit(X_train, y_train)
preds = gscv.predict(X_test)
```

3. Scatter plot the predictions against the actual values:

```
sp = dl.plotting.Subplotter(2, 2, context)
html = ch9util.scatter_predictions(preds, y_test, gscv.best_
params_,
                                    gscv.best_score_, sp.ax)
```

4. Plot a validation curve for a range of trial numbers:

```
trials = 10 * np.arange(5, 20)
ch9util.plot_validation(sp.next_ax(), gscv.best_estimator_,
                        X_train, y_train, 'max_trials', trials)
```

5. Plot a validation curve for a range of stop probabilities:

```
probs = 0.01 * np.arange(90, 99)
ch9util.plot_validation(sp.next_ax(), gscv.best_estimator_,
                        X_train, y_train, 'stop_probability',
probs)
```

6. Plot a validation curve for a range of consensus set sizes:

```
ninliers = 2 ** np.arange(4, 14)
ch9util.plot_validation(sp.next_ax(), gscv.best_estimator_,
                        X_train, y_train, 'stop_n_inliers',
ninliers)
HTML(html + sp.exit())
```

Refer to the following screenshot for the end result:

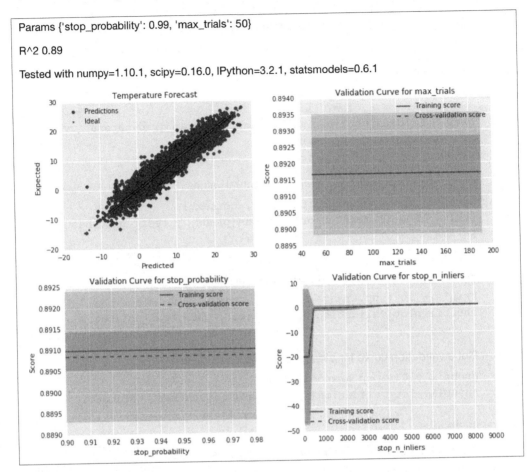

Params {'stop_probability': 0.99, 'max_trials': 50}

R^2 0.89

Tested with numpy=1.10.1, scipy=0.16.0, IPython=3.2.1, statsmodels=0.6.1

See also

▶ The Wikipedia page about the RANSAC algorithm at `https://en.wikipedia.org/wiki/RANSAC` (retrieved November 2015)

▶ The relevant scikit-learn documentation at `http://scikit-learn.org/stable/modules/generated/sklearn.linear_model.RANSACRegressor.html` (retrieved November 2015)

▶ The *Fitting a robust linear model* recipe

▶ The *Taking variance into account with weighted least squares* recipe

Bagging to improve results

Bootstrap aggregating or **bagging** is an algorithm introduced by Leo Breiman in 1994, which applies bootstrapping to machine learning problems. Bagging was also mentioned in the *Learning with random forests* recipe.

The algorithm aims to reduce the chance of overfitting with the following steps:

1. We generate new training sets from input training data by sampling with replacement.
2. Fit models to each generated training set.
3. Combine the results of the models by averaging or majority voting.

The scikit-learn `BaggingClassifier` class allows us to bootstrap training examples, and we can also bootstrap features as in the random forests algorithm. When we perform a grid search, we refer to hyperparameters of the base estimator with the prefix `base_estimator__`. We will use a decision tree as the base estimator so that we can reuse some of the hyperparameter configuration from the *Learning with random forests* recipe.

How to do it...

The code is in the `bagging.ipynb` file in this book's code bundle:

1. The imports are as follows:

```
import ch9util
from sklearn.ensemble import BaggingClassifier
from sklearn.grid_search import GridSearchCV
from sklearn.tree import DecisionTreeClassifier
import numpy as np
import dautil as dl
from IPython.display import HTML
```

2. Load the data and create a `BaggingClassifier`:

```
X_train, X_test, y_train, y_test = ch9util.rain_split()
clf = BaggingClassifier(base_estimator=DecisionTreeClassifier(
    min_samples_leaf=3, max_depth=4), random_state=43)
```

3. Grid search, fit, and predict as follows:

```
params = {
    'n_estimators': [320, 640],
    'bootstrap_features': [True, False],
    'base_estimator__criterion': ['gini', 'entropy']
}

gscv = GridSearchCV(estimator=clf, param_grid=params,
                    cv=5, n_jobs=-1)

gscv.fit(X_train, y_train)
preds = gscv.predict(X_test)
```

4. Plot the rain forecast confusion matrix as follows:

```
sp = dl.plotting.Subplotter(2, 2, context)
html = ch9util.report_rain(preds, y_test, gscv.best_params_,
sp.ax)
```

5. Plot a validation curve for a range of ensemble sizes:

```
ntrees = 2 ** np.arange(4, 11)
ch9util.plot_validation(sp.next_ax(), gscv.best_estimator_,
                        X_train, y_train, 'n_estimators', ntrees)
```

6. Plot a validation curve for the `max_samples` parameter:

```
nsamples = 2 ** np.arange(4, 14)
ch9util.plot_validation(sp.next_ax(), gscv.best_estimator_,
                        X_train, y_train, 'max_samples', nsamples)
```

7. Plot the learning curve as follows:

```
ch9util.plot_learn_curve(sp.next_ax(), gscv.best_estimator_,
                         X_train, y_train)

HTML(html + sp.exit())
```

Refer to the following screenshot for the end result:

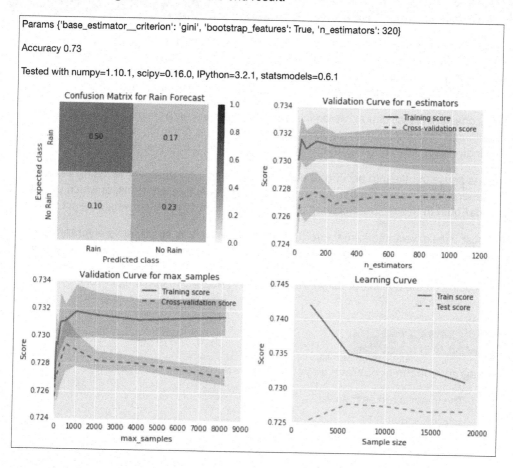

Params {'base_estimator__criterion': 'gini', 'bootstrap_features': True, 'n_estimators': 320}

Accuracy 0.73

Tested with numpy=1.10.1, scipy=0.16.0, IPython=3.2.1, statsmodels=0.6.1

See also

▸ The Wikipedia page for bagging at `https://en.wikipedia.org/wiki/Bootstrap_aggregating` (retrieved November 2015)

▸ The documentation for the `BaggingClassifier` at `http://scikit-learn.org/stable/modules/generated/sklearn.ensemble.BaggingClassifier.html` (retrieved November 2015)

Boosting for better learning

Strength in numbers is the reason why large countries tend to be more successful than small countries. That doesn't mean that a person in a large country has a better life. But for the big picture, the individual person doesn't matter that much, just like in an ensemble of decision trees the results of a single tree can be ignored if we have enough trees.

In the context of classification, we define **weak learners** as learners that are just a little better than a baseline such as randomly assigning classes. Although weak learners are weak individually, like ants, together they can do amazing things just like ants can.

It makes sense to take into account the strength of each individual learner using weights. This general idea is called **boosting**. There are many boosting algorithms, of which we will use **AdaBoost** in this recipe. Boosting algorithms differ mostly in their weighting scheme.

AdaBoost uses a weighted sum to produce the final result. It is an adaptive algorithm that tries to boost the results for individual training examples. If you have studied for an exam, you may have applied a similar technique by identifying the type of questions you had trouble with and focusing on the difficult problems. In the case of AdaBoost, boosting is done by tweaking the weak learners.

How to do it...

The program is in the `boosting.ipynb` file in this book's code bundle:

1. The imports are as follows:

```
import ch9util
from sklearn.grid_search import GridSearchCV
from sklearn.ensemble import AdaBoostRegressor
from sklearn.tree import DecisionTreeRegressor
import numpy as np
import dautil as dl
from IPython.display import HTML
```

2. Load the data and create an `AdaBoostRegressor` class:

```
X_train, X_test, y_train, y_test = ch9util.temp_split()
params = {
    'loss': ['linear', 'square', 'exponential'],
    'base_estimator__min_samples_leaf': [1, 2]
}
reg = AdaBoostRegressor(base_estimator=DecisionTreeRegressor(rand
om_state=28),
                        random_state=17)
```

3. Grid search, fit, and predict as follows:

```
gscv = GridSearchCV(estimator=reg,
                    param_grid=params, cv=5, n_jobs=-1)
gscv.fit(X_train, y_train)
preds = gscv.predict(X_test)
```

4. Scatter plot the predictions against the actual values:

```
sp = dl.plotting.Subplotter(2, 2, context)
html = ch9util.scatter_predictions(preds, y_test, gscv.best_
params_,
                        gscv.best_score_, sp.ax)
```

5. Plot a validation curve for a range of ensemble sizes:

```
nestimators = 2 ** np.arange(3, 9)
ch9util.plot_validation(sp.next_ax(), gscv.best_estimator_,
                        X_train, y_train, 'n_estimators',
nestimators)
```

6. Plot a validation curve for a range of learning rates:

```
learn_rate = np.linspace(0.1, 1, 9)
ch9util.plot_validation(sp.next_ax(), gscv.best_estimator_,
                        X_train, y_train, 'learning_rate', learn_
rate)
```

7. Plot the learning curve as follows:

```
ch9util.plot_learn_curve(sp.next_ax(), gscv.best_estimator_,
                        X_train, y_train)
HTML(html + sp.exit())
```

Refer to the following screenshot for the end result:

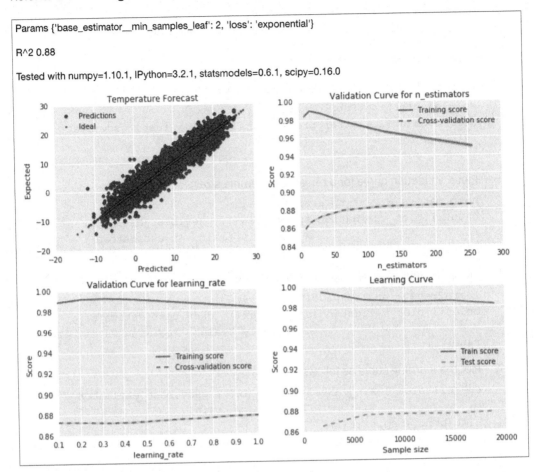

Params {'base_estimator__min_samples_leaf': 2, 'loss': 'exponential'}

R^2 0.88

Tested with numpy=1.10.1, IPython=3.2.1, statsmodels=0.6.1, scipy=0.16.0

See also

▶ The Wikipedia page about boosting at `https://en.wikipedia.org/wiki/ Boosting_%28machine_learning%29` (retrieved November 2015)

▶ The Wikipedia page about AdaBoost at `https://en.wikipedia.org/wiki/ AdaBoost` (retrieved November 2015)

▶ The documentation for the `AdaBoostRegressor` class at `http://scikit- learn.org/stable/modules/generated/sklearn.ensemble. AdaBoostRegressor.html` (retrieved November 2015)

Nesting cross-validation

If we are fitting data to a straight line, the parameters of the mathematical model will be the slope and intercept of the line. When we determine the parameters of a model, we fit the model on a subset of the data (training set), and we evaluate the performance of the model on the rest of the data (test set). This is called **validation** and there are more elaborate schemes. The scikit-learn `GridSearchCV` class uses k-fold cross-validation, for example.

Classifiers and regressors usually require extra parameters (hyperparameters) such as the number of components of an ensemble, which usually have nothing to do with the linear model as mentioned in the first sentence. It's a bit confusing to talk about models because we have models with plain parameters and a bigger model with hyperparameters.

Let's call the bigger model a level 2 model, although this is not standard nomenclature as far as I know. If we are using `GridSearchCV` to obtain the hyperparameters of the level 2 model, we have another set of parameters (not hyperparameters or level 1 parameters) to worry about—the number of folds and the metric used for comparison. Evaluation metrics have not passed the review yet (refer to *Chapter 10, Evaluating Classifiers, Regressors, and Clusters*), but there are more metrics than we used in this chapter. Also, we might worry whether we determined the hyperparameters on the same data as used to evaluate the results. One solution is to apply **nested cross-validation**.

Nested cross-validation consists of the following cross-validations:

▶   The inner cross-validation does hyperparameter optimization, for instance using grid search

▶   The outer cross-validation is used to evaluate performance and do statistical analysis

In this recipe, we will look at the following distributions:

▶   The distribution of all the scores

▶   The distribution of the best scores for each outer cross-validation iteration reported by `GridSearchCV`

▶   The distribution of the mean scores for each fold

▶   The distribution of the standard deviations of scores within a `GridSearchCV` iteration

How to do it...

The code is in the `nested_cv.ipynb` file in this book's code bundle:

1.   The imports are as follows:

```
from sklearn.grid_search import GridSearchCV
from sklearn.cross_validation import ShuffleSplit
from sklearn.cross_validation import cross_val_score
```

```
import dautil as dl
from sklearn.ensemble import ExtraTreesRegressor
from joblib import Memory
import numpy as np
from IPython.display import HTML

memory = Memory(cachedir='.')
```

2. Get the R-squared scores as described in the previous section:

```
@memory.cache
def get_scores():
    df = dl.data.Weather.load()[['WIND_SPEED', 'TEMP',
'PRESSURE']].dropna()
    X = df.values[:-1]
    y = df['TEMP'][1:]

    params = { 'min_samples_split': [1, 3],
            'min_samples_leaf': [3, 4]}

    gscv = GridSearchCV(ExtraTreesRegressor(bootstrap=True,
                                            random_state=37),
                    param_grid=params, n_jobs=-1, cv=5)
    cv_outer = ShuffleSplit(len(X), n_iter=500,
                            test_size=0.3, random_state=55)

    r2 = []
    best = []
    means = []
    stds = []

    for train_indices, test_indices in cv_outer:
        train_i = X[train_indices], y[train_indices]
        gscv.fit(*train_i)
        test_i = X[test_indices]
        gscv.predict(test_i)
        grid_scores = dl.collect.flatten([g.cv_validation_scores
            for g in gscv.grid_scores_])
        r2.extend(grid_scores)
        means.extend(dl.collect.flatten([g.mean_validation_score
            for g in gscv.grid_scores_]))
        stds.append(np.std(grid_scores))
        best.append(gscv.best_score_)

    return {'r2': r2, 'best': best, 'mean': means, 'std': stds}
```

3. Get the scores and load them into NumPy arrays:

```
scores = get_scores()
r2 = np.array(scores['r2'])
avgs = np.array(scores['mean'])
stds = np.array(scores['std'])
best = np.array(scores['best'])
```

4. Plot the distributions as follows:

```
sp = dl.plotting.Subplotter(2, 2, context)
dl.plotting.hist_norm_pdf(sp.ax, r2)
sp.label()

dl.plotting.hist_norm_pdf(sp.next_ax(), best)
sp.label()

dl.plotting.hist_norm_pdf(sp.next_ax(), avgs)
sp.label()

dl.plotting.hist_norm_pdf(sp.next_ax(), stds)
sp.label()
HTML(sp.exit())
```

Refer to the following screenshot for the end result (distributions of cross-validation results):

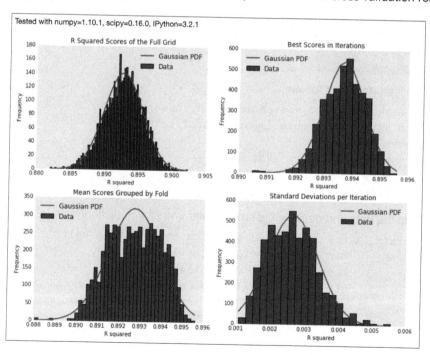

See also

▸ The Wikipedia page about cross-validation at `https://en.wikipedia.org/wiki/Cross-validation_%28statistics%29` (retrieved November 2015)

▸ The Wikipedia page about hyperparameter optimization at `https://en.wikipedia.org/wiki/Hyperparameter_optimization` (retrieved November 2015)

Reusing models with joblib

The joblib `Memory` class is a utility class that facilitates caching of function or method results to disk. We create a `Memory` object by specifying a caching directory. We can then decorate the function to cache or specify methods to cache in a class constructor. If you like, you can specify the arguments to ignore. The default behavior of the `Memory` class is to remove the cache any time the function is modified or the input values change. Obviously, you can also remove the cache manually by moving or deleting cache directories and files.

In this recipe, I describe how to reuse a scikit-learn regressor or classifier. The naïve method would be to store the object in a standard Python pickle or use joblib. However, in most cases, it is better to store the hyperparameters of the estimator.

We will use the `ExtraTreesRegressor` class as estimator. **Extra trees (extremely randomized trees)** are a variation of the random forest algorithm, which is covered in the *Learning with random forests* recipe.

How to do it...

1. The imports are as follows:

```
from sklearn.grid_search import GridSearchCV
from sklearn.ensemble import ExtraTreesRegressor
import ch9util
from tempfile import mkdtemp
import os
import joblib
```

2. Load the data and define a hyperparameter grid search dictionary:

```
X_train, X_test, y_train, y_test = ch9util.temp_split()
params = {'min_samples_split': [1, 3],
          'bootstrap': [True, False],
          'min_samples_leaf': [3, 4]}
```

3. Do a grid search as follows:

```
gscv = GridSearchCV(ExtraTreesRegressor(random_state=41),
                    param_grid=params, cv=5)
```

4. Fit and predict as follows:

```
gscv.fit(X_train, y_train)
preds = gscv.predict(X_test)
```

5. Store the best parameters found by the grid search:

```
dir = mkdtemp()
pkl = os.path.join(dir, 'params.pkl')
joblib.dump(gscv.best_params_, pkl)
params = joblib.load(pkl)
print('Best params', gscv.best_params_)
print('From pkl', params)
```

6. Create a new estimator and compare the predictions:

```
est = ExtraTreesRegressor(random_state=41)
est.set_params(**params)
est.fit(X_train, y_train)
preds2 = est.predict(X_test)
print('Max diff', (preds - preds2).max())
```

Refer to the following screenshot for the end result:

```
Best params {'min_samples_split': 1, 'min_samples_leaf': 4, 'bootstrap': True}
From pkl {'bootstrap': True, 'min_samples_leaf': 4, 'min_samples_split': 1}
Max diff 0.0
```

The code is in the `reusing_models.py` file in this book's code bundle.

See also

▸ The documentation for the `Memory` class at `https://pythonhosted.org/joblib/memory.html` (retrieved November 2015)

▸ The Wikipedia page about random forests at `https://en.wikipedia.org/wiki/Random_forest` (retrieved November 2015)

Hierarchically clustering data

In *Python Data Analysis*, you learned about clustering—separating data into clusters without providing any hints-which is a form of unsupervised learning. Sometimes, we need to take a guess for the number of clusters, as we did in the *Clustering streaming data with Spark* recipe.

There is no restriction against having clusters contain other clusters. In such a case, we speak of **hierarchical clustering**. We need a distance metric to separate data points. Take a look at the following equations:

$$(9.2) \quad \|a-b\|_2 = \sqrt{\sum_i (a_i - b_i)^2}$$

$$(9.3) \quad \min\{d(a,b) : a \in A, b \in B\}$$

In this recipe, we will use Euclidean distance (9.2), provided by the SciPy `pdist()` function. The distance between sets of points is given by the linkage criteria. In this recipe, we will use the single-linkage criteria (9.3) provided by the SciPy `linkage()` function.

How to do it...

The script is in the `clustering_hierarchy.ipynb` file in this book's code bundle:

1. The imports are as follows:

```
from scipy.spatial.distance import pdist
from scipy.cluster.hierarchy import linkage
from scipy.cluster.hierarchy import dendrogram
import dautil as dl
import matplotlib.pyplot as plt
```

2. Load the data, resample to annual values, and compute distances:

```
df = dl.data.Weather.load().resample('A').dropna()
dist = pdist(df)
```

3. Plot the hierarchical cluster as follows:

```
dendrogram(linkage(dist), labels=[d.year for d in df.index],
           orientation='right')
plt.tick_params(labelsize=8)
plt.xlabel('Cluster')
plt.ylabel('Year')
```

Refer to the following screenshot for the end result:

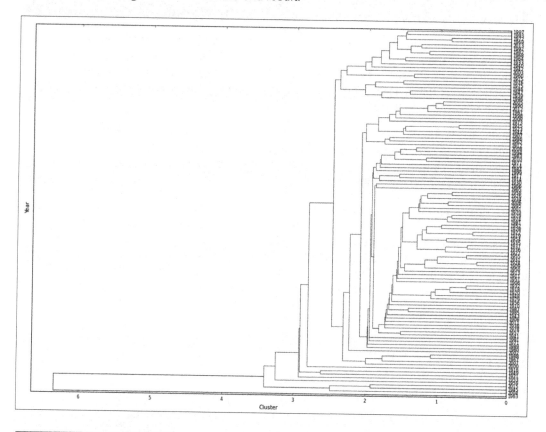

See also

- ▸ The Wikipedia page about hierarchical clustering at `https://en.wikipedia.org/wiki/Hierarchical_clustering` (retrieved November 2015)

- ▸ The documentation for the `pdist()` function at `https://docs.scipy.org/doc/scipy/reference/generated/scipy.spatial.distance.pdist.html` (retrieved November 2015)

- ▸ The documentation for the `linkage()` function at `https://docs.scipy.org/doc/scipy/reference/generated/scipy.cluster.hierarchy.linkage.html` (retrieved November 2015)

Taking a Theano tour

Theano is a Python library created by a machine learning group in Montreal and is often associated with deep learning, although that is not necessarily its core purpose. Theano is tightly integrated with NumPy and can run code on CPU or GPU. If you are interested in the GPU option, refer to the documentation listed in the *See also* section. Theano also supports symbolic differentiation through symbolic variables.

According to the its documentation, Theano is a cross between NumPy and SymPy. It is possible to implement machine learning algorithms with Theano, but it's not as easy or convenient as using scikit-learn. However, you may get the potential advantages of higher parallelism and numerical stability.

In this recipe, we will perform linear regression of temperature data using **gradient descent**. Gradient descent is an optimization algorithm that we can use in a regression context to minimize fit residuals. The gradient measures how steep a function is. The algorithm takes many steps proportional to how steep the gradient is in order to find a local minimum. We are trying to go downhill, but we don't know in which direction we can find a local minimum. So, going for a large move down should on average get us down faster, but there is no guarantee. In some cases, it may help to smooth the function (smoother hill), so we don't spend a lot of time oscillating.

Getting ready

Install Theano with the following command:

```
$ pip install --no-deps git+git://github.com/Theano/Theano.git
```

I tested the code with the bleeding edge version as of November 2015.

How to do it...

The code is in the `theano_tour.ipynb` file in this book's code bundle:

1. The imports are as follows:

   ```
   import theano
   import numpy as np
   import theano.tensor as T
   import ch9util
   from sklearn.cross_validation import train_test_split
   from sklearn.metrics import r2_score
   import dautil as dl
   from IPython.display import HTML
   ```

2. Load the temperature data and define Theano symbolic variables:

```
temp = dl.data.Weather.load()['TEMP'].dropna()
X = temp.values[:-1]
y = temp.values[1:]
X_train, X_test, y_train, y_test = train_test_split(X, y, random_
state=16)
w = theano.shared(0., name ='w')
c = theano.shared(0., name ='c')

x = T.vector('x')
y = T.vector('y')
```

3. Define prediction and cost (loss) functions to minimize:

```
prediction = T.dot(x, w) + c
cost = T.sum(T.pow(prediction - y, 2))/(2 * X_train.shape[0])
Define gradient functions as follows:
gw = T.grad(cost, w)
gc = T.grad(cost, c)

learning_rate = 0.01
training_steps = 10000
```

4. Define the training function as follows:

```
train = theano.function([x, y], cost, updates =
                            [(w, w - learning_rate * gw),
                             (c, c - learning_rate * gc)])
predict = theano.function([x], prediction)
```

5. Train the estimator as follows:

```
for i in range(training_steps):
    train(X_train.astype(np.float), y_train)
```

6. Predict and visualize the prediction as follows:

```
preds = predict(X_test)
r2 = r2_score(preds, y_test)
HTML(ch9util.scatter_predictions(preds, y_test, '', r2))
```

Refer to the following screenshot for the end result:

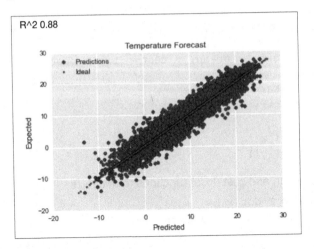

See also

- The Theano documentation at `http://deeplearning.net/software/theano/` (retrieved November 2015)

- The Wikipedia page about gradient descent at `https://en.wikipedia.org/wiki/Gradient_descent` (retrieved November 2015)

10
Evaluating Classifiers, Regressors, and Clusters

In this chapter, we will cover the following recipes:

- ▸ Getting classification straight with the confusion matrix
- ▸ Computing precision, recall, and F1-score
- ▸ Examining a receiver operating characteristic and the area under a curve
- ▸ Visualizing the goodness of fit
- ▸ Computing MSE and median absolute error
- ▸ Evaluating clusters with the mean silhouette coefficient
- ▸ Comparing results with a dummy classifier
- ▸ Determining MAPE and MPE
- ▸ Comparing with a dummy regressor
- ▸ Calculating the mean absolute error and the residual sum of squares
- ▸ Examining the kappa of classification
- ▸ Taking a look at the Matthews correlation coefficient

Introduction

Evaluating classifiers, regressors, and clusters is a critical multidimensional problem involving many aspects. Purely from an engineering perspective, we worry about speed, memory, and correctness. Under some circumstances, speed is everything. If memory is scarce, of course, we have to make that our priority. The world is a giant labyrinth full of choices, and you are sometimes forced to choose one model over others instead of using multiple models in an ensemble. We should, of course, inform our rational decision with appropriate evaluation metrics.

There are so many evaluation metrics out there that you would need multiple books to describe them all. Obviously, many of the metrics are very similar. Some of them are accepted and popular, and of those metrics, some are implemented in scikit-learn.

We will evaluate the classifiers and regressors from *Chapter 9, Ensemble Learning and Dimensionality Reduction*. We applied those estimators to the sample problem of weather forecasting. This is not necessarily a problem at which humans are good. Achieving human performance is the goal for some problems, such as face recognition, character recognition, spam classification, and sentiment analysis. As a baseline to beat, we often choose some form of random guessing.

Getting classification straight with the confusion matrix

Accuracy is a metric that measures how well a model has performed in a given context. Accuracy is the default evaluation metric of scikit-learn classifiers. Unfortunately, accuracy is one-dimensional, and it doesn't help when the classes are unbalanced. The rain data we examined in *Chapter 9, Ensemble Learning and Dimensionality Reduction*, is pretty balanced. The number of rainy days is almost equal to the number of days on which it doesn't rain. In the case of e-mail spam classification, at least for me, the balance is shifted toward spam.

A **confusion matrix** is a table that is usually used to summarize the results of classification. The two dimensions of the table are the predicted class and the target class. In the context of binary classification, we talk about positive and negative classes. Naming a class negative is arbitrary—it doesn't necessarily mean that it is bad in some way. We can reduce any multi-class problem to one class versus the rest of the problem; so, when we evaluate binary classification, we can extend the framework to multi-class classification. A class can either be correctly predicted or not; we label those instances with the words true and false accordingly.

We have four combinations of true, false, positive, and negative, as described in the following table:

	Predicted class	
Target class	**True positives**: It rained and we correctly predicted it.	**False positives**: We incorrectly predicted that it would rain.
	False negatives: It did rain, but we predicted that it wouldn't.	**True negatives**: It didn't rain, and we correctly predicted it.

How to do it...

1. The imports are as follows:

```
import numpy as np
from sklearn.metrics import confusion_matrix
import seaborn as sns
import dautil as dl
from IPython.display import HTML
import ch10util
```

2. Define the following function to plot the confusion matrix:

```
def plot_cm(preds, y_test, title, cax):
    cm = confusion_matrix(preds.T, y_test)
    normalized_cm = cm/cm.sum().astype(float)
    sns.heatmap(normalized_cm, annot=True, fmt='.2f', vmin=0,
vmax=1,
                xticklabels=['Rain', 'No Rain'],
                yticklabels=['Rain', 'No Rain'], ax=cax)
    cax.set_xlabel('Predicted class')
    cax.set_ylabel('Expected class')
    cax.set_title('Confusion Matrix for Rain Forecast | ' + title)
```

3. Load the target values and plot the confusion matrix for the random forest classifier, bagging classifier, voting, and stacking classifier:

```
y_test = np.load('rain_y_test.npy')
sp = dl.plotting.Subplotter(2, 2, context)

plot_cm(y_test, np.load('rfc.npy'), 'Random Forest', sp.ax)

plot_cm(y_test, np.load('bagging.npy'), 'Bagging', sp.next_ax())

plot_cm(y_test, np.load('votes.npy'),'Votes', sp.next_ax())

plot_cm(y_test, np.load('stacking.npy'), 'Stacking', sp.next_ax())
sp.fig.text(0, 1, ch10util.classifiers())
HTML(sp.exit())
```

Refer to the following screenshot for the end result:

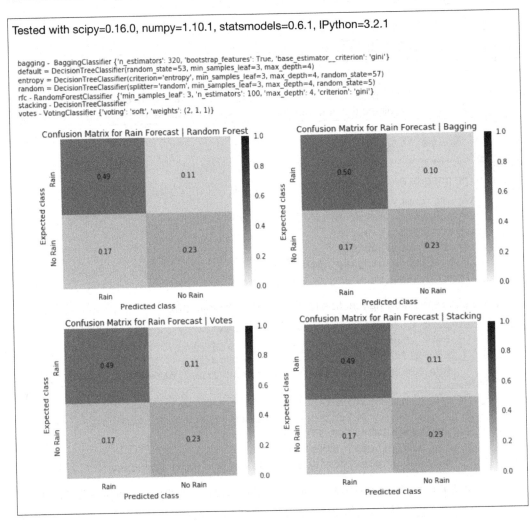

Tested with scipy=0.16.0, numpy=1.10.1, statsmodels=0.6.1, IPython=3.2.1

bagging - BaggingClassifier {'n_estimators': 320, 'bootstrap_features': True, 'base_estimator__criterion': 'gini'}
default = DecisionTreeClassifier(random_state=53, min_samples_leaf=3, max_depth=4)
entropy = DecisionTreeClassifier(criterion='entropy', min_samples_leaf=3, max_depth=4, random_state=57)
random = DecisionTreeClassifier(splitter='random', min_samples_leaf=3, max_depth=4, random_state=5)
rfc - RandomForestClassifier {'min_samples_leaf': 3, 'n_estimators': 100, 'max_depth': 4, 'criterion': 'gini'}
stacking - DecisionTreeClassifier
votes - VotingClassifier {'voting': 'soft', 'weights': (2, 1, 1)}

The source code is in the `conf_matrix.ipynb` file in this book's code bundle.

How it works

We displayed four confusion matrices for four classifiers, and the four numbers of each matrix seem to be repeating. Of course, the numbers are not exactly equal; however, you have to allow for some random variation.

▸ The Wikipedia page about the confusion matrix at `https://en.wikipedia.org/wiki/Confusion_matrix` (retrieved November 2015)

▸ The `confusion_matrix()` function documented at `http://scikit-learn.org/stable/modules/generated/sklearn.metrics.confusion_matrix.html` (retrieved November 2015)

Computing precision, recall, and F1-score

In the *Getting classification straight with the confusion matrix* recipe, you learned that we can label classified samples as true positives, false positives, true negatives, and false negatives. With the counts of these categories, we can calculate many evaluation metrics of which we will cover four in this recipe, as given by the following equations:

$$(10.1) \quad Accuracy = \frac{T_p + T_n}{T_p + T_n + F_p + F_n}$$

$$(10.2) \quad Precision = \frac{T_p}{T_p + F_p}$$

$$(10.3) \quad Recall = \frac{T_p}{T_p + T_n}$$

$$(10.4) \quad F_1 = 2 \cdot \frac{precision \cdot recall}{precision + recall}$$

These metrics range from zero to one, with zero being the worst theoretical score and one being the best. Actually, the worst score would be the one we get by random guessing. The best score in practice may be lower than one because in some cases we can only hope to emulate human performance, and there may be ambiguity about what correct classification should be, for instance, in the case of sentiment analysis (covered in the *Python Data Analysis* book).

▸ The accuracy (10.1) is the ratio of correct predictions.

▸ **Precision** (10.2) measures relevance as the likelihood of classifying a negative class sample as positive. Choosing which class is positive is somewhat arbitrary, but let's say that a rainy day is positive. High precision would mean that we labeled a relatively small number of non-rainy (negative) days as rainy. For a search (web, database, or other), it would mean a relatively high number of relevant results.

- ▶ **Recall** (10.3) is the likelihood of finding all the positive samples. If again, rainy days are our positive class, the more rainy days are classified correctly, the higher the recall. For a search, we can get a perfect recall by returning all the documents because this will automatically return all the relevant documents. A human brain is a bit like a database, and in that context, recall will mean the likelihood of remembering, for instance, how a certain Python function works.

- ▶ The **F1 score** (10.4) is the harmonic mean of precision and recall (actually, there are multiple variations of the F1 score). The G score uses the geometric mean; but, as far as I know, it is less popular. The idea behind the F1 score, related F scores and G scores, is to combine the precision and recall. That doesn't necessarily make it the best metric. There are other metrics you may prefer, such as the **Matthews correlation coefficient** (refer to the *Taking a look at the Matthews correlation coefficient* recipe) and **Cohen's kappa** (refer to the *Examining kappa of classification* recipe). When we facie the choice of so many classification metrics, we obviously want the best metric. However, you have to make the choice based on your situation, as there is no metric that fits all.

How to do it...

1. The imports are as follows:

```
import numpy as np
from sklearn import metrics
import ch10util
import dautil as dl
from IPython.display import HTML
```

2. Load the target values and calculate the metrics:

```
y_test = np.load('rain_y_test.npy')
accuracies = [metrics.accuracy_score(y_test, preds)
              for preds in ch10util.rain_preds()]
precisions = [metrics.precision_score(y_test, preds)
              for preds in ch10util.rain_preds()]
recalls = [metrics.recall_score(y_test, preds)
              for preds in ch10util.rain_preds()]
f1s = [metrics.f1_score(y_test, preds)
          for preds in ch10util.rain_preds()]
```

3. Plot the metrics for the rain forecasts:

```
sp = dl.plotting.Subplotter(2, 2, context)
ch10util.plot_bars(sp.ax, accuracies)
sp.label()
```

```
ch10util.plot_bars(sp.next_ax(), precisions)
sp.label()

ch10util.plot_bars(sp.next_ax(), recalls)
sp.label()

ch10util.plot_bars(sp.next_ax(), f1s)
sp.label()
sp.fig.text(0, 1, ch10util.classifiers())
HTML(sp.exit())
```

Refer to the following screenshot for the end result:

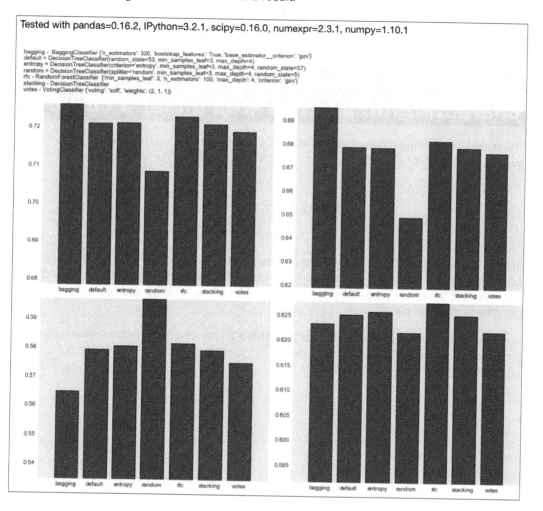

The code is in the `precision_recall.ipynb` file in this book's code bundle.

See also

- The Wikipedia page about precision and recall at `https://en.wikipedia.org/wiki/Precision_and_recall` (retrieved November 2015)

- The `precision_score()` function documented at `http://scikit-learn.org/stable/modules/generated/sklearn.metrics.precision_score.html` (retrieved November 2015)

- The `recall_score()` function documented at `http://scikit-learn.org/stable/modules/generated/sklearn.metrics.recall_score.html` (retrieved November 2015)

- The `f1_score()` function documented at `http://scikit-learn.org/stable/modules/generated/sklearn.metrics.f1_score.html` (retrieved November 2015)

Examining a receiver operating characteristic and the area under a curve

The **receiver operating characteristic** (**ROC**) is a plot of the recall (10.3) and the **false positive rate** (**FPR**) of a binary classifier. The FPR is given by the following equation:

$$(10.5) \quad FPR = \frac{F_p}{F_p + T_n}$$

In this recipe, we will plot the ROC for the various classifiers we used in *Chapter 9, Ensemble Learning and Dimensionality Reduction*. Also, we will plot the curve associated with random guessing and the ideal curve. Obviously, we want to beat the baseline and get as close as possible to the ideal curve.

The **area under the curve** (**AUC**, **ROC AUC**, or **AUROC**) is another evaluation metric that summarizes the ROC. AUC can also be used to compare models, but it provides less information than ROC.

How to do it...

1. The imports are as follows:

```
from sklearn import metrics
import numpy as np
import ch10util
import dautil as dl
from IPython.display import HTML
```

2. Load the data and calculate metrics:

```
y_test = np.load('rain_y_test.npy')
roc_aucs = [metrics.roc_auc_score(y_test, preds)
            for preds in ch10util.rain_preds()]
```

3. Plot the AUROC for the rain predictors:

```
sp = dl.plotting.Subplotter(2, 1, context)
ch10util.plot_bars(sp.ax, roc_aucs)
sp.label()
```

4. Plot the ROC curves for the rain predictors:

```
cp = dl.plotting.CyclePlotter(sp.next_ax())

for preds, label in zip(ch10util.rain_preds(),
                        ch10util.rain_labels()):
    fpr, tpr, _ = metrics.roc_curve(y_test, preds,
                                    pos_label=True)
    cp.plot(fpr, tpr, label=label)

fpr, tpr, _ = metrics.roc_curve(y_test, y_test)
sp.ax.plot(fpr, tpr, 'k', lw=4, label='Ideal')
sp.ax.plot(np.linspace(0, 1), np.linspace(0, 1),
           '--', label='Baseline')
sp.label()
sp.fig.text(0, 1, ch10util.classifiers())
HTML(sp.exit())
```

Refer to the following screenshot for the end result:

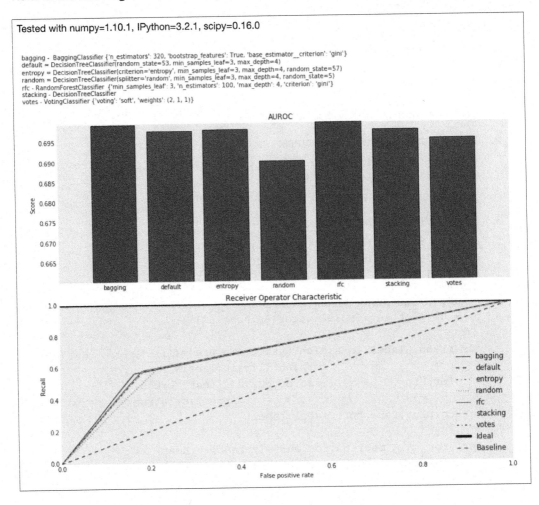

Tested with numpy=1.10.1, IPython=3.2.1, scipy=0.16.0

The code is in the `roc_auc.ipynb` file in this book's code bundle.

See also

▸ The Wikipedia page about the ROC at `https://en.wikipedia.org/wiki/Receiver_operating_characteristic` (retrieved November 2015)

▸ The `roc_auc_score()` function documented at `http://scikit-learn.org/stable/modules/generated/sklearn.metrics.roc_auc_score.html` (retrieved November 2015)

Visualizing the goodness of fit

We expect, or at least hope, that the residuals of regression are just random noise. If that is not the case, then our regressor may be ignoring information. We expect the residuals to be independent and normally distributed. It is relatively easy to check with a histogram or a QQ plot. In general, we want the mean of the residuals to be as close to zero as possible, and we want the variance of the residuals to be as small as possible. An ideal fit will have zero-valued residuals.

How to do it...

1. The imports are as follows:

```
import numpy as np
import matplotlib.pyplot as plt
import dautil as dl
import seaborn as sns
from scipy.stats import probplot
from IPython.display import HTML
```

2. Load the target and predictions for the boosting regressor:

```
y_test = np.load('temp_y_test.npy')
preds = np.load('boosting.npy')
```

3. Plot the actual and predicted values as follows:

```
sp = dl.plotting.Subplotter(2, 2, context)
cp = dl.plotting.CyclePlotter(sp.ax)
cp.plot(y_test)
cp.plot(preds)
sp.ax.set_ylabel(dl.data.Weather.get_header('TEMP'))
sp.label()
```

4. Plot the residuals on their own as follows:

```
residuals = preds - y_test
sp.next_ax().plot(residuals)
sp.label()
```

5. Plot the distribution of the residuals:

```
sns.distplot(residuals, ax=sp.next_ax())
sp.label()
```

6. Plot a QQ plot of the residuals:

```
probplot(residuals, plot=sp.next_ax())
HTML(sp.exit())
```

Refer to the following screenshot for the end result:

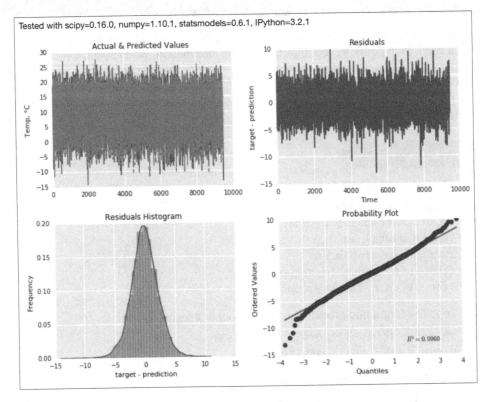

The code is in the `visualizing_goodness.ipynb` file in this book's code bundle.

See also

▸ The `probplot()` function documented at `https://docs.scipy.org/doc/scipy-0.16.0/reference/generated/scipy.stats.probplot.html` (retrieved November 2015)

Computing MSE and median absolute error

The **mean squared error (MSE)** and **median absolute error (MedAE)** are popular regression metrics. They are given by the following equations:

$$(10.6) \quad MSE = \frac{1}{n}\sum_{i=1}^{n}\left(\hat{Y}_i - Y_i\right)^2$$

$$(10.7) \quad MedAE(y, \hat{y}) = median\left(\left|y1 - \hat{y}1\right|, \ldots, \left|y_n - \hat{y}_n\right|\right)$$

The MSE (10.6) is analogous to population variance. The square root of the MSE (**RMSE**) is, therefore, analogous to standard deviation. The units of the MSE are the same as the variable under analysis—in our case, temperature. An ideal fit has zero-valued residuals and, therefore, its MSE is equal to zero. Since we are dealing with squared errors, the MSE has values that are larger or ideally equal to zero.

The MedAE is similar to the MSE, but we start with the absolute values of the residuals, and we use the median instead of the mean as the measure for centrality. The MedAE is also analogous to variance and is ideally zero or very small. Taking the absolute value instead of squaring potentially avoids numerical instability and speed issues, and the median is more robust for outliers than the mean. Also, taking the square tends to emphasize larger errors.

In this recipe, we will plot bootstrapped populations of MSE and MedAE for the regressors from *Chapter 9, Ensemble Learning and Dimensionality Reduction*.

How to do it...

1. The imports are as follows:

```
from sklearn import metrics
import ch10util
from IPython.display import HTML
import dautil as dl
from IPython.display import HTML
```

2. Plot the distributions of the metrics for the temperature predictors:

```
sp = dl.plotting.Subplotter(3, 2, context)
ch10util.plot_bootstrap('boosting',
                        metrics.mean_squared_error, sp.ax)
sp.label()

ch10util.plot_bootstrap('boosting',
                        metrics.median_absolute_error, sp.next_
ax())
sp.label()

ch10util.plot_bootstrap('etr',
                        metrics.mean_squared_error, sp.next_ax())
sp.label()

ch10util.plot_bootstrap('etr',
                        metrics.median_absolute_error, sp.next_
ax())
sp.label()
```

```
ch10util.plot_bootstrap('ransac',
                        metrics.mean_squared_error, sp.next_ax())

sp.label()

ch10util.plot_bootstrap('ransac',
                        metrics.median_absolute_error, sp.next_
ax())
sp.label()
sp.fig.text(0, 1, ch10util.regressors())
HTML(sp.exit())
```

Refer to the following screenshot for the end result:

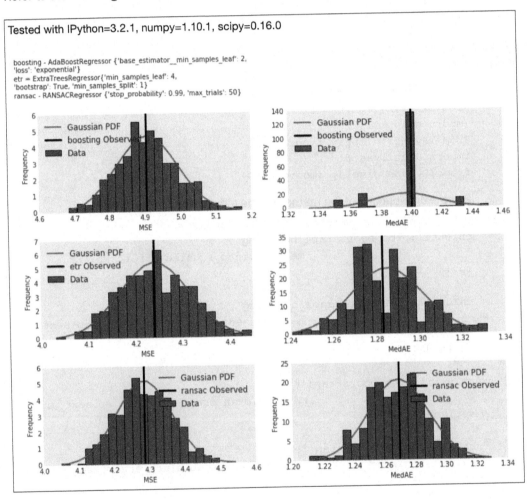

The code is in the `mse.ipynb` file in this book's code bundle.

See also

▸ The Wikipedia page about the MSE at `https://en.wikipedia.org/wiki/Mean_squared_error` (retrieved November 2015)

▸ The `mean_squared_error()` function documented at `http://scikit-learn.org/stable/modules/generated/sklearn.metrics.mean_squared_error.html` (retrieved November 2015)

▸ The `median_absolute_error()` function documented at `http://scikit-learn.org/stable/modules/generated/sklearn.metrics.median_absolute_error.html` (retrieved November 2015)

Evaluating clusters with the mean silhouette coefficient

Clustering is an unsupervised machine learning type of analysis. Although we don't know in general what the best clusters are, we can still get an idea of how good the result of clustering is. One way is to calculate the **silhouette coefficients** as defined in the following equation:

$$(10.8) \quad s(i) = \frac{b(i) - a(i)}{\max\{a(i), b(i)\}}$$

In the preceding equation, *a(i)* is the average dissimilarity of sample *i* with respect to other samples in the same cluster. A small *a(i)* indicates that the sample belongs in its cluster. *b(i)* is the lowest average dissimilarity of *i* to other cluster. It indicates the next best cluster for *i*. If the silhouette coefficients *s(i)* of a sample is close to 1, it means that the sample is properly assigned. The value of *s(i)* varies between -1 to 1. The average of the silhouette coefficients of all samples measures the quality of the clusters.

We can use the mean silhouette coefficient to inform our decision for the number of clusters of the K-means clustering algorithm. The K-means clustering algorithm is covered in more detail in the *Clustering streaming data with Spark* recipe in *Chapter 5, Web Mining, Databases and Big Data*.

How to do it...

1. The imports are as follows:

```
import dautil as dl
from sklearn.cluster import KMeans
from sklearn.metrics import silhouette_score
from sklearn.metrics import silhouette_samples
from IPython.display import HTML
```

2. Define the following function to plot the silhouette samples:

```
def plot_samples(ax, years, labels, i, avg):
    silhouette_values = silhouette_samples(X, labels)
    dl.plotting.plot_text(ax, years, silhouette_values,
                          labels, add_scatter=True)
    ax.set_title('KMeans k={0} Silhouette avg={1:.2f}'.format(i,
avg))
    ax.set_xlabel('Year')
    ax.set_ylabel('Silhouette score')
```

3. Load the data and resample it as follows:

```
df = dl.data.Weather.load().resample('A').dropna()
years = [d.year for d in df.index]
X = df.values
```

4. Plot the clusters for varying numbers of clusters:

```
sp = dl.plotting.Subplotter(2, 2, context)
avgs = []
rng = range(2, 9)

for i in rng:
    kmeans = KMeans(n_clusters=i, random_state=37)
    labels = kmeans.fit_predict(X)
    avg = silhouette_score(X, labels)
    avgs.append(avg)

    if i < 5:
        if i > 2:
            sp.next_ax()

        plot_samples(sp.ax, years, labels, i, avg)

sp.next_ax().plot(rng, avgs)
sp.label()
HTML(sp.exit())
```

Refer to the following screenshot for the end result:

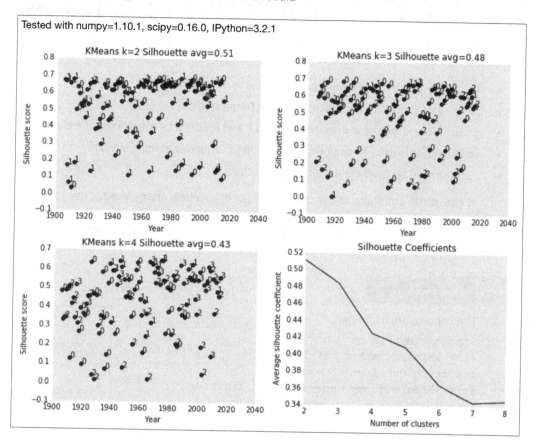

The code is in the `evaluating_clusters.ipynb` file in this book's code bundle.

See also

▸ The Wikipedia page about the silhouette coefficient at `https://en.wikipedia.org/wiki/Silhouette_%28clustering%29` (retrieved November 2015)

▸ The `silhouette_score()` function documented at `http://scikit-learn.org/stable/modules/generated/sklearn.metrics.silhouette_score.html` (retrieved November 2015)

Comparing results with a dummy classifier

The scikit-learn `DummyClassifier` class implements several strategies for random guessing, which can serve as a baseline for classifiers. The strategies are as follows:

- `stratified`: This uses the training set class distribution
- `most_frequent`: This predicts the most frequent class
- `prior`: This is available in scikit-learn 0.17 and predicts by maximizing the class prior
- `uniform`: This uses an uniform distribution to randomly sample classes
- `constant`: This predicts a user-specified class

As you can see, some strategies of the `DummyClassifier` class always predict the same class. This can lead to warnings from some scikit-learn metrics functions. We will perform the same analysis as we did in the *Computing precision, recall, and F1 score* recipe, but with dummy classifiers added.

How to do it...

1. The imports are as follows:

```
import numpy as np
from sklearn import metrics
import ch10util
from sklearn.dummy import DummyClassifier
from IPython.display import HTML
import dautil as dl
```

2. Load the data as follows:

```
y_test = np.load('rain_y_test.npy')
X_train = np.load('rain_X_train.npy')
X_test = np.load('rain_X_test.npy')
y_train = np.load('rain_y_train.npy')
```

3. Create the dummy classifiers and predict with them:

```
stratified = DummyClassifier(random_state=28)
frequent = DummyClassifier(strategy='most_frequent',
                           random_state=28)
prior = DummyClassifier(strategy='prior', random_state=29)
uniform = DummyClassifier(strategy='uniform',
                          random_state=29)
```

```
preds = ch10util.rain_preds()

for clf in [stratified, frequent, prior, uniform]:
    clf.fit(X_train, y_train)
    preds.append(clf.predict(X_test))
```

4. Calculate metrics with the predictions as follows:

```
accuracies = [metrics.accuracy_score(y_test, p)
                for p in preds]
precisions = [metrics.precision_score(y_test, p)
                for p in preds]
recalls = [metrics.recall_score(y_test, p)
            for p in preds]
f1s = [metrics.f1_score(y_test, p)
        for p in preds]
```

5. Plot the metrics for the dummy and regular classifiers:

```
labels = ch10util.rain_labels()
labels.extend(['stratified', 'frequent',
                'prior', 'uniform'])

sp = dl.plotting.Subplotter(2, 2, context)
ch10util.plot_bars(sp.ax, accuracies, labels, rotate=True)
sp.label()

ch10util.plot_bars(sp.next_ax(), precisions, labels, rotate=True)
sp.label()

ch10util.plot_bars(sp.next_ax(), recalls, labels, rotate=True)
sp.label()

ch10util.plot_bars(sp.next_ax(), f1s, labels, rotate=True)
sp.label()
sp.fig.text(0, 1, ch10util.classifiers(), fontsize=10)
HTML(sp.exit())
```

Refer to the following screenshot for the end result:

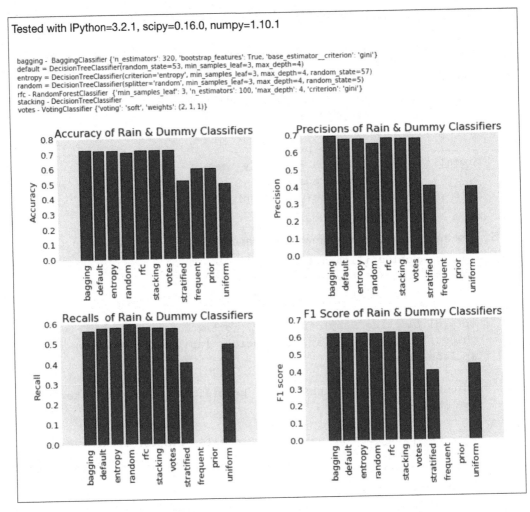

The code is in the `dummy_clf.ipynb` file in this book's code bundle.

See also

▶ The `DummyClassifier` class documented at `http://scikit-learn.org/stable/modules/generated/sklearn.dummy.DummyClassifier.html` (retrieved November 2015)

Determining MAPE and MPE

The **Mean Percentage Error (MPE)** and **Mean Absolute Percentage Error** (**MAPE**) express forecasting errors as ratios, and they are, therefore, dimensionless and easy to interpret. As you can see in the following equations, the disadvantage of MPE and MAPE is that we run the risk of dividing by zero:

$$(10.9) \quad MPE = \frac{100\%}{n} \sum_{t=1}^{n} \frac{a_t - f_t}{a_t}$$

$$(10.10) \quad MAPE = \frac{1}{n} \sum_{t=1}^{n} \left| \frac{A_t - F_t}{A_t} \right|$$

It is perfectly valid for the target variable to be equal to zero. For temperature, this happens to be the freezing point. Freezing often occurs in winter, so we either have to ignore those observations or add a constant large enough to avoid dividing by zero values. In the following section, it becomes clear that simply ignoring observations leads to strange bootstrap distributions.

How to do it...

1. The imports are as follows:

```
import ch10util
import dautil as dl
from IPython.display import HTML
```

2. Plot the bootstrapped metrics as follows:

```
sp = dl.plotting.Subplotter(3, 2, context)
ch10util.plot_bootstrap('boosting',
                        dl.stats.mape, sp.ax)
sp.label()

ch10util.plot_bootstrap('boosting',
                        dl.stats.mpe, sp.next_ax())
sp.label()

ch10util.plot_bootstrap('etr',
                        dl.stats.mape, sp.next_ax())
sp.label()

ch10util.plot_bootstrap('etr',
```

```
                                     dl.stats.mpe, sp.next_ax())
        sp.label()

        ch10util.plot_bootstrap('ransac',
                                dl.stats.mape, sp.next_ax())
        sp.label()

        ch10util.plot_bootstrap('ransac',
                                dl.stats.mpe, sp.next_ax())
        sp.label()
        sp.fig.text(0, 1, ch10util.regressors())
        HTML(sp.exit())
```

Refer to the following screenshot for the end result:

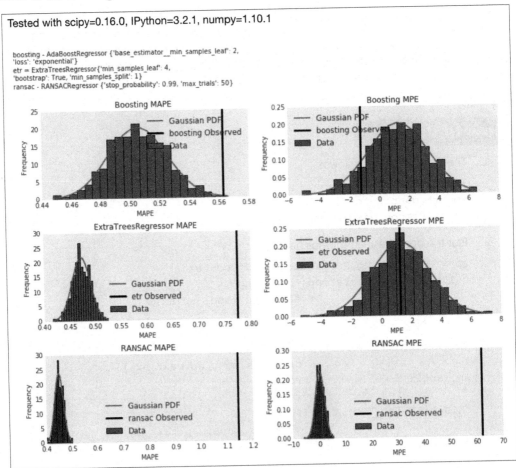

The code is in the `mape_mpe.ipynb` file in this book's code bundle.

See also

- ▸ The Wikipedia page about the MPE at `https://en.wikipedia.org/wiki/Mean_percentage_error` (retrieved November 2015)

- ▸ The Wikipedia page about the MAPE at `https://en.wikipedia.org/wiki/Mean_absolute_percentage_error` (retrieved November 2015)

Comparing with a dummy regressor

The scikit-learn `DummyRegressor` class implements several strategies for random guessing, which can serve as baseline for regressors. The strategies are as follows:

- ▸ `mean`: This predicts the mean of the training set.

- ▸ `median`: This predicts the median of the training set.

- ▸ `quantile`: This predicts a specified quantile of the training set when provided with the `quantile` parameter. We will apply this strategy by specifying the first and third quartile.

- ▸ `constant`: This predicts a constant value that is provided by the user.

We will compare the dummy regressors with the regressors from *Chapter 9, Ensemble Learning and Dimensionality Reduction*, using R-squared, MSE, MedAE, and MPE.

How to do it...

1. The imports are as follows:

```
import numpy as np
from sklearn.dummy import DummyRegressor
import ch10util
from sklearn import metrics
import dautil as dl
from IPython.display import HTML
```

2. Load the temperature data as follows:

```
y_test = np.load('temp_y_test.npy')
X_train = np.load('temp_X_train.npy')
X_test = np.load('temp_X_test.npy')
y_train = np.load('temp_y_train.npy')
```

3. Create dummy regressors using the available strategies and predict tempreture with them:

```
mean = DummyRegressor()
median = DummyRegressor(strategy='median')
q1 = DummyRegressor(strategy='quantile', quantile=0.25)
q3 = DummyRegressor(strategy='quantile', quantile=0.75)


preds = ch10util.temp_preds()


for reg in [mean, median, q1, q3]:
    reg.fit(X_train, y_train)
    preds.append(reg.predict(X_test))
```

4. Calculate R-squared, MSE, median absolute error, and mean percentage error for the regular and dummy regressors:

```
r2s = [metrics.r2_score(p, y_test) for p in preds]
mses = [metrics.mean_squared_error(p, y_test)
        for p in preds]
maes = [metrics.median_absolute_error(p, y_test)
        for p in preds]
mpes = [dl.stats.mpe(y_test, p) for p in preds]


labels = ch10util.temp_labels()
labels.extend(['mean', 'median', 'q1', 'q3'])
```

5. Plot the metrics as follows:

```
sp = dl.plotting.Subplotter(2, 2, context)
ch10util.plot_bars(sp.ax, r2s, labels)
sp.label()


ch10util.plot_bars(sp.next_ax(), mses, labels)
sp.label()


ch10util.plot_bars(sp.next_ax(), maes, labels)
sp.label()


ch10util.plot_bars(sp.next_ax(), mpes, labels)
sp.label()
sp.fig.text(0, 1, ch10util.regressors())
HTML(sp.exit())
```

Refer to the following screenshot for the end result:

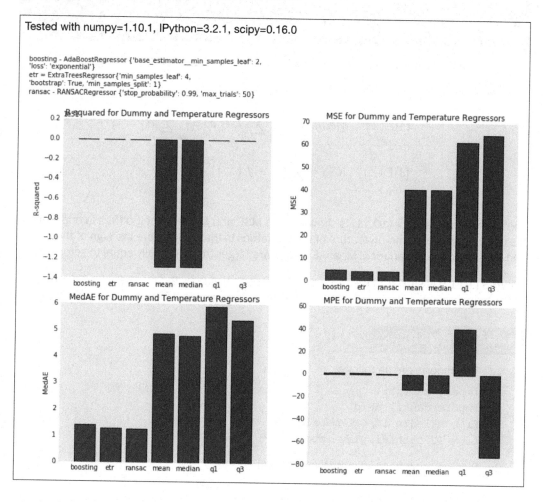

The code is in the `dummy_reg.ipynb` file in this book's code bundle.

See also

▸ The `DummyRegressor` class documented at `http://scikit-learn.org/stable/modules/generated/sklearn.dummy.DummyRegressor.html` (retrieved November 2015)

▸ The *Computing MSE and median absolute error* recipe in this chapter

▸ The *Determining MAPE and MPE* recipe in this chapter

Calculating the mean absolute error and the residual sum of squares

The **mean absolute error (MeanAE)** and **residual sum of squares (RSS)** are regression metrics given by the following equations:

$$(10.11) \quad MeanAE = \frac{1}{n}\sum_{t=1}^{n}|f_i - y_i| = \frac{1}{n}\sum_{i=1}^{n}|e_i|$$

$$(10.12) \quad RSS = \sum_{i=1}^{n}(y_i - f(x_i))^2$$

The mean absolute error (10.11) is similar to the MSE and MedAE, but it differs in one step of the calculation. The common feature of these metrics is that they ignore the sign of the error and are analogous to variance. MeanAE values are larger than or ideally equal to zero.

The RSS (10.12) is similar to the MSE, except we don't divide by the number of residuals. For this reason, you get larger values with the RSS. However, an ideal fit gives you a zero RSS.

How to do it...

1. The imports are as follows:

```
import ch10util
import dautil as dl
from sklearn import metrics
from IPython.display import HTML
```

2. Plot the bootstrapped metrics as follows:

```
sp = dl.plotting.Subplotter(3, 2, context)
ch10util.plot_bootstrap('boosting',
                        metrics.mean_absolute_error, sp.ax)
sp.label()

ch10util.plot_bootstrap('boosting',
                        dl.stats.rss, sp.next_ax())
sp.label()

ch10util.plot_bootstrap('etr',
                        metrics.mean_absolute_error, sp.next_ax())
sp.label()

ch10util.plot_bootstrap('etr',
                        dl.stats.rss, sp.next_ax())
```

```
sp.label()

ch10util.plot_bootstrap('ransac',
                        metrics.mean_absolute_error, sp.next_ax())
sp.label()

ch10util.plot_bootstrap('ransac',
                        dl.stats.rss, sp.next_ax())
sp.label()
sp.fig.text(0, 1, ch10util.regressors())
HTML(sp.exit())
```

Refer to the following screenshot for the end result:

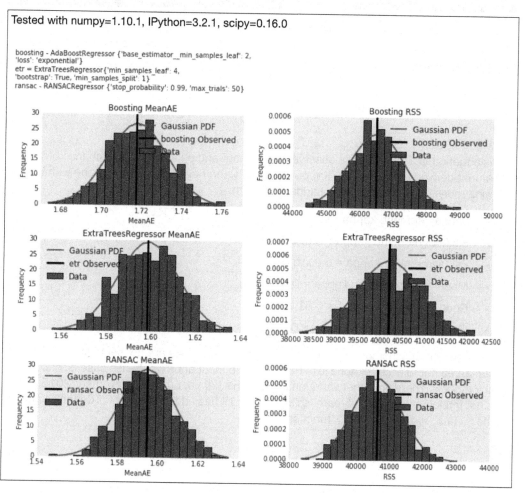

The code is in the `mae_rss.ipynb` file in this book's code bundle.

See also

▸ The Wikipedia page about the MeanAE at `https://en.wikipedia.org/wiki/Mean_absolute_error` (retrieved November 2015)

▸ The `mean_absolute_error()` function documented at `http://scikit-learn.org/stable/modules/generated/sklearn.metrics.mean_absolute_error.html` (retrieved November 2015)

▸ The Wikipedia page about the RSS at `https://en.wikipedia.org/wiki/Residual_sum_of_squares` (retrieved November 2015)

Examining the kappa of classification

Cohen's kappa measures the agreement between target and predicted class similar to accuracy, but it also takes into account random chance of getting the predictions. Cohen's kappa is given by the following equation:

$$(10.13) \quad K = \frac{p_o - p_e}{1 - p_e} = 1 - \frac{1 - p_o}{1 - p_e}$$

In this equation, p_0 is the relative observed agreement and p_e is the random chance of agreement derived from the data. Kappa varies between negative values and one with the following rough categorization from Landis and Koch:

▸ Poor agreement: kappa < 0

▸ Slight agreement: kappa = 0 to 0.2

▸ Fair agreement: kappa = 0.21 to 0.4

▸ Moderate agreement: kappa = 0.41 to 0.6

▸ Good agreement: kappa = 0.61 to 0.8

▸ Very good agreement: kappa = 0.81 to 1.0

I know of two other schemes to grade kappa, so these numbers are not set in stone. I think we can agree not to accept kappa less than 0.2. The most appropriate use case is, of course, to rank models. There are other variations of Cohen's kappa, but as of November 2015, they were not implemented in scikit-learn. scikit-learn 0.17 has added support for Cohen's kappa via the `cohen_kappa_score()` function.

How to do it...

1. The imports are as follows:

```
import dautil as dl
from sklearn import metrics
import numpy as np
import ch10util
from IPython.display import HTML
```

2. Compute accuracy, precision, recall, F1-score, and kappa for the rain predictors:

```
y_test = np.load('rain_y_test.npy')
accuracies = [metrics.accuracy_score(y_test, preds)
             for preds in ch10util.rain_preds()]
precisions = [metrics.precision_score(y_test, preds)
             for preds in ch10util.rain_preds()]
recalls = [metrics.recall_score(y_test, preds)
             for preds in ch10util.rain_preds()]
f1s = [metrics.f1_score(y_test, preds)
         for preds in ch10util.rain_preds()]
kappas = [metrics.cohen_kappa_score(y_test, preds)
             for preds in ch10util.rain_preds()]
```

3. Scatter plot the metrics against kappa as follows:

```
sp = dl.plotting.Subplotter(2, 2, context)
dl.plotting.plot_text(sp.ax, accuracies, kappas,
                    ch10util.rain_labels(), add_scatter=True)
sp.label()

dl.plotting.plot_text(sp.next_ax(), precisions, kappas,
                    ch10util.rain_labels(), add_scatter=True)
sp.label()

dl.plotting.plot_text(sp.next_ax(), recalls, kappas,
                    ch10util.rain_labels(), add_scatter=True)
sp.label()

dl.plotting.plot_text(sp.next_ax(), f1s, kappas,
                    ch10util.rain_labels(), add_scatter=True)
sp.label()
sp.fig.text(0, 1, ch10util.classifiers())
HTML(sp.exit())
```

Refer to the following screenshot for the end result:

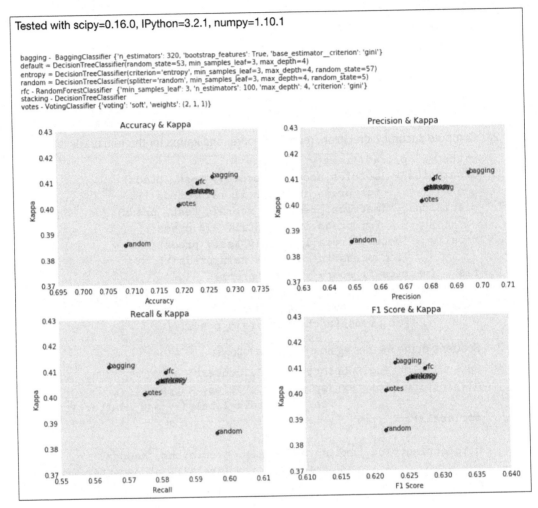

The code is in the `kappa.ipynb` file in this book's code bundle.

How it works

From the first two plots, we can conclude that the bagging classifier has the highest accuracy, precision, and kappa. All the classifiers have a kappa above 0.2, so they are at least somewhat acceptable.

See also

▶ The Wikipedia page about Cohen's kappa at `https://en.wikipedia.org/wiki/Cohen's_kappa` (retrieved November 2015)

Taking a look at the Matthews correlation coefficient

The **Matthews correlation coefficient (MCC)** or **phi coefficient** is an evaluation metric for binary classification invented by Brian Matthews in 1975. The MCC is a correlation coefficient for target and predictions and varies between -1 and 1 (best agreement). MCC is a very good way to summarize the confusion matrix (refer to the *Getting classification straight with the confusion matrix* recipe) as it uses all four numbers in it. The MCC is given by the following equation:

$$(10.14) \quad MCC = \frac{T_p \times T_n - F_p \times F_n}{\sqrt{\left(T_p + F_p\right)\left(T_p + F_n\right)\left(T_n + F_p\right)\left(T_n + F_n\right)}}$$

How to do it...

1. The imports are as follows:

```
import dautil as dl
from sklearn import metrics
import numpy as np
import ch10util
from IPython.display import HTML
```

2. Calculate accuracies, precisions, recalls, F1-scores, and Matthews correlation coefficients for the rain predictors:

```
y_test = np.load('rain_y_test.npy')
accuracies = [metrics.accuracy_score(y_test, preds)
              for preds in ch10util.rain_preds()]
precisions = [metrics.precision_score(y_test, preds)
              for preds in ch10util.rain_preds()]
recalls = [metrics.recall_score(y_test, preds)
           for preds in ch10util.rain_preds()]
f1s = [metrics.f1_score(y_test, preds)
       for preds in ch10util.rain_preds()]
mc = [metrics.matthews_corrcoef(y_test, preds)
      for preds in ch10util.rain_preds()]
```

3. Plot the metrics as follows:

```
sp = dl.plotting.Subplotter(2, 2, context)
dl.plotting.plot_text(sp.ax, accuracies, mc,
                      ch10util.rain_labels(), add_scatter=True)
sp.label()

dl.plotting.plot_text(sp.next_ax(), precisions, mc,
                      ch10util.rain_labels(), add_scatter=True)
sp.label()

dl.plotting.plot_text(sp.next_ax(), recalls, mc,
                      ch10util.rain_labels(), add_scatter=True)
sp.label()

dl.plotting.plot_text(sp.next_ax(), f1s, mc,
                      ch10util.rain_labels(), add_scatter=True)
sp.label()
sp.fig.text(0, 1, ch10util.classifiers())
HTML(sp.exit())
```

Refer to the following screenshot for the end result:

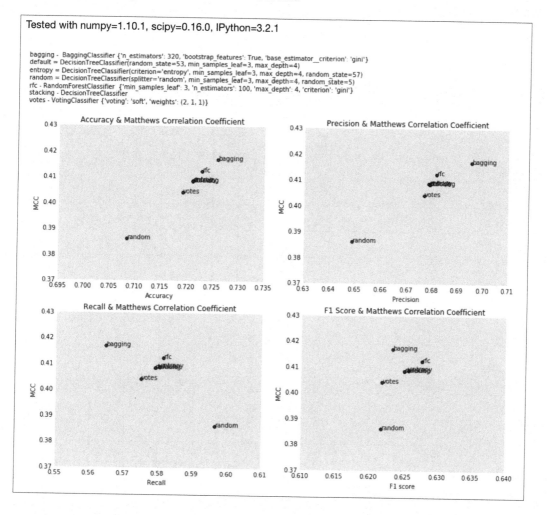

```
Tested with numpy=1.10.1, scipy=0.16.0, IPython=3.2.1

bagging - BaggingClassifier {'n_estimators': 320, 'bootstrap_features': True, 'base_estimator__criterion': 'gini'}
default = DecisionTreeClassifier(random_state=53, min_samples_leaf=3, max_depth=4)
entropy = DecisionTreeClassifier(criterion='entropy', min_samples_leaf=3, max_depth=4, random_state=57)
random = DecisionTreeClassifier(splitter='random', min_samples_leaf=3, max_depth=4, random_state=5)
rfc - RandomForestClassifier  {'min_samples_leaf': 3, 'n_estimators': 100, 'max_depth': 4, 'criterion': 'gini'}
stacking - DecisionTreeClassifier
votes - VotingClassifier {'voting': 'soft', 'weights': (2, 1, 1)}
```

The code is in the `matthews_correlation.ipynb` file in this book's code bundle.

See also

▸ The Wikipedia page about the MCC at `https://en.wikipedia.org/wiki/Matthews_correlation_coefficient` (retrieved November 2015)

▸ The `matthews_corrcoef()` function documented at `http://scikit-learn.org/stable/modules/generated/sklearn.metrics.matthews_corrcoef.html` (retrieved November 2015)

11
Analyzing Images

In this chapter, we will cover the following recipes:

- ▶ Setting up OpenCV
- ▶ Applying Scale-Invariant Feature Transform (SIFT)
- ▶ Detecting features with SURF
- ▶ Quantizing colors
- ▶ Denoising images
- ▶ Extracting patches from an image
- ▶ Detecting faces with Haar cascades
- ▶ Searching for bright stars
- ▶ Extracting metadata from images
- ▶ Extracting texture features from images
- ▶ Applying hierarchical clustering on images
- ▶ Segmenting images with spectral clustering

Introduction

Image processing is a very large field of study. The techniques used for image processing can often (with small changes) be applied to video analysis as well. We can view image processing as a special type of signal processing. Signal processing is covered in *Chapter 6, Signal Processing and Timeseries*. However, images pose special challenges, such as high dimensionality (we can define each image pixel to be a feature) and spatial dependence (pixel location matters).

The human visual system is very advanced compared to what computers can do. We are able to recognize objects, facial expressions, and object motion. Apparently, this has to do with predators and with their tendency to consume human flesh. Instead of trying to understand how human vision works, we will concentrate on finding features in images and clustering image pixels (segmenting) in this chapter.

In this chapter, we use the OpenCV library quite a lot, and since it is a fairly large library, I decided to create a special Docker container for this chapter only. As you probably know already, I made a Docker image called `pydacbk`. Well, the Docker container for this chapter is named `pydacbk11`.

Setting up OpenCV

OpenCV (**Open Source Computer Vision**) is a library for computer vision created in 2000, and is currently maintained by Itseez. OpenCV is written in C++, but it also has bindings for Python and other programming languages. OpenCV supports many operating systems and GPUs. There is not enough space in this chapter to cover all the features of OpenCV. Even a single book is probably not enough—for Pythonistas, I recommend *OpenCV Computer Vision with Python* by Joseph Howse.

Some of the third-party patented algorithms in the OpenCV 2.x.x package, such as SIFT and SURF (refer to the relevant recipes in this chapter), have been moved to a special GitHub repository. You still can use them, but you need to explicitly include them in the installation process.

The OpenCV build process has many options. If you are unsure which options are the best for you, read the OpenCV documentation or use the appropriate package manager for your operating system. In general, you should not use too many options. Although you have the flexibility to turn off certain modules, other modules may depend on them, which could lead to a cascade of errors.

Getting ready

If you are on Windows or Fedora, read the corresponding tutorials at `http://docs.opencv.org/3.0.0/da/df6/tutorial_py_table_of_contents_setup.html` (retrieved December 2015). For the Ubuntu-based Docker container, I needed to install some prerequisites with the following commands:

```
$ apt-get update
$ apt-get install -y cmake make git g++
```

The following instructions serve as an example and make some assumptions about your setup. For instance, it assumes that you are using Anaconda with Python 3. For convenience, I organized all the instructions in a single shell script for the Ubuntu-based Docker container; however, if you prefer, you can also type each line separately in a terminal.

1. Download the code of the core OpenCV project (if you don't have Git, you can also download the code from the GitHub website):

```
$ cd /opt
$ git clone https://github.com/Itseez/opencv.git
$ cd opencv
$ git checkout tags/3.0.0
```

2. Download the code of the (third-party) contributions to OpenCV (if you don't have Git, you can also download the code from the GitHub website):

```
$ cd /opt
$ git clone https://github.com/Itseez/opencv_contrib
$ cd opencv_contrib
$ git checkout tags/3.0.0
$ cd /opt/opencv
```

3. Make a build directory and navigate to it:

```
$ mkdir build
$ cd build
```

4. This step shows some of the build options available to you (you don't have to use all these options):

```
$ ANACONDA=~/anaconda
$ cmake -D CMAKE_BUILD_TYPE=RELEASE \
    -D BUILD_PERF_TESTS=OFF \
    -D BUILD_opencv_core=ON \
    -D BUILD_opencv_python2=OFF \
    -D BUILD_opencv_python3=ON \
    -D BUILD_opencv_cuda=OFF \
    -D BUILD_opencv_java=OFF \
    -D BUILD_opencv_video=ON \
    -D BUILD_opencv_videoio=ON \
    -D BUILD_opencv_world=OFF \
    -D BUILD_opencv_viz=ON \
    -D WITH_CUBLAS=OFF \
```

```
    -D WITH_CUDA=OFF \

    -D WITH_CUFFT=OFF \

    -D WITH_FFMPEG=OFF \

    -D PYTHON3_EXECUTABLE=${ANACONDA}/bin/python3 \

    -D PYTHON3_LIBRARY=${ANACONDA}/lib/libpython3.4m.so \

    -D PYTHON3_INCLUDE_DIR=${ANACONDA}/include/python3.4m \

    -D PYTHON3_NUMPY_INCLUDE_DIRS=${ANACONDA}/lib/python3.4/site-
packages/numpy/core/include \

    -D PYTHON3_PACKAGES_PATH=${ANACONDA}/lib/python3.4/site-
packages \

    -D BUILD_opencv_latentsvm=OFF \

    -D BUILD_opencv_xphoto=OFF \

    -D BUILD_opencv_xfeatures2d=ON \

    -D OPENCV_EXTRA_MODULES_PATH=/opt/opencv_contrib/modules \

/opt/opencv
```

5. Run the `make` command (with 8 cores) and install as follows:

```
$ make -j8
$ sudo make install
```

How it works

The previous instructions assumed that you are installing OpenCV for the first time. If you are upgrading from OpenCV 2.x.x, you will have to take extra precautions. Also, I assumed that you don't want certain options and are using Anaconda with Python 3. The following table explains some of the build options we used:

Option	Description
BUILD_opencv_python2	Support for Python 2
BUILD_opencv_python3	Support for Python 3
BUILD_opencv_java	Support for the OpenCV Java bindings
PYTHON3_EXECUTABLE	The location of the Python 3 executable
PYTHON3_LIBRARY	The location of the Python 3 library
PYTHON3_INCLUDE_DIR	The location of the Python 3 `include` directory
PYTHON3_NUMPY_INCLUDE_DIRS	The location of the NumPy `include` directories
PYTHON3_PACKAGES_PATH	The location of the Python 3 packages
BUILD_opencv_xfeatures2d	Support for certain third-party algorithms, such as SIFT and SURF
OPENCV_EXTRA_MODULES_PATH	The location of the code of the OpenCV third-party contributions

There's more

If you don't have enough space, for instance in a Docker container, then you can clean up with the following commands:

```
$ rm -rf /opt/opencv
$ rm -rf /opt/opencv_contrib
```

Applying Scale-Invariant Feature Transform (SIFT)

The SIFT algorithm (1999) finds features in images or videos and is patented by the University of British Columbia. Typically, we can use the features for classification or clustering. SIFT is invariant with respect to translation, scaling, and rotation.

The algorithm's steps are as follows:

1. Blur the image at different scales using a Gaussian blur filter.
2. An **octave** corresponds to doubling the standard deviation of the filter. Group the blurred images by octave and difference them.
3. Find the local extremas across the scale for the differenced images.
4. Compare each pixel related to local extrema to the neighboring pixels in the same scale and neighboring scales.
5. Select the largest or smallest value from the comparison.
6. Reject points with low contrast.
7. Interpolate candidate key points (image features) to get the position on the original image.

Getting ready

Follow the instructions in the *Setting up OpenCV* recipe.

How to do it...

1. The imports are as follows:
   ```
   import cv2
   import matplotlib.pyplot as plt
   import dautil as dl
   from scipy.misc import face
   ```

2. Plot the original image as follows:

```
img = face()
plt.title('Original')
dl.plotting.img_show(plt.gca(), img)
gray = cv2.cvtColor(img, cv2.COLOR_BGR2GRAY)
```

3. Plot the grayscaled image as follows:

```
plt.figure()
plt.title('Gray')
dl.plotting.img_show(plt.gca(), gray, cmap=plt.cm.gray)
```

4. Plot the image with keypoints (blue) as follows:

```
sift = cv2.xfeatures2d.SIFT_create()
(kps, descs) = sift.detectAndCompute(gray, None)
img2 = cv2.drawKeypoints(gray, kps, None, (0, 0, 255))

plt.figure()
plt.title('With Keypoints')
dl.plotting.img_show(plt.gca(), img2)
```

Refer to the following screenshot for the end result:

The program is in the `applying_sift.ipynb` file in this book's code bundle.

See also

- The Wikipedia page about SIFT at `https://en.wikipedia.org/wiki/Scale-invariant_feature_transform` (retrieved December 2015)

- The SIFT algorithm documented at `http://docs.opencv.org/3.0.0/da/df5/tutorial_py_sift_intro.html` (retrieved December 2015)

Detecting features with SURF

Speeded Up Robust Features (**SURF**) is a patented algorithm similar to and inspired by SIFT (refer to the *Applying Scale-Invariant Feature Transform* recipe). SURF was introduced in 2006 and uses Haar wavelets (refer to the *Applying the discrete wavelet transform* recipe). The greatest advantage of SURF is that it is faster than SIFT.

Take a look at the following equations:

$$(11.1) \quad S(x,y) = \sum_{i=0}^{x} \sum_{j=0}^{y} I(i,j)$$

$$(11.2) \quad H(p,\sigma) = \begin{pmatrix} L_{xx}(p,\sigma) & L_{xy}(p,\sigma) \\ L_{xy}(p,\sigma) & L_{yy}(p,\sigma) \end{pmatrix}$$

$$(11.3) \quad \sigma_{approx} = Current\ filter\ size * \left(\frac{Base\ Filter\ Scale}{Base\ Filter\ Size} \right)$$

The algorithm steps are as follows:

1. Transform the image if necessary to get the grayscale equivalent.

2. Calculate the **integral image** at different scales, which is the sum of the pixels above and to the left of a pixel, as shown in equation (11.1). The integral image replaces the Gaussian filter in SIFT.

3. Define the **Hessian matrix** (11.2) containing second-order derivatives of the grayscale image as function of pixel location p and scale σ (11.3).

4. **Determinants** are values related to square matrices. The determinant of the Hessian matrix corresponds to a local change in a point. Select points with the largest determinant.

5. The scale σ is defined by 11.3, and just as with SIFT, we can define scale octaves. SURF works by varying the size of the filter kernel, while SIFT varies the image size. Interpolate the maximums from the previous step in the scale and image space.

6. Apply the Haar wavelet transform to a circle around key points.

7. Use a sliding window to sum responses.

8. Determine orientation from the response sums.

Getting ready

Follow the instructions in the *Setting up OpenCV* recipe.

How to do it...

1. The imports are as follows:

```
import cv2
import matplotlib.pyplot as plt
import dautil as dl
```

2. Plot the original image as follows:

```
img = cv2.imread('covers.jpg')
plt.title('Original')
dl.plotting.img_show(plt.gca(), img)
```

3. Plot the grayscaled image as follows:

```
gray = cv2.cvtColor(img, cv2.COLOR_BGR2GRAY)

plt.figure()
plt.title('Gray')
dl.plotting.img_show(plt.gca(), gray, cmap=plt.cm.gray)
surf = cv2.xfeatures2d.SURF_create()
(kps, descs) = surf.detectAndCompute(gray, None)
img2 = cv2.drawKeypoints(gray, kps, None, (0, 0, 255))
```

4. Plot the image with keypoints (blue) as follows:

```
plt.figure()
plt.title('With Keypoints')
dl.plotting.img_show(plt.gca(), img2)
```

Refer to the following screenshot for the end result:

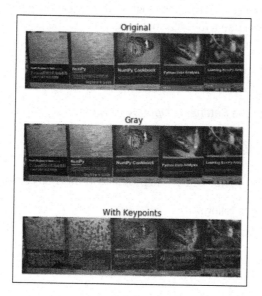

The code is in the `applying_surf.ipynb` file in this book's code bundle.

See also

- The Wikipedia page about SURF at `https://en.wikipedia.org/wiki/Speeded_up_robust_features` (retrieved December 2015)

- The Wikipedia page about the integral image at `https://en.wikipedia.org/wiki/Summed_area_table` (retrieved December 2015)

- The Wikipedia page about the Hessian matrix at `https://en.wikipedia.org/wiki/Hessian_matrix` (retrieved December 2015)

- The Wikipedia page about the determinant at `https://en.wikipedia.org/wiki/Determinant` (retrieved December 2015)

- The SURF algorithm documented at `http://docs.opencv.org/3.0.0/df/dd2/tutorial_py_surf_intro.html` (retrieved December 2015)

Quantizing colors

In ancient times, computer games were practically monochromatic. Many years later, the Internet allowed us to download images, but the Web was slow, so compact images with few colors were preferred. We can conclude that restricting the number of colors is traditional. Color is a dimension of images, so we can speak of dimensionality reduction if we remove colors from an image. The actual process is called **color quantization**.

Usually, we represent **RGB** (**red**, **green**, and **blue**) values in three-dimensional space for each pixel and then cluster the points. For each cluster, we are left with a corresponding average color. In this recipe, we will use k-means clustering (refer to the *Clustering streaming data with Spark* recipe), although this is not necessarily the best algorithm.

Getting ready

Follow the instructions in the *Setting up OpenCV* recipe.

How to do it...

The code is in the `quantizing_colors.ipynb` file in this book's code bundle:

1. The imports are as follows:

```
import numpy as np
import cv2
import matplotlib.pyplot as plt
import dautil as dl
from scipy.misc import face
```

2. Plot the original image as follows:

```
sp = dl.plotting.Subplotter(2, 2, context)
img = face()
dl.plotting.img_show(sp.ax, img)
sp.label()
Z = img.reshape((-1, 3))

Z = np.float32(Z)
```

3. Apply k-means clustering and plot the result:

```
criteria = (cv2.TERM_CRITERIA_MAX_ITER, 7, 1.0)

for k in [2, 4, 8]:
    _, label, center = cv2.kmeans(Z, k, None, criteria, 7,
                        cv2.KMEANS_RANDOM_CENTERS)

    center = np.uint8(center)
    res = center[label.flatten()]
    res2 = res.reshape((img.shape))

    dl.plotting.img_show(sp.next_ax(), res2)
    sp.label()
```

Refer to the following screenshot for the end result:

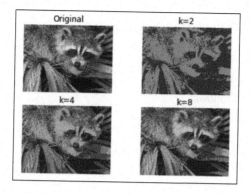

See also

- The Wikipedia page about color quantization at `https://en.wikipedia.org/wiki/Color_quantization` (retrieved December 2015)
- The `kmeans()` function documented at `http://docs.opencv.org/3.0.0/d5/d38/group__core__cluster.html#ga9a34dc06c6ec9460e90860f15bcd2f88` (retrieved December 2015)

Denoising images

Noise is a common phenomenon in data and also in images. Of course, noise is undesirable, as it does not add any value to our analysis. We typically assume that noise is normally distributed around zero. We consider a pixel value to be the sum of the true value and noise (if any). We also assume that the noise values are independent, that is, the noise value of one pixel is independent of another pixel.

One simple idea is to average pixels in a small window, since we suppose the expected value of noise to be zero. This is the general idea behind blurring. We can take this idea a step further and define multiple windows around a pixel, and we can then average similar patches.

OpenCV has several denoising functions and usually we need to specify the strength of the filter, the size of the search window, and the size of the template window for similarity checks. You should be careful not to set the filter strength too high because that may make the image not only cleaner, but also a bit blurred.

Getting ready

Follow the instructions in the *Setting up OpenCV* recipe.

How to do it...

1. The imports are as follows:

    ```
    import cv2
    import matplotlib.pyplot as plt
    from sklearn.datasets import load_sample_image
    import numpy as np
    import dautil as dl
    ```

2. Plot the original image as follows:

    ```
    img = load_sample_image('china.jpg')
    dl.plotting.img_show(plt.gca(), img)
    plt.title('Original')
    Z = img.reshape((-1, 3))
    ```

3. Add noise to the image and plot the noisy image:

    ```
    np.random.seed(59)
    noise = np.random.random(Z.shape) < 0.99

    noisy = (Z * noise).reshape((img.shape))

    plt.figure()
    plt.title('Noisy')
    dl.plotting.img_show(plt.gca(), noisy)
    ```

4. Clean the image and display it:

    ```
    cleaned = cv2.fastNlMeansDenoisingColored(noisy, None, 10, 10, 7,
    21)
    plt.figure()
    plt.title('Cleaned')
    dl.plotting.img_show(plt.gca(), cleaned)
    ```

Refer to the following screenshot for the end result:

The code is in the `denoising_images.ipynb` file in this book's code bundle.

See also

▸ The `fastNlMeansDenoisingColored()` function documented at `http://docs.opencv.org/3.0.0/d1/d79/group__photo__denoise.html#ga21abc1c8b0e15f78cd3eff672cb6c476` (retrieved December 2015)

Extracting patches from an image

Image segmentation is a procedure that splits an image into multiple segments. The segments have similar color or intensity. The segments also usually have a meaning in the context of medicine, traffic, astronomy, or something else.

The easiest way to segment images is with a threshold value, which produces two segments (if values are equal to the threshold, we put them in one of the two segments). **Otsu's thresholding** method minimizes the weighted variance of the two segments (refer to the following equation):

$$(11.4) \quad \sigma_w^2(t) = \omega_w^2(t)\sigma_1^2(t) + \omega_2(t)\sigma_2^2(t)$$

If we segment images, it is a good idea to remove noise or foreign artifacts. With **dilation** (see the *See also* section) we can find parts of the image that belong to the background and the foreground. However, dilation leaves us with unidentified pixels.

Getting ready

Follow the instructions in *Setting up OpenCV*.

How to do it...

1. The imports are as follows:

```
import numpy as np
import cv2
from matplotlib import pyplot as plt
from sklearn.datasets import load_sample_image
import dautil as dl
from IPython.display import HTML
```

2. Plot the original image as follows:

```
sp = dl.plotting.Subplotter(2, 2, context)
img = load_sample_image('flower.jpg')
dl.plotting.img_show(sp.ax, img)
sp.label()
```

3. Plot the Otsu threshold image as follows:

```
gray = cv2.cvtColor(img, cv2.COLOR_BGR2GRAY)
_, thresh = cv2.threshold(gray, 0, 255,
                          cv2.THRESH_OTSU)

dl.plotting.img_show(sp.next_ax(), thresh)
sp.label()
```

4. Plot the image with foreground and background distracted as follows:

```
kernel = np.ones((3, 3), np.uint8)
opening = cv2.morphologyEx(thresh, cv2.MORPH_OPEN,
                           kernel, iterations=2)

bg = cv2.dilate(opening, kernel, iterations=3)

dist_transform = cv2.distanceTransform(opening, cv2.DIST_L2, 5)
_, fg = cv2.threshold(dist_transform, 0.7 * dist_transform.max(),
                      255, 0)

fg = np.uint8(fg)
rest = cv2.subtract(bg, fg)

dl.plotting.img_show(sp.next_ax(), rest)
sp.label()
```

5. Plot the image with markers as follows:

```
_, markers = cv2.connectedComponents(fg)
markers += 1
markers[rest == 255] = 0

dl.plotting.img_show(sp.next_ax(), markers)
sp.label()

HTML(sp.exit())
```

Refer to the following screenshot for the end result:

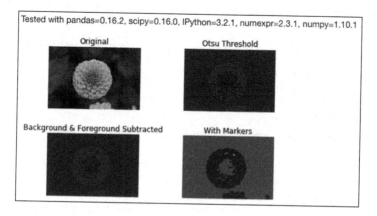

The code is in the `extracting_patches.ipynb` file in this book's code bundle.

- ▶ The Wikipedia page about image segmentation at `https://en.wikipedia.org/wiki/Image_segmentation` (retrieved December 2015)

- ▶ The Wikipedia page about Otsu's method at `https://en.wikipedia.org/wiki/Otsu's_method` (retrieved December 2015)

- ▶ The Wikipedia page about dilation at `https://en.wikipedia.org/wiki/Dilation_%28morphology%29` (retrieved December 2015)

Detecting faces with Haar cascades

Faces are an identifying feature of human anatomy. Strictly speaking, many animals also have faces, but that is less relevant for most practical applications. **Face detection** tries to find (rectangular) areas in an image that represent faces. Face detection is a type of **object detection**, because faces are a type of object.

Most face detection algorithms are good at detecting clean fron-facing faces because most training images fall in that category. Tilted faces, bright lights, or noisy images may cause problems for face detection. It is possible to deduce age, gender, or ethnicity (for instance, the presence of epicanthic folds) from a face, which of course is useful for marketing.

A possible application could be analyzing profile pictures on social media sites. OpenCV uses a **Haar feature-based cascade classifiers system** to detect faces. The system is also named the **Viola–Jones object detection framework** after its inventorsr who proposed it in 2001.

The algorithm has the following steps:

1. Haar feature selection: Haar features are similar to Haar wavelets (as covered in the *Applying the discrete wavelet transform* recipe in *Chapter 6, Signal Processing and Timeseries*).

2. Creating an integral image (refer to the *Detecting features with SURF* recipe).

3. Adaboost training (refer to the *Boosting for better learning* recipe in *Chapter 9, Ensemble Learning and Dimensionality Reduction*).

4. Cascading classifiers.

When we look at face images, we can create heuristics related to brightness.

For instance, the nose region is brighter than regions directly to its left and right. Therefore, we can define a white rectangle covering the nose and black rectangles covering the neighboring areas. Of course the Viola-Jones system doesn't know exactly where the nose is, but by defining windows of varying size and seeking corresponding white and black rectangles, there is a chance of matching a nose. The actual Haar features are defined as the sum of brightness in a black rectangle and the sum of brightness in a neighboring rectangle. For a 24 x 24 window, we have more than 160 thousand features (roughly 24 to the fourth power).

The training set consists of a huge collection of positive (with faces) images and negative (no faces) images. Only about 0.01% of the windows (in the order of 24 by 24 pixels) actually contain faces. The cascade of classifiers progressively filters out negative image areas stage by stage. In each progressive stage, the classifiers use progressively more features on less image windows. The idea is to spend the most time on image patches that contain faces. The original paper by Viola and Jones had 38 stages with 1, 10, 25, 25, and 50 features in the first five stages. On average, 10 features per image window were evaluated.

In OpenCV, you can train a cascade classifier yourself, as described in http://docs. opencv.org/3.0.0/dc/d88/tutorial_traincascade.html (retrieved December 2015). However, OpenCV has pre-trained classifiers for faces, eyes, and other features. The configuration for these classifiers is stored as XML files, which can be found in the folder where you installed OpenCV (on my machine, /usr/local/share/OpenCV/haarcascades/).

Getting ready

Follow the instructions in *Setting up OpenCV*.

How to do it...

1. The imports are as follows:

```
import cv2
from scipy.misc import lena
import matplotlib.pyplot as plt
import numpy as np
import dautil as dl
import os
from IPython.display import HTML
```

2. Define the following function to plot the image with a detected face (if detected):

```
def plot_with_rect(ax, img):
    img2 = img.copy()

    for x, y, w, h in face_cascade.detectMultiScale(img2, 1.3, 5):
        cv2.rectangle(img2, (x, y), (x + w, y + h), (255, 0, 0),
    2)

    dl.plotting.img_show(ax, img2, cmap=plt.cm.gray)
```

3. Download the XML configuration file and create a classifier:

```
# dir = '/usr/local/share/OpenCV/haarcascades/'
base = 'https://raw.githubusercontent.com/Itseez/opencv/master/
data/'
url = base + 'haarcascades/haarcascade_frontalface_default.xml'
path = os.path.join(dl.data.get_data_dir(),
                    'haarcascade_frontalface_default.xml')

if not dl.conf.file_exists(path):
    dl.data.download(url, path)

face_cascade = cv2.CascadeClassifier(path)
```

4. Plot the original image with a detected face:

```
sp = dl.plotting.Subplotter(2, 2, context)
img = lena().astype(np.uint8)
plot_with_rect(sp.ax, img)
sp.label()
```

5. Plot the slightly rotated image (detection fails):

```
rows, cols = img.shape
mat = cv2.getRotationMatrix2D((cols/2, rows/2), 21, 1)
rot = cv2.warpAffine(img, mat, (cols, rows))
plot_with_rect(sp.next_ax(), rot)
sp.label()
```

6. Plot the image with noise added (detection fails):

```
np.random.seed(36)
noisy = img * (np.random.random(img.shape) < 0.6)
plot_with_rect(sp.next_ax(), noisy)
sp.label()
```

7. Plot the blurred image with a detected face:

```
blur = cv2.blur(img, (9, 9))
plot_with_rect(sp.next_ax(), blur)
sp.label()

HTML(sp.exit())
```

Refer to the following screenshot for the end result:

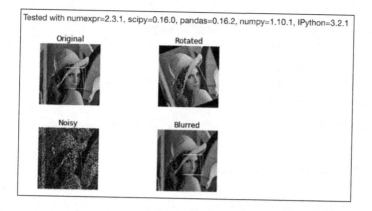

The code is in the `detecting_faces.ipynb` file in this book's code bundle.

See also

▸ The Wikipedia page about face detection at `https://en.wikipedia.org/wiki/Face_detection` (retrieved December 2015)

▸ The Wikipedia page about the Viola-Jones framework at `https://en.wikipedia.org/wiki/Viola%E2%80%93Jones_object_detection_framework` (retrieved December 2015)

Searching for bright stars

Many stars are visible at night, even without using a telescope or any other optical device. Stars are, in general, larger than planet Earth, but in certain stages of their evolution, they can be smaller. Due to the large distance, they appear as tiny dots. Often, these dots consist of two (a binary system) or more stars. Not all stars emit visible light and not all starlight can reach us.

There are many approaches that we can take to find bright stars in a starry sky image. In this recipe, we will look for local maximums of brightness, which are also above a threshold. To determine brightness, we will convert the image to the HSV color space. In this color space, the three dimensions are hue, saturation, and value (brightness). The OpenCV `split()` function image values in a color space into the constituent values, for example, hue, saturation, and brightness. This is a relatively slow operation. To find maximums, we can apply the SciPy `argrelmax()` function.

Getting ready

Follow the instructions in the *Setting up OpenCV* recipe.

How to do it...

1. The imports are as follows:

```
import dautil as dl
import os
import cv2
import matplotlib.pyplot as plt
from scipy.signal import argrelmax
import numpy as np
from IPython.display import HTML
```

2. Define the following function to scan the horizontal or vertical axis for local brightness peaks:

```
def scan_axis(v, axis):
    argmax = argrelmax(v, order=int(np.sqrt(v.shape[axis])),
                       axis=axis)

    return set([(i[0], i[1]) for i in np.column_stack(argmax)])
```

3. Download the image to analyze:

```
dir = dl.data.get_data_dir()
path = os.path.join(dir, 'night-927168_640.jpg')
base = 'https://pixabay.com/static/uploads/
photo/2015/09/06/10/19/'
url = base + 'night-927168_640.jpg'

if not dl.conf.file_exists(path):
    dl.data.download(url, path)
```

4. Extract the brightness values from the image:

```
img = cv2.imread(path)
hsv = cv2.cvtColor(img, cv2.COLOR_BGR2HSV)

h, s, v = cv2.split(hsv)

# Transform for normalization
v = v.astype(np.uint16) ** 2
```

5. Plot a histogram of the brightness values:

```
sp = dl.plotting.Subplotter(2, 2, context)
sp.ax.hist(v.ravel(), normed=True)
sp.label()
```

6. Plot a histogram of the brightness values for axis 0:

```
dl.plotting.hist_norm_pdf(sp.next_ax(), v.mean(axis=0))
sp.label()
```

7. Plot a histogram of the brightness values for axis 1:

```
dl.plotting.hist_norm_pdf(sp.next_ax(), v.mean(axis=1))
sp.label()
```

8. Plot the image with points we believe to contain bright stars:

```
points = scan_axis(v, 0).intersection(scan_axis(v, 1))

limit = np.percentile(np.unique(v.ravel()), 95)

kp = [cv2.KeyPoint(p[1], p[0], 1) for p in points
        if v[p[0], p[1]] > limit]
with_kp = cv2.drawKeypoints(img, kp, None, (255, 0, 0))

dl.plotting.img_show(sp.next_ax(), with_kp)
sp.label()

HTML(sp.exit())
```

Refer to the following screenshot for the end result:

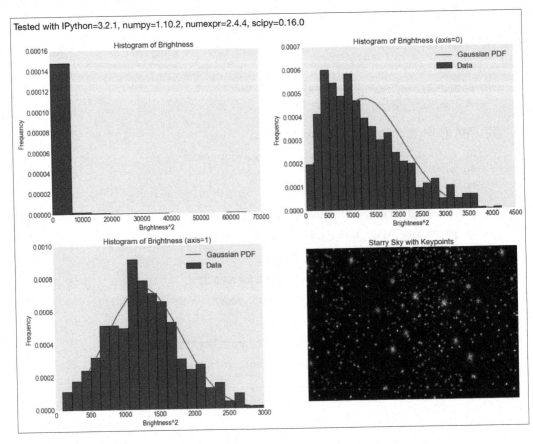

The code is in the `searching_stars.ipynb` file in this book's code bundle.

See also

▶ The Wikipedia page about HSL and HSV at `https://en.wikipedia.org/wiki/HSL_and_HSV` (retrieved December 2015)

▶ The `argrelmax()` function documented at `https://docs.scipy.org/doc/scipy-0.16.0/reference/generated/scipy.signal.argrelmax.html` (retrieved December 2015)

▶ The `split()` function documented at `http://docs.opencv.org/3.0-rc1/d2/de8/group__core__array.html#ga0547c7fed86152d7e9d0096029c8518a` (retrieved December 2015)

Extracting metadata from images

Digital photos often contain extra textual metadata, for example, timestamps, exposure information, and geolocations. Some of this metadata is editable by the camera owner. In the context of marketing, for instance, it can be useful to extract the metadata from profile (or other) images on social media websites. Purportedly, whistle blower Edward Snowden claimed that the American NSA is collecting EXIF metadata from global online data.

Getting ready

In this recipe, we will use ExifRead to extract the EXIF metadata.

Install ExifRead as follows:

```
$ pip install ExifRead
```

I tested the code with ExifRead 2.1.2.

How to do it...

1. The imports are as follows:

   ```
   import exifread
   import pprint
   ```

2. Open the image as follows:

   ```
   f = open('covers.jpg', 'rb')
   ```

3. Print the tags and keys as follows:

   ```
   # Return Exif tags
   tags = exifread.process_file(f)
   print(tags.keys())
   pprint.pprint(tags)
   f.close()
   ```

Refer to the following end result:

```
dict_keys(['EXIF Flash', 'Image Make', 'EXIF Contrast',
'EXIF DateTimeOriginal', 'Image ResolutionUnit', 'EXIF
ComponentsConfiguration', 'EXIF ISOSpeedRatings', 'Image
ExifOffset', 'Image ImageDescription', 'EXIF MaxApertureValue',
'EXIF ExposureBiasValue', 'Image YResolution', 'Image
Orientation', 'EXIF DateTimeDigitized', 'EXIF MeteringMode',
'EXIF Sharpness', 'EXIF WhiteBalance', 'EXIF ExposureTime',
'Image Model', 'EXIF SceneCaptureType', 'Image Software', 'EXIF
SceneType', 'EXIF SubjectDistanceRange', 'EXIF LightSource', 'EXIF
```

```
FocalLengthIn35mmFilm', 'Image XResolution', 'Image DateTime',
'EXIF FileSource', 'EXIF ExposureProgram', 'EXIF FocalLength',
'EXIF FNumber', 'EXIF Saturation', 'EXIF ExifImageWidth', 'EXIF
ExposureMode', 'EXIF DigitalZoomRatio', 'EXIF FlashPixVersion',
'EXIF ExifVersion', 'EXIF ColorSpace', 'EXIF CustomRendered', 'EXIF
GainControl', 'EXIF CompressedBitsPerPixel', 'EXIF ExifImageLength'])
{'EXIF ColorSpace': (0xA001) Short=sRGB @ 406,
 'EXIF ComponentsConfiguration': (0x9101) Undefined=YCbCr @ 298,
 'EXIF CompressedBitsPerPixel': (0x9102) Ratio=2 @ 650,
 'EXIF Contrast': (0xA408) Short=Normal @ 550,
 'EXIF CustomRendered': (0xA401) Short=Normal @ 466,
 'EXIF DateTimeDigitized': (0x9004) ASCII=0000:00:00 00:00:00 @ 630,
 'EXIF DateTimeOriginal': (0x9003) ASCII=0000:00:00 00:00:00 @ 610,
 'EXIF DigitalZoomRatio': (0xA404) Ratio=0 @ 682,
 'EXIF ExifImageLength': (0xA003) Long=240 @ 430,
 'EXIF ExifImageWidth': (0xA002) Long=940 @ 418,
 'EXIF ExifVersion': (0x9000) Undefined=0220 @ 262,
 'EXIF ExposureBiasValue': (0x9204) Signed Ratio=0 @ 658,
 'EXIF ExposureMode': (0xA402) Short=Auto Exposure @ 478,
 'EXIF ExposureProgram': (0x8822) Short=Program Normal @ 238,
 'EXIF ExposureTime': (0x829A) Ratio=10/601 @ 594,
 'EXIF FNumber': (0x829D) Ratio=14/5 @ 602,
 'EXIF FileSource': (0xA300) Undefined=Digital Camera @ 442,
 'EXIF Flash': (0x9209) Short=Flash fired, auto mode @ 370,
 'EXIF FlashPixVersion': (0xA000) Undefined=0100 @ 394,
 'EXIF FocalLength': (0x920A) Ratio=39/5 @ 674,
 'EXIF FocalLengthIn35mmFilm': (0xA405) Short=38 @ 514,
 'EXIF GainControl': (0xA407) Short=None @ 538,
 'EXIF ISOSpeedRatings': (0x8827) Short=50 @ 250,
 'EXIF LightSource': (0x9208) Short=Unknown @ 358,
 'EXIF MaxApertureValue': (0x9205) Ratio=3 @ 666,
 'EXIF MeteringMode': (0x9207) Short=Pattern @ 346,
 'EXIF Saturation': (0xA409) Short=Normal @ 562,
 'EXIF SceneCaptureType': (0xA406) Short=Standard @ 526,
 'EXIF SceneType': (0xA301) Undefined=Directly Photographed @ 454,
 'EXIF Sharpness': (0xA40A) Short=Normal @ 574,
 'EXIF SubjectDistanceRange': (0xA40C) Short=0 @ 586,
 'EXIF WhiteBalance': (0xA403) Short=Auto @ 490,
 'Image DateTime': (0x0132) ASCII=0000:00:00 00:00:00 @ 184,
 'Image ExifOffset': (0x8769) Long=204 @ 126,
 'Image ImageDescription': (0x010E) ASCII=          @ 134,
 'Image Make': (0x010F) ASCII=NIKON @ 146,
 'Image Model': (0x0110) ASCII=E7900 @ 152,
 'Image Orientation': (0x0112) Short=Horizontal (normal) @ 54,
 'Image ResolutionUnit': (0x0128) Short=Pixels/Inch @ 90,
```

```
'Image Software': (0x0131) ASCII=E7900v1.1 @ 174,
'Image XResolution': (0x011A) Ratio=300 @ 158,
'Image YResolution': (0x011B) Ratio=300 @ 166}
```

The code is in the `img_metadata.py` file in this book's code bundle.

See also

▸ The Wikipedia page about EXIF at `https://en.wikipedia.org/wiki/Exchangeable_image_file_format` (retrieved December 2015)

▸ The documentation for ExifRead at `https://github.com/ianare/exif-py` (retrieved December 2015)

Extracting texture features from images

Texture is the spatial and visual quality of an image. In this recipe, we will take a look at **Haralick texture features**. These features are based on the **co-occurrence matrix** (11.5) defined as follows:

$$(11.5) \quad C\Delta x, \Delta y\left(i, j\right) = \sum_{p=1}^{n}\sum_{q=1}^{m}\begin{cases}1, & if\ I\left(p,q\right) = i\ and\ I\left(p+\Delta x, q+\Delta y\right) = j \\ 0, & Othere\end{cases}$$

$$Angular\ 2nd\ Moment = \sum_{j}\sum_{i} p\left[i,j\right]^2$$

$$(11.6) \qquad Contrast = \sum_{n=0}^{Ng-1} n^2 \left\{\sum_{i=1}^{Ng}\sum_{j=1}^{Ng} p\left[i,j\right]\right\}, where\left|i-j\right| = n$$

$$Correlation = \frac{\sum_{i=1}^{Ng}\sum_{j=1}^{Ng}\left(ij\right)p\left[i,j\right] - \mu_x\mu_y}{\sigma_x\sigma_y}$$

$$Entropy = -\sum_{i}\sum_{j} p\left[i,j\right]log\left(p\left[i,j\right]\right)$$

In equation 11.5, *i* and *j* are intensities, while *p* and *q* are positions. The Haralick features are 13 metrics derived from the co-occurrence matrix, some of them given in equation 11.6. For a more complete list, refer to `http://murphylab.web.cmu.edu/publications/boland/boland_node26.html` (retrieved December 2015).

We will calculate the Haralick features with the mahotas API and apply them to the handwritten digits dataset of scikit-learn.

Getting ready

Install mahotas as follows:

```
$ pip install mahotas
```

I tested the code with mahotas 1.4.0.

How to do it...

1. The imports are as follows:

```
import mahotas as mh
import numpy as np
from sklearn.datasets import load_digits
import matplotlib.pyplot as plt
from tpot import TPOT
from sklearn.cross_validation import train_test_split
import dautil as dl
```

2. Load the scikit-learn digits data as follows:

```
digits = load_digits()
X = digits.data.copy()
```

3. Create Haralick features and add them:

```
for i, img in enumerate(digits.images):
    np.append(X[i], mh.features.haralick(
        img.astype(np.uint8)).ravel())
```

4. Fit and score a model with TPOT (or my fork, as discussed in *Chapter 9, Ensemble Learning and Dimensionality Reduction*):

```
X_train, X_test, y_train, y_test = train_test_split(
    X, digits.target, train_size=0.75)

tpot = TPOT(generations=6, population_size=101,
            random_state=46, verbosity=2)
tpot.fit(X_train, y_train)

print('Score {:.2f}'.format(tpot.score(X_train, y_train, X_test,
y_test)))
```

5. Plot the first original image as follows:

```
dl.plotting.img_show(plt.gca(), digits.images[0])
plt.title('Original Image')
```

6. Plot the core features for that image:

```
plt.figure()
dl.plotting.img_show(plt.gca(), digits.data[0].reshape((8, 8)))
plt.title('Core Features')
```

7. Plot the Haralick features for that image too:

```
plt.figure()
dl.plotting.img_show(plt.gca(), mh.features.haralick(
    digits.images[0].astype(np.uint8)))
plt.title('Haralick Features')
```

Refer to the following screenshot for the end result:

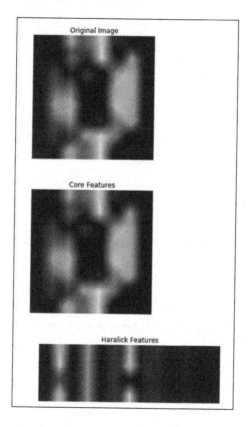

The code is in the `extracting_texture.ipynb` file in this book's code bundle.

- ▶ The Wikipedia page about image texture at `https://en.wikipedia.org/wiki/Image_texture` (retrieved December 2015)
- ▶ The Wikipedia page about the co-occurrence matrix at `https://en.wikipedia.org/wiki/Co-occurrence_matrix` (retrieved December 2015)

Applying hierarchical clustering on images

We encountered the concept of hierarchical clustering in *Chapter 9*, *Ensemble Learning and Dimensionality Reduction*. In this recipe, we will segment an image by hierarchically clustering it. We will apply **agglomerative clustering** $O(n^3)$, which is a type of hierarchical clustering.

In agglomerative clustering, each item is assigned its own cluster at initialization. Later, these clusters merge (agglomerate) and move up the hierarchy as needed. Obviously, we only merge clusters that are similar by some measure.

After initialization, we find the pair that are closest by some distance metric and merge them. The merged cluster is a higher-level cluster consisting of lower-level clusters. After that, we again find the closest pair and merge them, and so on. During this process, clusters can have any number of items. We stop clustering after we reach a certain number of clusters, or when the clusters are too far apart.

How to do it...

1. The imports are as follows:

```
import numpy as np
from scipy.misc import ascent
import matplotlib.pyplot as plt
from sklearn.feature_extraction.image import grid_to_graph
from sklearn.cluster import AgglomerativeClustering
import dautil as dl
```

2. Load an image and load it into an array:

```
img = ascent()
X = np.reshape(img, (-1, 1))
```

3. Cluster the image with the number of cluster set to 9 (a guess):

```
connectivity = grid_to_graph(*img.shape)
NCLUSTERS = 9
ac = AgglomerativeClustering(n_clusters=NCLUSTERS,
                             connectivity=connectivity)
```

```
ac.fit(X)
label = np.reshape(ac.labels_, img.shape)
```

4. Plot the image with cluster segments superimposed:

```
for l in range(NCLUSTERS):
    plt.contour(label == l, contours=1,
                colors=[plt.cm.spectral(l/float(NCLUSTERS)), ])

dl.plotting.img_show(plt.gca(), img, cmap=plt.cm.gray)
```

Refer to the following screenshot for the end result:

The code is in the `clustering_hierarchy.ipynb` file in this book's code bundle.

- ▸ The `AgglomerativeClustering` class documented at `http://scikit-learn.org/stable/modules/generated/sklearn.cluster.AgglomerativeClustering.html` (retrieved December 2015)
- ▸ The Wikipedia page about hierarchical clustering at `https://en.wikipedia.org/wiki/Hierarchical_clustering` (retrieved December 2015)

Segmenting images with spectral clustering

Spectral clustering is a clustering technique that can be used to segment images. The scikit-learn `spectral_clustering()` function implements the normalized graph cuts spectral clustering algorithm. This algorithm represents an image as a graph of units. "Graph" here is the same mathematical concept as in *Chapter 8, Text Mining and Social Network Analysis*. The algorithm tries to partition the image, while minimizing segment size and the ratio of intensity gradient along cuts.

How to do it...

1. The imports are as follows:

```
import numpy as np
import matplotlib.pyplot as plt
from sklearn.feature_extraction.image import img_to_graph
from sklearn.cluster import spectral_clustering
from sklearn.datasets import load_digits
```

2. Load the digits data set as follows:

```
digits = load_digits()
img = digits.images[0].astype(float)
mask = img.astype(bool)
```

3. Create a graph from the image:

```
graph = img_to_graph(img, mask=mask)
graph.data = np.exp(-graph.data/graph.data.std())
```

4. Apply spectral clustering to get three clusters:

```
labels = spectral_clustering(graph, n_clusters=3)
label_im = -np.ones(mask.shape)
label_im[mask] = labels
```

5. Plot the original image as follows:

```
plt.matshow(img, False)
plt.gca().axis('off')
plt.title('Original')
```

6. Plot the image with the three clusters as follows:

```
plt.figure()
plt.matshow(label_im, False)
plt.gca().axis('off')
plt.title('Clustered')
```

Refer to the following screenshot for the end result:

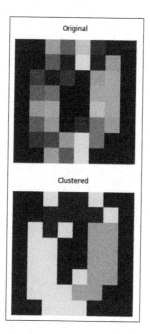

The code is in the `clustering_spectral.ipynb` file in this book's code bundle.

See also

- The Wikipedia page about spectral clustering at `https://en.wikipedia.org/wiki/Spectral_clustering` (retrieved December 2015)
- The `spectral_clustering()` function documented at `http://scikit-learn.org/stable/modules/generated/sklearn.cluster.spectral_clustering.html` (retrieved December 2015)

12
Parallelism and Performance

In this chapter, we will cover the following recipes:

- ▶ Just-in-time compiling with Numba
- ▶ Speeding up numerical expressions with Numexpr
- ▶ Running multiple threads with the `threading` module
- ▶ Launching multiple tasks with the `concurrent.futures` module
- ▶ Accessing resources asynchronously with the `asyncio` module
- ▶ Distributed processing with `execnet`
- ▶ Profiling memory usage
- ▶ Calculating the mean, variance, skewness, and kurtosis on the fly
- ▶ Caching with a least recently used cache
- ▶ Caching HTTP requests
- ▶ Streaming counting with the Count-min sketch
- ▶ Harnessing the power of the GPU with OpenCL

Introduction

The ENIAC, built between 1943 and 1946, filled a large room with eighteen thousand tubes and had a 20-bit memory. We have come a long way since then. The growth has been exponential as also predicted by Moore's law. Whether we are dealing with a self-fulfilling prophecy or a fundamental phenomenon is, of course, hard to say. Purportedly, the growth is starting to decelerate.

Given our current knowledge of technology, thermodynamics, and quantum mechanics, we can set hard limits for Moore's law. However, our assumptions may be wrong; for instance, scientists and engineers may come up with fundamentally better techniques to build chips. (One such development is quantum computing, which is currently far from widespread.) The biggest hurdle is heat dissipation, which is commonly measured in units of kT, with k the Boltzmann constant (about 10-23 J/K) and T in Kelvin (freezing point is 273.15 K). The heat dissipation per bit for a chip is at least kT (10-20 J at 350 K). Semi-conductors in the 1990s consumed at least a hundred thousand kT. A computational system undergoes changes in energy levels during operation. The smallest tolerable difference in energy is roughly 100 kT. Even if we somehow manage to avoid this limit, we will soon be operating close to atomic levels, which for quantum mechanical reasons is not practical (information about particles is fundamentally limited), unless we are talking about a quantum computer. Currently, the consensus is that we will reach the limit within decades. Another consideration is the complex wiring of chips. Complex wiring lowers the life expectancy of chips considerably.

This chapter is about software performance; however, there are other more important software aspects, such as maintainability, robustness, and usability. Betting on Moore's law is risky and not practical, since we have other possibilities to improve performance. The first option is to do the work in parallel as much as possible using multiple machines, cores on a single machine, GPUs, or other specialized hardware such as FPGAs. For instance, I am testing the code on an eight-core machine. As a student, I was lucky enough to get involved in a project with the goal of creating a grid. The grid was supposed to bring together university computers into a single computational environment. In a later phase, there were plans to connect other computers too, a bit like the SETI project. (As you know, many office computers are idle during weekends and at night, so why not make them work too?)

Currently, of course, there are various commercial cloud systems, such as those provided by Amazon and Google. I will not discuss those because I feel that these are more specialized topics, although I did cover some Python-specific cloud systems in *Python Data Analysis*.

The second method to improve performance is to apply caching, thereby avoiding unnecessary function calls. I covered the joblib library, which has a caching feature, in *Chapter 9, Ensemble Learning and Dimensionality Reduction*. Python 3 has brought us new features for parallelism and caching.

The third method is getting close to the metal. As you know, Python is a high-level programming language with a virtual machine and interpreter. Python has an extra layer, which a language unlike what C has. When I was a student, we were taught that C is a high-level language, with assembler and machine code as the lower levels. As far as I know, these days, practically nobody codes in assembler. Via Cython (covered in *Python Data Analysis*) and similar software, we can compile our code to obtain performance on a par with C and C++. Compiling is a hassle and is problematic because it reduces portability due to platform dependence. A common solution is to automate compiling with shell scripts and make files. Numba and other similar projects make life even easier with just-in-time compiling, although with some limitations.

Just-in-time compiling with Numba

The Numba software performs just-in-time compiling using special function decorators. The compilation produces native machine code automatically. The generated code can run on CPUs and GPUs. The main use case for Numba is math-heavy code that uses NumPy arrays.

We can compile the code with the `@numba.jit` decorator with optional function signature (for instance, `int32(int32)`). The types correspond with similar NumPy types. Numba operates in the `nopython` and `object` modes. The `nopython` mode is faster but more restricted. We can also release the **Global Interpreter Lock** (**GIL**) with the `nogil` option. You can cache the compilation results by requesting a file cache with the `cache` argument.

The `@vectorize` decorator converts functions with scalar arguments into NumPy ufuncs. Vectorization gives extra advantages, such as automatic broadcasting, and can be used on a single core, multiple cores in parallel, or a GPU.

Getting ready

Install Numba with the following command:

```
$ pip/conda install numba
```

I tested the code with Numba 0.22.1.

How to do it...

1. The imports are as follows:
   ```python
   from numba import vectorize
   from numba import jit
   import numpy as np
   ```

2. Define the following function to use the `@vectorize` decorator:
   ```python
   @vectorize
   def vectorize_version(x, y, z):
       return x ** 2 + y ** 2 + z ** 2
   ```

3. Define the following function to use the `@jit` decorator:
   ```python
   @jit(nopython=True)
   def jit_version(x, y, z):
       return x ** 2 + y ** 2 + z ** 2
   ```

4. Define some random arrays as follows:

```
np.random.seed(36)
x = np.random.random(1000)
y = np.random.random(1000)
z = np.random.random(1000)
```

5. Measure the time it takes to sum the squares of the arrays:

```
%timeit x ** 2 + y ** 2 + z ** 2
%timeit vectorize_version(x, y, z)
%timeit jit_version(x, y, z)
jit_version.inspect_types()
```

Refer to the following screenshot for the end result:

```
The slowest run took 10.80 times longer than the fastest. This could mean that an intermediat
e result is being cached
100000 loops, best of 3: 8.56 µs per loop
The slowest run took 44363.89 times longer than the fastest. This could mean that an intermed
iate result is being cached
100000 loops, best of 3: 2.87 µs per loop
The slowest run took 97089.67 times longer than the fastest. This could mean that an intermed
iate result is being cached
1000000 loops, best of 3: 1.82 µs per loop
jit_version (array(float64, 1d, C), array(float64, 1d, C), array(float64, 1d, C))
---------------------------------------------------------------------
# File: <ipython-input-2-85851b86f297>
# --- LINE 5 ---

@jit(nopython=True)

# --- LINE 6 ---

def jit_version(x, y, z):

    # --- LINE 7 ---
    # label 0
    #    x = arg(0, name=x)   :: array(float64, 1d, C)
    #    y = arg(1, name=y)   :: array(float64, 1d, C)
    #    z = arg(2, name=z)   :: array(float64, 1d, C)
    #    $const0.2 = const(int, 2)   :: int64
    #    $const0.5 = const(int, 2)   :: int64
```

The code is in the `compiling_numba.ipynb` file in this book's code bundle.

How it works

The best time measured is 1.82 microseconds on my machine, which is significantly faster than the measured time for normal Python code. At the end of the screenshot, we see the result of the compilation, with the last part omitted because it is too long and difficult to read. We get warnings, which are most likely caused by CPU caching. I left them on purpose, but you may be able to get rid of them using much larger arrays that don't fit in the cache.

See also

▶ The Numba website at `http://numba.pydata.org/` (retrieved January 2016)

Speeding up numerical expressions with Numexpr

Numexpr is a software package for the evaluation of numerical array expressions, which is also installed when you install pandas, and you may have seen it announced in the watermark of other recipes (tested with Numexpr 2.3.1). Numexpr tries to speed up calculations by avoiding the creation of temporary variables because reading the variables can be a potential bottleneck. The largest speedups are expected for arrays that can't fit in the CPU cache.

Numexpr splits large arrays into chunks, which fit in the cache, and it also uses multiple cores in parallel when possible. It has an `evaluate()` function, which accepts simple expressions and evaluates them (refer to the documentation for the complete list of supported features).

How to do it...

1. The imports are as follows:

```
import numexpr as ne
import numpy as np
```

2. Generate random arrays, which should be too large to hold in a cache:

```
a = np.random.rand(1e6)
b = np.random.rand(1e6)
```

3. Evaluate a simple arithmetic expression and measure execution time:

```
%timeit 2 * a ** 3 + 3 * b ** 9
%timeit ne.evaluate("2 * a ** 3 +3 * b ** 9 ")
```

Refer to the following screenshot for the end result:

```
10 loops, best of 3: 71.3 ms per loop
100 loops, best of 3: 3.05 ms per loop
```

The code is in the `speeding_numexpr.ipynb` file in this book's code bundle.

How it works

We generated random data that should not fit in a cache to avoid caching effects and because that is the best use case for Numexpr. The size of the cache differs from one machine to another, so if necessary use a larger or smaller size for the arrays. In the example, we put a string containing a simple arithmetic expression, although we could have used a slightly more complex expression. For more details, refer to the documentation. I tested the code with a machine that has eight cores. The speedup is larger than a factor of eight, so it's clearly due to Numexpr.

See also

▶ The Numexpr website at `https://pypi.python.org/pypi/numexpr` (retrieved January 2016)

Running multiple threads with the threading module

A computer process is an instance of a running program. Processes are actually heavyweight, so we may prefer threads, which are lighter. In fact, threads are often just subunits of a process. Processes are separated from each other, while threads can share instructions and data.

Operating systems typically assign one thread to each core (if there are more than one), or switch between threads periodically; this is called **time slicing**. Threads as processes can have different priorities and the operating system has daemon threads running in the background with very low priority.

It's easier to switch between threads than between processes; however, because threads share information, they are more dangerous to use. For instance, if multiple threads are able to increment a counter at the same time, this will make the code nondeterministic and potentially incorrect. One way to minimize risks is to make sure that only one thread can access a shared variable or shared function at a time. This strategy is implemented in Python as the GIL.

How to do it...

1. The imports are as follows:

```
import dautil as dl
import ch12util
from functools import partial
from queue import Queue
```

```
from threading import Thread
import matplotlib.pyplot as plt
import numpy as np
from scipy.stats import skew
from IPython.display import HTML

STATS = []
```

2. Define the following function to resample:

```
def resample(arr):
    sample = ch12util.bootstrap(arr)
    STATS.append((sample.mean(), sample.std(), skew(sample)))
```

3. Define the following class to bootstrap:

```
class Bootstrapper(Thread):
    def __init__(self, queue, data):
        Thread.__init__(self)
        self.queue = queue
        self.data = data
        self.log = dl.log_api.conf_logger(__name__)

    def run(self):
        while True:
            index = self.queue.get()

            if index % 10 == 0:
                self.log.debug('Bootstrap {}'.format(
                    index))

            resample(self.data)
            self.queue.task_done()
```

4. Define the following function to perform serial resampling:

```
def serial(arr, n):
    for i in range(n):
        resample(arr)
```

5. Define the following function to perform parallel resampling:

```
def threaded(arr, n):
    queue = Queue()

    for x in range(8):
        worker = Bootstrapper(queue, arr)
        worker.daemon = True
        worker.start()

    for i in range(n):
        queue.put(i)

    queue.join()
```

6. Plot distributions of moments and execution times:

```
sp = dl.plotting.Subplotter(2, 2, context)
temp = dl.data.Weather.load()['TEMP'].dropna().values
np.random.seed(26)
threaded_times = ch12util.time_many(partial(threaded, temp))
serial_times = ch12util.time_many(partial(serial, temp))

ch12util.plot_times(sp.ax, serial_times, threaded_times)

stats_arr = np.array(STATS)
ch12util.plot_distro(sp.next_ax(), stats_arr.T[0], temp.mean())
sp.label()

ch12util.plot_distro(sp.next_ax(), stats_arr.T[1], temp.std())
sp.label()

ch12util.plot_distro(sp.next_ax(), stats_arr.T[2], skew(temp))
sp.label()

HTML(sp.exit())
```

Refer to the following screenshot for the end result:

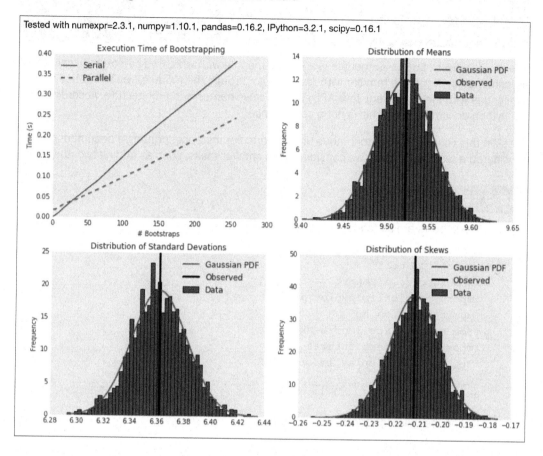

The code is in the `running_threads.ipynb` file in this book's code bundle.

See also

▸ The documentation for Python threading at `https://docs.python.org/3/library/threading.html` (retrieved January 2016)

Launching multiple tasks with the concurrent.futures module

The `concurrent.futures` module is a Python module with which we can execute callables asynchronously. If you are familiar with Java and go through the module, you will notice some similarities with the equivalent Java API, such as class names and architecture. According to the Python documentation, this is not a coincidence.

A task in this context is an autonomous unit of work. For instance, printing a document can be considered a task, but usually we consider much smaller tasks, such as adding two numbers.

How to do it...

1. The imports are as follows:

```
import dautil as dl
import ch12util
from functools import partial
import matplotlib.pyplot as plt
import numpy as np
from scipy.stats import skew
import concurrent.futures
from IPython.display import HTML


STATS = []
```

2. Define the following function to resample:

```
def resample(arr):
    sample = ch12util.bootstrap(arr)
    STATS.append((sample.mean(), sample.std(), skew(sample)))
```

3. Define the following class to bootstrap:

```
class Bootstrapper():
    def __init__(self, data):
        self.data = data
        self.log = dl.log_api.conf_logger(__name__)

    def run(self, index):
        if index % 10 == 0:
            self.log.debug('Bootstrap {}'.format(
                index))

        resample(self.data)
```

4. Define the following function to perform serial resampling:

```
def serial(arr, n):
    for i in range(n):
        resample(arr)
```

5. Define the following function to perform parallel resampling:

```
def parallel(arr, n):
    executor = concurrent.futures.ThreadPoolExecutor(max_
workers=8)
    bootstrapper = Bootstrapper(arr)

    for x in executor.map(bootstrapper.run, range(n)):
        pass

    executor.shutdown()
```

6. Plot distributions of moments and execution times:

```
rain = dl.data.Weather.load()['RAIN'].dropna().values
np.random.seed(33)
parallel_times = ch12util.time_many(partial(parallel, rain))
serial_times = ch12util.time_many(partial(serial, rain))

sp = dl.plotting.Subplotter(2, 2, context)
ch12util.plot_times(sp.ax, serial_times, parallel_times)

STATS = np.array(STATS)
ch12util.plot_distro(sp.next_ax(), STATS.T[0], rain.mean())
sp.label()

ch12util.plot_distro(sp.next_ax(), STATS.T[1], rain.std())
sp.label()

ch12util.plot_distro(sp.next_ax(), STATS.T[2], skew(rain))
sp.label()
HTML(sp.exit())
```

Refer to the following screenshot for the end result:

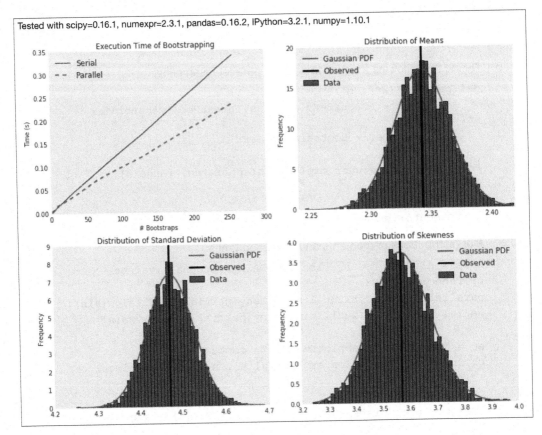

The code is in the `launching_futures.ipynb` file in this book's code bundle.

See also

► The documentation for the `concurrent.futures` module at `https://docs.python.org/3/library/concurrent.futures.html` (retrieved January 2016)

Accessing resources asynchronously with the asyncio module

It is a basic fact of life that I/O (for example, file or database access) is slow. I/O is not only slow, but also unpredictable. In a common scenario, we wait for data (from a web service or sensors) and write the data to the filesystem or a database. In such a situation, we can find ourselves to be I/O bound—spending more time waiting for the data than actually processing it. We can poll for data periodically or act on event triggers (either check your watch or set an alarm). GUIs usually have special threads that wait for user input in an infinite loop.

The Python `asyncio` module for asynchronous I/O uses the concept of **coroutines** with a related function decorator. A brief example of this module was also given in the *Scraping the web* recipe of *Chapter 5, Web Mining, Databases, and Big Data*. Subroutines can be thought of as a special case of coroutines. A subroutine has a start and exit point, either through an early exit with a return statement or by reaching the end of the subroutine definition. In contrast, a coroutine can yield with the `yield from` statement by calling another coroutine and then resuming execution from that exit point. The coroutine is letting another coroutine take over, as it were, and is going back to sleep until it is activated again.

Subroutines can be placed on a single stack. However, coroutines require multiple stacks, which makes understanding the code and potential exceptions more complex.

How to do it...

The code is in the `accessing_asyncio.ipynb` file in this book's code bundle:

1. The imports are as follows:

```
import dautil as dl
import ch12util
from functools import partial
import matplotlib.pyplot as plt
import numpy as np
from scipy.stats import skew
import asyncio
import time
from IPython.display import HTML

STATS = []
```

2. Define the following function to resample:

```python
def resample(arr):
    sample = ch12util.bootstrap(arr)
    STATS.append((sample.mean(), sample.std(), skew(sample)))
```

3. Define the following class to bootstrap:

```python
class Bootstrapper():
    def __init__(self, data, queue):
        self.data = data
        self.log = dl.log_api.conf_logger(__name__)
        self.queue = queue

    @asyncio.coroutine
    def run(self):
        while not self.queue.empty():
            index = yield from self.queue.get()

            if index % 10 == 0:
                self.log.debug('Bootstrap {}'.format(
                    index))

            resample(self.data)
            # simulates slow IO
            yield from asyncio.sleep(0.01)
```

4. Define the following function to perform serial resampling:

```python
def serial(arr, n):
    for i in range(n):
        resample(arr)
        # simulates slow IO
        time.sleep(0.01)
```

5. Define the following function to perform parallel resampling:

```python
def parallel(arr, n):
    q = asyncio.Queue()

    for i in range(n):
        q.put_nowait(i)

    bootstrapper = Bootstrapper(arr, q)
    policy = asyncio.get_event_loop_policy()
    policy.set_event_loop(policy.new_event_loop())
    loop = asyncio.get_event_loop()
```

```
            tasks = [asyncio.async(bootstrapper.run())
                    for i in range(n)]

            loop.run_until_complete(asyncio.wait(tasks))
            loop.close()
```

6. Plot distributions of moments and execution times:

```
pressure = dl.data.Weather.load()['PRESSURE'].dropna().values
np.random.seed(33)
parallel_times = ch12util.time_many(partial(parallel, pressure))
serial_times = ch12util.time_many(partial(serial, pressure))

dl.options.mimic_seaborn()
ch12util.plot_times(plt.gca(), serial_times, parallel_times)

sp = dl.plotting.Subplotter(2, 2, context)
ch12util.plot_times(sp.ax, serial_times, parallel_times)

STATS = np.array(STATS)
ch12util.plot_distro(sp.next_ax(), STATS.T[0], pressure.mean())
sp.label()

ch12util.plot_distro(sp.next_ax(), STATS.T[1], pressure.std())
sp.label()

ch12util.plot_distro(sp.next_ax(), STATS.T[2], skew(pressure))
sp.label()
HTML(sp.exit())
```

Refer to the following screenshot for the end result:

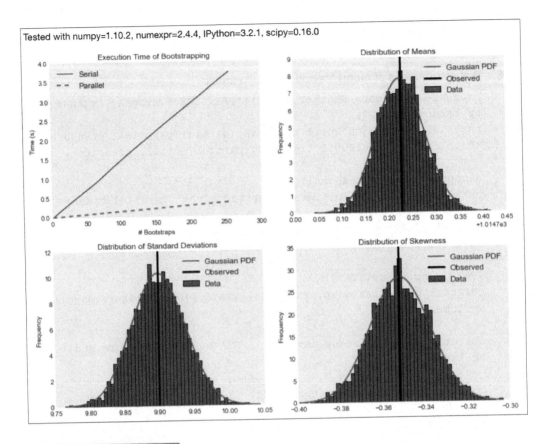

Tested with numpy=1.10.2, numexpr=2.4.4, IPython=3.2.1, scipy=0.16.0

▶ The documentation for the `asyncio` module at `https://docs.python.org/3/library/asyncio.html` (retrieved January 2016)

▶ The related Wikipedia page at `https://en.wikipedia.org/wiki/Coroutine` (retrieved January 2016)

Distributed processing with execnet

The `execnet` module has a share-nothing model and uses **channels** for communication. Channels in this context are software abstractions used to send and receive messages between (distributed) computer processes. `execnet` is most useful for combining heterogeneous computing environments with different Python interpreters and installed software. The environments can have different operating systems and Python implementations (CPython, Jython, PyPy, or others).

In the **shared nothing architecture**, computing nodes don't share memory or files. The architecture is therefore totally decentralized with completely independent nodes. The obvious advantage is that we are not dependent on any one node.

Getting ready

Install execnet with the following command:

```
$ pip/conda install execnet
```

I tested the code with execnet 1.3.0.

How to do it...

1. The imports are as follows:

```
import dautil as dl
import ch12util
from functools import partial
import matplotlib.pyplot as plt
import numpy as np
import execnet

STATS = []
```

2. Define the following helper function:

```
def run(channel, data=[]):
    while not channel.isclosed():
        index = channel.receive()

        if index % 10 == 0:
            print('Bootstrap {}'.format(
                index))

        total = 0

        for x in data:
            total += x

        channel.send((total - data[index])/(len(data) - 1))
```

3. Define the following function to perform serial resampling:

```
def serial(arr, n):
    for i in range(n):
        total = 0

        for x in arr:
            total += x

        STATS.append((total - arr[i])/(len(arr) - 1))
```

4. Define the following function to perform parallel resampling:

```
def parallel(arr, n):
    gw = execnet.makegateway()
    channel = gw.remote_exec(run, data=arr.tolist())

    for i in range(n):
        channel.send(i)
        STATS.append(channel.receive())

    gw.exit()
```

5. Plot distributions of means and execution times:

```
ws = dl.data.Weather.load()['WIND_SPEED'].dropna().values
np.random.seed(33)
parallel_times = ch12util.time_many(partial(parallel, ws))
serial_times = ch12util.time_many(partial(serial, ws))

%matplotlib inline
dl.options.mimic_seaborn()
ch12util.plot_times(plt.gca(), serial_times, parallel_times)
plt.legend(loc='best')

plt.figure()
STATS = np.array(STATS)
ch12util.plot_distro(plt.gca(), STATS, ws.mean())
plt.title('Distribution of the Means')
plt.legend(loc='best')
```

Refer to the following screenshot for the end result:

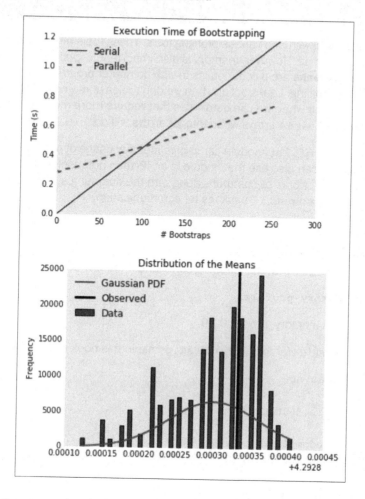

The code is in the `distributing_execnet.ipynb` file in this book's code bundle.

See also

- The execnet website at `http://codespeak.net/execnet/` (retrieved January 2016)

- The related Wikipedia page at `https://en.wikipedia.org/wiki/Shared_nothing_architecture` (retrieved January 2016)

Profiling memory usage

In *Python Data Analysis*, we used various profiling tools. These tools mostly had to do with measuring execution times. However, memory is also important, especially if we don't have enough of it. **Memory leaks** are a common issue with computer programs that we can find by performing memory profiling. Leaks occur when we don't release memory that is not needed. Problems also may occur when we use data types that require more memory than we need, for instance, NumPy `float64` arrays when integer arrays will do.

The Python `memory_profiler` module can profile memory usage of code line by line. Once you install it, you can also use the module in an IPython notebook via various magic commands. The module works by communicating with the operating system. On Windows, you will require the Python `psutil` package for communication.

Getting ready

Install `memory_profiler` with the following command:

```
$ pip install memory-profiler
```

I tested the code with memory_profiler 0.39.

Create a script to profile (refer to the `mem_test.py` file in this book's code bundle):

```
import numpy as np


def test_me():
    a = np.random.random((999, 99))
    b = np.random.random((99, 99))
    a.ravel()
    b.tolist()
```

How to do it...

1. The imports are as follows:
    ```
    import dautil as dl
    from mem_test import test_me
    ```

2. Load the IPython extension as follows:
    ```
    %load_ext memory_profiler
    ```

3. Profile the test script line-by-line with the following command:
    ```
    %mprun -f test_me test_me()
    ```

Refer to the following screenshot for the end result:

```
Line #     Mem usage     Increment   Line Contents
================================================
     4     108.5 MiB      0.0 MiB     def test_me():
     5     109.3 MiB      0.8 MiB         a = np.random.random((999, 99))
     6     109.3 MiB      0.0 MiB         b = np.random.random((99, 99))
     7     109.3 MiB      0.0 MiB         a.ravel()
     8     109.5 MiB      0.2 MiB         b.tolist()
```

The code is in the `profiling_memory.ipynb` file in this book's code bundle.

See also

▸ The memory_profiler website at `https://pypi.python.org/pypi/memory_profiler` (retrieved January 2016)

Calculating the mean, variance, skewness, and kurtosis on the fly

Mean, variance, skewness, and kurtosis are important quantities in statistics. Some of the calculations involve sums of squares, which for large values may lead to overflow. To avoid loss of precision, we have to realize that variance is invariant under shift by a certain constant number.

When we have enough space in memory, we can directly calculate the moments, taking into account numerical issues if necessary. However, we may want to not keep the data in memory because there is a lot of it, or because it is more convenient to calculate the moments on the fly.

An online and numerically stable algorithm to calculate the variance has been provided by Terriberry (Terriberry, Timothy B. (2007), *Computing Higher-Order Moments Online*). We will compare this algorithm, although it is not the best one, to the implementation in the `LiveStats` module. If you are interested in improved algorithms, take a look at the Wikipedia page listed in the *See also* section.

Take a look at the following equations:

$$(12.1) \quad \delta = x - m$$

$$(12.2) \quad m\backslash' = m + \frac{\delta}{n}$$

$$(12.3) \quad M_2\backslash' = M_2 + \delta^2 \frac{n-1}{n}$$

$$(12.4) \quad M_3\backslash' = M_3 + \delta^3 \frac{(n-1)(n-2)}{n^2} - \frac{3\delta M_2}{n}$$

$$(12.5) \quad M_4\backslash' = M_4 + \frac{\delta^4(n-1)(n^2-3n+3)}{n^3} + \frac{6\delta^2 M_2}{n^2} - \frac{4\delta M_3}{n}$$

$$(12.6) \quad g_1 = \frac{\sqrt{nM_3}}{M_2^{3/2}}$$

$$(12.7) \quad g_2 = \frac{nM_4}{M_2^2} - 3$$

Skewness is given by 12.6 and kurtosis is given by 12.7.

Getting ready

Install LiveStats with the following command:

```
$ pip install LiveStats
```

I tested the code with LiveStats 1.0.

How to do it...

1. The imports are as follows:

```
from livestats import livestats
from math import sqrt
import dautil as dl
import numpy as np
from scipy.stats import skew
from scipy.stats import kurtosis
import matplotlib.pyplot as plt
```

2. Define the following function to implement the equations for the moments calculation:

```
# From https://en.wikipedia.org/wiki/
# Algorithms_for_calculating_variance
def online_kurtosis(data):
    n = 0
    mean = 0
    M2 = 0
    M3 = 0
    M4 = 0
    stats = []

    for x in data:
        n1 = n
        n = n + 1
        delta = x - mean
        delta_n = delta / n
        delta_n2 = delta_n ** 2
        term1 = delta * delta_n * n1
        mean = mean + delta_n
        M4 = M4 + term1 * delta_n2 * (n**2 - 3*n + 3) + \
            6 * delta_n2 * M2 - 4 * delta_n * M3
        M3 = M3 + term1 * delta_n * (n - 2) - 3 * delta_n * M2
        M2 = M2 + term1
        s = sqrt(n) * M3 / sqrt(M2 ** 3)
        k = (n*M4) / (M2**2) - 3
        stats.append((mean, sqrt(M2/(n - 1)), s, k))

    return np.array(stats)
```

3. Initialize and load data as follows:

```
test = livestats.LiveStats([0.25, 0.5, 0.75])

data = dl.data.Weather.load()['TEMP'].\
    resample('M').dropna().values
```

4. Calculate the various statistics with LiveStats, the algorithm mentioned in the previous section, and compare with the results when we apply NumPy functions to all the data at once:

```
ls = []
truth = []

test.add(data[0])
```

```
for i in range(1, len(data)):
    test.add(data[i])
    q1, q2, q3 = test.quantiles()

    ls.append((test.mean(), sqrt(test.variance()),
            test.skewness(), test.kurtosis(), q1[1], q2[1],
q3[1]))
    slice = data[:i]
    truth.append((slice.mean(), slice.std(),
                skew(slice), kurtosis(slice),
                np.percentile(slice, 25), np.median(slice),
                np.percentile(slice, 75)))

ls = np.array(ls)
truth = np.array(truth)
ok = online_kurtosis(data)
```

5. Plot the results as follows:

```
dl.options.mimic_seaborn()
cp = dl.plotting.CyclePlotter(plt.gca())
cp.plot(ls.T[0], label='LiveStats')
cp.plot(truth.T[0], label='Truth')
cp.plot(data)
plt.title('Live Stats Means')
plt.xlabel('# points')
plt.ylabel('Mean')
plt.legend(loc='best')

plt.figure()

mses = [dl.stats.mse(truth.T[i], ls.T[i])
        for i in range(7)]
mses.extend([dl.stats.mse(truth.T[i], ok[1:].T[i])
            for i in range(4)])
dl.plotting.bar(plt.gca(),
                ['mean', 'std', 'skew', 'kurt',
                'q1', 'q2', 'q3',
                'my_mean', 'my_std', 'my_skew', 'my_kurt'], mses)
plt.title('MSEs for Various Statistics')
plt.ylabel('MSE')
```

Refer to the following screenshot for the end result:

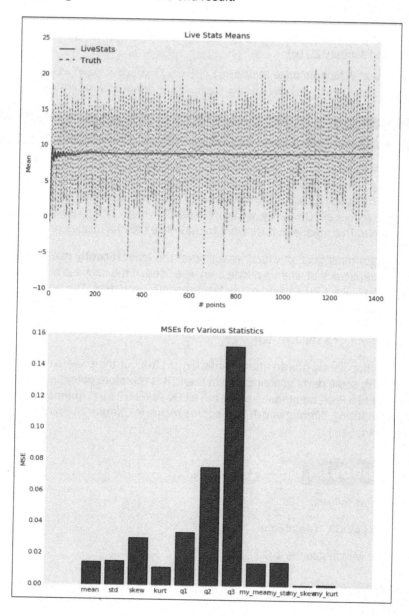

The code is in the `calculating_moments.ipynb` file in this book's code bundle.

See also

► The LiveStats website at `https://bitbucket.org/scassidy/livestats` (retrieved January 2016)

► The related Wikipedia page at `https://en.wikipedia.org/wiki/Algorithms_for_calculating_variance` (retrieved January 2016)

Caching with a least recently used cache

Caching involves storing results, usually from a function call, in memory or on disk. If done correctly, caching helps by reducing the number of function calls. In general, we want to keep the cache small for space reasons. If we are able to find items in cache, we talk about hits; otherwise, we have misses. Obviously, we want to have as many hits as possible and as few misses as possible. This means that we want to maximize the hits-misses ratio.

Many caching algorithms exist, of which we will cover the **least recently used** (**LRU**) algorithm. This algorithm keeps track of when a cache item was used. If the cache is about to exceed its maximum specified size, LRU gets rid of the least recently used item. The reasoning is that these items are possibly older and, therefore, not as relevant any more. There are several variations of LRU. Other algorithms do the opposite—removing the most recent item, the least frequently used item, or a random item.

The standard Python library has an implementation of LRU, but there is also a specialized Python library with some parts implemented in C and it is therefore potentially faster. We will compare the two implementations using the NLTK `lemmatize()` method (refer to the *Stemming, lemmatizing, filtering and TF-IDF scores* recipe in *Chapter 8, Text Mining and Social Network Analysis*).

Getting ready

Install fastcache as follows:

```
$ pip/conda install fastcache
```

I tested the code with fastcache 1.0.2.

How to do it...

1. The imports are as follows:

```
from fastcache import clru_cache
from functools import lru_cache
from nltk.corpus import brown
from nltk.stem import WordNetLemmatizer
```

```
import dautil as dl
import numpy as np
from IPython.display import HTML
```

2. Define the following function to cache:

```
def lemmatize(word, lemmatizer):
    return lemmatizer.lemmatize(word.lower())
```

3. Define the following function to measure the effects of caching:

```
def measure(impl, words, lemmatizer):
    cache = dl.perf.LRUCache(impl, lemmatize)
    times = []
    hm = []

    for i in range(5, 12):
        cache.maxsize = 2 ** i
        cache.cache()
        with dl.perf.StopWatch() as sw:
            _ = [cache.cached(w, lemmatizer) for w in words]

        hm.append(cache.hits_miss())
        times.append(sw.elapsed)
        cache.clear()

    return (times, hm)
```

4. Initialize a list of words and an NLTK `WordNetLemmatizer` object:

```
words = [w for w in brown.words()]
lemmatizer = WordNetLemmatizer()
```

5. Measure the execution time as follows:

```
with dl.perf.StopWatch() as sw:
    _ = [lemmatizer.lemmatize(w.lower()) for w in words]

plain = sw.elapsed

times, hm = measure(clru_cache, words, lemmatizer)
```

6. Plot the results for different cache sizes:

```
sp = dl.plotting.Subplotter(2, 2, context)
sp.ax.plot(2 ** np.arange(5, 12), times)
sp.ax.axhline(plain, lw=2, label='Uncached')
sp.label()
```

```
sp.next_ax().plot(2 ** np.arange(5, 12), hm)
sp.label()

times, hm = measure(lru_cache, words, lemmatizer)
sp.next_ax().plot(2 ** np.arange(5, 12), times)
sp.ax.axhline(plain, lw=2, label='Uncached')
sp.label()

sp.next_ax().plot(2 ** np.arange(5, 12), hm)
sp.label()
HTML(sp.exit())
```

Refer to the following screenshot for the end result:

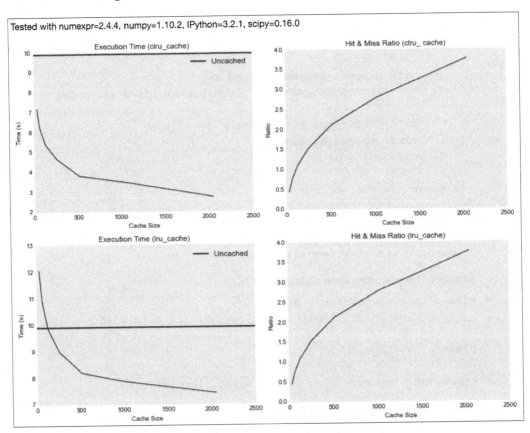

The code is in the `caching_lru.ipynb` file in this book's code bundle.

See also

- ▸ The related Wikipedia page at `http://en.wikipedia.org/wiki/Cache_algorithms` (retrieved January 2016)
- ▸ The fastcache website at `https://pypi.python.org/pypi/fastcache` (retrieved January 2016)
- ▸ The `functools.lru_cache` documentation at `https://docs.python.org/3/library/functools.html#functools.lru_cache` (retrieved January 2016)

Caching HTTP requests

Sometimes data is made available via a web service over HTTP. The advantage is that we don't have to care that much about the technologies that the sending party is using. This is comparable to the way e-mail, for instance, works. However, we have to explicitly request information via an HTTP GET (often) or HTTP POST (uppercase by convention) method. Whenever we request a web page or download a file, we usually perform a GET request. The web server on the other side has to process the request. If there are many requests, we can potentially slow down the server, so organizations often take measures to prevent this. It may mean that further requests from you will be blocked.

Avoiding issuing the same request multiple times is advantageous for efficiency reasons too. Web browsers solve this with a cache, and we can do the same with the `requests-cache` package. The cache is stored in a SQLite database by default.

A common use case that we will not cover is that of periodically retrieving information with HTTP. Obviously, we don't want to retrieve content if nothing has changed. The HTTP protocol provides efficient mechanisms to determine whether content was modified. A web server, however, is not required to report content changes.

Getting ready

Install requests-cache with the following command:

```
$ pip install --upgrade requests-cache
```

I tested the code with requests-cache 0.4.10.

How to do it...

1. The imports are as follows:

   ```
   import requests
   import requests_cache
   ```

2. Install the cache (this creates a SQLite database by default):

   ```
   requests_cache.install_cache()
   ```

3. Request a website that builds the cache:

   ```
   %time requests.get('http://google.com')
   ```

4. Request the same website that should now come from the local cache:

   ```
   %time requests.get('http://google.com')
   ```

5. Clear the cache as follows:

   ```
   requests_cache.clear()
   ```

6. Request the website yet again (the cache should be empty now):

   ```
   %time requests.get('http://google.com')
   ```

Refer to the following screenshot for the end result:

```
CPU times: user 14 ms, sys: 5.51 ms, total: 19.5 ms
Wall time: 42.1 ms
CPU times: user 3.56 ms, sys: 1 ms, total: 4.57 ms
Wall time: 5.29 ms
CPU times: user 14.4 ms, sys: 4.28 ms, total: 18.7 ms
Wall time: 952 ms
```

The code is in the `caching_requests.ipynb` file in this book's code bundle.

See also

- The related Wikipedia page at `https://en.wikipedia.org/wiki/HTTP_ETag` (retrieved January 2016)
- The requests-cache website at `https://pypi.python.org/pypi/requests-cache` (retrieved January 2016)

Streaming counting with the Count-min sketch

Streaming or online algorithms are useful as they don't require as much memory and processing power as other algorithms. This chapter has a recipe involving the calculation of statistical moments online (refer to *Calculating the mean, variance, skewness, and kurtosis on the fly*).

Also, in the *Clustering streaming data with Spark* recipe of Chapter 5, *Web Mining, Databases, and Big Data*, I covered another streaming algorithm.

Streaming algorithms are often approximate for fundamental reasons or because of roundoff errors. You should, therefore, try to use other algorithms if possible. Of course in many situations approximate results are good enough. For instance, it doesn't matter whether a user has 500 or 501 connections on a social media website. If you just send thousands of invitations, you will get there sooner or later.

Sketching is something you probably know from drawing. In that context, sketching means outlining rough contours of objects without any details. A similar concept exists in the world of streaming algorithms.

In this recipe, I cover the *Count-min sketch* (2003) by Graham Cormode and S. Muthu Muthukrishnan, which is useful in the context of ranking. For example, we may want to know the most viewed articles on a news website, trending topics, the ads with the most clicks, or the users with the most connections. The naive approach requires keeping counts for each item in a dictionary or a table. Dictionaries use hashing functions to calculate identifying integers, which serve as keys. For theoretical reasons, we can have collisions—this means that two or more items have the same key. The Count-min sketch is a two-dimensional tabular data structure that is small on purpose, and it uses hashing functions for each row. It is prone to collisions, leading to overcounting.

When an event occurs, for instance someone views an ad, we do the following:

1. For each row in the sketch, we apply the related hashing function using, for instance, the ad identifier to get a column index.
2. Increment the value corresponding with the row and column.

Each event is clearly mapped to each row in the sketch. When we request the count, we follow the opposite path to obtain multiple counts. The lowest count gives an estimate for the count of this item.

The idea behind this setup is that frequent items are likely to dominate less common items. The probability of a popular item having collisions with unpopular items is larger than of collisions between popular items.

How to do it...

1. The imports are as follows:

```
from nltk.corpus import brown
from nltk.corpus import stopwords
import dautil as dl
from collections import defaultdict
import matplotlib.pyplot as plt
import numpy as np
from IPython.display import HTML
```

2. Store the words of the NLTK Brown and stop words corpora in lists:

```
words_dict = dl.collect.IdDict()
dd = defaultdict(int)
fid = brown.fileids(categories='news')[0]
words = brown.words(fid)
sw = set(stopwords.words('english'))
```

3. Count the occurrence of each stopword:

```
for w in words:
    if w in sw:
        dd[w] += 1
```

4. Plot the distribution of count errors for various parameters of the Count-min sketch:

```
sp = dl.plotting.Subplotter(2, 2, context)
actual = np.array([dd[w] for w in sw])
errors = []

for i in range(1, 4):
    cm = dl.perf.CountMinSketch(depth=5 * 2 ** i,
                                width=20 * 2 ** i)

    for w in words:
        cm.add(words_dict.add_or_get(w.lower()))

    estimates = np.array([cm.estimate_count(words_dict.add_or_
get(w))
                          for w in sw])
    diff = estimates - actual
    errors.append(diff)

    if i > 1:
        sp.next_ax()
```

```
    sp.ax.hist(diff, normed=True,
            bins=dl.stats.sqrt_bins(actual))
    sp.label()

    sp.next_ax().boxplot(errors)
    sp.label()
    HTML(sp.exit())
```

Refer to the following screenshot for the end result:

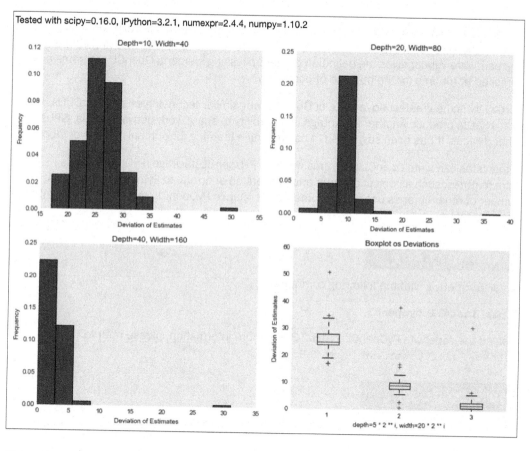

The code is in the `stream_demo.py` file in this book's code bundle.

See also

▸ The related Wikipedia page at `https://en.wikipedia.org/wiki/Count%E2%80%93min_sketch` (retrieved January 2016)

Harnessing the power of the GPU with OpenCL

Open Computing Language (**OpenCL**), initially developed by Apple Inc., is an open technology standard for programs, which can run on a variety of devices, including CPUs and GPUs that are available on commodity hardware, such as the machine I am using for this recipe. Since 2009, OpenCL has been maintained by the Khronos Compute Working Group. Many hardware vendors, including the one I am partial to, have an implementation of OpenCL.

OpenCL is a language resembling C (actually, there are multiple C dialects or versions) with functions called **kernels**. Kernels can run in parallel on multiple processing elements. The hardware vendor gives the definition of the processing element. OpenCL programs are compiled at runtime for the purpose of portability.

Portability is the greatest advantage of OpenCL over similar technologies such as CUDA, which is an NVIDIA product. Another advantage is the ability to share work between CPUs, GPUs, and other devices. It has been suggested to use machine learning for optimal division of labor.

Pythonistas can write OpenCL programs with the PyOpenCL package. PyOpenCL adds extra features, such as object cleanup and conversion of errors, to Python exceptions. A number of other libraries use and in some ways enhance PyOpenCL (refer to the PyOpenCL documentation).

Getting ready

Install `pyopencl` with the following command:

```
$ pip install pyopencl
```

I tested the code with PyOpenCL 2015.2.3. For more information, please refer to `https://wiki.tiker.net/OpenCLHowTo`.

How to do it...

The code is in the `opencl_demo.ipynb` file in this book's code bundle:

1. The imports are as follows:

   ```
   import pyopencl as cl
   from pyopencl import array
   import numpy as np
   ```

2. Define the following function to accept a NumPy array and perform a simple computation:

```
def np_se(a, b):
    return (a - b) ** 2
```

3. Define the following function to do the same calculation as in the previous step using OpenCL:

```
def gpu_se(a, b, platform, device, context, program):
```

4. Create a queue with profiling enabled (only for demonstration) and buffers to shuffle data around:

```
queue = cl.CommandQueue(context,
                          properties=cl.command_queue_
properties.
                          PROFILING_ENABLE)
mem_flags = cl.mem_flags
a_buf = cl.Buffer(context,
                  mem_flags.READ_ONLY | mem_flags.COPY_HOST_
PTR,
                  hostbuf=a)
b_buf = cl.Buffer(context,
                  mem_flags.READ_ONLY | mem_flags.COPY_HOST_
PTR, hostbuf=b)
error = np.empty_like(a)
destination_buf = cl.Buffer(context,
                              mem_flags.WRITE_ONLY,
                              error.nbytes)
```

5. Execute the OpenCL program and profile the code:

```
exec_evt = program.mean_squared_error(queue, error.shape,
None,
                                        a_buf, b_buf,
destination_buf)
exec_evt.wait()
elapsed = 1e-9*(exec_evt.profile.end - exec_evt.profile.start)

print("Execution time of OpenCL: %g s" % elapsed)

cl.enqueue_copy(queue,
                error, destination_buf)

return error
```

6. Generate random data as follows:

```
np.random.seed(51)
a = np.random.rand(4096).astype(np.float32)
b = np.random.rand(4096).astype(np.float32)
```

7. Access CPU and GPUs. This part is hardware dependent, so you may have to change these lines:

```
platform = cl.get_platforms()[0]
device = platform.get_devices()[2]
context = cl.Context([device])
```

8. Define a kernel with the OpenCL language:

```
program = cl.Program(context, """
    __kernel void mean_squared_error(__global const float *a,
    __global const float *b, __global float *result)
    {
        int gid = get_global_id(0);
        float temp = a[gid] - b[gid];
        result[gid] =  temp * temp;
    }
    """).build()
```

9. Calculate squared errors with NumPy and OpenCL (GPU) and measure execution times:

```
gpu_error = gpu_se(a, b, platform, device, context, program)

np_error = np_se(a, b)
print('GPU error', np.mean(gpu_error))
print('NumPy error', np.mean(np_error))
%time np_se(a, b)
```

Refer to the following screenshot for the end result:

```
Execution time of OpenCL: 1.0528e-05 s
GPU error 0.168414
NumPy error 0.168414
CPU times: user 16 µs, sys: 5 µs, total: 21 µs
Wall time: 25 µs
```

See also

▶ The PyOpenCL website at `http://documen.tician.de/pyopencl/` (retrieved January 2016)

Glossary

This appendix is a brief glossary of technical concepts used throughout *Python Data Analysis* and this book.

American Standard Code for Information Interchange (ASCII) was the dominant encoding standard on the Internet until the end of 2007, with UTF-8 (8-bit Unicode) taking over. ASCII is limited to the English alphabet and has no support for other alphabets.

Analysis of variance (ANOVA) is a statistical data analysis method invented by statistician Ronald Fisher. This method partitions the data of a continuous variable using the values of one or more corresponding categorical variable to analyze variance. ANOVA is a form of linear modeling.

Anaconda is a free Python distribution for data analysis and scientific computing. It has its own package manager, **conda**.

The **Anscombe's quartet** is a classic example, which illustrates why visualizing data is important. The quartet consists of four datasets with similar statistical properties. Each dataset has a series of *x* values and dependent *y* values.

The **bag-of-words model**: A simplified model of text, in which text is represented by a bag (a set in which something can occur multiple times) of words. In this representation, the order of the words is ignored. Typically, word counts or the presence of certain words are used as features in this model.

Beta in finance is the slope of a linear regression model involving the returns of the asset and the returns of a benchmark, for instance, the S & P 500 index.

Caching involves storing results, usually from a function call, in memory or on disk. If done correctly, caching helps by reducing the number of function calls. In general, we want to keep the cache small for space reasons.

A **clique** is a subgraph that is complete. This is equivalent to the general concept of cliques, in which every person knows all the other people.

Clustering aims to partition data into groups called clusters. Clustering is unsupervised in the sense that the training data is not labeled. Some clustering algorithms require a guess for the number of clusters, while other algorithms don't.

Cohen's kappa measures agreement between the target and predicted class (in the context of classification)—similar to accuracy, but it also takes into account the random chance of getting the predictions. Kappa varies between negative values and one.

A **complete graph** is a graph in which every pair of nodes is connected by a unique connection.

The **confusion matrix** is a table usually used to summarize the results of classification. The two dimensions of the table are the predicted class and the target class.

Contingency table: A table containing counts for all combinations of the two categorical variables.

The **cosine similarity** is a common distance metric to measure the similarity of two documents. For this metric, we need to compute the inner product of two feature vectors. The cosine similarity of vectors corresponds to the cosine of the angle between vectors, hence the name.

Cross-correlation measures the correlation between two signals using a sliding inner product. We can use cross-correlation to measure the time delay between two signals.

The **Data Science Toolbox** (**DST**) is a virtual environment based on Ubuntu for data analysis using Python and R. Since DST is a virtual environment, we can install it on various operating systems.

The **discrete cosine transform** (**DCT**) is a transform similar to the Fourier transform, but it tries to represent a signal by a sum of cosine terms only.

The **efficient-market hypothesis** (**EMH**) stipulates that you can't, on average, "beat the market" by picking better stocks or timing the market. According to the EMH, all information about the market is immediately available to every market participant in one form or another and is immediately reflected in asset prices.

Eigenvalues are scalar solutions to the equation $Ax = ax$, where A is a two-dimensional matrix and x is a one-dimensional vector.

Eigenvectors are vectors corresponding to eigenvalues.

Exponential smoothing is a low-pass filter, which aims to remove noise.

Face detection tries to find (rectangular) areas in an image that represent faces.

Fast Fourier transform (**FFT**): A fast algorithm to compute Fourier transforms. FFT is *O(N log N)*, which is a huge improvement on older algorithms.

Filtering is a type of signal processing technique, involving the removal or suppression of part of the signal. Many filter types exist, including the median and Wiener filters.

Fourier analysis is based on the **Fourier series**, named after the mathematician Joseph Fourier. The Fourier series is a mathematical method to represent functions as an infinite series of sine and cosine terms. The functions in question can be real or complex valued.

Genetic algorithms are based on the biological theory of evolution. This type of algorithm is useful for searching and optimization.

GPUs (**graphical processor units**) are specialized circuits used to display graphics efficiently. Recently, GPUs have been used to perform massively parallel computations (for instance, to train neural networks).

Hadoop Distributed File System (**HDFS**) is the storage component of the Hadoop framework for big data. HDFS is a distributed filesystem, which spreads data on multiple systems, and is inspired by Google File System, used by Google for its search engine.

A **hive plot** is a visualization technique for plotting network graphs. In hive plots, we draw edges as curved lines. We group nodes by some property and display them on radial axes.

Influence plots take into account residuals, influence, and leverage for individual data points, similar to bubble plots. The size of the residuals is plotted on the vertical axis and can indicate that a data point is an outlier.

Jackknifing is a deterministic algorithm to estimate confidence intervals. It falls under the family of resampling algorithms. Usually, we generate new datasets under the jackknifing algorithm by deleting one value (we can also delete two or more values).

JSON (**JavaScript Object Notation**) is a data format. In this format, data is written down using JavaScript notation. JSON is more succinct than other data formats, such as XML.

K-fold cross-validation is a form of cross-validation involving k (a small integer number) random data partitions called **folds**. In k iterations, each fold is used once for validation, and the rest of the data is used for training. The results of the iterations can be combined at the end.

Linear discriminant analysis (**LDA**) is an algorithm that looks for a linear combination of features in order to distinguish between classes. It can be used for classification or dimensionality reduction by projecting to a lower-dimensional subspace.

Learning curve: A way to visualize the behavior of a learning algorithm. It is a plot of training and test scores for a range of training data sizes.

Logarithmic plots (or log plots) are plots that use a logarithmic scale. This type of plot is useful when the data varies a lot, because they display orders of magnitude.

Logistic regression is a type of a classification algorithm. This algorithm can be used to predict probabilities associated with a class or an event occurring. Logistic regression is based on the **logistic function**, which has output values in the range from zero to one, just like in probabilities. The logistic function can therefore be used to transform arbitrary values into probabilities.

The **Lomb-Scargle periodogram** is a frequency spectrum estimation method that fits sines to data, and it is frequently used with unevenly sampled data. The method is named after Nicholas R. Lomb and Jeffrey D. Scargle.

The **Matthews correlation coefficient** (**MCC**) or **phi coefficient** is an evaluation metric for binary classification invented by Brian Matthews in 1975. The MCC is a correlation coefficient for target and predictions and varies between -1 and 1 (best agreement).

Memory leaks are a common issue of computer programs, which we can find by performing memory profiling. Leaks occur when we don't release memory that is not needed.

Moore's law is the observation that the number of transistors in a modern computer chip doubles every 2 years. This trend has continued since Moore's law was formulated, around 1970. There is also a second Moore's law, which is also known as Rock's law. This law states that the cost of R&D and manufacturing of integrated circuits increases exponentially.

Named-entity recognition (**NER**) tries to detect names of persons, organizations, locations, and others in text. Some NER systems are almost as good as humans, but it is not an easy task. Named entities usually start with upper case, such as Ivan. We should therefore not change the case of words when applying NER.

Object-relational mapping (**ORM**): A software architecture pattern for translation between database schemas and object-oriented programming languages.

Open Computing Language (**OpenCL**), initially developed by Apple Inc., is an open technology standard for programs, which can run on a variety of devices, including CPUs and GPUs that are available on commodity hardware.

OpenCV (**Open Source Computer Vision**) is a library for computer vision created in 2000 and currently maintained by Itseez. OpenCV is written in C++, but it also has bindings to Python and other programming languages.

Opinion mining or **sentiment analysis** is a research field with the goal of efficiently finding and evaluating opinions and sentiment in text.

Principal component analysis (**PCA**), invented by Karl Pearson in 1901, is an algorithm that transforms data into uncorrelated orthogonal features called principal components. The **principal components** are the eigenvectors of the covariance matrix.

The **Poisson distribution** is named after the French mathematician Poisson, who published it in 1837. The Poisson distribution is a discrete distribution usually associated with counts for a fixed interval of time or space.

Robust regression is designed to deal better with outliers in data than ordinary regression. This type of regression uses special robust estimators.

Scatter plot: A two-dimensional plot showing the relationship between two variables in a Cartesian coordinate system. The values of one variable are represented on one axis, and the other variable is represented by the other axis. We can quickly visualize correlation this way.

In the **shared-nothing architecture**, computing nodes don't share memory or files. The architecture is therefore totally decentralized, with completely independent nodes. The obvious advantage is that we are not dependent on any one node. The first commercial shared-nothing databases were created in the 1980s.

Signal processing is a field of engineering and applied mathematics that deals with the analysis of analog and digital signals corresponding to variables that vary with time.

Structured Query Language (**SQL**) is a specialized language for relational database querying and manipulation. This includes creating, inserting rows in, and deleting tables.

Short-time Fourier transform (**STFT**): The STFT splits a signal in the time domain into equal parts and then applies the FFT to each segment.

Stop words: Common words with low information value. Stop words are usually removed before analyzing text. Although filtering stop words is common practice, there is no standard definition of stop words.

The **Spearman rank correlation** uses ranks to correlate two variables with the Pearson correlation. Ranks are the positions of values in sorted order. Items with equal values get a rank, which is the average of their positions. For instance, if we have two items of equal value assigned positions 2 and 3, the rank is 2.5 for both items.

Spectral clustering is a clustering technique that can be used to segment images.

The **star schema** is a database pattern that facilitates reporting. Star schemas are appropriate for the processing of events such as website visits, ad clicks, or financial transactions. Event information (metrics such as temperature or purchase amount) is stored in fact tables linked to much smaller-dimension tables. Star schemas are denormalized, which places the responsibility of integrity checks on the application code. For this reason, we should only write to the database in a controlled manner.

Term frequency-inverse document frequency (**tf-idf**) is a metric measuring the importance of a word in a corpus. It is composed of a term frequency number and an inverse document frequency number. The term frequency counts the number of times a word occurs in a document. The inverse document frequency counts the number of documents in which the word occurs and takes the inverse of the number.

Time series: An ordered list of data points, starting with the oldest measurements. Usually, each data point has a related timestamp.

Violin plots combine box plots and kernel-density plots or histograms in one type of plot.

Winsorising is a technique to deal with outliers and is named after Charles Winsor. In effect, Winsorising clips outliers to given percentiles in a symmetric fashion.

B

Function Reference

This appendix is a short reference of functions not meant as exhaustive documentation, but as an extra aid in case you are temporarily unable to look up the documentation. These functions are organized by package for various libraries.

IPython

The following displays a Python object in all frontends:

```
IPython.core.display.display(*objs, **kwargs)
```

The following renders HTML content:

```
IPython.display.HTML(TextDisplayObject)
```

The following displays interactive widgets connected to a function. The first parameter is expected to be a function:

```
IPython.html.widgets.interaction.interact (__interact_f=None,
**kwargs)
```

The following arguments to this function are widget abbreviations passed in as keyword arguments, which build a group of interactive widgets tied to __interact_f and places the group in a container:

```
IPython.html.widgets.interaction.interactive (__interact_f, **kwargs)
```

Matplotlib

The following method is used to get or set axis properties. For example, `axis('off')` turns off the axis lines and labels:

```
matplotlib.pyplot.axis(*v, **kwargs)
```

The following argument creates a new figure:

```
matplotlib.pyplot.figure(num=None, figsize=None, dpi=None,
facecolor=None, edgecolor=None, frameon=True, FigureClass=<class
'matplotlib.figure.Figure'>, **kwargs)
```

The following argument turns the plot grids on or off:

```
matplotlib.pyplot.grid(b=None, which='major', axis='both', **kwargs)
```

The following argument plots a histogram:

```
matplotlib.pyplot.hist(x, bins=10, range=None, normed=False,
weights=None, cumulative=False, bottom=None, histtype='bar',
align='mid', orientation='vertical', rwidth=None, log=False,
color=None, label=None, stacked=False, hold=None, **kwargs)
```

The following displays an image for array-like data:

```
matplotlib.pyplot.imshow(X, cmap=None, norm=None, aspect=None,
interpolation=None, alpha=None, vmin=None, vmax=None, origin=None,
extent=None, shape=None, filternorm=1, filterrad=4.0, imlim=None,
resample=None, url=None, hold=None, **kwargs)
```

The following shows a legend at an optionally specified location (for instance, `plt.legend(loc='best')`):

```
matplotlib.pyplot.legend(*args, **kwargs)
```

The following argument creates a two-dimensional plot with single or multiple *x, y* pairs and corresponding optional format string:

```
matplotlib.pyplot.plot(*args, **kwargs)
```

The following creates a scatter plot of two arrays:

```
matplotlib.pyplot.scatter(x, y, s=20, c='b', marker='o', cmap=None,
norm=None, vmin=None, vmax=None, alpha=None, linewidths=None,
verts=None, hold=None, **kwargs)
```

The following argument displays a plot:

```
matplotlib.pyplot.show(*args, **kw)
```

The following argument creates subplots given the row number, column number, and index number of the plot. All these numbers start at one. For instance, `plt.subplot(221)` creates the first subplot in a two-by-two grid:

```
matplotlib.pyplot.subplot(*args, **kwargs)
```

The following argument puts a title on the plot:

```
matplotlib.pyplot.title(s, *args, **kwargs)
```

NumPy

The following creates a NumPy array with evenly spaced values within a specified range:

```
numpy.arange([start,] stop[, step,], dtype=None)
```

The following argument returns the indices that would sort the input array:

```
numpy.argsort(a, axis=-1, kind='quicksort', order=None)
```

The following creates a NumPy array from an array-like sequence, such as a Python list:

```
numpy.array(object, dtype=None, copy=True, order=None, subok=False,
ndmin=0)
```

The following argument calculates the dot product of two arrays:

```
numpy.dot(a, b, out=None)
```

The following argument returns the identity matrix:

```
numpy.eye(N, M=None, k=0, dtype=<type 'float'>)
```

The following argument loads NumPy arrays or pickled objects from .npy, .npz or pickles. A memory-mapped array is stored in the filesystem and doesn't have to be completely loaded in memory. This is especially useful for large arrays:

```
numpy.load(file, mmap_mode=None)
```

The following argument loads data from a text file into a NumPy array:

```
numpy.loadtxt(fname, dtype=<type 'float'>, comments='#',
delimiter=None, converters=None, skiprows=0, usecols=None,
unpack=False, ndmin=0)
```

The following calculates the arithmetic mean along the given axis:

```
numpy.mean(a, axis=None, dtype=None, out=None, keepdims=False)
```

The following argument calculates the median along the given axis:

```
numpy.median(a, axis=None, out=None, overwrite_input=False)
```

The following creates a NumPy array of specified shape and data type, containing ones:

```
numpy.ones(shape, dtype=None, order='C')
```

The following performs a least squares polynomial fit:

```
numpy.polyfit(x, y, deg, rcond=None, full=False, w=None, cov=False)
```

The following changes the shape of a NumPy array:

```
numpy.reshape(a, newshape, order='C')
```

The following argument saves a NumPy array to a file in the NumPy .npy format:

```
numpy.save(file, arr)
```

The following argument saves a NumPy array to a text file:

```
numpy.savetxt(fname, X, fmt='%.18e', delimiter=' ', newline='\n',
header='', footer='', comments='# ')
```

The following argument sets printing options:

```
numpy.set_printoptions(precision=None, threshold=None, edgeitems=None,
linewidth=None, suppress=None, nanstr=None, infstr=None,
formatter=None)
```

The following argument returns the standard deviation along the given axis:

```
numpy.std(a, axis=None, dtype=None, out=None, ddof=0, keepdims=False)
```

The following selects array elements from input arrays based on a Boolean condition:

```
numpy.where(condition, [x, y])
```

The following creates a NumPy array of specified shape and data type, containing zeros:

```
numpy.zeros(shape, dtype=float, order='C')
```

pandas

The following creates a fixed frequency datetime index:

```
pandas.date_range(start=None, end=None, periods=None, freq='D',
tz=None, normalize=False, name=None, closed=None)
```

The following argument generate various summary statistics, ignoring `NaN` values:

```
pandas.DataFrame.describe(self, percentile_width=None,
percentiles=None, include=None, exclude=None)
```

The following creates a `DataFrame` object from a dictionary of array-like objects or dictionaries:

```
pandas.DataFrame. from_dict(data, orient='columns', dtype=None)
```

The following argument finds NaN and None values:

```
pandas.isnull(obj)
```

The following argument merges `DataFrame` objects with a database-like join on columns or indices:

```
pandas.merge(left, right, how='inner', on=None, left_on=None,
right_on=None, left_index=False, right_index=False, sort=False,
suffixes=('_x', '_y'), copy=True)
```

The following creates a `DataFrame` object from a CSV file:

```
pandas.read_csv(filepath_or_buffer, sep=',', dialect=None,
compression=None, doublequote=True, escapechar=None, quotechar='"',
quoting=0, skipinitialspace=False, lineterminator=None,
header='infer', index_col=None, names=None, prefix=None,
skiprows=None, skipfooter=None, skip_footer=0, na_values=None, na_
fvalues=None, true_values=None, false_values=None, delimiter=None,
converters=None, dtype=None, usecols=None, engine='c', delim_
whitespace=False, as_recarray=False, na_filter=True, compact_
ints=False, use_unsigned=False, low_memory=True, buffer_lines=None,
warn_bad_lines=True, error_bad_lines=True, keep_default_na=True,
thousands=Nment=None, decimal='.', parse_dates=False, keep_date_
col=False, dayfirst=False, date_parser=None, memory_map=False,
nrows=None, iterator=False, chunksize=None, verbose=False,
encoding=None, squeeze=False, mangle_dupe_cols=True, tupleize_
cols=False, infer_datetime_format=False)
```

Scikit-learn

The following argument turns `seed` into a `numpy.random.RandomState` instance:

```
sklearn.utils.check_random_state(seed)
```

The following performs a grid search over given hyperparameter values for an estimator:

```
sklearn.grid_search.GridSearchCV estimator, param_grid, scoring=None,
fit_params=None, n_jobs=1, iid=True, refit=True, cv=None, verbose=0,
pre_dispatch='2*n_jobs', error_score='raise')
```

The following argument splits arrays into random train and test sets:

```
sklearn.cross_validation.train_test_split(*arrays, **options)
```

The following returns the accuracy classification score:

```
sklearn.metrics.accuracy_score(y_true, y_pred, normalize=True, sample_
weight=None)
```

SciPy

The following computes the relative maxima of data:

```
scipy.signal.argrelmax(data, axis=0, order=1, mode='clip')
```

The following argument calculates the kurtosis of a dataset:

```
scipy.stats.kurtosis(a, axis=0, fisher=True, bias=True)
```

The following applies a median filter on an array:

```
scipy.signal.medfilt(volume, kernel_size=None)
```

The following argument calculates the skewness of a data set:

```
scipy.stats.skew(a, axis=0, bias=True)
```

Seaborn

The following argument plots a univariate distribution of observations:

```
seaborn.distplot(a, bins=None, hist=True, kde=True, rug=False,
fit=None, hist_kws=None, kde_kws=None, rug_kws=None, fit_kws=None,
color=None, vertical=False, norm_hist=False, axlabel=None, label=None,
ax=None)
```

The following argument plots tabular data as a color-encoded matrix:

```
seaborn.heatmap(data, vmin=None, vmax=None, cmap=None, center=None,
robust=False, annot=False, fmt='.2g', annot_kws=None, linewidths=0,
linecolor='white', cbar=True, cbar_kws=None, cbar_ax=None,
square=False, ax=None, xticklabels=True, yticklabels=True, mask=None,
**kwargs)
```

The following argument plots data and the corresponding linear regression model fit:

```
seaborn.regplot(x, y, data=None, x_estimator=None, x_bins=None, x_
ci='ci', scatter=True, fit_reg=True, ci=95, n_boot=1000, units=None,
order=1, logistic=False, lowess=False, robust=False, logx=False,
x_partial=None, y_partial=None, truncate=False, dropna=True, x_
jitter=None, y_jitter=None, label=None, color=None, marker='o',
scatter_kws=None, line_kws=None, ax=None)
```

The following argument restores all matplotlib RC parameters to the default settings:

```
seaborn.reset_defaults()
```

The following argument restores all matplotlib RC parameters to the original settings:

```
seaborn.reset_orig()
```

The following argument plots the residuals of a linear regression:

```
seaborn.residplot(x, y, data=None, lowess=False, x_partial=None,
y_partial=None, order=1, robust=False, dropna=True, label=None,
color=None, scatter_kws=None, line_kws=None, ax=None)
```

The following argument sets aesthetic parameters:

```
seaborn.set(context='notebook', style='darkgrid', palette='deep',
font='sans-serif', font_scale=1, color_codes=False, rc=None)
```

Statsmodels

The following argument downloads and returns the R dataset from the Internet:

```
statsmodels.api.datasets.get_rdataset(dataname, package='datasets',
cache=False)
```

The following argument plots a Q-Q plot:

```
statsmodels.api.qqplot(data, dist, distargs=(), a=0, loc=0, scale=1,
fit=False, line=None, ax=None)
```

The following argument creates an ANOVA table for one or more fitted linear models:

```
statsmodels.stats.anova.anova_lm()
```

Online Resources

The following is a short list of resources including presentations, links to documentation, freely available IPython Notebooks, and data.

IPython notebooks and open data

For more information on IPython notebooks and open data, you can refer to the following:

- Data science Python notebooks available at `https://github.com/donnemartin/data-science-ipython-notebooks` (retrieved January 2016)

- A collection of tutorials and examples for solving and understanding machine learning and pattern classification tasks available at `https://github.com/rasbt/pattern_classification` (retrieved January 2016)

- Awesome public datasets available at `https://github.com/caesar0301/awesome-public-datasets` (retrieved January 2016)

- UCI machine learning datasets available at `https://archive.ics.uci.edu/ml/datasets.html` (retrieved January 2016)

- Gallery of interesting IPython notebooks available at `https://github.com/ipython/ipython/wiki/A-gallery-of-interesting-IPython-Notebooks` (retrieved January 2016)

Mathematics and statistics

- Linear algebra tutorials from Khan Academy available at `https://www.khanacademy.org/math/linear-algebra` (retrieved January 2016)

- Probability and statistics tutorials from Khan Academy at `https://www.khanacademy.org/math/probability` (retrieved January 2016)

- Coursera course on linear algebra, which uses Python, available at `https://www.coursera.org/course/matrix` (retrieved January 2016)

- *Introduction to probability* by Harvard University, available at `https://itunes.apple.com/us/course/statistics-110-probability/id502492375` (retrieved January 2016)

- The statistics wikibook at `https://en.wikibooks.org/wiki/Statistics` (retrieved January 2016)

- *Electronic Statistics Textbook*. Tulsa, OK: StatSoft. WEB: `http://www.statsoft.com/textbook/` (retrieved January 2016)

Presentations

- *Statistics for hackers* by Jake van der Plas, available at `https://speakerdeck.com/jakevdp/statistics-for-hackers` (retrieved January 2016)

- *Explore Data: Data Science + Visualization* by Roelof Pieters, available at `http://www.slideshare.net/roelofp/explore-data-data-science-visualization` (retrieved January 2016)

- *High Performance Python (1.5hr) Tutorial at EuroSciPy 2014* by Ian Ozsvald, available at `https://speakerdeck.com/ianozsvald/high-performance-python-1-dot-5hr-tutorial-at-euroscipy-2014` (retrieved January 2016)

- *Mastering Linked Data* by Valerio Maggio, available at `https://speakerdeck.com/valeriomaggio/mastering-linked-data-with-ptyhon-at-pydata-berlin-2014` (retrieved January 2016)

- *Fast Data Analytics with Spark and Python* by Benjamin Bengfort, available at `http://www.slideshare.net/BenjaminBengfort/fast-data-analytics-with-spark-and-python` (retrieved January 2016)

- *Social network analysis with Python* by Benjamin Bengfort, available at `http://www.slideshare.net/BenjaminBengfort/social-network-analysis-with-python` (retrieved January 2016)

- SciPy 2015 conference list of talks, available at `https://www.youtube.com/playlist?list=PLYx7XA2nY5Gcpabmu61kKcToLz0FapmHu` (retrieved January 2016)

- Statistical inference in Python, available at `https://sites.google.com/site/pyinference/home/scipy-2015` (retrieved January 2016)

- *Ibis: Scaling Python Analytics on Hadoop and Impala* by Wes McKinney, available at `http://www.slideshare.net/wesm/ibis-scaling-python-analytics-on-hadoop-and-impala` (retrieved January 2016)

- *PyData: The Next Generation* by Wes McKinney, available at `http://www.slideshare.net/wesm/pydata-the-next-generation` (retrieved January 2016)

- *Python as the Zen of Data Science* by Travis Oliphant, available at `http://www.slideshare.net/teoliphant/python-as-the-zen-of-data-science` (retrieved January 2016)

- *PyData Texas 2015 Keynote* by Peter Wang, available at `http://www.slideshare.net/misterwang/pydata-texas-2015-keynote` (retrieved January 2016)

- *What's new in scikit-learn 0.17* by Andreas Mueller, available at `http://www.slideshare.net/AndreasMueller7/whats-new-in-scikitlearn-017` (retrieved January 2016)

- *Tree models with Scikit-learn: Great models with little assumptions* by Gilles Loupe, available at `http://www.slideshare.net/glouppe/slides-46767187` (retrieved January 2016)

- *Mining Social Web APIs with IPython Notebook (Data Day Texas 2015)* by Matthew Russell, available at `http://www.slideshare.net/ptwobrussell/mining-social-web-ap-iswithipythonnotebookddtx2015` (retrieved January 2016)

- *Docker for data science* by Calvin Giles, available at `http://www.slideshare.net/CalvinGiles/docker-for-data-science` (retrieved January 2016)

- *10 more lessons learned from building Machine Learning systems* by Xavier Amatriain, available at `http://www.slideshare.net/xamat/10-more-lessons-learned-from-building-machine-learning-systems` (retrieved January 2016)

- *IPython & Project Jupyter: A language-independent architecture for open computing and data science* by Fernando Perez, available at `https://speakerdeck.com/fperez/ipython-and-project-jupyter-a-language-independent-architecture-for-open-computing-and-data-science` (retrieved January 2016)

- *Scikit-learn for easy machine learning: the vision, the tool, and the project* by Gael Varoquaux, available at `http://www.slideshare.net/GaelVaroquaux/slides-48793181` (retrieved January 2016)

- *Big Data, Predictive Modeling and tools* by Olivier Grisel, available at `https://speakerdeck.com/ogrisel/big-data-predictive-modeling-and-tools` (retrieved January 2016)

- *Data Science Python Ecosystem* by Christine Doig, available at `https://speakerdeck.com/chdoig/data-science-python-ecosystem` (retrieved January 2016)

- *New Trends in Storing Large Data Silos in Python* by Francesc Alted, available at `https://speakerdeck.com/francescalted/new-trends-in-storing-large-data-silos-in-python` (retrieved January 2016)

- *Distributed Computing on your Cluster with Anaconda - Webinar 2015* by Continuum Analytics, available at `http://www.slideshare.net/continuumio/distributed-computing-on-your-cluster-with-anaconda-webinar-2015` (retrieved January 2016)

D

Tips and Tricks for Command-Line and Miscellaneous Tools

In this book we used various tools, such as the IPython notebook and Unix shell commands. We have a short list of tips, which is not meant to be exhaustive. For working with databases, I recommend the DbVisualiser software available at `https://www.dbvis.com/` (retrieved January 2016). It supports all the major database products and operating systems. Also, I like to use text expanders in a desktop environment.

IPython notebooks

I explained a minimal workflow for notebooks. Also, I made simple IPython widgets, which were used throughout the book, so I will describe them here. To run the IPython notebook code, follow these steps:

1. Start the IPython notebook either with your GUI or with the following command:

   ```
   $ jupyter notebook
   ```

2. Run the code either cell by cell or in one run.

I made a widget that sets some of the matplotlib properties. The settings are stored in the `dautil.json` file in the current folder. These files should also be part of the code bundle.

The other IPython widget helps with setting up subplots. It takes care of setting titles, legends, and labels. I consider these strings to be configuration and, therefore, store them in the `dautil.json` files too.

Command-line tools

Some of these tools have GUI alternatives that are not always mentioned. In my opinion, it is a good idea to learn about using command-line tools even if you decide afterwards that you prefer the GUI options. Linux is one of the many popular operating systems that support CLI. You can find good documentation about Linux tools at `http://tldp.org/` (retrieved January 2016). Most information on the website is generic and useful on other operating systems as well, such as OS X.

Navigation is often cumbersome in the CLI world. I find bashmarks a good tool to help you with that. You can find bashmarks at `https://github.com/huyng/bashmarks` (retrieved January 2016). The steps to install bashmarks are as follows:

1. Type the following in a terminal:

   `$ git clone git://github.com/huyng/bashmarks.git`

2. Now, type this in the terminal:

   `$ cd bashmarks`

3. Next, type the following:

   `$ make install`

4. Source either in a configuration file or just the current session:

   `$ source ~/.local/bin/bashmarks.sh`

The following table lists the bashmarks commands:

Command	Description
`s <bookmark_name>`	This saves the current directory as `bookmark_name`
`g <bookmark_name>`	This goes to the directory associated with `bookmark_name`
`p <bookmark_name>`	This prints the directory associated with `bookmark_name`
`d <bookmark_name>`	This deletes the bookmark
`l`	This lists all available bookmarks

The alias command

The `alias` command allows you to define a short mnemonic for a long command. For instance, we can define the following alias to start the IPython server when we type `ipnb`:

`$ alias ipnb='ipython notebook'`

We can define aliases for the current session only, but usually we define aliases in the `.bashrc` startup file (the dot in the file name means that it is a hidden file) found in the home directory. If you find yourself having many aliases, it may be useful to create a file containing all the aliases. You can then source this file from `.bashrc`.

Command-line history

The command-line history is a mechanism to minimize the number of keystrokes. You can read more about it at `http://www.tldp.org/LDP/GNU-Linux-Tools-Summary/html/x1712.htm` (retrieved January 2016).

To simply execute the last run command, type the following again:

```
$ !!
```

Depending on which shell mode (`vi` or `emacs`) you are in, you may prefer other ways to navigate the history. The up and down arrows on your keyboard should also let you navigate history.

A common use case is to search for a long command we executed in the past and run it again. We can search through history, as follows:

```
$ history|grep <search for something>
```

You can of course shorten this using the aliasing mechanism or with a desktop text expander. The search gives a list of commands with numbers ranked in chronological order. You can execute, for instance, the command numbered `328`, as follows:

```
$ !328
```

If, for example, you wish to execute the last command that started with `python`, type the following:

```
$ !python
```

Reproducible sessions

Chapter 1, Laying the Foundation for Reproducible Data Analysis explained the value of reproducible analysis. In this context, we have the `script` command, which is a way to capture commands and the output of a session.

Docker tips

Docker is a great technology, but we have to be careful not to make our images too big and to remove image files when possible. The `docker-clean` script at `https://gist.github.com/michaelneale/1366325a7737c4cb80b0` (retrieved January 2016) helps reclaim space.

I found it useful to have an install script, which is just a regular shell script, and I added it to the `Dockerfile` as follows:

```
ADD install.sh /root/install.sh
```

Python creates `__pycache__` directories for the purpose of optimization (we can disable this option in various ways). These are not strictly needed and can be easily removed as follows:

```
find /opt/conda -name \__pycache__ -depth -exec rm -rf {} \;
```

Anaconda puts a lot of files in its `pkgs` directory, which we can remove as follows:

```
rm -r /opt/conda/pkgs/*
```

Some people recommend removing test code; however, in certain rare cases, the non-test code depends on the test code. Also, it is useful to have the test code just in case.

There are some gotchas to be aware of when working with Docker. For instance, we have to set the `PATH` environment variable as follows:

```
export PATH=/usr/local/sbin:/usr/local/bin:/usr/sbin:/usr/bin:/sbin:/bin:${PATH}
```

For Python scripts, we also need to set the language settings as follows:

```
ENV LANG=C.UTF-8
```

It is generally recommended to specify the package version when you install software with `pip` or `conda`, such as like this:

```
$ conda install scipy=0.15.0
$ pip install scipy==0.15.0
```

When installing with `conda`, it is also recommended that you install multiple packages at once in order to avoid installing multiple versions of common dependencies:

```
$ conda install scipy=0.15.0 curl=7.26.0
```

My Docker setup for the main Docker repository consists of a `Dockerfile` script and an install script (`install.sh`). The contents of the `Dockerfile` are as follows:

```
FROM continuumio/miniconda3

ADD install.sh /root/install.sh
RUN sh -x /root/install.sh

ENV LANG=C.UTF-8
```

I execute the install script with the –x switch, which gives more verbose output.

The contents of `install.sh` are as follows:

```
export PATH=/usr/local/sbin:/usr/local/bin:/usr/sbin:/usr/bin:/sbin:/
bin:${PATH}
apt-get install -y libgfortran3
conda config --set always_yes True
conda install beautiful-soup bokeh=0.9.1 execnet=1.3.0 \
fastcache=1.0.2 \
    joblib=0.8.4 jsonschema ipython=3.2.1 lxml mpmath=0.19 \
    networkx=1.9.1 nltk=3.0.2 numba=0.22.1 numexpr=2.3.1 \
    pandas=0.16.2 pyzmq scipy=0.16.0 seaborn=0.6.0 \
    sqlalchemy=0.9.9 statsmodels=0.6.1 terminado=0.5 tornado
conda install matplotlib=1.5.0 numpy=1.10.1 scikit-learn=0.17
pip install dautil==0.0.1a29
pip install hiveplot==0.1.7.4
pip install landslide==1.1.3
pip install LiveStats==1.0
pip install mpld3==0.2
pip install pep8==1.6.2
pip install requests-cache==0.4.10
pip install tabulate==0.7.5

find /opt/conda -name \__pycache__ -depth -exec rm -rf {} \;
rm -r /opt/conda/pkgs/*

mkdir -p /.cache/dautil/log
mkdir -p /.local/share/dautil
```

Index

A

AdaBoost
about 286
reference link 288
AdaBoostRegressor class
reference link 288
agglomerative clustering 360
AgglomerativeClustering class
reference link 361
aggregated counts
fitting, to Poisson distribution 72-75
aggregated data
fitting, to gamma distribution 71, 72
Alembic
URL 148
alias command 420
American Standard Code for Information
Interchange (ASCII) 142, 401
Anaconda
about 2, 401
setting up 2-4
URL 3
Analysis of variance (ANOVA)
about 101
one-way ANOVA 99
two-way ANOVA 99
used, for evaluating relations between
variables 99-101
analytic signal
reference link 176
angle() function
reference link 176
Anscombe's quartet
graphing 36-39
reference link 39

Apache Spark 160
approximation 197
arbitrary precision
used, for linear algebra 131, 132
using, for optimization 128, 129
argrelmax() function
reference link 174, 354
association tables
implementing 144-147
assortativity coefficient, graph
calculating 258, 259
reference link 259
asyncio module
reference link 380
used, for accessing resources
asynchronously 377-380
autoregressive models
reference link 223
used, for determining market
efficiency 221-223
average clustering coefficient
about 257
estimating 257, 258
average_clustering() function
reference link 258

B

bagging
reference link 285
used, for improving results 283, 284
bagging (bootstrap aggregating) 276
BaggingClassifier
reference link 285
bag-of-words model
reference link 244

Bartlett's method 170
bashmark commands
  d <bookmark_name> 420
  g <bookmark_name> 420
  l 420
  p <bookmark_name> 420
  reference link 420
  s <bookmark_name> 420
basic terms database
  implementing 248-252
Bayesian analysis 75
Beaufort scale
  reference link 118
Benevolent Dictator for Life (BDFL) 139
beta
  about 214, 401
  reference link 215
betweenness centrality
  determining 255, 256
  reference link 256
betweenness_centrality() function
  reference link 256
bias
  determining 75-78
binary variable
  correlating, with point biserial
    correlation 97-99
binomial distribution 75
Bokeh installation
  reference link 51
Bokeh plots
  reference link 53
boosting
  about 286
  reference link 288
  used, for better learning 286, 287
Boot2Docker 8
bootstrap aggregating 283
Box-Cox transformation
  reference link 114
  used, for normalization 112-114
box plots
  and kernel density plots, combining with
    violin plots 54, 55
bright stars
  searching for 351-354

bucketing 118
build options
  BUILD_opencv_java 336
  BUILD_opencv_python2 336
  BUILD_opencv_python3 336
  BUILD_opencv_xfeatures2d 336
  OPENCV_EXTRA_MODULES_PATH 336
  PYTHON3_EXECUTABLE 336
  PYTHON3_INCLUDE_DIR 336
  PYTHON3_LIBRARY 336
  PYTHON3_NUMPY_INCLUDE_DIRS 336
  PYTHON3_PACKAGES_PATH 336

C

Cache algorithms
  reference link 393
caching 401
Calmar ratio
  about 206
  reference link 208
  stocks, ranking with 206, 207
Capital Asset Pricing Model (CAPM)
  about 214
  reference link 215
cascade classifier
  reference link 349
categorized corpus
  creating 236-238
CategorizedPlaintextCorpusReader
  reference link 239
centrality 254
central tendency, of noisy data
  measuring 109-111
cepstrum
  about 185
  reference link 188
chebyfit() function
  reference link 130
clip() function
  reference link 106
clique
  about 259, 402
  reference link 260
clique number, graph
  obtaining 259, 260

closeness centrality
  about 254
  reference link 255
clustering 402
clustering coefficient
  about 257
  reference link 258
code style
  standardizing 30-33
Cohen's kappa
  about 304, 402
  examining 326-329
  reference link 329
ColorBrewer tool
  reference link 40
color quantization
  about 341
  reference link 343
colors
  quantizing 341, 343
command-line history
  about 421
  reference link 421
command-line tools 420
common tab separated values (TSV) 58
community package
  reference link 56
complete graph
  about 259, 402
  reference link 260
concurrent.futures module
  reference link 376
  used, for launching multiple tasks 374-376
conda 401
confidence intervals
  of mean, determining 81-83
  of standard deviation, determining 81, 82
  of variance, determining 81, 82
  reference link 83
confusion matrix
  about 300, 402
  reference link 303
  used, for summarizing results of
    classification 300-302
confusion_matrix() function
  reference link 303
consensus set 280

contingency table
  about 99, 402
  reference link 101
continuous variable
  correlating, with point biserial
    correlation 97-99
continuumio/miniconda3 image
  URL 10
co-occurrence matrix
  about 357
  reference link 360
coroutines
  about 377
  reference link 380
corpora
  download link 236
correlate() function
  reference link 176
correlation coefficient 329
cosine similarity
  about 261, 402
  reference link 264
cosine_similarity() function
  reference link 264
Count-min sketch
  reference link 397
  used, for streaming counting 395-397
cross-correlation 175, 176, 402
cross-validation
  nesting 289-292
  reference link 292
custom magics
  URL 13

D

d3.js
  used for visualizing via mpld3 49-51
data
  clustering hierarchically 294
  clustering, with Spark 161-165
  fitting, to exponential distribution 68-70
  rebinning 118, 119
  transforming, with logarithms 116, 117
  transforming, with power ladder 114-116
  winsorizing 107, 108
  winsorizing, reference link 108

data access
  standardizing 30-33
data analysis 36
database indices
  reference link 151
database migration scripts
  setting up 147, 148
data points
  highlighting, with influence plots 62-64
Data Science Toolbox (DST)
  about 4, 402
  installing 4-6
DbVisualiser software
  reference link 419
decision tree learning 276
degree 258
degree_assortativity_coefficient() function
  reference link 259
degree distribution
  about 258
  reference link 259
density() function
  reference link 254
detail coefficients 197
determinants
  about 339
  reference link 341
DFFITS
  reference link 65
dilation
  about 346
  reference link 348
dimension tables
  star schema, implementing 153-157
discrete cosine transform (DCT)
  about 168, 402
  reference link 190
  used, for analyzing signals 188-190
discrete wavelet transform (DWT)
  applying 197-200
  reference link 200
distance
  reference link 65
distributed processing
  execnet, using 380-383

Docker
  URL 8
  URL, for user guide 10
docker-clean script
  reference link 422
Docker images
  Python applications, sandboxing 8, 9
docker tips 422, 423
document graph, with cosine similarity
  creating 261-264
dummy classifier
  comparing with 316-318
  strategies 316
DummyClassifier class
  reference link 318
dummy regressor
  comparing with 321-323
  strategies 321
DummyRegressor class
  reference link 323
Duncan dataset
  reference link 114

E

ECDF class
  reference link 86
efficient-market hypothesis (EMH)
  about 216, 402
  reference link 218
eigenvalues 402
eigenvectors 402
ensemble learning 266, 272
equal weights 2 asset portfolio
  optimizing 230-233
execnet
  reference link 383
  used, for distributed processing 380-383
EXIF
  reference link 357
ExifRead
  reference link 357
exponential distribution
  data, fitting into 68-70
  reference link 70

exponential smoothing
  about 177-179, 402
  reference link 179
  smoothing factor 177
extra trees (extremely randomized trees) 292
extreme values
  exploring 87-90

F

F1-score
  computing 303-305
f1_score() function
  reference link 306
face detection
  about 348, 402
  reference link 351
fact
  star schema, implementing 153-157
false positive rate (FPR) 306
Fano factor
  about 170
  reference link 172
fastcache
  reference link 393
Fast Fourier transform (FFT) 403
fastNlMeansDenoisingColored() function
  reference link 345
fat tailed distribution
  reference link 208
features
  recursively eliminating 266-268
filtering 240, 403
findroot() function
  reference link 130
Fisher transformation 91
folds 403
Fourier analysis 403
fourier() function
  reference link 133
Fourier series 403
frequency spectrum 168
frequency spectrum, of audio
  analyzing 185-187
frequentist approach 75
functools.lru_cache
  reference link 393

G

gamma distribution
  about 68
  aggregated data, fitting 71, 72
  for SciPy documentation, reference link 72
  reference link 72
generalized extreme value distribution (GEV)
  about 87
  reference link 90
genetic algorithms 278, 403
genetic programming 278
geographical maps
  displaying 58-60
  reference link 58
ggplot2
  about 60
  reference link 61
ggplot2-like plots
  reference link 60
  using 60-62
Global Interpreter Lock (GIL) 367
goodness of fit
  visualizing 309, 310
graphical processor units (GPU)
  about 403
  harnessing, with Open Computing Language
    (OpenCL) 398-400
gradient descent
  about 296
  reference link 298
graph_clique_number() function
  reference link 260
graphs
  reference link 254
Gross Domestic Product (GDP) 58, 116

H

Haar cascades
  used, for detecting faces 348, 350
Haar feature-based cascade classifiers
    system 348
Haar wavelet 197
Hadoop Distributed File System (HDFS)
  URL 160
  using 159, 160

Haralick texture features
about 357
reference link 357
hat-matrix 63
heat dissipation 366
heatmaps
creating 51-53
Hertzsprung-Russell diagram
about 104
reference link 106
Hessian matrix
about 339
reference link 341
hierarchical clustering
about 294
applying, on images 360, 361
reference link 295, 361
hiveplot package
reference link 56
hive plots
about 55
used, for visualizing network graphs 55-57
HSL and HSV
reference link 354
HTML entities
dealing with 142-144
HTTP requests
caching 393, 394
reference link 394
Hurst exponent
about 197
reference link 200
hyperparameter optimization
about 266
reference link 292

I

image
denoising 343, 345
hierarchical clustering, applying 360, 361
metadata, extracting from 355-357
patches, extracting from 345-347
segmenting, with spectral clustering 361-363
texture features, extracting from 357-360
image processing 333

image segmentation
about 345
reference link 348
image texture
reference link 360
indices
adding, after table creation 150, 151
individual stocks
correlating, with broader market 211-213
influence plots
about 403
used, for highlighting data points 62-65
instantaneous phase
about 174
reference link 176
integral image
about 339
reference link 341
interquartile mean (IQM) 109
inverse document frequency 240
IPython
about 407
configuring 13-15
reference link 13-15
URL 11
IPython Notebook
about 10
used, for tracking package history 10-13
used, for tracking package versions 10-13
IPython notebook widgets
interacting with 43-46
reference link 47

J

jackknife resampling
reference link 83
jackknifing 81, 403
Java Runtime Environment (JRE) 159
JavaScript Object Notation (JSON) 403
joblib
installation link 61
used, for reusing models 292, 293
Just in time compiling
Numba, using 367, 368

K

kernel density
estimating 78-80
estimating, reference link 80
kernel density plots
and box plots, combining with violin
plots 54, 55
kernels 398
K-fold cross-validation 403
K-means clustering
reference link 165
kmeans() function
reference link 343
kurtosis
calculating 385-389

L

LDA
reference link 272
learning curves 266 403
least recently used (LRU) cache
used, for caching 390-392
leaves 276
lemmatization
about 240-243
reference link 244
leverage 63
linear algebra
arbitrary precision, using for 131, 132
linear discriminant analysis (LDA)
about 403
applying, for dimension reduction 271, 272
linkage() function
reference link 295
liquidity
stocks, ranking with 204, 205
LiveStats
reference link 390
lmplot() function
reference link 39
logarithmic plots 404
logarithms
used, for transforming data 116, 117
logging
for robust error checking 16-18
reference link 19

logistic function 404
logit() function
applying, for transforming
proportions 120, 121
lombscargle() function
reference link 185
Lomb-Scargle periodogram
about 183, 404
reference link 185
using 183, 184
lu_solve() function
reference link 133
lxml documentation
URL 144

M

main sequence 104
mathematics and statistics
reference links 416
matplotlib
configuring 24-28
references 28
URL 25
matplotlib color maps
reference link 42, 43
selecting 42, 43
matrix of scatterplots
viewing 47-49
matthews_corrcoef() function
reference link 331
Matthews correlation coefficient (MCC)
about 304, 329, 331
reference link 331
maximum clique 259
maximum drawdown 206
**maximum likelihood estimation
(MLE) method 73**
mean
calculating 385-389
mean absolute deviation (MAD) 70
mean_absolute_error() function
reference link 326
mean absolute error (MeanAE)
calculating 324, 325
reference link 326

Mean Absolute Percentage Error (MAPE)
  determining 319, 320
  reference link 321
Mean Percentage Error (MPE)
  determining 319, 320
  reference link 321
mean silhouette coefficient
  used, for evaluating clusters 313-315
mean_squared_error() function
  reference link 313
mean squared error (MSE)
  computing 310-312
  reference link 313
medfilt() documentation
  reference link 196
median_absolute_error() function
  reference link 313
median absolute error (MedAE)
  computing 310-312
mel frequency spectrum
  about 188
  reference link 188
mel scale
  about 185
  reference link 188-190
Memory class
  reference link 293
memory leaks 384, 404
memory_profiler module
  reference link 385
  used, for profiling memory usage 384, 385
memory usage
  profiling, with memory_profiler
      module 384, 385
metadata
  extracting, from images 355-357
Miniconda 2
models
  reusing, with joblib 292, 293
Modern Portfolio Theory (MPT)
  about 231
  reference link 233
Monte Carlo method
  about 83
  reference link 86
Moore's law 404

moving block bootstrapping time series data
  about 193-195
  reference link 196
mpld3
  d3.js, used for visualization via 49-51
mpmath 104
multiple models
  majority voting 273-275
  stacking 272-275
multiple tasks
  launching, with concurrent.futures
      module 374-376
multiple threads
  running, with threading module 370-373

N

named entities
  recognizing 244-246
named-entity recognition (NER)
  about 244
  reference link 244
nested cross-validation 289
network graphs
  visualizing, with hive plots 55-57
NetworkX
  reference link 56
news articles
  tokenizing, in sentences 239
  tokenizing, in words 239, 240
n-grams 240
noisy data
  central tendency, measuring 109-111
non-ASCII text
  dealing with 142-144
non-negative matrix factorization (NMF)
  documentation link 248
  reference link 248
  used, for extraction of topics 246-248
non-parametric runs test
  used, for examining market 216-218
Numba
  used, for Just in time compiling 367-369
numerical expressions
  speeding up, with Numexpr 369, 370

Numexpr
reference link 370
used, for speeding up numerical
expressions 369, 370
NumPy
about 409, 410
URL 16
NumPy print options
seeding 28, 29
URL 30

O

object detection 348
object-relational mapping (ORM) 136
octave 337
Open Computing Language (OpenCL)
about 404
used, for harnessing GPU 398-400
Open Source Computer Vision (OpenCV)
reference link 334
setting up 334-337
Ostu's thresholding method
about 346
reference link 348
outliers
about 104
clipping 104, 105
filtering 104, 105
reference link 104

P

pandas
about 410
configuring 22, 23
URL 22
pandas library
about 22
URL 22
PCA class
reference link 270
pdist() function
reference link 295
peaks
analyzing 172-174

Pearson's correlation
reference link 94
used, for correlating variables 91-94
pep8 analyzer
URL 31
using 30
periodogram() function
reference link 170
periodograms
used, for performing spectral
analysis 168-170
presentations
reference links 416, 417
phase synchronization
measuring 174-176
phi coefficient 404
point biserial correlation
reference link 99
used, for correlating binary variable 97, 98
used, for correlating continuous
variable 97, 98
Poisson distribution
about 405
aggregated counts, fitting 72-74
reference link 75
posterior distribution 75
power ladder
used, for transforming data 114, 115
power spectral density
estimating, with Welch's method 170-172
precision
computing 303-305
reference link 306
precision_score() function
reference link 306
principal component analysis (PCA)
about 404
applying, for dimension reduction 269
reference link 270
principal component regression (PCR)
about 269
reference link 270
principal components 269, 404
prior distribution 75
probability weights
used, for sampling 83-86

probplot() function
  reference link 310
Proj.4
  reference link 58
proportions
  transforming, by applying logit()
    function 120-122
PyOpenCL
  reference link 400
PyOpenCL 2015.2.3
  reference link 398
Python applications
  sandboxing, with Docker images 8, 9
Python threading
  reference link 373

R

R
  homepage link 61
RandomForestClassifier class
  reference link 279
random forests
  about 276
  reference link 279, 293
  used, for learning 276-279
random number generators
  seeding 28, 29
RANdom SAmple Consensus algorithm. *See*
    RANSAC algorithm
random walk hypothesis (RWH) 219
random walks
  reference link 220
  testing for 219, 220
RANSAC algorithm
  reference link 282
  used, for fitting noisy data 279-281
recall
  computing 303-305
  reference link 306
recall_score() function
  reference link 306
receiver operating characteristic (ROC)
  examining 306, 307
  reference link 308
reports
  standardizing 30-33

reproducible data analysis 2
reproducible sessions 421
requests-cache website
  reference link 394
rescaled range
  reference link 200
residual sum of squares (RSS)
  calculating 324, 325
  reference link 326
Resilient Distributed Datasets (RDDs) 160
resources
  accessing asynchronously, with asyncio
    module 377-379
returns 202
returns statistics
  analyzing 208-210
RFE class
  reference link 268
RGB (red, green and blue) 342
risk and return
  exploring 214
risk-free rate 214
robust error checking
  with logs 16-18
robust linear model
  fitting 122-124
robust regression 122, 405
roc_auc_score() function
  reference link 308

S

savgol_filter() function
  reference link 182
Savitzky-Golay filter
  about 180
  reference link 182
Scale-Invariant Feature Transform (SIFT)
  about 337
  applying 337, 338
  documentation, reference link 339
  reference link 339
scatter plot 405
scikit-learn
  about 60, 411
  URL 28, 30

scikit-learn documentation
reference link 80
SciPy 412
SciPy documentation
for exponential distribution, reference link 70
for Poisson distribution 75
seaborn 412
seaborn color palettes
about 39-41
reference link 42
selecting 39
search engine indexing
reference link 252
security market line (SML) 214
Selenium
URL 139
using 136
shapefile format 58
shared nothing architecture
about 381
reference link 383
shared-nothing architecture 405
Sharpe ratio
about 204
reference link 206
stocks, ranking with 204, 205
short-time Fourier transform (STFT) 185, 405
signal processing 405
signals
analyzing, with discrete cosine transform
(DCT) 188-190
silhouette coefficients
about 313
reference link 315
silhouette_score() function
reference link 315
simple and log returns
computing 202, 203
reference link 203
skewness
calculating 385-389
smoothing
evaluating 180-182
social network closeness centrality
calculating 254, 255
social network density
computing 252-254

software aspects 366
software performance
improving 366
**Solving a Problem in the Doctrine of
Chances essay**
reference link 78
Sortino ratio
about 206, 207
reference link 208
stocks, ranking with 206, 207
Spark
data, clustering 161-165
setting up 160, 161
URL 161
Spearman rank correlation
about 405
reference link 97
used, for correlating variables 94-96
spectral analysis
performing, with periodograms 168-170
reference link 170
spectral clustering
about 405
reference link 363
used, for segmenting images 361-363
spectral_clustering() function
reference link 363
Speeded Up Robust Features (SURF)
detecting 339-341
reference link 341
split() function
reference link 354
SQLAlchemy
reference link 153
stacking
about 273
reference link 275
Stanford Network Analysis Project (SNAP)
about 55
reference link 55
star schema
about 153, 405
implementing, with dimension
tables 153-157
implementing, with fact 153-157
URL 158

statsmodels
about 413
documentation, reference link 80
stemming 240-243
STFT
reference link 188
stock prices database
populating 225-229
tables, creating for 223-225
stop words
about 405
reference link 244
streaming algorithms 395
Structured Query Language (SQL) 405

T

table column
adding, to existing table 148, 149
tables
creating, for stock prices database 223, 224
tabulate PyPi
URL 33
term frequency 240
term frequency-inverse document frequency
   (tf-idf) 405
test web server
setting up 151-153
texture features
extracting, from images 357-360
TF-IDF
reference link 244
TF-IDF scores 240-243
TfidfVectorizer class
reference link 244
Theano
about 296, 297
documentation link 298
installing 296
threading module
used, for running multiple threads 370-373
time series 406
time series data
block bootstrapping 191-193
block bootstrapping, reference link 193
time slicing 370

tmean()
reference link 111
topic models
about 246
reference link 248
trend smoothing factor 177
trima()
reference link 111
trimean 109
trimmed mean 109
truncated mean 109
two-way ANOVA
reference link 101

U

unigrams 240
unit testing
about 19
performing 19-21
unittest library
URL 21
unittest.mock library
URL 21

V

Vagrant
about 4
reference link 6
URL 5
validation 289
validation curves 266
variables
correlating, with Pearson's correlation 91-93
correlating, with Spearman rank
   correlation 94-96
relations evaluating, with ANOVA 99-101
variance
calculating 385-389
reference link 390
Viola-Jones object detection framework
about 348
reference link 351

violin plots
about 54, 406
box plots and kernel density plots,
combining with 54, 55
reference link 55
VirtualBox
about 4, 6
URL 5
virtualenv
virtual environment, creating with 6-8
virtual environment
creating, with virtualenv 6-8
creating, with virtualenvwrapper 6-8
URL 8
virtualenvwrapper
URL 8
virtual environment, creating with 6-8
VotingClassifier class
reference link 275

W

Wald-Wolfowitz runs test
about 216
reference link 218
watermark extension
using 11
weak learners 286
web
scraping 139-141

web browsing
simulating 136-139
weighted least squares
about 125
used, for taking variance into
account 125, 126
welch() function
reference link 172
Welch's method
reference link 172
used, for estimating power spectral
density 170-172
winsorising 107, 108, 406
Within Cluster Sum of Squares (WCSS) 162
Within Set Sum Squared Error (WSSSE) 162
WordNetLemmatizer class
reference link 244

X

XPath
URL 139

Y

YAML
about 4
URL 4

CPSIA information can be obtained
at www.ICGtesting.com
Printed in the USA
LVOW05s2259290916
506808LV00003B/39/P

9 781785 2822